1 MONTH OF
FREE
READING

at

www.ForgottenBooks.com

By purchasing this book you are eligible for one month membership to ForgottenBooks.com, giving you unlimited access to our entire collection of over 1,000,000 titles via our web site and mobile apps.

To claim your free month visit:

www.forgottenbooks.com/free103013

ISBN 978-1-5283-7455-2
PIBN 10103013

This book is a reproduction of an important historical work. Forgotten Books uses
state-of-the-art technology to digitally reconstruct the work, preserving the original format
whilst repairing imperfections present in the aged copy. In rare cases, an imperfection in
the original, such as a blemish or missing page, may be replicated in our edition. We do,
however, repair the vast majority of imperfections successfully; any imperfections that
remain are intentionally left to preserve the state of such historical works.

THE -

CHARTER OF THE NATIONS;

OR,

FREE TRADE AND ITS RESULTS:

AN ESSAY

ON THE RECENT COMMERCIAL POLICY OF THE UNITED
KINGDOM,

TO WHICH THE COUNCIL OF THE NATIONAL ANTI-CORN LAW LEAGUE
AWARDED THEIR FIRST PRIZE.

BY HENRY DUNCKLEY, M.A.

It droppeth, as the gentle rain from heaven,
Upon the place beneath: it is twice bless'd,
It blesseth him that gives, and him that takes
Merchant of Venice.

𝕃ondon:

W. AND F. G. CASH, 5, BISHOPSGATE WITHOUT.
DUBLIN: JAMES M'GLASHAN.
EDINBURGH: JOHN MENZIES.

MDCCCLIV.

PREFACE.

———

THE advertisement which is prefixed to this volume
will sufficiently explain the circumstances in which
it originated. It is the good or bad fortune of a
person in the position of the author to be unable
to avail himself of that harmless artifice by which,
under the guise of an apology, an attempt is
sometimes made to disarm the inexorable critic.
If a man has a right to disparage himself, he
has certainly no right to disparage others, and
if anything he has written is judged worthy of
publication by those whose practical acquaintance
with the subject to which it relates entitles their
opinion to the utmost respect, it is at least his
privilege to be silent. An opposite course, moreover, might easily be construed into an act of mock
humility, or an ingenious attempt to exalt himself
by an implied acquaintance with faults which such
persons have either not perceived, or indulgently
overlooked.

Though justly proud of the preference which was unanimously awarded to his production, the author has not the slightest wish to make it, if that were possible, a screen between the public and himself. Perhaps it is only a decent pride that would dispose any one rather to be censured for his own sake than to be praised for another's; at least it is a weakness. which he confesses.

In entering upon the perusal of the following essay, the reader is respectfully reminded that it professes to deal exclusively with facts, and with such only as fall within an answer to the question : "What has accrued; or may be expected to accrue, from our Free Trade policy?" It formed no part of the prescribed plan to enter, even incidentally, upon an argumentative vindication of Free Trade principles. However needful such a vindication may be abroad, where the question has been scarcely at all discussed, it is unnecessary to say how obsolete it would have been here, after the information which has been diffused through the exertions of the Anti-Corn Law League. Still less was it permitted the author to digress upon matters, however attractive, connected with the general theory of trade, the history of British manufactures, or the prospects of commerce, as resulting from the social condition of foreign populations, or the geographical facilities and vast productiveness of half-settled portions of the globe. These are fields which it would have been equally pleasant and useful to traverse, but to have included them within the present volume would have been beside its main object, which is simply to show that Free Trade, as it has been recognised by the British legislature, is a good thing, and to commend it to the attention of other nations by exhibiting its happy consequences among ourselves. In striving to win our brethren of other lands to the cause which we have at length espoused, we point to the facts which are contained in this volume as a proof of our disinterestedness. It will be seen that our arguments are not inspired by fear; that, in calling upon them to break down their tariffs, we are not in the position of mendicants begging for bread. On the contrary, our friendly overtures are made at the era of our greatest prosperity; we invite other nations to join us at the very time that we are better able than we ever were to stand alone; we ask for commercial concessions when, if they should, unhappily, be refused, we are most prepared to do without them. Commercially and socially the British Empire was never in a more flourishing condition; never were we so wealthy, or amassing wealth more rapidly. No doubt if the principles of Free Trade were generally adopted, our own country would participate in the greater prosperity that would ensue, but the lion's share of the booty would not be ours; it would fall to the lot of those great and highly civilised communities whose fine energies are now crippled by the iron bondage of monopoly; who, to make one producer rich, are making twenty consumers poor, and who, to maintain a rivalry in which nature never designed them to excel, overlook the means of real superiority which lie within their grasp, foolishly content to purchase delusive wealth at the cost of a failing exchequer, a half-clad populace, and an impoverished land.

It may be proper, in a work of this nature, to say one word respecting the sources from which the author has derived his information. In tracing the effects of the earlier and partial concessions which were made to Free Trade principles, he has chiefly had occasion to refer to the able and well-known work of the late G. R. Porter, entitled " The Progress of the Nation," in connexion with the Annual Reports of the Manchester Chamber of Commerce, and the older volumes of the *Manchester Guardian*. The commercial statistics for the last ten or twelve years have been drawn from parliamentary documents, illustrated occasionally by information gleaned from other sources, including one or two special communications from the office of the Board of Trade. Statements respecting the rate of wages, the condition of particular branches of industry and particular districts, etc., have been furnished by gentlemen in various parts of the kingdom, in whose intelligence and veracity the author could fully confide, and to whom he takes this opportunity of returning his sincere thanks. For the important assistance to be derived from a faithful record of contemporary facts, elucidated by powerful writing, it is almost superfluous to mention the *Times*, to which everybody is indebted, and the *Economist*, the able and accredited organ of commerce.

The author is happy to state that a translation of his essay into the Dutch language is already in progress, and will shortly be introduced to the Dutch public under the auspices of the Hon. T. Van Borse, ex-Minister of Finance, to whom the cause of commercial freedom is indebted for unremitting exertions to establish the Free Trade system in the Netherlands. The Dutch experienced more injury, perhaps, than any other nation from the severity of our old restrictive legislation, especially the Navigation Act, and now that the days of commercial and political jealousy are over, it will be a happy augury indeed if they join us in denouncing a system from which both have equally suffered. England will welcome a coadjutor with whom she once aspired, in a dream of republican ambition, to be politically one, and in Free Trade a union may be realized, which, while it will not imperil the independence, or compromise the just dignity of either party, will promote in no small degree the best interests of the world.

Salford, August 1st, 1854.

CONTENTS.

PART I.

CHAPTER I.

EXTERNAL CONNEXION OF FREE TRADE WITH THE PAST.

CHAPTER II.

INWARD SIGNIFICANCE OF FREE TRADE.

CHAPTER III.

RISE, PROGRESS, AND TRIUMPH OF THE FREE TRADE MOVEMENT.

PART II.

EFFECTS OF FREE TRADE ON THE COMMERCE, MANUFACTURES, AND OTHER INDUSTRIAL INTERESTS OF THE BRITISH EMPIRE .

CHAPTER I.

CHAPTER II.

PAGE

PART III.

RESULTS AND TENDENCIES OF FREE TRADE—SOCIAL, POLITICAL, AND RELIGIOUS

CHAPTER I.

ACTUAL RESULTS OF FREE TRADE.

b

CHAPTER II.

PROSPECTIVE RESULTS OF FREE TRADE.

CHARTER OF THE NATIONS,

PART I.

FREE TRADE IN ITS HISTORICAL RELATIONS.

A GREAT event, like the abolition of those monopolies which long shackled the industrial interests of this country, can never be fully understood by itself. Even though our chief object may be only to obtain a correct estimate of its results, yet still, if our labours are to have a permanent value, it will be necessary to carry our inquiries higher than the immediate cause. If a person wished to conjecture approximately the weight of the vast body of water that rushes over the falls of Niagara, he would not content himself with ascertaining the width and depth of the stream at the point of projection; he would ascend the rapids, and find out the height of its source. Such an investigation of previous facts is still more necessary when historical and moral elements enter into the subject to be considered, since in this case the connexion is less evident, while it is also more instructive and important. True it is that the most trivial events have a connexion with the past, and, in a metaphysical sense, the link of causation is equally strong in those slight incidents which chequer the life of a peasant, and those mighty revolutions in the course of which empires rise or fall. The present, in its faintest outlines and minutest details, as well as in its leading features, is but the produce of the past; and, so amazing is the wisdom which balances the opposing tendencies of human society, that the free agency of the individual is one of the vital forces of a growth as sure and regular as those which we admire in the forest glade. In a moral point of view, however, the historical connexion is strongest in those movements which are most important. Great events are but the mature form of what has long been virtually in existence; we see in them, not the ephemeral products of the passing hour, but the offspring of ages, the epitomes of all time.

In order, therefore, to see clearly the nature of Free Trade, as recently recognised by the Legislature, we shall first view it in an historical light; considering consecutively its Outward Connexion with the Past; its Inward Significance; and its Rise, Progress, and Triumph.

CHAPTER I.

THE OUTWARD CONNEXION OF FREE TRADE WITH THE PAST.

1. To whatever extent the Free Trade movement has been indebted for its recent success to the enlightened energy of its abettors, and the imperative requirements of the present age, it is impossible, even on the most superficial survey, to separate it from the past progress of science, art, and industry in these realms. Commencing with this view of the subject, we cannot but remark at the outset that the triumph of Free Trade is closely connected with the growth of enlightened opinions in reference to the origin and distribution of national wealth. This important department of inquiry, which has of late years occupied so prominent a place in the discussions of the legislature, received scarcely any notice till the middle of the last century, when it began to attract the attention of some of the most distinguished philosophers of France. But though indebted for its first cultivation to Quesnai, Turgot, D'Alembert, Mirabeau, and other economists of the French School, the science of Political Economy is in reality the offspring of this country, since it found amongst us, not only the clearest and most impartial

exposition of its principles, but, what was of still greater importance, the practical application of those principles on the widest scale, and the most complete demonstration of their utility. The rationale of inquiry established by Bacon, and the objective turn which was given to the speculative thought of the last century by the metaphysics of Locke, point out the remoter origin of economical science ; at the same time it was indebted for the prominence which it then obtained to the awful state into which France was plunged by a long career of extravagance and military despotism. The finances of that country were then fast becoming desperate, the lower classes of the population were steeped in wretchedness, and economical questions were forced into discussion as the only way of saving the state from ruin. Unhappily, the disease was found too strong for the remedy ; an age of revolutions supervened, in which the institutions of feudalism were swept away. It is instructive, however, to reflect that the same causes which produced the French Revolution, contributed also to the cultivation of a science which will ultimately be the means of raising the social condi. tion of all nations, and uniting them permanently in the arts of peace.

2. It was most likely in consequence of the intimacy which subsisted between Adam Smith and the French Economists, that the former was first led to apply his accomplished mind to the problems of Political Economy, and the result at length appeared in his "Inquiry into the Nature and the Causes of the Wealth of Nations," "the most comprehensive and perfect work," to quote the language of Dugald Stewart, "that has yet appeared on the general principles of any branch

of legislation." Notwithstanding the luminous style and the vein of felicitous illustration which characterise this performance, the views it expounds did not become immediately popular; but its principles, nevertheless, matured in silence the opinions of the inquiring few, and occasionally, as in the orations of Fox and Burke, threw a ray of light on the hitherto unknown regions of revenue and trade. For some time, any formal application of the science to the business of the House of Commons was listened to with impatience, till the general distress which prevailed in the country sub-sequent to the conclusion of peace in 1815, the in-fluence of Mr. Huskisson, and the financial abilities of Mr. Ricardo, procured for its truths a respectful hearing, and succeeded in inaugurating a new com-mercial policy. The " Inquiry into the Wealth of Nations" may be regarded as the forerunner of Free Trade, and the firm hold which the principles of that work have now taken of the popular mind, constitutes the safest guarantee that ere long the last vestige of Protection shall disappear from the Statute Book.

3. A scientific exposition of the laws of trade would, however, have done comparatively little towards the attainment of commercial freedom, if our trade itself, by the magnitude of its operations, and the importance of its dependent interests, had not made their applica-tion a matter of necessity. Here a new order of cir-cumstances demands attention. The most important of these is the remarkable fitness of this country to become a seat of manufactures, and the emporium of a world-wide commerce. Consecrated in the purposes of Providence to the beneficent task of expounding to the world the laws of trade, the land we inhabit was

so arranged as to afford to every species of industrial enterprise the most favourable sphere of development. Although denied the warm temperature and luxuriant vegetation of tropical climes, it would be impossible to find a spot on which greater natural advantages have been bestowed. Every facility seems at hand for starting us on a manufacturing career; under whatever aspect we regard our native soil, it is rich in the materials of commerce. Those metals which are of greatest utility in the useful arts, and the coal which is requisite in working them, are distributed conveniently, and in inexhaustible abundance, throughout the land. We have plenty of stone, lime, slate, clay, and the various earths which are necessary to the manufacture of glass and earthenware. Our salt mines supply us with more of that mineral than we can ourselves consume; our soil affords us plentiful crops of corn, while the British fleece has been celebrated as an article of commerce from the earliest times. With our insulated position we have a greater line of sea coast, and a greater number of capacious harbours, as compared with the extent of land surface, than any other nation in the world. At the same time the geographical arrangement of the country, while it renders no part difficult of access, has divided it into separate districts, each of which, in accordance with the principle of the division of labour, has been appropriated by a particular manufacture, and thus economy of time and capital has been produced, as well as that frequent intercourse among persons of the same trade, which is so eminently favourable to excellence. The narrow extent of our inland territory, scarcely any part of which is more than a few hours' distance from an excellent sea-port, is another important contribution to that outburst of productive energy which has broken for ever the bondage of fiscal restriction; and when we reflect that the cotton of Georgia can be brought to our factories in almost the same time as would be required to land it on the quays of New York, we feel it is no chance result that England has become the world's instructress in the principles of an enlightened commercial policy.

4. But though these circumstances conspired to render Britain an extensive seat of manufacturing ingenuity, we should probably never have reached our present position if it had not been for one particular species of manufacture, the sudden growth and important results of which entitle it to a place among the most remarkable phenomena on record. Our treasures of iron and coal, our crystal mountain streams, and convenient outlets to the ocean, could hardly have failed to render us distinguished in the annals of commerce, but if Providence had never planted the cotton shrub we should in all probability never have known that prodigious expansion of trade which has distinguished the last hundred years. In that case our exports would probably have been little more than half their present amount; our command over the productions of foreign climes would have been proportionally less; population would have advanced at a slower rate; those majestic masses of men which stretch, like a living zone, through our central districts, would have had no existence; and the magic impulse which has been felt during that period in every department of national energy, which has affected more or less our literature, our laws, our social condition, our

political institutions, making us almost a new people, would never have been communicated.   The agent by which this change has been brought about is sufficiently insignificant; even antiquity, whose prerogative it has ever been to ennoble whatever it touches, has as yet conferred no dignity on *cotton*.   Our aristocratic aversion to it scarcely gives way when we are told that, thousands of years ago, it afforded clothing to the inhabitants of Hindostan, adorned the walls of Persian palaces, presented a theme of wonder to the father of history, and furnished the shrouds* in which the Egyptians wrapped their dead.   But though destitute of fashionable renown, it has already acquired one of a still higher kind.   This wondrous plant has become one of the most powerful agents of civilisation, and, associated with human skill, has given a broad and ineffaceable impress to the condition of the world. Its useful lustre was wisely reserved till the close of the feudal epoch, as if to show that the decaying institutions of the middle ages would not involve in their ruin the extinction of society; that their overthrow would rather resemble the release of an imprisoned soul, whose energies had long been anxious to burst into freer action, and that the olive branch of industry can effect changes at once more rapid, more extensive, and more durable than those which follow the bloody path of conquest.

5. Our natural advantages, combined with the introduction of cotton, lie at the root of that remarkable

---

* We are aware that this point is disputed.   For an able statement of the argument on both sides see art. COTTON, by Dr. Royle, of King's College, in Kitto's "Cyclopædia of Biblical Literature."

development of our manufacturing energy which at length created a necessity for Free Trade, but another and equally important circumstance was required to carry it to perfection—the mechanical inventions and chemical discoveries which render so illustrious the latter part of the eighteenth century. The successive introduction of the water-frame, the spinning-jenny, the mule, and the power-loom, produced a total change in the textile manufactures. A still higher place must be assigned to the steam-engine, an invention which seems the necessary complement of every other, which renders art prolific, and arms the softest touch of genius with demiurgic power. These inventions were worthily sustained by corresponding advances in other departments of science. Above all, the chemical researches of Black, Priestley, Dalton, and Berthollet, to the last of whom we are indebted for that application of the properties of oxymuriatic acid which has revolutionised the whole process of bleaching, contributed very powerfully to promote the excellence of our manufactures. These inventions and discoveries must, indeed, be regarded as the proximate cause of our commercial greatness; but for these it would have been impossible to have met the demands of our own markets, without bestowing a thought on the openings for profitable enterprise which might have been offered abroad. Their joint effect on the progress of trade resembles the marvels of romance much more than the sober facts of history. From a few hundred pounds' weight, our importation of cotton wool has increased to more than six hundred millions, and the value of our cotton manufacture is equal to one-half the value of our entire exports of manufactured

produce.   But not in one department of manufacture
alone has the impetus of improved machinery been
felt; it has extended itself to almost every branch of
industry, resulting everywhere in cheaper production,
wider markets, increased employment, and accumulated capital.

6. The most important result of the inventions of
the last century, considered in a political and social
point of view, is the influence they have exerted on
the increase and distribution of the population.   We
cannot doubt that, in this respect, a great change has
been brought about.   No century since the Conquest
has done half so much to revolutionise the modes of
subsistence, and with them the prevalent habits and
manners of the people, as that which closed with
1850.   During this period the population has multiplied at a quicker ratio than at any preceding epoch.
From 1801, the year when the first returns on this subject were made to Parliament, to 1841, the period of
the last census which was taken before the commencement of our Free Trade policy, the population of
the United Kingdom advanced from 16,338,102, to
27,041,031, being at the rate of 65½ per cent., and it is
probable that if the requisite data could be procured,
the same ratio would be found to hold good for the
twenty-five years immediately preceding the former
date.   The comparative value of this ratio of increase
will be better appreciated by a simple calculation.
Mr. Hallam estimates the population of England,
at the accession of Henry VII., in 1485, at three
millions.*   Now, if from this period, down to 1845, the

---

* "Constitutional History," Chapter I.

population had increased in the same ratio as it is ascertained to have done during the first forty years of the present century, the population of one part of the United Kingdom alone would have been 250,000,000. The rapid growth of the population during the period referred to is evidenced in part by the sudden rise and expansion of towns. Within the memory of some persons still living the populous hives of industry in the north were not a third of their present size. Leeds, Bradford, Sheffield, Halifax, Huddersfield had then scarcely lost that rural character which distinguished them three centuries ago, and grass was still growing on a great part of the space which is now covered with the crowded thoroughfares of Manchester. The population of this latter town in 1773, according to the estimate of Dr. Price, was, including Salford, only 27,246, not more than a fourteenth of its present amount. A spectator, taking his stand at the back of the amphitheatre of hills which closes the valley of the Irwell towards the east, would have looked in vain for those vast masses of factory piles which now chequer the landscape. Stockport, Ashton, Oldham, and Rochdale; Bolton, Bury, Blackburn, and Burnley, either of which is now equal in size and social importance to half a dozen of the ancient type of country boroughs, were then villages as compared with their present extent. But this rapid growth in the size of towns indicates something more than a quicker rate of increase in the population: it brings before us an important social change which has been effected, during the last hundred years, in the relative proportion of persons employed in the pursuits of agriculture, and those which are connected with commerce. Dur-

ing the twenty years, 1811—1831, the centesimal proportion of families employed in agricultural pursuits,
fell from 35·2 to 25·9 ; or, from constituting more
than one-third of the entire population at the commencement of that period, they sank to little more than
one-fourth at its close. During the same interval,
while the increase of families on the whole population
was 34 per cent., the centesimal increase of those
employed in agriculture was no more than $7\frac{1}{2}$. The
revolution thus noiselessly produced furnishes the key
to our present political position. This silent transfer
of the population to the seats of manufacturing
industry destroyed the exclusiveness of aristocratic
power, and commenced that era of popular education
and enfranchisement the full results of which can be
gathered only by future generations.

7. The growth of trade, together with the increase
and re-distribution of the population, has wrought a
great change in the structure of British society, and
points us to another cause of the concession of Free
Trade. That phase of social life in which the bulk
of the people depend for their livelihood upon
agriculture, is unquestionably more simple than one
in which they support themselves by manufactures.
Such a state of things, especially when connected with
the laws of entail, which form an essential part of the
feudal system, never fails to repress the growth of
population, to render difficult or impossible free
personal intercourse between large bodies of men,
to check combination as a principle of popular effort,
and, generally, to keep the mass of the people in
dependence on their hereditary employers. Trade, on
the other hand, especially when it is carried on with

foreign countries, introduces some complication into the mode of procuring subsistence. The workman, instead of parting with his labour in almost direct exchange for food, has to sell it, through several hands, in distant markets, and his ability to supply his wants depends really upon the willingness of the foreigner to employ him. In these circumstances he becomes, perforce, a politician. His attention is drawn as naturally to questions of Customs and Excise, as that of the farm labourer to the state of the weather in the time of harvest. It is evident that when a million of such workmen are engrafted on any population, a new political power has sprung up, which, whether constitutionally represented or not, will necessarily have great weight in the future decisions of the legislature. The same circumstances which lead such an important section of the people to the formation of political opinions, furnish them also with the means of placing them in the most prominent and imperative aspect before the community. Fifty thousand persons residing within one square mile will ripen faster than the same number spread through half a county; while the rapidity with which, in the former case, plans may be formed, the ease and secrecy with which intercourse of any kind may be carried on, and the courage which is always kindled by conscious prowess, render the prevalent wishes of the one class much more formidable than those of the other. It is by no means necessary to the political weight of these advantages that they should be actually wielded. The robber shuns the place where arms *are kept.* The possession of power, where this is undoubted, is sufficient to command respect. The manufacturing districts have, happily, not often been in a state even bordering on insurrection, but who will say that what the multitudes therein gathered *could* do, and in supposable circumstances *might* do, has exerted no influence on the minds of our legislators ? A wise statesman looks well to the actual elements of the population for which he frames laws, and the concentration in a few vast masses of several millions of men, of quickened wants, and rapidly advancing intelligence, is a phenomenon which he cannot permit himself to despise. The production of such a phenomenon is the highest political significance of trade, and through this channel it has become with us the omnipotent procurer of its own freedom.

8. We are now brought to the last in that series of great events which cleared the way for the enfranchisement of commerce, viz., the legislative recognition of the political power which had been called into existence by the events of the last hundred years. In a country which has raised "the press" to the dignity of a "fourth estate," and in which public opinion has obtained the force of paramount law, the House of Commons is not the only agency by which an efficient control can be exercised over public measures ; yet still it can hardly be questioned that if the Reform Bill had never passed into law, a Free Trade policy could not have been so speedily or so pacifically won. We say nothing here respecting the intrinsic merits of that measure, save that the friends of healthy progress can hardly regard it as final. The country will probably pronounce ere long that another advance is necessary, but still it is the Reform Bill

which gave us the opportunity of confronting monopoly in the highest seats of power, and before the audience of the world. Day after day, during the Free Trade struggle, the people caught some new argument from the echoes of St. Stephen's, which gradually overcame the prejudices and silenced the arguments of Protection. Exposed there to the constant assault of men who had first practised on the exchange the shrewdness and common sense which distinguished them in the senate, self-interest was obliged to have recourse to superhuman ingenuity in order to mask its motives, and the honest champions of the corn laws were driven from one post to another, till their discomfiture was manifest to the nation, and avowed conversion became the only way of escaping with a vestige of credit for disinterestedness and capacity. These discussions, transferred to the newspapers, and dispersed within a few hours into every city, village, and hamlet in the empire, carried on the education of the people in the principles of Free Trade, and prepared them for anticipating the legislature in a unanimous verdict of approval. How different would the case have been if the seats of Manchester, Stockport, Rochdale and Birmingham had been filled by the nominees of Gatton and Old Sarum! Then indeed the settlement of the question might have been transferrred to another field, and the victory secured by means of very different weapons.

In the events which we have thus rapidly glanced at, as tending to necessitate the ultimate triumph of Free Trade, we cannot but be struck with one general fact, viz., the harmonious co-operation of dissimilar circumstances in the accomplishment of one grand purpose, and the hidden link which connects the properties of matter, the efforts of science, and the gifts of genius with the political and social well-being of mankind. The present commercial elevation of Great Britain is of world-wide interest; we shall not exaggerate its true character if we regard it as inaugurating a new era in the condition and prospects of our race. On these heights sits Freedom, exulting in the achievements of her oldest sons, and bidding the nations share in, and emulate the peaceful triumphs they have won.* But on what basis has Providence raised this mountain-pile of grandeur? —We see it in our mineral treasures, in the inventions of such men as Wyatt, Arkwright, Hargreaves, Watt, and Stephenson; in the enterprise and self-reliance of our capitalists; in the energy and skill of myriads of industrious artisans; in, may we not add, the practical sagacity and indomitable perseverance which distinguish the Saxon mind. On such foundations has Providence reared the fabric which time will consecrate not to wealth only, but to whatever can humanize and bless the world.

* Tennyson: "Of old sat Freedom on the heights," &c. Poems, p. 177.

CHAPTER II.

INWARD SIGNIFICANCE OF FREE TRADE.

FROM the outward connexions which unite Free Trade with the past, we proceed to consider its inward significance as an historical event. The clue which will best conduct us through this part of our inquiry is suggested by the question—What social and political tendencies does Free Trade represent?—Of what principles is it the triumph?—In what respect may it be regarded as the symbol of national progress? It is under this aspect that the Free Trade movement will appear most interesting to posterity. To them, the events which occurred in immediate connexion with it, although of most importance to us, will resemble the slight undulations which the eye can trace on the surface of the rising wave, while the movement itself will appear like those majestic billows which carry the eye backward to a distant shore.

1. Looking at the Free Trade movement under this aspect, we recognise it as marking that period in the progress of trade, at which its laws are clearly understood; when the growing intelligence of those who are engaged in it works out its emancipation

C

from self-imposed restriction, and asks from legislation no other boon than free scope for its unfettered energies. In trade, as in everything else relating to practical life, we are endowed with certainin born instincts, which, if faithfully followed, never fail to lead us right. As in art the sense of beauty, as in morals the sense of rectitude, so in exchange the dictates of self-interest, controlled of course by justice, are an unerring guide. But circumstances sometimes conspire to darken these perceptions, and to involve the brightest truths awhile in a cloud of error. This has been the case pre-eminently with the principles of trade, as they were first planted and developed in Europe. The feudal origin of most modern states was very unfavourable to the growth of correct views of commercial policy. The flood of invasion which successively swept over every province of the Roman Empire, destroyed whatever industry had previously flourished, and reduced the entire population, except a few despots, to the condition of slaves. For a long period all commerce was suspended, nor was it possible to think of accumulating wealth, when life and property lay at the mercy of the sword. After a long interval, order at length began to be re-established, but still the influences under which trade ventured to raise its head were exceedingly unfavourable to its healthy progress. Cooped up in towns, frowned upon by the shadow of baronial castles, prevented by heavy tolls from free inland intercourse, and crushed by extortionate exactions for the slender privilege of continuing unenslaved, the tradesmen and merchants of those days were naturally led to fight monopoly with its own weapons. Weak, they sought the refuge of the weak. Protection then indeed had a valid meaning. As the only method of successfully coping with the barbarous spirit of the age, they copied the example of their feudal superiors, became exclusive and aristocratic, turned every trade into a " mystery" accessible only to the initiated, wrapt every species of handicraft in the bondage of unjust laws, and forgetting that, if labour is property, freedom to enter upon it is also a right, enforced long apprenticeships and the permissive sanction of guilds. When at length the burgesses of enfranchised towns obtained a place in parliament, their legislative policy betrayed the same narrow spirit. Their demands, when rendered weighty by their growing opulence, were found too often on the side of commercial restriction. Universal freedom of trade was an idea far in advance of the age, and every branch of labour therefore sought, by acquiring exclusive advantages for itself, to counterbalance those which were enjoyed by others. In those times wealthy merchants often laid hold of the necessities of the Court, and, by means of opportune bribes, secured some profitable monopoly to themselves. Sometimes an individual was found sufficiently intelligent and patriotic to expose these evils, but, generally speaking, a tendency to rely on unjust preferences was in that age characteristic of the trading spirit. Deprived of an open field, oppressed by feudal domination, it sought to repay injustice with injustice, and in the attempt inflicted on itself still deeper wounds. But such mistakes can only occur during the infancy of commerce; experience has a never-failing tendency to correct the first dictates of selfishness, and to show that a just policy is also that

which pays best.   Increasing knowledge has rebuked
the narrow spirit of our ancestors, and brought to light
the true science of trade.   Accordingly, the exclusive
privileges of guilds have been abolished, every man
has now an equal right to ply his trade in our cities
and corporate towns, the stringent laws which once
regulated apprenticeship have been considerably re-
laxed, and in a variety of kindred measures the great
principle of Free Trade in labour has been recognised
by the state.   In other respects, also, the theory of
trade has experienced considerable development.   No
person now regards wealth as synonymous with the
precious metals, or supposes that the path to opulence
lies in withdrawing from every branch of foreign
traffic which will not yield us a balance of gold.
There are now few persons who do not admit that, as
a mercantile people, it is our policy to allow our
neighbours every possible opportunity of profitable
trade, and that to buy in the cheapest market the
world affords, and to sell in the dearest, is a natural
right, as it is also the universal law of well-being alike
to individuals and communities.

2. The Free Trade movement is thus connected with
the past, as signalising the complete self-development
and self-emancipation of commerce, but it is equally
significant, in an historical point of view, as marking
an epoch in the progress of civil freedom.   Freedom
of trade is properly included in the freedom of the
individual.   It forms part of that right of free action
which is the inalienable possession of every man.
Buying and selling are merely modes of exchanging
our own property for the property of others, and in
this process we naturally owe obedience to no man-

dates but such as spring from the obligations of morality. Moreover, in every community which has made any progress in civilisation, the exchange of commodities is very nearly allied to subsistence, and to fetter it with restrictions is in some measure to cripple the right to live. Accordingly, this is a province on which the state has no right to enter. Precincts which lie so near the existence and freedom of the individual are too sacred to endure the presence of the legislative power. The assumed right to tax in any way, or for any purpose, the process of exchange, is questionable in point of justice as well as policy. Property is taxable for state purposes, but not the operations by which property is acquired. This is, when strictly viewed, as unwarrantable an infringement on the liberty of the subject as any species of enforced obedience to despotic power.

If these remarks are true, all laws which aim at diverting trade from its natural channels; which step in between the seller and the buyer, with a view to make them act otherwise than a regard to their own interests would lead them to act; nay, every species of impost which falls upon the process of exchange, is essentially unjust, and at variance with the genius of a free state. The origin of such laws is to be found in conquest, by which the conqueror always acquires an imaginary right to the lives and property of the vanquished. To this we may ascribe those vexatious proceedings by which many of our earlier monarchs strove to make trade the slave of their ignorant tyranny, and the entire system of taxation which, till within a few years, has hitherto been pursued, is traceable to the same source. Legislative enactments directed against the cultivation of this article, the importation or exportation of another, or fixing the place, terms, and manner of sale in reference to a third ; the stimulus of drawbacks and bounties, and the quietus of prohibitory duties ; all this may properly be stigmatised as impolitic, but it is more, it is unjust ; it is a civil wrong ; it violates the inalienable right of free action ; it is at best but a wily badge of serfdom, one of the relics of a feudal age.   When William the Conqueror obtained possession of England, he became, by a victor's right, lord of the land and its occupants. The merchant, in his eye, was but a kind of serf, as much the property of his feudal superior as the helots of agriculture.   To have spared the lives of the conquered was regarded as an act of grace, and if the usages of war gave him a command over their lives, how much more did they invest him with an undisputed right to control their actions? Hence, when trade began to revive, he brought it, without a struggle, beneath the feudal yoke; the throne assumed the unquestioned prerogative of imposing on it any conditions which might suit its interest, its ignorance, or its caprice.   The most absurd regulations were framed, the most mischievous laws were enacted, so that, in looking back, the historian is led to wonder that trade could by any means survive them.   Meanwhile the exchequer fed itself on the industry of the people, every new want was met by some new impost, and that fiscal fabric—indirect taxation—was slowly reared, which some political writers have ventured to praise because it was an *invisible* incubus on the energies of the country.

The pretensions of despotism are inconsistent with

the diffusion of knowledge and the advance of civilisation, and one of the first indications of national progress is the growth of correct views respecting the legitimate province of the legislative power. Ever since the Conquest a tide has been setting in, beneath which the landmarks of tyranny have successively disappeared. Every succeeding age has witnessed the exercise of a more enlightened discrimination in defining the sphere of the civil ruler; contemporaneously with the development of the theory of trade, there has occurred a development of the theory of politics, and the recent repeal of those laws which fettered commerce marks the point of progress which has been reached in both. The state is finally expelled from the circle of private interests, justice between man and man is recognised as its sole province, and its resources are henceforth to be drawn, not from oppressive imposts on industry, wrapped in puerile concealment, but from assessments openly and honestly levied, and voluntarily acquiesced in as the price which a free man pays for benefits conferred.

3. While the Free Trade movement marks the effect of past experience in assimilating our commercial and political practice to the dictates of science, it is still more interesting as the sign of a great change in popular opinion, which has been slowly ripening for centuries, and which is now issuing in the social as well as, political enfranchisement of industry. In every state which has either been founded, or entirely revolutionised, by conquest, the pursuits of trade have always been coupled with inferiority of social position. Perhaps this statement might be made still more comprehensive, since every

people who have been enthusiastically attached to warlike pursuits, have regarded the occupations of handicraft and traffic with a certain measure of contempt. This is the true spirit of barbarism, in which justice yields to violence, and mere animal prowess is exalted above intellectual and moral worth. In those rude ages where civilisation takes its rise, the warrior alone corresponds to the popular type of nobleness; the strong arm which can wield the sword, and the reckless daring which can face with exultation the dangers of battle, seem to unite every feature of heroic perfection; all else is drivelling and mean. If society advances without interruption from this primary state, it is long indeed before the peaceful pursuits of industry are thought compatible with the maintenance of aristocratic rank. The trader may become wealthy, and clothed in consequence with some degree of consideration, but till the prejudices of barbarism are dispelled from the public mind, he will always be placed under a ban of degradation, and his pacific honours will be deemed infinitely less brilliant than those which, however justly legitimated by time, were founded originally on a robber's right, and were reached through rivers of blood.

Such false sentiments do not remain exclusively among the classes with whom they originated. Acting on the ambition which is innate in the human breast, they impregnate the ranks beneath, till a sympathetic tinge is communicated to the very bottom of the social scale. Hence the pitiable prejudices which, till a recent period, were extensively spread abroad through English society, and which, in some quarters, where they are fostered by more than ordinary ignorance, are not yet extinct. Hence the cold reserve and superb disdain which high-bred grandeur has often assumed, at the mention of a person who, though superior in every quality which can render a man valuable to the community, had the insufferable misfortune to be " only a tradesman." Happily those days are passing away, trade has now a chivalry of its own ; a chivalry whose stars are radiant with the more benignant lustre of justice, happiness, and religion, and whose titles will outlive the barbarous nomenclature of Charlemagne. Trade can be scorned no longer ; it has burst forth with the splendour of heaven-made genius, and compelled the reluctant homage of all ranks. The presence of a self-elevated man is no longer regarded as derogatory to any circle, however hallowed by the prestige of hereditary greatness and historic fame. Thanks to the lofty spirit of British patriotism, which burns with as pure a flame in the palace as by the peasant's hearth, the commercial phenomena of our age have met with a graceful recognition, and our constitutional honours are rapidly being shared by men whose title to distinction has been won in the beneficent pursuits of industry.

4. This social enfranchisement of trade is associated with one which is at least of equal importance— its release from political disability. We have mentioned the legislative act which extended the electoral franchise to the populous towns in our manufacturing districts as one of the immediate causes of the Free Trade triumph, but contemplated from a different point of view it is itself the effect of a tendency which

attained a still greater triumph in the repeal of the corn laws. It is contrary to the genius of a feudal state that property acquired by trade should be invested with political power. This, accordingly, was the principle of Norman legislation. The king and his barons, the former being the absolute owner of the soil, and the latter the persons to whom it was given in fief, were clothed, *de facto*, with the entire authority of the realm; the landed interest then was absolute. Circumstances, however, soon rendered a modification of the system necessary. The nation whose political destinies were placed at the feet of the conqueror of Hastings possessed a vigorous life, the energies of which could not long be repressed. Burgesses were soon found by the side of barons in the councils of the sovereign, and trade began to exert some influence, however small, on the course of legislation. By this step the legitimacy of an entirely new title to political power was distinctly recognised, and a blow was given to the feudal system thus early in the period of its naturalisation amongst us, beneath which it was at last to crumble away. Still, the innovation, though important, was not of sufficient magnitude to attract opposition; it was an insertion of the thin edge of the wedge, and gave little notice of the destructive separation which was sooner or later to ensue; the landed interest was no longer absolute, but it was still immensely paramount to every other. Time passed on, and amid the wasting wars which consigned many a gallant lineage to oblivion, trade was silently extending its operations, and rising to greater influence in the state. The naval victories of Elizabeth, the zeal for maritime discovery which distinguished the sixteenth century, and the gradual application of juster principles to the management of commerce, increased the wealth of the mercantile and manufacturing portion of the community; while the civil struggles of the seventeenth century finally secured for them a continually increasing share of political power; still, such was the vast influence of the landed interest, that its permanent ascendancy seemed as yet unthreatened. In the eighteenth century the process was quickened. Towards its close our manufacturing energy broke out with almost miraculous power. The result of this was that our ancient municipal regime suddenly became antiquated. Those small boroughs which had hitherto been the sole representatives of the trading spirit, whose associations, at once Celtic, Roman, and Saxon, carried the mind back to a period compared with which the throne itself was but of yesterday, and whose chartered privileges and aristocratic connexions had rendered them the most conservative element in the state, found themselves at once thrown into the shade by those leviathan communities which had sprung up, unfavoured and unfranchised, in the once obscure wilds of the north. The effect of this revolution was to change the equipoise of wealth. Vast as was the value of those territorial possessions which upheld the feudal power of the aristocracy, it was now rivalled by interests which had hitherto kept at an humble distance. Industry now stood side by side with hereditary opulence; the owner of ten thousand spindles confronted the lord of ten thousand acres; the one grasping the steam-engine, the other the plough; each surrounded by an equal number of dependents, and bearing an equal share in the burdens and dangers of the state. Now the time had arrived when the shadow of an injustice between such rivals could no longer be endured. The suppliant of twenty generations back has now himself become a hero, who offers his hand with honest pride to the descendant of mail-clad barons, but will be his inferior no more. Trade shall no longer pay a tribute to the soil; the exchequer shall no longer become the agent, through the medium of taxation, of depressing one great national interest for the sake of raising the revenues of another; but justice, even-handed, shall deal out the same to all. This is the meaning of commercial freedom; it is the establishment of amicable relations, on the basis of perfect equity, between classes which had hitherto been antagonistic to each other. Free Trade thus annihilates one of the last remaining vestiges of serfdom, closes an era of disunion and distrust, in which haughty reserve on the one side has been repaid too well with defiance and hate on the other; an era full of bitterness to individuals and of danger to the commonwealth; and inaugurates a new state of things, in which all petty rivalries will cease, and all ranks cordially join in the patriotic task of advancing to the uttermost of their power the honour and happiness of their common country.

CHAPTER III.

THE RISE, PROGRESS, AND TRIUMPH OF THE FREE TRADE MOVEMENT.

HAVING considered the outward connexions of the Free Trade movement with the past, and its inward significance, we proceed now to sketch its actual rise, progress, and triumph. The revolution we are about to trace has been a rapid one. Ten years ago those who are now among the most eloquent and conscientious advocates of Free Trade were its determined opponents. Hence the Free Trade movement stands before us with the distinctness of a drama : we see it calling into play the most energetic elements of the human character ; the men who acted the chief parts in it constituted a galaxy of statesmen such as our country has been seldom able to boast, and they are still, with one great exception, among the most conspicuous on the stage of public affairs. At its commencement the bulk of the people regarded its principles with uncon- cern; in both sections of the legislature it had to contend with hostile majorities; and a party, strong in numbers, wealth, hereditary power, and above all, in parliamentary tact and genius, were its sworn foes.

But in the course of seven or eight years the scene was totally changed, the nation was enthusiastic in its favour. At the sacrifice of the dearest political ties a band of distinguished statesmen stood forward in its support, throwing around themselves, and the cause they espoused, the purest lustre by a manly retractation of past errors, and the triumph of commercial freedom was completed by the transfer of its principles to the statute book. If we wished merely to contemplate the effects of Free Trade upon the physical well-being of the people, it would still be incumbent upon us briefly to trace the progress and unfold the workings of such a change. But our plan is more comprehensive; we recognise in the success of the Free Trade movement the creation of a vast moral power, which has already communicated itself to our national life, and is pregnant with the most important consequences to the political condition and prospects of the coming age. Accordingly, starting with the consolidation of our restrictive system in 1815, we propose briefly to delineate its leading features, point out the successive modifications which it has undergone, and describe the measures by which it was ultimately overthrown.

Commencing with the date we have just named, the Free Trade movement divides itself, chronologically, into four distinct periods. The first of these, extending from the close of the war to 1822, may be termed the *dark ages* of Protection, during which its maxims ruled the legislature with absolute sway, and produced their genuine fruits in popular suffering and sedition. The second, dating from the liberal measures of Mr., afterwards Lord, Wallace, and extending to the period of Mr. Huskisson's retirement from office, was distinguished by the first attempts on the part of the government to develope a Free Trade policy, and gave cheering indications that the lessons of experience were silently moulding the convictions of our rising statesmen. The third interval has for its landmark on one side the absorption of all agitation for minor objects in the grand struggle for a reform of the House of Commons, and on the other, the subsidence of the movement into one for cheap bread, the rise of the Anti-Corn Law League, and the resignation of the Melbourne ministry in 1841. While the fourth extends from the accession of Sir Robert Peel to the present time, and embraces the leading events which constitute the Free Trade triumph, from the significant alterations of the tariff in 1842, to the entire repeal of the Corn and Navigation Laws in 1846 and 1849. These periods do not merely succeed each other; they are bound by an organic connexion. We have first, the experiment of absolute monopoly and prohibition; next, symptoms of misgiving, and a consequent relaxation of our restrictive system, though in the face of much opposition, and to an extent altogether incommensurate with the necessities of the case. During the following interval we see the spirit of popular discontent dashing impetuously against the pillars of the constitution, seeking the means of redressing social grievances in a fresh distribution of political power; while in the closing scene of the drama those grievances stand out isolated from all political questions, and by means of the newly obtained franchise are levelled for ever. Such is a succinct outline of the period which must now pass more in detail, but still as briefly as possible, under review.

I. The close of the revolutionary wars may be regarded as the commencement of a new epoch in the commercial and manufacturing career of this country. One of the most remarkable effects of that contest was the wall of separation which it raised, both in an economical and political point of view, between the times which preceded it and those which were to follow. In the blood of its armies Europe had blotted out its old recollections ; the landmarks of its former policy were overflowed ; international legislation was brought back again to its normal state, and an entirely new path had to be struck out. The commercial position of Great Britain was especially interesting. The victories of Nelson had all but annihilated the navies of every continental power, and left us, with the single exception of a rival across the Atlantic, the undisputed masters of the sea. The long continuance of hostilities had depressed every foreign manufacturing interest which might have entered into successful competition with our own, and constituted the British Isles the workshop of the world. In order to maintain this proud position, it was above all things requisite that we should enter into relations of friendly and equitable intercourse with other nations, and freely admit in exchange for our own produce whatever they had to offer. Such a policy would no doubt have been attended with the happiest results. It would have confined the capital of our neighbours to the production of raw material, or to those kinds of handicraft in which peculiar advantages permitted them to excel ; it would have prevented the rise of that commercial jealousy which has thwarted so many of our best laid plans, and exposed our trade to such extreme dangers; it would, above all, have brought the states of Europe into closer and more beneficent contact, broken down the absurd barriers of national prejudice, diminished incalculably the chances of war, and, by rendering useless the maintenance of vast forces by sea and land, removed a crushing weight from the common industry of the world. Unhappily, this was *not* the course adopted; narrow views and selfish dictates resumed another thirty years' lease of power, and the accumulated evils arising from this ratification of old errors were found necessary to force upon us the measures of common sense.

It is difficult to conceive of a more distressing and humiliating picture than that which is afforded by the commercial attitude of this country at the era of which we speak. We see a people, acknowledged, in point of manufacturing resources and skill, to occupy the highest place, sheltering themselves behind protective duties; striving, with puerile selfishness, to make its impregnability more secure; a people whose very existence depended on profitable exchange, on buying in the cheapest and selling in the dearest market, astutely raising, to their own disadvantage, the price of all foreign commodities; restraining themselves by law from purchasing those articles as cheaply as other nations, and then, not unfrequently taxing themselves again in their excise duties, so that the highest price which could be obtained for their exported produce barely equalled, in many cases, the cost of manufacture. This love of imposts was omniscient; it seized on every article which by any stretch of possibility an Englishman could want.

Considerably more than a thousand different kinds of foreign produce were prohibited from enriching us, unless they purchased that privilege at the custom-house. Among the more important of these may be mentioned sugar, on which differential duties pressed in favour of our own colonies; timber, which, when brought from the countries bordering on the Baltic, was subject to imposts varying from 100 to 500 per cent., in order to give precedence in the market to that of inferior quality supplied from Canada; tea, of which a large proportion paid into the exchequer 300 per cent. on its original cost. Besides these may be mentioned glass, tanned hides, a variety of valuable drugs, such as cochineal and indigo, which were extensively used in manufacturing processes; cattle, sheep, meat, and all articles which could be employed as common food, together with every kind of foreign manufacture capable of being brought into competition with our own. Two sections of our protective code deserve, however, special notice : the one as affecting an article of food most nearly connected with human subsistence; the other from its generic importance to every branch of commerce; we refer to the laws affecting corn and navigation.

1. From the end of the fourteenth century down to our own times, CORN has been the subject of incessant and ever-varying legislation. Previous to the former period one uniform rule seems to have prevailed; the prohibition of all exportation of corn without a special license from the crown. In the year 1394, a law passed permitting the free exportation of corn, vesting however in the crown a discretional power of forbidding it, a power which was annulled in 1436, and the right

of exportation, whenever the home price of wheat should not exceed six shillings and eightpence per quarter, rendered absolute. In 1463 we meet with the earliest statute relating to the importation of corn, this being declared illegal except when its price should exceed the sum just named. Seventy-one years subsequent to the passing of this measure, an act was adopted which abrogated all previous legislation, and restored the law to its original state, but in 1554 exportation was again permitted, and by successive acts of parliament the price within which it might take place was raised from six shillings and eightpence to fifty-three shillings and fourpence. The change of prices consequent on the importation of the precious metals had by this time rendered obsolete the prohibitory statute of 1463, but in 1670 a prohibitory duty was laid on the importation of wheat so long as its home price was under the sum last named, and the heavy impost of eight shillings per quarter after it reached that point, and till it rose to eighty shillings per quarter. Even this excessive measure of protection, with the right of exportation extended, was thought insufficient to shield the interests of our agriculturalists from injury, and immediately after the Revolution an act passed the legislature by which, within certain limits, a bounty of five shillings was allowed on every quarter of wheat exported, and, ten years after, the custom-house duties on the exportation of corn were entirely remitted. In 1773, the price at which wheat was allowed to be imported at a nominal duty of sixpence per quarter was reduced from eighty shillings to forty-eight shillings, but in 1791 the limit of importation on those easy terms was raised to fifty-four shillings, and when the price fell to fifty shillings, importation was altogether forbidden.* In 1804, the price at which wheat could be imported was raised to sixty-six shillings per quarter, and that at which it was met by duties wholly prohibitory to sixty-three shillings. The high prices which prevailed till the close of the war rendered this statute practically inoperative, and in the years 1813 and 1814 the agricultural interest exerted itself to the utmost to obtain more efficient protection. They succeeded then in carrying a bill which set the exportation of corn quite free from legislative restriction, whatever its price might be at home, and in 1815, amid prodigious popular excitement, which rendered it necessary to surround the Houses of Parliament with soldiers, after protracted opposition, coupled with an eloquent protest against it, which was entered on the journal of the House of Lords, a law passed by which the importation of wheat for home consumption was absolutely prohibited till its home price reached eighty shillings per quarter. It has been said that the motives which disposed the majority of the legislature to adopt this course, had an important relation to the peculiar monetary character of the epoch. The excessive issue of inconvertible securities by the Bank of England had caused a great depreciation in the value of the currency. The circulation of the Bank of England, which in 1797 was little more than eight millions and a half, amounted in 1815 to more than twenty-seven millions in notes alone. In antici-

* "History of British Commerce," by G. L. Craik, M.A. chap. lx.

pating a return to cash payments, and the universal fall of prices which would ensue, the landed interest insisted upon a measure which would insure them the same returns in a metallic currency as they had received in the depreciated paper currency ; a measure which, in other words, would permit them with safety to practise a fraud upon the rest of the nation by compelling them to pay for their food at a higher scale of prices, when every other kind of payment was fixed according to a lower scale. But whatever outward form the reasons on which the adoption of the measure was urged might assume, it is certain that their essence lay in the grossest self-interest; a degree of self-interest so intense as to wither up the common sense of rectitude which makes us feel instinctively that theft is theft. Both the measure itself, and the legislature which passed it, deserve the severest reprobation. It is impossible to separate from the former the guilt of frequent crimes. By occasioning an unnatural scarcity of food it led to the perpetration of innumerable acts of violence which received in too many instances an expiation on the scaffold, and thus, in common with the blackest misdeeds which stain humanity, having originated in selfishness it ended in blood.

2. The laws affecting NAVIGATION, which, at the period whence we commence our survey, were in full force, cannot lay claim to an equally ancient date, or an history equally chequered. They were passed in the Rump Parliament, in 1651, and continued essentially unaltered for nearly two centuries. The immediate occasion of framing them was no doubt a combination of political and commercial jealousy.

The Dutch had gained possession of nearly all the carrying trade between the West Indies and Europe, and were, moreover, attached to the political interests of the exiled heir of the British Crown. In such narrow and transient views did that policy originate which came at length to be regarded as the palladium of our greatness. Thus easily can the passions of a moment, when allied with party interests, set off with great names, and seen through the haze of antiquity, be passed off as the dictates of superhuman wisdom. It has tended to prolong the reputation of the navigation laws that they received the approval of Adam Smith.* His approval, however, is inconsistent with his own principles; he has told us how we ought to estimate monopolies. The act of navigation declared that no merchandise of Asia, Africa, or America should be imported into any of the possessions of Great Britain except in English-built ships, belonging to English subjects, navigated by an English commander, and having a majority of the crew Englishmen. It further enacted that no goods, the growth or manufacture of any country in Europe, should be imported into Great Britain except in English ships, or in ships belonging to the country in which the goods were produced, or from which they were commonly imported. Early in the reign of Charles II. the act was confirmed and extended. The restrictions which previously affected only the importation of goods into this country were now laid on the exportation of goods from England to foreign countries, and by subsequent regulations these disa-

---

* "Wealth of Nations," B. iv. ch. 2.

bilities on foreign shipping were further increased by discriminating duties on the articles imported in them, and by heavier port dues. A slight change in the application of these laws became necessary when we recognised the independence of our American colonies, the latter then assuming the same relation to this country as the states of continental Europe, and one of the first acts of Congress was to retaliate upon our exclusiveness by a statute framed in exact accordance with our own.

Such was the character of our commercial legislation at the commencement of the year 1815, but, notwithstanding the clamour for Protection on the part of the agricultural interest, which resulted, as we have seen, in the enactment of a more stringent corn law, indications were not wholly wanting about the same period that a change was at hand. One of the most promising of these was the modification which had just been made in the East India Company's Charter. That powerful association had hitherto engrossed the whole of the trade to East India and China. Private enterprise had thus been shut out of a most profitable field, and the people of this country had been obliged to pay for the ambition and extravagance which had marked our Indian administration by exorbitant prices on articles of daily food.* A portion of this monopoly was continued till 1833, but the trade to the Presidencies of Madras, Calcutta, and Bombay, together with the port of

* Yet at this time it was declared "a high crime and misdemeanour" for an Englishman, "directly or indirectly, to go, sail, or repair to, or be found in, the East Indies" without a licence. 33 George III. c. 52, s. 132.

Penang, was thrown open in 1814. The following year an important change was effected in our relations with the United States. Thus far, since the retaliatory measures of Congress to which we have just adverted, the governments of the two countries had vigorously maintained the battle against each other's mercantile interest, with incalculable vexation and loss on both sides. A useless set of ships had always to be kept in pay, because either nation refused to export its commodities in the vessels of the other. American vessels, after discharging their cargo at the docks of Liverpool, had to return loaded with ballast, while, perhaps, all the way, within hailing distance, the vessels of Great Britain were carrying our own manufactures to the States, themselves to return empty in like manner, and similarly accompanied by American ships freighted with American produce. If this absurdity had been acted on a narrower scale it would have appeared matchless; a folly like this had nothing wherewith to screen itself from derision except its magnitude. But this was not all that the two rival nations did towards annihilating each other's commerce. The only privilege as yet conceded on both sides, that of bringing over their respective produce in their own vessels, was rendered as nugatory as possible by heavy discriminating dues and imposts. Interpreting the conduct of both nations in the spirit of their petty and truly barbarous policy, it would appear as if a British vessel at New York, and an American vessel at Liverpool, were respectively looked upon as proper subjects for every species of cozenage and oppression. At length the evil worked its own correction. Such a state of things could no longer be tolerated, and a convention which was signed in 1815 placed the ships of both nations in a position of perfect reciprocal equality. This step was followed, after a lapse of six or seven years, by similar arrangements with other countries. In 1823 Prussia announced its intention of retaliating upon British shipping and merchandise, unless those belonging to Prussian subjects were forthwith released from the · heavy disabilities imposed upon them in British ports. This spirited conduct led to a correspondence, which resulted in the " Reciprocity of Duties Act," by virtue of which the crown was empowered to extend to other countries the principles which had already been applied in the convention of 1815 to our intercourse with the United States. Treaties in conformity with this measure were entered into the following year with the Netherlands, Prussia, and Denmark, and in the course of the next five years with the Hanse Towns, France, Mexico, and Austria.*

II. These indications that more enlightened views were gradually gaining the ascendant in our commercial policy, were confirmed by the measure which, in 1822, passed the legislature under the auspices of Mr. Wallace, and by the still more important changes which were effected by Mr. Huskisson in 1825. Mr. Wallace's measures were intended to mitigate still further the pressure of the navigation laws, and to give to our colonies greater freedom of intercourse with each other and with foreign countries. By these enactments, certain descriptions of goods were allowed to be imported into this country, from any European

* Porter's " Progress of the Nation."

port, in ships belonging to the port of shipment. Dutch vessels, which had hitherto been prohibited from entering any English port with cargo, were placed on the same footing as the ships of other nations. South American produce, which could formerly be imported only from certain ports of Spain and Portugal, was now permitted to be brought direct from the places of growth. In certain important branches of traffic, the privilege was now granted to our West Indian Colonies of trading direct in British vessels with any port of Europe or Africa, instead of confining their operations, as they had thus far been compelled to do, to the markets of Great Britain. Mr. Huskisson began his commercial changes in 1824, by a revision of the laws relating to the silk trade. Previous to that year our domestic manufactures in silk had been protected by an entire prohibition of silk articles, the produce of the foreign loom; by heavy duties on thrown silk, or silk in the first stage of manufacture, and even by bounties on silk exports which were granted in the reign of George I. The prohibition of silk manufactures dated from 1765, and such goods were expressly excluded from the treaty of commerce which was made with France in 1786. By the law of 1824 the prohibition of silk goods of foreign manufacture was changed into protective duties of 30 per cent. *ad valorem*, the duty of four shillings per pound on raw silk was reduced to one penny, and that of fourteen shillings and eight pence per pound on thrown silk, to three shillings and sixpence. It was provided, however, that these changes should not take full effect till 1826. In 1825 the same principles were embodied in more extensive measures. Foreign manufactures, instead of being totally excluded from the British market, were placed under maximum duties of 30 per cent. *ad valorem*, and at the same time the duties chargeable on those raw materials which were extensively employed in our manufactures were repealed or greatly reduced.

These important changes on the part of the Government, indicating a disposition extensively to modify, if not wholly to abandon, the protective system, which had hitherto been jealously preserved intact, was not wholly spontaneous. Ever since the passing of the corn laws in 1815, the condition of the poorer classes, especially in the manufacturing districts, had been such as to excite the liveliest solicitude. Probably no darker period, in a social and political point of view, is to be found in the annals of this country than that which elapsed between 1815 and 1820. By December, 1816, the price of wheat had risen to one hundred and three shillings and seven pence per quarter. In January, 1817, the average price was one hundred and four shillings and one penny, and in June it had reached one hundred and twelve shillings and eight pence per quarter. So high a range of prices reduced vast numbers of the poorer classes to the brink of starvation, and murmurs of discontent were soon heard in every part of the kingdom. Soup kitchens were opened in destitute districts, coal and clothing were gratuitously distributed, and other benevolent efforts were made to give some relief to the sufferings of the poor, but such palliatives were secretly regarded with derision by the mass of those they were meant to aid; help was scorned in the instinctive cry for

justice; the puerility of first creating scarcity by act
of Parliament, and then endeavouring to mitigate it
by philanthropy, gave an air of insincerity to all
professions of compassion on the part of the wealthier
classes; an intense eagerness for political changes
seized upon the famished multitudes who were
congregated in our large towns, and the manufacturing districts became the theatres of wide-
spread conspiracies, which threatened the safety
and even the existence of the state. On the 14th
November, 1816, five thousand men assembled at
Peter's Fields, Manchester, to take into consideration
the distressed condition of the country. The following
month was distinguished by the celebrated riot of
Spa Fields, and early in the next year the Habeas
Corpus Act was suspended. On the 17th March a
vast number of people again met at Peter's Fields,
Manchester, with the avowed determination of march-
ing, *en masse*, to London, to petition the Prince
Regent for a redress of grievances. Rumours of "a
most daring and traitorous conspiracy" agitated the
public mind: it was fully believed that a simultaneous
rising was resolved upon throughout the northern and
midland counties; a large body of men were actually
stopped by the military on their march to Nottingham,
and three of the ringleaders underwent the revolting
penalty annexed to the crime of treason. The distress which was felt at this period may be inferred
from the fact that the " Gazette" usually contained
the names of from forty to sixty bankrupts, and that
at the Manchester August Sessions more than 371
persons were brought up for trial. This era of excitement reached its climax August 16th, 1819, in the

famous assembly at Peterloo, Manchester, where more than a hundred thousand of the labouring population met to deliberate upon their wrongs, and were dispersed by military violence.

Such a series of outbreaks was not without its effect on the more enlightened and patriotic members of the government. It was easy to comprehend the philosophy of the popular discontent. Our manufactures were fettered by fiscal restrictions; a declining commerce and a rapidly increasing population issued in a glut of labour and consequent low wages, while heavy imposts prevented the plenty which might exist elsewhere from touching our shores. In the misery which marked this period we recognise much of the secret force which set the Free Trade movement stirring. Meanwhile the attention of government was directed to our commercial restrictions from other quarters. In the year 1820 a petition was presented to the legislature by a number of the leading mercantile firms of the metropolis, which embodied a distinct enunciation of Free Trade principles, and prayed that every restrictive regulation of trade not essential to the revenues, all duties merely protective from foreign competition, and the excess of such duties as were partly for the purpose of revenue and partly for the purpose of protection, might be repealed. Thus the measures to which we have adverted were not only forced upon the government as a remedy for social distress, they were a concession to the growing demand for commercial freedom, and though far from inaugurating Free Trade, must be considered as a great approximation towards it. They resemble the fissures and rents in some ancient edifice, which tell us that its day of splendour is gone, and that ere long its turreted roofs will fall. We recognise in them the first misgivings which generally precede the entire dethroning of an error; the result of its first reluctant submission to the test of truth. These experiments were the commencing throes of that convulsion which twenty years later tore asunder the fabric of monopoly.

During the six years which followed the adoption of Mr. Huskisson's measures, the public mind became increasingly absorbed in the great question of Parliamentary Reform. Economical theories gave way once more to the discussion of political rights. The impression had now become deeper and stronger than ever, that the people were inadequately represented in the House of Commons, and that no improvements could be made in legislation till the influence of the aristocratic element in that assembly was considerably diminished. Sentiments of this kind had long been prevalent among the operative portion of the population; they now began to rally in their support the conservative patriotism of the middle classes. Still, it was no mere love of change, not even an abstract sense of political justice, which originated the cry for reform; social evils, and foremost among them the hated corn laws, lay at the root of the determination to modify our political institutions. The people were not mistaken as to the cause of their privations. In the first impulse of indignation, they had attacked machinery, but reflection soon told them that their sufferings were the natural result of *laws* which forced them to be idle by destroying trade, and raised the price of food to a height which good wages would barely have enabled them to reach. They found here one case at least in which a change in the existing law was absolutely necessary to their physical and social well-being. How then was this change to be brought about ? The parties composing the legislature were resolved, with few exceptions, to maintain the law as it was, because any change would interfere with their own interests. They might be appealed to on the score of justice, but with them, such was the force of prejudice, even justice, in reference to this matter, had a conventional meaning, being regarded as the mere synonym of class ascendancy. In these circumstances, one course alone remained — change the constitution of the House of Commons ; make it what it professes to be, a people's assembly ; let Sheffield, Birmingham, and Manchester be represented in the stead of places not possessing a twentieth of their vast population. If this change could once be effected, every other desirable change seemed easy. A long series of unjust enactments might then be blotted from the statute book. Accordingly, during the gloomy period we have described, the corn laws were the real object of assault. Parliamentary reform was desired chiefly as the means of breaking a landlord's monopoly of the people's food, and bursting the fetters which bound our trade. This was the true meaning of the Luddite riots at Nottingham, the blanketeering expedition in Lancashire, and the massacre of Peterloo ; this was the secret of the enormous power which was wielded by Cobbett, Hunt and their associates, and which afterwards displayed its embattled front in the political unions of 1831.

Thus the agitation which has disquieted the nation for the last half-century, has been closely connected with the maintenance of our protective policy, and even the great achievement of Parliamentary reform was but a stage in the progress of legislation towards Free Trade.

III. The subsidence of the Reform agitation again restored economical questions to their old footing, and brings us to the period at which the Free Trade movement began to assume a more defined shape, and exercise a more decisive control over the course of legislation. It cannot be said, however, that merely political matters absorbed all the vigour of the Reform administration. Our tariff, though dealt with *sotto voce*, had not been altogether forgotten. During the connexion of Lord Sydenham with the Board of Trade, changes were adopted affecting more than 700 articles of importation. Among the most important of these was the readjustment of our wine duties with France, to the beneficial effects of which we shall advert hereafter. In the department of excise, also, various changes of a useful tendency were effected, and one great revolution, which will ever be remembered with gratitude, and the effect of which in facilitating business, fostering the growth of sentiment, binding society together, and tending to humanise the world, is past all value,—we refer to the postal reforms which were carried out through the enlightened energy of Mr. Rowland Hill. We might, perhaps, without exaggeration, place this amongst the most powerful auxiliaries of Free Trade. The means of conveying *thought* cheaply and expeditiously from place to place, seem so indispensable to the success of a movement which sought to combine all classes of the community in an intelligent protest against monopoly; which aimed at sending its missives of argument and patriotic persuasion to every farmstead from Penzance to the Orkneys; that one is compelled to regard the measure which placed them at the service of Free Trade as a special prearrangement of infinite wisdom. It is the proud boast of Free Trade, that it could profit by such a measure. Truth alone loves the open day,—the means of presenting herself, disarrayed, to the scrutiny of all minds, a privilege which selfishness and error would gladly waive, is grasped by her as the surest weapon of victory.

1. About the year 1840 various circumstances combined to render an important modification of the corn laws necessary, and a feeling rapidly gained strength which would be satisfied with nothing short of their total repeal. A succession of bad harvests had raised the price of food. Importation of foreign wheat had taken place to a very considerable extent. From the commencement of 1838 to the end of 1841, the average annual import of all kinds of grain amounted to 3,400,000 quarters; the aggregate quantity of foreign wheat alone which was brought into our market during that period having been 9,434,620 quarters, while the aggregate quantity imported during the previous four years was only 362,000 quarters. If this had been bought in the ordinary course of trade no inconvenience would have been felt; but the influence of the corn laws precluded our merchants from making wheat a common article of exchange, since they kept it from yielding to the usual law of supply and demand. In seasons of scarcity corn had to be procured far

E

beyond the extent to which our productions could be given in exchange, and the consequence was a drain of gold and a derangement of the currency. This actually occurred during the years 1838, 1839, and 1840. The payments for foreign wheat in those years amounted to ten millions sterling, and our financial relations were still further embarrassed by over-importation of American securities, and the prevalence of over-trading in France and Belgium. The effect of these circumstances was a drain on the Bank of England, which reduced its stock of gold from £10,126,000 in April, 1838, to £7,073,000 in the corresponding month of 1839, and to £2,522,000 in the October following. In this state of the money market, trade experienced fearful depression. Wages were low, employment irregular, and provisions dear; discontent brooded fiercely in the minds of the factory population, and threatened a destructive outbreak erelong. Social animosities were kindled, Chartist agitation was rife, conspiracies and insurrections, incendiary speeches and midnight drills, were again the order of the day. The worst feature of the discontents which prevailed was the dissatisfaction of the workpeople with their employers, while the latter, placed between an exasperated populace and commercial restrictions, were totally helpless. It need scarcely be added that crime and pauperism were advancing. The number of criminals in 1841 was twenty per cent. greater than in 1838. Our foreign trade was declining. Retaliatory tariffs had been established by Russia and Sweden, America was about to do the same, and France, to use the language of Lord Palmerston, had made every article of produce a subject of Protection, " down to needles and fish-hooks."* While these circumstances urged upon our legislature the necessity of establishing our trade upon a more satisfactory footing, the present time seemed to offer peculiar facilities for making the attempt. Our treaties with Brazil were on the point of expiring, the United States were about to reconsider their tariff, and the Zollverein would be open, in the following year, on discussing the question of its renewal, to a readjustment of those duties which pressed so heavily on British manufactures. But a still more cogent argument was furnished by the state of the national finances. This faithful index of the public weal already indicated too surely that protective duties were fast destroying our commerce, and that imposts on articles of consumption, instead of replenishing the exchequer, operated chiefly against the subsistence of the people. For several years the disproportion between our income and expenditure had gone on increasing, till, in 1841, there was a deficiency of £2,101,370. Thus the social condition of the people, the growing excitement of popular feeling, the aspect of trade, the posture of our commercial relations, and the embarrassment of our finances, all conspired to show that we had reached a crisis in which timidity and half-measures would no longer suffice, and nothing but a bold yet prudent course could save the common-wealth.

2. Nothing could have contributed more at this crisis to strengthen the anti-corn law agitation, than the Report of the Committee of the House of

* Speech in the House of Commons, May 17, 1841.

Commons, in 1840, on Import Duties. Their labours
rendered accessible a mass of valuable information
as to the state of our foreign trade, and laid bare to
every reflecting mind the injuries it sustained through
a policy which at once prevented us from selling
cheap and compelled us to buy dear ; which first taxed
the raw material, then levied duties on the manufactured article, and finally commissioned an array
of custom-house officers to repel the purchaser. It
was proved before the Committee that $94\frac{1}{2}$ per cent.
of the custom-house revenue was raised on seventeen
articles only, while more than eleven hundred articles
were subjected to imposts for the sake of raising the
remaining $5\frac{1}{2}$ per cent. But this was not the only
startling fact which came to light. Of £22,000,000,
the average amount of our custom-house revenue in
recent years, it appeared that above £20,000,000 was
raised on raw material and food. Thus our legislation
had been a two-edged sword in the vitals of industry ;
on the one hand forbidding the free use of the articles
required in our manufactures, and on the other
enhancing the cost of labour by raising the price of
subsistence. Moreover, the artificial dearness produced by excessive taxation materially diminished, in
another way, the resources of the country. In the
opinion of Mr. McGregor, between four and five
millions sterling were annually carried out of the
kingdom by persons of fortune, and spent in France,
Switzerland, and other parts of the continent. But
the most important part of the evidence adduced
before the Committee related to a change which was
proved to be going on in our manufacturing relations
with foreign states. This, even more than the want

of a healthy progress in the amount of our transactions, threatened soon to work a very decisive change, to say the least, in our domestic industry. For fifteen years we had been besought to adopt a more liberal course; Prussia, Holland, Germany, and the United States had been anxious to obtain such a relaxation of our tariff as would have enabled them to exchange their raw products for our manufactures, but, foiled in their efforts, they had begun to manufacture for themselves. In Saxony, Bavaria, Wurtemburg, the Rhenish provinces of Prussia, as well as Russia and Switzerland, factories had been erected, filled with British machinery, and often placed under the oversight of an experienced workman from this country, and every exertion made, under the shelter of protective imposts, to drive us from the markets of the continent. Our skilled artizans were to be found in the United States, in Brazil, in the neighbourhood of Constantinople and St. Petersburg, everywhere teaching the foreigner to render himself independent of selfish Britain. We shall have to refer to these facts in answering the taunt of the now defeated protectionist that foreign states have not all at once repealed their protective laws in response to our adoption of Free Trade, and we shall then tell him that it is his work, which he did too well, which we have not as yet succeeded wholly in undoing. But, for the present, it was no wonder that the operatives of Lancashire were unemployed; no wonder that, instead of the cheerful hum of industry, one might hear there the terrible language of despair, and read in multitudes of frenzied faces resolves which fill the patriot's soul with horror. From the year 1828 to 1838 the increase in our exports of cotton goods was only 25 per cent.; while the increase in our exportation of *cotton twist*, that part upon which least labour had been expended, was 114 per cent. Dividing the nine years, 1831—1839, into three equal periods, the value of the machinery exported during the second was considerably more than double that exported during the first, and that exported during the third more than five times greater. Comparing our exports in 1827 with those of 1838, it was found that the proportion of *finished* goods to the whole, was, in the former year, 82·56 per cent., and in the latter year only 73·80. Separating our foreign from our colonial exports, it was proved that, while the proportion between the articles which had employed much labour, and those which had employed little labour, remained the same in the latter, in the former it had considerably changed—finished articles, which, in 1827, constituted 81·95 per cent. of the whole, having sunk to 69·12 per cent in 1838. Separating still further our exports to the north of Europe from the rest of our foreign trade, it was found that the proportion of finished goods to the whole had fallen from 61·78 per cent. at the former period, to 39·16 at the latter. Such facts, however dry on paper, have a terrible meaning in reality. They are the statistics of starvation, inspired, even to the calm eye of the historian, with pallid fury, and sending, happily from afar, along the flowery pathways of better times, the grim voices of misery and death.

3. The necessity of attempting forthwith an extensive modification of our commercial system was rendered still more absolute by the decisive change which was taking place in the state of public opinion.

Hitherto the cry against the corn laws had been partial; it had issued chiefly from those whose interests were manifestly injured by their continuance; other classes had been comparatively silent. This apathy was, in some, the result of selfishness, but in the majority of ignorance. The agricultural party firmly believed that high rents were bound up with protective duties on corn, while our Chambers of Commerce had not been altogether free from the illusion that the protective system was on the whole friendly to their interests. Errors of a kindred nature were thickly strewn throughout the country. The tenant farmer had been taught to grasp the corn laws as the only chance of escaping the workhouse; the unenlightened instincts of the agricultural labourer had been diligently whetted against Free Trade, till he almost regarded the prohibition of foreign corn as his birthright, a melancholy compensation, in his case, for the loss of every other. The population of the numerous boroughs situated in farming districts, and dependent on the neighbouring gentry for support, were easily persuaded that the repeal of the corn laws would be the ruin of their trade. Even the intelligent operatives of such cities as Norwich and Coventry, the nature of whose occupations laid them most open to foreign competition, were not without apprehensions of the results of unrestricted freedom of exchange, and those apprehensions naturally checked their zeal for its acquisition. The maxim, *ubi explorari vera non possunt, falsa per metum augurantur*, was most aptly illustrated in the feelings with which those sections of the operative class who did not possess the facilities for acquiring knowledge, including in this term the

stern lessons of experience, peculiar to the manufacturing districts, regarded a hand to hand wrestle
with the foreigner. Wages, they argued, were low
enough, but then they might be lower. Privations,
when not keen enough to produce despair, often
inspire a timorous apprehensiveness of worse, the
effect of which is a disposition favourable rather to
endurance than ameliorative effort. Among the
multitudinous thousands of Lancashire and Yorkshire
the former effect was produced; among the numerous
classes engaged in the minor kinds of handicraft
throughout the kingdom the latter. By 1842 this
state of things was rapidly passing away. Men of all
ranks were joining the Free Traders. The leading
statesmen of the party which had hitherto been pledged
to the maintenance of Protection, were becoming sus-
picious in their movements; their assertions were
less confident and absolute than formerly, and their
behaviour conveyed the impression that their convictions were not quite in harmony with the position
which circumstances forced them to occupy. Gentlemen of rank and fortune, whose interests were entirely
identified with the soil, were now found, with increasing
frequency, on the side of repeal. The whole question
was becoming better understood, and, as soon as it
was understood, its simplicity challenged conviction.
Henceforth, not only a few manufacturers in those
parts of the kingdom which had been considered the
hotbed of democracy, and whose demands were ascribed to a selfish disregard of the national interests,
but merchants, farmers, landowners, tradesmen, men
distinguished in science and letters, the operative
armies of the north, and the aristocratic citizens of

the south, led on by the mighty vanguard of the press, were arming in a common crusade against the spirit of monopoly.

4. This result was no doubt brought about by the co-operation of a great variety of causes. On the more inquiring classes, the experiments in Free Trade which we have already described, and to the effects of which we shall presently more fully advert, had not been spent in vain. Literature had also done its share in effecting the change. The writings of Adam Smith and Jeremy Bentham, expounded and popularised by their numerous disciples, had communicated correct views on economical questions through every conceivable avenue of thought. Among those who were mainly instrumental in bringing about this change, a distinguished place is due to Colonel Perronet Thompson, whose logic, equally convincing and humorous, as displayed in his Catechism of the Corn Laws, and Political Essays, at once unmasked and ridiculed the fallacies of Protection. Even poetry had lent its aid, and the flashes of terrific ire which broke through the rugged verse of the Anti-Corn Law Rhymer, carried illumination to minds beyond the reach of logic, or kindled into burning sentiment the knowledge which reading and sad experience had accumulated in the bosoms of thousands. But the glory of completing this revolution, of concentrating existing opposition into a formidable array, of carrying the war, by means of the platform and the press, into the strongest entrenchments of the foe, and of so guiding the contest as to be in a position ultimately to demand a surrender at discretion, is due to an association whose name will ever be famous in British

history,—the ANTI-CORN LAW LEAGUE. Besides the obvious impropriety of attempting its eulogy in these pages, the achievements of this powerful confederacy are yet too recent, and its distinguished leaders occupy too prominent a place in present movements, to admit of full justice being now done to the wisdom, the energy, and the patriotism which they displayed. This must be done at some future day, and history will not forget to do it. It is impossible, however, to separate the Anti-Corn Law League from the downfall of protection, and any view of that great occurrence which did not include it would be shorn of its brightest lustre and its noblest lesson.

In the year 1838, a number of gentlemen, chiefly resident in Manchester, resolved to form themselves into an association for the purpose of seeking the abolition of the corn laws. The immediate occasion in which the Manchester and Salford Anti-Corn Law Association originated, was an entertainment given to Dr. Bowring, a gentleman so well known for his statistical labours, and varied erudition. It was then the middle of September; the progress of the Whig Government towards commercial reform had been characteristically slow, and it was resolved to have a " demonstration" previous to the next session of parliament, for the purpose of bringing the great question of repeal prominently before the attention of the legislature and the nation. Accordingly, on Wednesday, 23rd January, 1839, eight hundred gentlemen, including fourteen members of parliament, and other distinguished advocates of Free Trade, dined together at the Corn Exchange, Manchester. On the following day, delegates assembled from all parts of the kingdom, and, after passing a series of declaratory resolutions, adjourned till the 14th of February, when they met again at Brown's Hotel, Westminster. On the following day Mr. C. P. Villiers presented a petition for the repeal of the corn laws, signed by 40,000 persons, and moved "that John Benjamin Smith, Robert Hyde Greg, and others, be heard at the bar of the House by their witnesses, agents, or counsel, in support of the allegations of the petition." The motion was negatived by a majority of 189. Upon this the delegates returned to Manchester, a crowded meeting was held at the Corn Exchange, and it was resolved that they should reassemble in London, to await the result of Mr. Villiers' motion for " a committee of the whole House to take into consideration the laws affecting the importation of corn." This motion was negatived by a majority of 147; and a still more decided tone was adopted during the same month, in the House of Lords, when a motion, introduced by Earl Fitzwilliam, affirming " that the corn act had failed to secure the steadiness in the price of grain which is essential to the best interests of the country," found only 24 supporters in a House of 244 members. These votes were an unmistakable indication of the determined hostility to Free Trade which actuated the legislature. Under these circumstances the delegates returned to their constituents, and the Anti-Corn Law League was formed. A subscription was forthwith set on foot to raise " the sinews of war ;" able lecturers were dispatched alike into the manufacturing towns and rural districts ; the following month a newspaper devoted to the progress of the movement made its appearance, under the

name of the Anti-Bread-Tax Circular; and by the
close of the year 300 lectures had been delivered,
150,000 copies of various pamphlets circulated, and
120,000 copies of the Circular printed and sent out
into every corner of the country.

Such an energetic commencement was a fit earnest
of the spirited exertions which were to follow. The.
simplicity and power evinced in these opening movements convey impressions bordering on the morally
sublime. We discern in them nothing artificial, no
parade of strength, no laborious attempts at the
emphatic: they were a spontaneous outburst, at once
natural and politic, partaking of the force without the
fury of popular agitation, an embodying of all that is
irresistible in roused passion, and all that is calm and
far-seeing in ripened wisdom. It was indeed a very
triumph of directness and singleness of purpose, a
complete demonstration of the political capacities of
commerce. A company of merchants and manufacturers suddenly entered upon public life, committing themselves to a contest with experienced
statesmen, presenting as striking a contrast to the
ordinary class of politicians as Franklin did among
the starched diplomatists of France and Austria. But
with them, as with him, common sense proved flexible
to every purpose; everything was easy in their hands;
every resource was skilfully brought under tribute;
every snare avoided with a prudence which set
espionage at defiance; every difficulty vanquished with
an ease which made resistance at length appear hopeless. Their object was a noble one; they aimed, it
is true, at the abolition of the corn laws, but, in order
to this, they aimed at the enlightenment of the nation.

Relinquishing the aid of ignorance, and the inglorious victory which might have been won by a display of physical force, they sought to make the people aware of their true interests, and magnanimously postponed success till the cry for commercial freedom should attain a unanimity which no government could resist. The variety and novelty of their measures demonstrated at once their practical skill, and the extensive sympathy which was already felt on behalf of the movement. Within a few months of each other two expressions of public sentiment occurred, very different in their character, but equally bold and full of meaning. While the House of Commons were debating the superiority of a sliding scale to a fixed duty, an assembly of ministers of religion, convened from every part of the country, the flower of the denominations they represented, solemnly repudiated as impious the laws which taxed the bread of the starving poor. Amid the impressive rites of devotion, the spirit of monopoly was fearlessly brought to the touchstone of sacred truth, and laden with a Christian's curse. Not long afterwards, in the same neighbourhood, industry contributed in its own way, to its own enfranchisement. While Sir Robert Peel was proposing his tariff in 1842, the ladies of the United Kingdom presented a graceful offering at the shrine of Free Trade. The Anti-Corn Law Bazaar, which was then held at Manchester, though inferior to its successor at Covent Garden, gave an unparalleled demonstration of the firm hold which the movement had taken of the national mind. Here another phase of its many-sidedness came to view. Trifles, pleasantries, antiquarian lore, the numerous products of the boudoir, autographs, marbles, pictures, books, costly furniture, in short, almost every conceivable article, from Jeremy Bentham's pencil to a mummy's necklace, was there offered for sale, that its equivalent might go to untax the people's bread. Are such incidents trivial? In truth they are far otherwise. Every question which thus masters the religious and fire-side sympathies of England is virtually settled. The cause which could thus, by men of large intellect and irreproachable piety, be embalmed in prayer, and draw to its aid the cheerful hearts and energies of a thousand homes, had already secured the victory; its triumph was merely a question of time.

5. It was in these circumstances that, in 1841, the late Viscount Melbourne, then at the head of Her Majesty's government, sanctioned the introduction into Parliament of a measure for revising the tariff with reference to corn. The duty then existing on that article was determined by the sliding scale established in 1828, during the administration of the late Duke of Wellington. In virtue of that arrange-ment the tax on corn varied from twenty-four shillings and eightpence per quarter, when the price of the latter was sixty-two shillings, down to two shillings and eight-pence, when the home price was seventy-two shillings per quarter, a nominal duty of one shilling per quarter being charged when the price was above seventy-three shillings. Instead of this species of sliding scale, Lord John Russell moved in the House of Commons the adoption of a fixed duty of eight shillings per quarter. The ground on which the ministerial party based their support of this measure was, that by admitting foreign corn at a lower price, we should

promote the activity of our manufactures, and alleviate existing distress, while, on the other hand, the fixity of the impost would prevent the fluctuations to which the value of wheat had been exposed, and impart a greater degree of certainty to the interests concerned in its growth and purchase. The proposition encountered at once the most determined opposition on the part of the agricultural interest, backed by the formidable party in the House of Commons of which Sir Robert Peel was the acknowledged leader. It is important, however, to bear in mind the peculiar position of political parties at this juncture. A clear view of the relation in which the great conservative statesman stood to the question of Free Trade, as involved in the discussions of 1841, will throw important light on his subsequent policy. In opposing the measures of the Whig government Sir Robert Peel and his associates had taken up protective ground, but the immediate reason of this was that such a position gave them the best chance of beating their political foes. The corn laws were, in fact, the field on which the main battle of Conservatism had to be fought. Ever since the passing of the Reform Bill the Tories had endeavoured to recruit their shattered ranks. The Registration Courts had been prophetically pointed out as the avenue of legislative power. This suggestion of Sir Robert Peel's had been zealously acted on by his followers, and under his guidance a rare combination of talent in the House of Commons had so improved the reaction always consequent on any great political change, and so consolidated every available fragment of power, that within four years of the triumphant majorities of Earl Grey, Sir Robert Peel already saw his way open to the Treasury Bench. Disappointed at that time in his expectation of being able to retain office, he returned to his former task, relying upon discipline and tact for victory in the inevitably approaching conflict. The anticipated struggle reached its climax in 1841; it happened to occur in connexion with the corn laws, but it might have happened in connexion with any other question, and, whatever the particular question might have been, there is no doubt that its real merits would have been, for a time, completely subordinate to party views. The Whigs were to be driven from office, and the corn laws afforded the most convenient cudgel for accomplishing the feat. We are far from accusing a late .illustrious statesman of political dishonesty; but we know that imperceptible shades of difference often conduct the mind from truth to error: and that opinions are often unconsciously held before they are fully recognised. Knowing this, and remembering in addition the state of parties, the important modifications which were made in our commercial code the very next session, and the studious reserve which Sir Robert Peel maintained respecting the principles of Protection, we cannot but believe that his incipient conversion to Free Trade dates from an earlier period than 1841, and that his opposition to the half-measures of the Whig government was inspired at least as much by political necessity, as by unfaltering confidence in the maxims which had thus far guided his public career.

IV. 1. In order fully to comprehend the position and the duties of Government at this crisis, it will be proper to pause for a moment, and survey the actual condition of the country. The period of Sir R. Peel's accession to office was one of greater depression than our industrial interests had ever before experienced. The state seemed precipitately falling to decay; it was as though the very spirit of death paralysed all the movements of capital; we stood like some ancestral oak, arrested in the mid-career of spring-tide vegetation by some fatal shock, and from whose branches the vital sap is suddenly withdrawn. Never again may such a dismal time darken the path of Old England! The distress which was then endured by the nation sounds more like the wild creation of a tragic fancy than a recital of sober facts. Nor was it the privations which were actually endured that palsied the people's energies, so much as the apparent impossibility of escaping from them. The effects of a financial crisis, or a bad harvest, however severe for a time, can be endured, because they are in their nature temporary. When the crash is once over, the capitalist, like a farmer in the wake of a hurricane, can begin work again with a fair prospect of success. But adversity did not spring from transient causes; for ten or twenty years before, several of our staple trades had shown symptoms of decay, and dark as the present moment undoubtedly was, the deeper darkness of midnight lay beyond. The root of the evil was found in protective laws; so long as these existed genius and industry might contend in vain.

Passing rapidly through the land, let us ask what was the condition of that extensive and wealthy district of which Leeds and Bradford are the principal centres. In the township of Leeds alone, and within four years, thirty-nine persons or firms connected with

the woollen manufacture became bankrupt, with liabilities amounting, in the aggregate, to half a million
sterling. To these we must add the failures of
eighteen flax and tow spinners, sixteen machine makers,
sixteen wool-staplers, and nine stuff and worsted spinners, all of which occurred within the same time, and
in the same town. Six shillings and eight pence is
above the average amount of the dividends which were
paid on this enormous mass of insolvency, and the
total loss accruing from these cases alone, cannot be
set down at less than a million sterling. In Bradford,
one-fourth of the mills were idle, and the value of mill
property had declined full thirty per cent. So little
machinery was wanted, that the wages of machine
makers had fallen, in five years, to little more than
one-half, and the trade itself seemed on the verge of
extinction. In the populous district of Thornton
Road, thirty-one firms failed or compounded with their
creditors, and fourteen others declined business; their
total amount of bad debts being more than a million
and a half. Passing into the neighbourhood of Nottingham, we find, in that town alone, 10,580 persons,
nearly a fifth of the population, receiving parochial
relief, with a reduction of wages, through a period of
six years, of as much as twenty-five per cent. Entering the region of hardwares, the various trades of
Birmingham show the same depressed condition.
Silver-workers, platers, screw-makers, brass-founders,
and those engaged in the coal and iron trades, were
now receiving only a half, and in some cases only a
third, of the rate of wages paid them a few years
earlier. On a Saturday night many a master had to
carry his goods to the pawnbroker, before he could pay

his men. A stranger wandering through the town might count in fifteen streets upwards of four hundred empty houses, and not a week passed without some instance of death by starvation gaining a melancholy publicity through the medium of a coroner's verdict. Of the vast trade in iron which Wolverhampton formerly carried on with the United States, only one sixth remained. From injuries sustained in the same quarter, Sheffield had lost more than a fourth of its staple industry; wages had declined some forty per cent., pauperism was doubled, and in the course of five years no less than £20,000 was expended by four trades alone in the relief of unemployed workmen. Transferring ourselves into the woollen districts of Gloucester, Somerset, and Wilts, we meet the same picture. At Frome, from 1831 to 1841, population had considerably decreased, rents were fifty per cent. lower, one-sixth of the houses were unoccupied, and the only item of increase was the poor-rate. Of Bradford, Stroud, Uley, Wootton, the same tale could be told. Comparing the whole county of Gloucester at the two periods just mentioned, we find a diminution of fifty per cent. in the number of looms employed, and the number of manufacturers who still held their ground was less than the number of those who had failed during that short interval. In Coventry one-third of the population was unemployed; in Spitalfields 8000 looms were idle, and 24,000 persons thrown upon parochial relief; in the whole of the metropolis one thousand letter-press compositors and nine thousand tailors were altogether without work. Other trades throughout the kingdom were in the same condition. To visit the iron works of Scotland, the colliers of Staffordshire, the glovers of Yeovil, the carpet weavers of Kendal, the glass-blowers of Warrington, the shawl weavers of Paisley, and the flax spinners of Dundee, would only be to encounter similar proofs of the entire prostration of industry. In Paisley, for example, no less than thirty failures took place within a few weeks, in less than a year two-thirds of the whole number of manufacturers became insolvent, while one-third of a population which is distinguished, even in the north, for industry and ingenuity, were thrown upon the public for support.

It was, however, in the manufacturing districts of Lancashire that the vials of wretchedness seemed poured out to their last dregs. It is unnecessary, after the facts we have given, to look at the commercial statistics of the case; we will confine ourselves to a few of their social results. In Bolton, only a third of the people were fully employed, the poor-rate had been tripled in five years, fifteen hundred houses within the borough were unoccupied, and wages had experienced an immense decline. We might infer from these facts alone the condition of the working classes, but we have at hand the surer test of figures. The net earnings of 1003 families averaged only 1s. 2d. a head per week; more than half the beds in their possession were filled with straw; they had among them 466 blankets, not quite one to every ten persons—while only one-half could boast the humble luxury of a change of linen. At Stockport, Ashton, Oldham and the other large towns, the picture of misery was but slightly varied. In Wigan, the receipts of 2000 families were only sufficient, if all laid out in bread, to buy each individual 22 ounces a day. The spectacle of distress which meets us when we turn to Manchester is projected on a gigantic scale, and filled up with more harrowing details. At the instance of a number of charitable gentlemen, 12,000 families were brought under visitation, and the mass of destitution which was thus brought to light almost exceeds belief. To buy themselves bread thousands had parted with every stick of furniture and every rag of clothing beyond the merest wants of decency. The value of the property thus pledged by the section of the population just mentioned was probably not less than £28,000. " It was indeed a touching spectacle," says the philanthropic gentleman to whom we are indebted for some of these facts, "to see the care with which the poor creatures brought forth from some concealed part of their scanty dress, or from some hidden corner of their wretched abode, the bundles of tickets which formed their humble title-deeds to articles of personal or household use with which, one after another, they had been obliged to part, and of which they had little chance of ever becoming again possessed." We could easily fill our pages with narratives of suffering which would move the hardest heart to tears; we might tell how skilled workmen, capable now of earning, at the regular rate of wages paid in their trade, from 18s. to 25s. a week, and withal sober, intelligent and religious, were driven to subsist upon mere vegetable refuse; how many a family, reduced and broken-hearted, sunk in misery from which they could not flee, wasted away to the grave, leaving one, perhaps, behind, the helpless spectator of all their sufferings, who had often bitterly cursed the hour that awoke within his bosom the fond

emotions of a parent, and had found in madness a
sad asylum from his woes. We forbear to enter upon
such details, but the reader will perhaps pardon the insertion of one unvarnished fact, which we select from
the rest because it speaks chiefly to the judgment, and
accurately illustrates the condition of thousands of
the industrial classes at the period to which we refer.
" We visited one house," says the narrator, " occupied
by thirteen persons, father, mother, and eleven children. The house was without the least vestige of
furniture ; every article, even the lock from the door,
had been sold to purchase bread. Three shillings
per week was the amount of their regular income, the
wages of one of the sons who was employed as an
errand boy. Four shillings and sixpence was all they
had to live upon for a whole week,—the boy's wages,
and eighteenpence obtained by the sale of their last
remaining articles of furniture. This was expended
by Wednesday, and for the next three days, till the
Saturday evening, the period of our visit, the whole
of the family had subsisted on 2¼d. worth of meal,
which (having sold their pan) was prepared for
use by mixing it with cold water. The father of
this family bears an excellent character. He had
been for several years employed in chemical works.
His employers, compelled by declining business
reluctantly to discharge him, had done their utmost
to serve him, even offering to guarantee his trust-
worthiness to the extent of £400. No employment,
however, can be obtained, and his daily vocation is
to watch for coal-carts, in order that, by the most
menial toil, he may carry home a few pence to his
famishing family."

2. Such was the state of things when, on the accession of Sir Robert Peel to power, the nation at once looked for some comprehensive scheme of commercial reform. An instinctive faith in the expansiveness of his views overcame the misgiving which the relation he sustained to the great agricultural interest was calculated to excite, and prepared the public mind, not indeed for the adoption of a Free Trade policy, but for some relaxation of the imposts which pressed so heavily on our commerce. Accordingly, the utmost anxiety prevailed to know the nature of his plans. When he rose to unfold them, on the ninth of February, 1842, it might almost be said that a nation pressed to hear. Inside the House of Commons every spot was occupied at an early hour, while dense crowds assembled outside, eagerly catching every stray rumour which reached them from within. Messengers were waiting, ready to convey the earliest announcement to the more distant districts of the kingdom, where the most intense excitement prevailed in reference to the forthcoming measures. The permanent importance of those measures, and the prominent place they will always hold in the development of Free Trade, render it necessary that we should accurately, though briefly, state them. The key to the ministerial proposals which were then made is found in the necessity which existed for devising some steps in order to recruit the exhausted exchequer. The deficiency for the current year amounted to £2,550,000; instead of meeting this by laying on fresh taxes in the department of the customs or excise, which experience had taught us to expect would be burdensome rather than productive,

it was proposed to lay a tax of sevenpence in the pound on all incomes above £150 per year. This, it was calculated, would not only cover the deficiency which had arisen in the annual income, but also furnish a considerable surplus, to be applied in abating such duties as were most oppressive to general interests. The tariff was classified, for the purpose of revision, under twenty different heads. The first division comprised various imported articles used as food, of which corn was the most important, and in reference to which it was proposed to substitute a mitigated sliding-scale. The basis assumed for this ingenious piece of mechanism was fifty shillings as the price per quarter in the home market, and at this point the duty was reduced from thirty-six shillings and eight pence, its former amount, to twenty shillings. When the price of wheat was fifty-one shillings per quarter, the duty sank to nineteen shillings; at fifty-two, fifty-three, and fifty-four shillings respectively, the duty remained stationary at eighteen shillings. At fifty-five shillings per quarter the duty again began sliding till the price reached sixty-six shillings, when it rose gradually to the highest point of ascent, importation being declared free whenever the price exceeded seventy-three shillings. It was argued that this arrangement would have the advantage of rendering the importation of corn profitable when the price stood at sixty shillings per quarter, at which the duty levied on the old system was virtually prohibitive. Still, it was far from meeting the demands of the crisis. To relieve the pressure of the corn laws on our manufacturing interests, it was necessary to make corn an article of traffic, which it never could become in connexion with the intricacy and uncertainty of a sliding scale. Next to corn, the most important articles of food affected by the proposed tariff were live animals, hitherto prohibited, but which were now to be admitted at varying rates of duty; butter, cheese, and several kinds of salted meat. No change was made in sugar, but the duty on coffee was considerably reduced. Duties on the importation of timber, to the amount of £600,000 annually, were repealed, and those previously levied on stage coaches were reduced by £70,000. Other imposts on a variety of articles, including woollen goods exported, woollen yarn, silk, and iron goods, were repealed. The total number of articles affected by the modified tariff now presented to the legislature amounted to 1,200. Many of these were used exclusively in manufacturing operations, and it was confidently affirmed that the general reduction of the duties previously imposed upon them, would not only be a relief to the manufacturer, but, by stimulating consumption, at length make up for the loss which would temporarily accrue to the exchequer. These measures were valuable, but infinitely more so the implied superiority of direct over indirect taxation.

3. The ministerial proposals were received with complete satisfaction by no section of the industrial community. On the one hand, the low scale of duties to be imposed on corn gave umbrage to the agricultural interest, a significant proof of which was seen in the secession of the Duke of Buckingham from the cabinet. The reduction of the import duties, moreover, though inconsiderable in amount, involved such a decided recognition of the principles of Free

Trade, that the Protectionist party could not regard it
without some apprehension of ulterior designs.   Their
confidence in Sir Robert Peel began to waver; they
recollected with dismay the unexpected part he took
in carrying the Roman Catholic Emancipation Bill,
and could not but feel alarmed lest the pressing
circumstances of the times should furnish him with
a plea for a similar act of apostacy.   Among the more
far-seeing of the Conservative body other sentiments
were beginning to prevail.   An opinion was rapidly
gaining ground that Protection was opposed to the
spirit of the age, that Free Trade had become a political
and social necessity, that the only point actually left
to the discretion of the Government was the particular
moment at which the concession should be made, and
that, henceforth, whatever class of politicians might
be in power, there must be, in all fiscal matters, a
substantial identity of measures.   These thoughts,
however, were passing on one side only; the other,
composed of the various sections of the manufacturing
interest, were much further advanced.   The absolute
necessity of Free Trade had long been an article of
their political creed : a necessity growing out of their
sufferings, and the invincible determination those
sufferings had inspired.   By this class the ministerial
measures were regarded with gloomy discontent.   The
attempts of the Premier to gloss over the distress which
had so long existed in the manufacturing districts,
indicated, in their opinion, a discreditable want of
feeling ; they could not help comparing his conduct,
in this respect, with that of Canning in 1826, who,
on rising to move that the corn then in bond should
be admitted duty free, thus began his address—" The

accounts, Sir, which we are daily receiving from certain districts of the distress of the working population, are such as must *come home to the feelings of any man.*" Admirable words at such a crisis!—more powerful even than statutes to inspire the nation with confidence in its rulers, since they are more comprehensive than specific measures, and include within themselves a pledge of every concession which may be found necessary for the public good. The apparent apathy of Sir Robert Peel increased the cheerless effect of his measures. Never, in the manufacturing districts, had an equal amount of depression been felt before. No business was done on the Manchester Exchange; cotton spinners and manufacturers who had hitherto kept their work-people employed, were heard to talk of closing their establishments, or greatly reducing the already reduced rate of wages.* This was but a sample of the feeling which prevailed elsewhere; the markets of Liverpool were overspread with gloom; in the populous districts of Ashton and Staleybridge; Bolton, Bury, and Rochdale; Leeds, Bradford, and Huddersfield, the probability of a further decline of wages contributed to swell the tide of discontent. In Manchester a requisition, requesting the mayor to call a Town's Meeting, received more than a thousand signatures in four hours, and in the crowded assemblage which was soon convened, resolutions were adopted condemning the policy of Government, and demanding the unconditional repeal of the corn laws, while similar expressions of opinion broke forth simultaneously from every large town in the United Kingdom.

* "Manchester Guardian" for 1841-42, *passim.*

It is unnecessary to follow minutely the advances towards complete freedom of commerce which were made during the period which elapsed from 1842 to December, 1845 : suffice it to say, that each session evinced more clearly the leaning of the Prime Minister towards Free Trade, and the determination of the country to rest satisfied with nothing less than its entire adoption.　In 1843 the Canadian Corn Bill diminished still more the protection afforded to agriculture.　In opening the budget of 1844 the Chancellor of the Exchequer thus expressed himself :—" Without pretending to say that I can at this moment decide what may be the result of the great reduction of duty made in 1842, yet, when I look at the list of articles on which the duty was reduced, and find that the consumption has increased in almost every one of them, there being only *five* in respect of which consumption has decreased, I am sanguine as to the successful result of the experiment." Accordingly, in this session, duties were reduced on glass, wool, currants, coffee, vinegar, and marine assurance, amounting to an aggregate of £450,000.　In the session of 1845 the same reductory course was pursued.　The cotton duty, among others, was repealed at an estimated loss to the revenue of £680,000; and that on the exportation of coals at an estimated loss of £118,000.　The loss on 430 minor articles amounted to £380,000.

4. The close of the year 1845 brings us to the commencement of that bold policy which conducted the nation well-nigh at once to the summit of commercial freedom, and probably anticipated by some years the natural period at which the spirit of monopoly would have met its doom.　The agitation

had hitherto been carried on by human agency, but it seemed as if reserved for Providence to conduct it to the final issue. In the mode of doing this a stern propriety was observed. Men, in their short-sightedness, or still more wretched selfishness, had withheld the bounties of heaven from their fellow-men: the common Parent closed his hand, that all might feel, in the presence of a common danger, the impiety of denying to any those gifts for which all alike are dependent upon his compassion. In the autumn of 1845 the first rumours began to spread of a probable failure in the potato crop. The potato had long been an article of such importance that an extensive deficiency in its usual amount of produce would have been severely felt by any country accustomed to employ it as food, but it was of special consequence to us, since millions in the sister isle were all but absolutely dependent upon it for subsistence. To them a failure in the potato crop was the same as a failure of the corn crops would have been to any other portion of the United Kingdom; it was even worse, since grain admits of being stored up from year to year, so that seasons of plenty come to the assistance of seasons of dearth, but potatoes never last even to the commencement of a second year's harvest. In 1845 the early crop of potatoes in Ireland was gathered in a sound state, but the "people's crop," so called because it is kept for home consumption, which is gathered later, shewed decided symptoms of disease. The next year the failure was still more decisive. Professors Lindley and Playfair, the commissioners appointed by Government, reported that one-half had been wholly destroyed, and that after setting aside one-eighth for seed, only three-eighths remained for the year's consumption. The suddenness with which the disease performed its work is very striking. "On the 29th of last month," wrote Father Mathew, " I travelled from Cork to Dublin; this doomed plant then bloomed in all the luxuriance of an abundant harvest. Returning on the 3rd of August (only five days after), I beheld with sorrow a wide waste of putrifying vegetation. In many places the wretched people were sitting on the fences of their decaying gardens, wringing their hands, and wailing bitterly the destruction which had left them foodless." The magnitude of the crisis may be gathered from the fact that, apart from vast contributions from private sources, Government spent ten millions in attempting to mitigate the famine, and that in the month of July, 1847, three millions of people, of whom three-fourths were adults, were in receipt of rations from relief committees. Such was the pressure of circumstances on Sir Robert Peel in the autumn of 1845. Accordingly, on the 1st of November, he proposed in the Cabinet that the duties on the import of foreign grain should be suspended for a limited period, either by an order in council, or a legislative enactment, Parliament in either case to be summoned without delay. He also thought that " any new laws to be enacted should contain within themselves the principle of *gradual reduction and final repeal*." At this time only three members of the Cabinet supported his proposition. It was renewed soon after, when the Earl of Derby, then Lord Stanley, stood almost alone in his opposition. On the 6th of December, Sir Robert Peel resigned office, but, Lord

John Russell having been unable to form a ministry, he resumed it again, with most of his colleagues, and commenced the following session by making an open avowal of his Free Trade policy.

5. It cannot be doubted that, in adopting such a course, Sir Robert Peel acted under the strongest necessity, but it was a necessity which sprang only in part from the Irish famine. That event rendered the step he took immediately imperative, and, when once taken, forbade its being retraced; but a discernment less keen than his own was sufficient to perceive that the corn laws must soon fall. The attitude of the Anti-Corn Law League at this moment was more menacing than it had been at any former period, and its menace was of just such a character as the minister could most fully appreciate—one of calm, self-conscious, moral power. Its pacific resolves, studiously confined within the spirit, as well as the letter, of the laws, and backed by the growing enthusiasm and unanimity of the people, were more terrific to injustice than a million of armed men. With inimitable tact and heroic patience, the Free Traders determined to fight the battle out by the slow but sure methods provided by the constitution. They had wealth enough for any purpose; the constitution recognised wealth as a valid title to political power; they would therefore purchase freeholds, and master the county constituencies. In 1844 they had raised £100,000 for carrying on the agitation, and at the moment when Sir Robert Peel resumed office, a fund of a quarter of a million was in progress, towards which £60,000 was contributed at a single meeting in Manchester. While the lapse of time seemed to recruit,

rather than to exhaust the financial power of the
League, it also multiplied its weapons in the sphere
of logic.   Unanswerable experiments had now proved
the expediency of Free Trade.   As far as it had been
tried its result had undeniably been to extend our
commerce, and promote the general interests of the
country.   We see here the true, and, at the same
time, the most legitimate source to which the altered
measures of Government may be ascribed.   Referring
to the Irish famine, Sir Robert Peel said, " I will not
give to that cause too much weight, I will not withhold the homage which is due to reason.and truth by
denying that my opinions on the subject of protection, have undergone a change.   My opinions have
been modified by the experience of the last three years.
I have had an opportunity of comparing the results
of the principle which has been followed during those
years, viz., the gradual removal of protection from
domestic industry.   I have had an opportunity of
comparing periods of abundance and comparatively
low prices, with periods of scarcity and high prices,
and I am led to the conclusion that the grounds of
public policy on which Protection has been defended
are not tenable ; at least I cannot defend them."
The close of the address from which this passage is
taken presents us with a noble instance of independence in a statesman, and was peculiarly appro-
priate to the circumstances which then surrounded
the illustrious convert to Free Trade:—" While honour
and a sense of public duty require it, I do not shrink
from office. I am ready to incur its responsibilities,
to bear its sacrifices, to confront its honourable perils ;
but I will not maintain it with limited power and

shackled authority. I will not stand at the helm during the tempestuous night, if that' helm is not allowed freely to traverse. I will not undertake to direct the course of the vessel by observations taken in 1842. I will reserve to myself the unfettered right of judging what will be for the public interest. I do not desire to be the minister of England, but while I am minister I will hold office by no servile tenure; I will hold office unshackled by any other obligation than that of consulting the public interest, and providing for the public safety."

6. The two great measures for which we are indebted to Sir Robert Peel's government, are the Corn Importation Bill, and the Customs' Duties Bill, both of which passed simultaneously through the legislature, and received the royal assent on the 26th of June, 1846. The former instituted a reduced sliding scale on foreign corn, ranging, in the case of wheat, from four shillings a quarter when the price was fifty-three shillings a quarter, to ten shillings when the price fell to forty-eight shillings. Other grain was admitted at proportionate rates of duty, and the whole arrangement was to last no longer than 1849, after which period the duty on all was to be merely nominal, while corn imported from the British colonies was reduced to the nominal duty at once. The Customs' Duties Bill was of a more complicated character, owing to the great variety of articles included in it. Its more important sections are those which refer to the importation of live animals, since, next to corn, they enter most largely into human subsistence. These were to be admitted in future entirely free of duty, as also were beef, fresh or salted,

G

bacon, and various other kinds of preserved meats. Of articles relating to clothing; silk, thrown and dyed; single or tram organzine or crape silk; thread; manufactures of cotton or wool, or of both intermixed, were also freed from former imposts, while several kinds of furniture wood, enamel, gelatine, and dressed hides, were admitted on the same terms. Timber was an important article in the new tariff. We have noticed already the reductions made in the imposts formerly levied on this commodity; these were still further lowered to twenty shillings per load, in the case of hewn timber, from April 5, 1847, and fifteen shillings per load from April 5, 1848. Other descriptions of timber, such as battens, deals, staves, firewood, handspikes, etc., were subjected to duties proportionally reduced. The extensive effect of these changes will be at once foreseen. The tariff was now an altogether different thing from what it was when Sir Robert Peel first began to reform it in 1842. Then it contained more than 1,200 articles, now it did not contain a sixth of that number. The Sugar Duties Bill, which obtained the royal assent on the 18th of August, can scarcely be termed a Free Trade measure; since, though it enacted a reduced rate of duty, it practically recognised the principle of protection to our colonial interests against the extensive sugar growers of Brazil; it was, moreover, entirely supplanted by the New Sugar Duties Bill, which afterwards passed through the legislature under the auspices of Lord John Russell. The passing of the two former measures fixed a limit to the ministry of Sir Robert Peel. The Whigs seized the opportunity afforded them by the Irish Coercion Bill of escaping from a forced coalition, and on the 29th of June, the Premier announced the resignation of himself and his colleagues.

7. One of the first acts of the new ministry was to apply the principles of Free Trade to the colonial and shipping interests of the United Kingdom. The Sugar Act of Sir Robert Peel was annulled by a new measure, establishing, by a reduction extending over several years, entire equality between colonial and foreign produce; and in 1849 the royal assent was given to the repeal of the famous Act of Navigation, which for two centuries had been regarded as the bulwark of our naval ascendancy. These two important measures completed the fabric which the repeal of the corn laws had begun, and fully committed the nation to its new career. It is true that numerous regulations at variance with the spirit of Free Trade still remained in the statute book, but after the destruction of the greater monopolies of corn, sugar, and ships, their disappearance was rendered a mere question of time. In this light the accession of the Whig Ministry to power was fortunate for the country; steps less decided in reference to the colonial and shipping interests than those they took, would have exposed our entire Free Trade policy to peril. The master grievance of the corn laws once disposed of, those which pressed less heavily on the people would have enjoyed, in all probability, a renewed lease of power, and the course of legislation being thus rendered inconsistent, less difficulty would have been felt by an administration intensely protective, in attempting a return to Protection. Such a retrograde course is now impossible; the effects of recent legislation will soon array the stoutest defenders of

monopoly in favour of Free Trade ; the British farmer will have no greater desire to see the resuscitation of the corn laws, and the British shipowner no greater desire to see the revival of the navigation act, than the manufacturers of Lancashire to petition to Parliament for protection against the muslins and cashmeres of India.

8. Whatever meed of gratitude we owe the ministry of Lord Russell, for the decision they displayed in carrying out the policy of Sir Robert Peel, it is unquestionably to the latter of these statesmen that our thanks are chiefly due. But for his honesty and patriotism, the legislative triumph of Free Trade could not have been so safely or so speedily achieved. The sacrifices which it cost him to act as he acted, are such as no man could appreciate but himself, and such as probably no British statesman had ever been called upon to make before; but however costly the price may have been at which he followed out his convictions of duty, he received an equal recompense in the popularity, as lasting as it was unprecedented, which forthwith attached itself to his name. The moment of his exit from power was the proudest in his career. He had ceased to be the idol of a party, only to receive instead the intelligent homage of an entire nation; the recriminations of apostacy which assailed him on the part of his former friends, were silenced by the applause which greeted on all sides the magnanimity which had consulted the public welfare at the cost of power, and the people forgave him the dubious crime of infidelity to faction, for the sake of his loyalty to truth. It was his happiness to die at the zenith of his fame ; his greatest achieve-

ments, almost as soon as they were performed, became historical; time already seems to have interposed an age between his epoch and our own, and the nation's gratitude has acquired a touch of tenderness which is usually the product of centuries. Other actors have appeared upon the stage, and other plans are agitated; the destiny of the commonwealth, more glorious than that of its most illustrious sons, must steadily fulfil its course, and we stand already within the shadow of greater events; but the name of PEEL is one which will not die, and the last words he uttered as Prime Minister of England will be treasured up in memories more faithful than the marbles on which they are inscribed:—" Within a few hours, probably, that power which I have held for a period of five years will be surrendered into the hands of another, without repining and without complaint; with a more lively recollection of the support and confidence I have received, than of the opposition which, during a recent period, I have encountered. I shall, I fear, leave office with a name severely censured by many honourable men, who, on public principle, deeply regret the severance of party ties, who deeply regret that severance, not from any interested or personal motive, but because they believe fidelity to a party, the existence of a great party, and the maintenance of a great party, to be a powerful instrument of good government. I shall surrender power severely censured, I fear, by many honourable men, who, from no interested motives, have adhered to the principle of Protection, because they look upon it as of importance to the welfare and interest of the country. I shall leave a name execrated, I know, by every monopolist, who, professing honourable opinions, would maintain protection for his own individual benefit; but it may be I shall leave a name sometimes remembered with expressions of good will, in the abodes of those whose lot it is to earn their daily bread by the sweat of their brow; when they shall recruit their exhausted energies with abundant and untaxed food, the sweeter because no longer leavened by a sense of injustice."*

While we cheerfully recognise the services of Lord John Russell and Sir Robert Peel in the final stage of the anti-corn law struggle, it is not to either of these statesmen that posterity will assign the honour of its success. With a candour which did him infinite credit, Sir Robert Peel acknowledged this in the speech with which he resigned office. A combination of parties, aided by the influence of government, carried the repeal of the corn laws, but it is to the spirit of the age, and to the band of courageous and enlightened men by whose efforts its energies were roused, that we must accord the chief merit of the victory. Every age is pervaded by sentiments of which contemporary generations are but half conscious; sentiments which, although not recognised, have a real hold upon the popular intellect, exert a formative influence upon the growth of events, and act as the invisible pioneers of humanity in the path of improvement. Themselves the product of the past, existing institutions have been partially modified by the circumstances out of which they sprang, and thus there has

---

* Speech of Sir Robert Peel, in the House of Commons, June 29, 1846.

been created a correspondence between the material forms of society and their own tendencies, which helps the latter onward to their fruition. Great men are great, chiefly because they recognise these sentiments in their logical completeness, and nobly dare everything in carrying them out. But in doing this they do not always act with absolute freedom. Events, partly the offspring of the very sentiments which they are half-willing and half-afraid to recognise, overmaster them, and compel them to bring their homage. Such was the case with the statesmen to whom we have referred. A great alternative was placed before them. Would they, or would they not, embody in their conduct the sentiments of the age, in a point on which those sentiments had become imperative? The penalty of refusal was political extinction; the age *would* move on,—were they willing to move with it? Either they must surrender the helm of state, and, instead of managing the current, drift down it like helpless waifs, while men of tougher sinew take their place; or else they must become as little children, acknowledge their errors, learn the lessons of the times more accurately, and freely inhale the new influences which descend from the constellations of the dawning day. While we admire the magnanimity which does not hesitate before such a choice, let us do full justice to the circumstances which frame it, and compel a decision on the one side or on the other.

Public opinion—not parliamentary opinion—repealed the corn laws. Argument had done its utmost on the floor of the House of Commons, a sense of justice had been appealed to in vain, the accession of great names, and the prestige of immense wealth, rendered the Anti-Corn Law League an object of positive terror to its opponents; yet still, there the question lay, insoluble, and within less than a year of the time when a bill for the repeal of the corn laws became the law of the land, having passed its third reading in the House of Commons by a majority of 98, a motion to the same effect, introduced by Mr. Villiers, was negatived by a majority of 132, so that within that brief period we are to imagine a change of legislative conviction equal to 230 votes. But while this was the state of Parliamentary majorities, a power had risen outside which could not be withstood; a power which combined irrefragable logic with the irresistible force of enlightened millions; a power so marvellously elaborated and so well directed as to threaten destruction to any institution, however venerable, that long opposed its progress, and yet so admirably controlled that it put forth no direct intimidation, and thus gave to its antagonists an opportunity for a voluntary and self-respectful acquiescence. For the possibility of creating this power, we are indebted to the admirable freedom of the British constitution, more particularly to the right of association and the liberty of the press; but its actual creation was the work of the Anti-Corn Law League. Apart from the exertions of this confederacy in enlightening the popular mind, it would have been long before the true principles of political economy would have been embodied in legislation. Conviction was going on in the right track, but at how slow a pace! " Le public," says Victor Cousin, " veut bien marcher, mais non pas courir; il veut bien permettre qu'on améliore ses idées, mais non pas qu'on les détruise brusquement: jamais le même individu n'a complètement changé; la société ne change complètement que par les changements partiels et progressifs des diverses générations." Such is the law by which the growth of opinion is ordinarily regulated, but on the subject of Free Trade the statesmen of England have furnished an important exception. Political conversion has been so common of late as greatly to modify the maxims by which we estimate the morality of public men. Scarcely can we point to a single individual on either side of the House of Commons, who is, or has been, a Cabinet Minister, who has not read his recantation. Not that our legislators showed themselves to be extravagantly endowed with the anticipative instincts of genius; they did not scent the truth afar; their arguments were seldom employed in convincing the obtuser intellects of the people; when they at last endorsed the opinion that Government should not intermeddle with the price of corn, they were not so universally in advance of the age as to excite apprehensions for the safety of the House of Commons from the presence of menacing mobs outside. On the contrary, the legislature was the last to yield; Sir Robert Peel did not throw himself upon the verdict of the country till that verdict had been most unmistakably pronounced.

It is equally exhilarating and instructive to contemplate the process by which public opinion was gradually, but rapidly, brought to decide the question. Commencing with a small circle of intelligent, independent, and single-minded men, correct opinions, together with a sense of their vital importance, quickly pervaded our manufacturing towns, and changed them into

centres of aggressive effort. Then the county constituencies in manufacturing districts began to give way,
and in such influential districts as South Lancashire
and the West Riding of Yorkshire, the " League " was
on the eve of complete success. Presently a sympathetic movement was discernible in boroughs which
had hitherto been exclusively under the influence of
the agricultural interest, till at length crowded assem-
blages of tenant farmers, convened perhaps in shire-
halls to give their coerced support to Protection, gave
a unanimous verdict for Free Trade. Meanwhile
significant accessions had taken place from among
the monied phalanx of the metropolis, and the territorial aristocracy. Such men as Earl Fitzwilliam, the
Marquis of Westminster, and Samuel Jones Lloyd,
openly espoused the side of the "League;" the old
episcopal city of Durham sent a Dissenter and Quaker
to Parliament in the person of John Bright; and the
City of London itself, after a contest of unparalleled
vigour, returned a candidate pledged to Free Trade.
Public meetings were now held in every part of the
kingdom; an advocate of the "League" had only to
announce a lecture, and he was sure of a battle, a
victory, and an ovation; while the large number of
assemblies which were thus held simultaneously,
seemed to convert the nation into a standing *comitia*,
where almost daily some decision opposed to the
policy of ministers was ratified by the public voice.
By these methods public opinion was rapidly assuming an imperiousness which would brook no denial;
a storm was gathering before which Government must
either bend or break. Such an array of sentiment
would have rendered error itself invincible; how

mighty then did it render truth! No wonder that convictions which asked but a candid hearing to win a place in the understanding of everybody, made rapid progress when aided by so powerful an ally. But this omnipotent opinion was not of spontaneous growth; its maturity was hastened by the Anti-Corn Law League. It was this "new power in the state," in other words, some fifty Englishmen, convened, on their own responsibility, at Newall Buildings, Manchester, that wrought a revolution second in importance to none which has transpired since 1688. We make no attempt to rebut the charges which were flung at the League during years of party rancour. Those charges, canvassed on constitutional grounds, are its true glory. In its hands the right of association was pacifically and legally carried to its highest pitch, and by its triumph public opinion was finally confirmed in virtual sovereignty over the other authorities of the state. Its actions vindicate themselves; they can never be imitated except when to do less would be treason to the duties which free men owe their country. Its roll of membership was as justifiable an instrument as the famous invitation to the Prince of Orange, which bore among its signatures the names of a Cavendish, a Sidney, and a Russell. It would be a shameful stint of praise merely to say that the Convention of 1688 and the Anti-Corn Law League of 1845, are acquitted on the score of expediency; the nation assigns them a place among the noblest efforts of patriotism, and the deeds of both will find a permanent record on the brightest pages of our illustrious annals.

In awarding to individuals their meed of praise for

the part they took in this great struggle, we may not forget a brighter laurel which we will join in placing on the brow of our common country.   The possibility of forming such a confederacy as the Anti-Corn Law League, and of keeping its machinery within the letter and spirit of the law, evinces the political maturity at which the people have arrived, and points us to the educational influence of free institutions enjoyed through many successive generations.   Such an organization would not have been possible in any other European state.   In despotic states it could have had no aim but the exercise of coercive power over the prerogatives of the crown, and would have been sacrificed at its birth to the fears of government; while in countries which are nominally under a constitutional regime, but less habituated to its occasional exigencies, the movement would have been from the outset one of pure factiousness, and no opportunity would have been lost of securing its triumph by physical force.   " The first notion which presents itself to a party, as well as to an individual, when it has acquired a consciousness of its own strength, is that of violence : the notion of persuasion arises at a later period, and is derived from experience."*   In aiming at persuasion, instead of coercion, the Anti-Corn Law League nobly illustrated the conscious power which becomes at length inherent in a people long accustomed to be free, and set an example which will serve for ever as a beacon and a pole-star to other nations.

* De Tocqueville.

PART II.

THE EFFECTS OF FREE TRADE ON THE COMMERCIAL, MANUFACTURING, AND OTHER INDUSTRIAL INTERESTS OF THE BRITISH EMPIRE.

THE eve of every great change is usually an occasion for special effusions of the prophetic spirit. At such seasons fear and interest usually combine to make men seers. It is difficult to commit ourselves fully to an untried course, which involves, at the same time, results of great magnitude, without feeling some measure of apprehension, and if we express our thoughts at all at such a crisis, the darker probabilities are usually allowed to tinge the language in which they are conveyed. Moreover, some persons have the presence of mind to exert their ingenuity on occasions of this nature. Determined at all events to be winners in the result, they loudly prophesy ill, that they may be sure to gain, if not by the falsification of their prophecy, at least by its fulfilment. But if the interests of any considerable party are likely to be affected to any serious extent by the proposed changes, then, though those changes may be likely to prove

on the whole very beneficial, the most sombre predictions will be hazarded respecting them. To the
dark fancy of its opponents it will seem laden with all
kinds of calamities; in their strains of warning prosaic expression will achieve a temporary triumph over
the sister arts, and the solemn invocations of Milton's
muse, and the speaking terrors of Michael Angelo,
wax tame beside the creations of their gloomy eloquence.

To this rule the change which abolished the
monopoly of the people's food, and established our
commerce on the broad principles of freedom, was no
exception. As soon as it was plainly resolved upon,
the most dismal forebodings were uttered in Parliament and reechoed through the land. As one Free
Trade measure after another was proposed, the prospects of the nation, beheld through the medium of
Protectionist harangues, grew visibly darker, till at
length the eye turned away affrighted from scenes of
hopeless wretchedness and ruin. To judge by the
same test, there was not a single interest which would
not suffer; agriculture would receive a fatal shock;
farms would be abandoned, rents would fall, and the
owners of baronial mansions be forced to quit them
in despair. Our shipping, exposed to foreign competition, would cease to find employment; noble
vessels would lie uselessly in our harbours; the seamen of foreign nations would supplant the British tar,
while, in the event of war, our shores, deprived by
the destruction of our mercantile marine of the protection anciently afforded by our "wooden walls,"
would be unable to resist the descent of an invading
force. Besides, it was urged, the fall of prices would

soon bring down the rate of wages, and the unrestricted admission of foreign manufactures would take the means of subsistence out of the hands of our own operatives. Secure of a market here, on account of our absolute need of his produce, the foreigner would be able to part with his goods without making any adequate purchases in return ; thus the country would be drained of gold, and the operations of industry checked for want of capital. Then, in the opinion of the opponents of Free Trade, the retributive catastrophe would draw nigh. Overwhelmed with pauperism and bankruptcy, the energies of trade would give way; the Nemesis of wasted acres and pawned coronets would pour her last vials on the seats of our manufactures, and the blind cupidity of cotton-lords receive the dregs of the cup they had forced on the acceptance of others. Such were the predictions in the midst of which our Free Trade policy was entered upon; we are now about to inquire how far they have been sustained or reversed by facts.

CHAPTER I.

EFFECTS OF THE PARTIAL APPLICATION OF FREE TRADE
PRINCIPLES PREVIOUS TO 1840.

In proceeding to consider those facts in our industrial and social condition which constitute an experimental justification of our Free Trade policy, it would be altogether wrong to omit those which happened previous to the era at which the corn laws were abolished. Several considerations concur to show that we ought to commence our review at a higher point. In the first place, it cannot be doubted that the triumph of Free Trade in 1846 was mainly owing to the success of those experiments by which its principles had already been put to the test. The arguments which were urged on its behalf, though backed by almost demonstrative proof, would not have succeeded so quickly in rousing the enthusiasm of the masses, or carrying such important changes through the legislature, if they had not borrowed irrefragable force from the unvarying experience of twenty years. In this, even more than in the wealth of its leaders, the eloquence of its advocates, the wisdom of its plans, or the justice of its cause, lay the prodigious strength of the Anti-Corn Law League. Moreover, a review of the earlier effects of Free Trade, when partially adopted, is requisite in order to render an appeal to facts decisive. It has been urged, for instance, that our prosperity is only temporary; that it springs from an accidental abundance of gold, or a speculating mania, and that in a year or two we shall witness a relapse, with other assertions of the same kind. The possibility that this prediction may receive a partial fulfilment, though from causes quite distinct from Free Trade, and the certainty that, if such a reverse happen, the fragments of the Protectionist party will at once raise a cry for Protection, force us in common prudence to show that our present prosperity is not a chance event, but one which might have been clearly foretold; that under a Free Trade policy the national industry revives just as surely as vegetation renews itself under the warm breezes and fertilizing rains of spring. In a word, it is desirable to show, by an impartial appeal to past as well as present facts, that Free Trade stands on the immovable basis of inductive science; that it would be just as reasonable to accept the Ptolemaic system as the true philosophy of the heavens, or the physics of the schoolmen as a true exposition of the laws of nature, as to admit the theories of Protection in questions relating to industry and commerce.

Before commencing our inquiry, it will be useful to consider the different forms under which the principles of Free Trade may be recognised in practice. Free Trade rests upon this simple axiom:—The interference of the legislative power with the process of exchange is, *per se*, invariably pernicious; except for

H

purposes of state necessity it ought not to be touched
at all, and, with reference even to this exception, it
is a political problem of the first moment to find out
the least amount of interference which will suffice,
or to discover some better way of replenishing the
national exchequer.   Accordingly, when any article,
or branch of traffic, is monopolised by individuals for
their own benefit, Free Trade stigmatises the preference as a violation of morals, and a loss to the
commonwealth.   When, for example, duties are levied
on foreign manufactures with the avowed object of
protecting our own, Free Trade asserts, not only that
the impost is a fraud on the public, but that the
manufactures so protected would do better without
the protection afforded than with it; and that, even
if they suffered for a time from the effects of foreign
competition, the general trade of the country would
be a gainer to a much greater extent, as official
returns would doubtless demonstrate.   On the other
hand, when duties are levied for the purpose of
. meeting the pecuniary wants of the state, Free Trade
insists on the inexpediency of any rate of taxation
which checks consumption; its maxim on this point
is that, within certain limits, low taxes are more
profitable than high taxes, since the greater cheapness
of the article in the former case ensures its being
used by a much greater proportion of the population.
These doctrines have always been the creed of Free
Traders, and the question is now, whether they are
true in point of fact?   Have these expectations been
realised, or have they been found delusive?   The case
is exempt from the shadow of ambiguity; the issue is
one of mere experience.   When protection has been

withdrawn from any branch of manufacture, has it flourished or declined? In proportion as we have applied the principles of commercial freedom, has there, or has there not, been a consequent increase of trade? Have we bought in such a case a larger quantity of the produce of other nations, and sold them a larger quantity of ours? Have protected interests, when the protection has been withdrawn, become extinct, or have they survived the shock, and become more vigorous than before? Again, have the highest taxes been found most profitable to the exchequer? Has consumption advanced under them? When they were reduced was a corresponding deficiency observed in the revenue? On the contrary, has not the revenue uniformly increased under such circumstances? Extending our view to the state of trade, and the general condition of the people, has not the greatest prosperity, in these respects, been observed in those branches of manufacture which were unprotected, and, in other branches, has not a great improvement taken place on every relaxation of protective duties? In proportion as the principles of Free Trade have been applied to the pursuits of the entire population, has our commerce declined, have the comforts of the poor been diminished, has political discontent increased? These are merely questions of fact, and we ask them, first, respecting a period when the gold discoveries of California and Australia were among the secrets of futurity; when ingenuity was undoubtedly required to pronounce white black, or to palm upon one event the natural results of another.

I. Taking in chronological order the more important relaxations of our restrictive system prior to

1846, we commence with the opening of the trade to the East Indies in 1814, with which we may connect the similar opening of the Chinese trade in 1833. Previous to the former date, our entire commerce with the vast and affluent markets of Continental Asia had been monopolised by the East India Company. A few favoured individuals, possessing no just claim to such a preference, were constituted the sole link between this country and those famous realms whose wealth had fired the imagination of Columbus, and been a source of opulence to every nation whose merchants had gained a footing on their shores. The pernicious effects of this monopoly were equal to its injustice. Most of the articles included in it, such as tea, coffee, sugar, pepper, cotton, silk, and indigo, were of the greatest importance, either as food or articles of manufacture, and the comparatively small quantities imported, as well as the consequent enhancement of the price, entailed privation and pecuniary loss upon the British consumer. Moreover, inconsiderable as our imports were from that part of the world, our exports did not amount to a fourth of their value; a circumstance which can only be ascribed to the prohibition of free commercial intercourse, and which speedily vanished on a change of system.

In fact, one of the first effects of this change was a rapid and steady growth in the exportation of manufactured produce to the East Indies. In 1814 its value amounted to no more than £1,874,690, but in the very next year it increased by nearly thirty-seven per cent.; in 1817, by nearly eighty-one per cent.; in 1827 by one hundred and forty-seven per cent.; and in 1844, including China, by more than three hundred and ten per cent. In 1815, the quantity of cotton goods sent to India was 818,208 yards; —in 1829 it amounted to 37,566,736 yards, an increase of 4491 per cent.;—in the former year only eight pounds' weight of cotton twist was exported to India; in the latter the quantity exported thither amounted to 4,549,219 lbs. In 1814, our imports of cotton wool " from places east of the Cape" were below three millions of pounds; in 1833 they reached thirty millions, and in 1844 nearly ninety millions. In 1833, the East India Company was entirely deprived of its commercial character, and the whole of our trade to that part of the world became entirely dependent on private enterprise. The results of this change have triumphantly demonstrated the utility of commercial freedom. Since that period several entirely new branches of traffic have sprung up; linseed, rum, tobacco, and sheep's wool, which up to 1833 formed no part of our imports from India, have become articles of considerable importance. " The quantity of coffee," says the late Mr. Porter, writing in 1846, " is nearly trebled; the quantities of lac dye and shellac respectively have been quadrupled; hemp is more than doubled; and hides are increased threefold. Indigo has not undergone any material alteration, but the quantities of pepper and rice are doubled. The sugar trade, from being quite insignificant, has lately become one of the most important branches of commerce." Since that period a great improvement has taken place in many articles of Indian produce, especially in rice and tallow; while the experiments which have been made in the growth of flax promise soon to render it an article of export to Europe.

II. After the opening of the East India trade, the next important inroad on the principles of monopoly was made by the treaties of reciprocity with various countries, which were entered into by the British Government between the years 1815 and 1830, and the repeal, in 1822, of several clauses of the Navigation Act. We have already explained the nature of those concessions, let us look at their results. To appreciate these it must be remarked, that the object of the navigation act and its subsidiary statutes was in reality to favour one branch of industrial enterprise at the expense of others. When higher imposts were laid upon articles brought to us in foreign vessels than when imported in British vessels, the immediate effect was to raise the price of foreign freights, and so to work the carrying trade of the world into the hands of our own shipowners. No doubt a political motive first suggested the step, but whatever effect it may have had in keeping up the number of British seamen, and thus increasing the efficiency of our marine, this could be produced only by giving those persons who were connected with the building and sale of British vessels a monopoly of a great portion of the traffic carried on with our shores, and the monopoly was kept up by raising the price of all articles brought hither in the ships of other nations. Hence, when, in the case of thirty different states, these unjust distinctions were abolished by the reciprocity acts, we had no right to conclude that the effect of their abolition would be on the whole pernicious, even though our own shipowners should be ruined by it. Such a result might have taught us that the building of ships was not our proper vocation; that other nations could build them at a cheaper rate, and that our merchants, when left to themselves, had prudently availed themselves of the cheaper means of transit, on the very same principle which would lead them to choose the cheapest mode of conveying them from the warehouse to the wharf; but we could not have concluded from the ruin of our shipbuilders and shipowners that the consequences of Free Trade in ships were, on the whole, pernicious. On the contrary, if, while our shipping interests had declined, the amount of tonnage employed in our foreign trade had greatly increased, we might have inferred that capital had been turned into a more profitable channel, and that Free Trade had increased the wealth of the nation by enabling it to substitute a more for a less gainful species of industry. But if *both* these results occurred; if, while our general trade increased, our shipping interest more than maintained its ground, we have then an *à fortiori* argument of the strongest kind wherewith to demonstrate the utility of the change.

A few facts will show that this was actually the case. In 1821 the British shipping engaged in the foreign trade of the United States amounted to an aggregate of 55,188 tons, constituting rather more than seven per cent. on the whole of the shipping thus engaged belonging to the Union. In 1844 this proportion had increased to nearly 39 per cent., and the absolute amount of tonnage to more than three quarters of a million. During the interval of those dates the increase of American shipping was 158 per cent., while the increase of British shipping amounted to 1289 per cent., being an annual increase on the former of rather more than six per cent., and in the latter of fifty-six per cent., a rate of increase nine times in favour of our own shipowners. If we examine the proportion of British and foreign shipping employed during the same period in our own foreign trade, with a view to ascertain the combined effect of the numerous concessions made to the shipping interests of other countries, we find that, in 1821, the proportion of foreign tonnage which entered the ports of the United Kingdom was 21 per cent., while in 1844 it had only increased to 28 per cent., or an annual average increase of ·3 per cent. Lest we should exaggerate the value of even this small increase it should be remembered, that the various reciprocity acts brought us into competition with states whose commerce was just beginning to recover from the disastrous effects of a long war. During the continuance of hostilities nearly the whole of the carrying trade of Europe had neccesarily been thrown into our hands. This, however, could not be regarded as a natural or final arrangement; it was to be expected that, as soon as the return of peace would allow, the marine of other countries would claim its share in carrying on their national traffic. Hence, the increase which took place in the amount of foreign shipping engaged in the foreign trade of this country during the period just mentioned, must be ascribed in a great measure to the natural progress of a branch of native industry from a normal state, rather than to any disadvantage resulting to our own shipowners from the relaxation of the navigation act. Besides this, it must be borne in mind that several of the states with which we formed treaties of reciprocity are among the oldest naval powers of Europe; that many of them possess superior advantages in ship-building, owing to their having an unlimited supply of the finest timber, an advantage which was relatively increased at the period of which we write by the heavy differential duties which were laid upon the importation of Baltic timber into this country. But, setting aside these considerations, and making no allowance either for the peculiar position of the marine of foreign states on the return of peace, or our own relative disadvantages as ship-builders, the small annual increase which occurred in the proportion of foreign to British shipping engaged in our own trade, taken in connexion with the vast enlargement of our commerce during the same period, triumphantly demonstrates the uselessness of Protection. From 1821 to 1844, while the proportion of foreign shipping employed in our foreign trade increased only from 21 to 28 per cent, the entire amount of tonnage employed increased as much as 155 per cent.; and it is impossible to think that this rate of increase would have been experienced if the old system of mutual restriction had been maintained. If, during that period, the tonnage of foreign shipping increased by 675,826 tons, the increase in the tonnage of British shipping was three times as great, so that by permitting our neighbours to put one penny into their pockets, we had put three-pence into our own. "In 1825 we had a large trade, British shipping was employed to a greater amount than in any previous year, and the proportion of British to each 100 tons employed fell from 79·83 in 1821 to 67·88 in 1825. In 1826 we had a languid trade;

fewer British ships found employment, but the proportion in each 100 tons rose to 72·67. It will
hardly be contended by the advocates of the late
navigation law that a large proportion of British
when compared with foreign shipping trading to our
ports, is, under these circumstances, of advantage to
the shipowners, if, in order to engross this larger
proportion they must submit to a positive decrease
of employment for their vessels. They will not surely
be so blind to their interests as to conceive it better
to engross 70 per cent. of a trade represented by 3,
than to be limited to 65 per cent. of a trade represented by 4."*

III. From the relaxation of the navigation act, in
1822, we pass to the extensive fiscal changes effected
by Mr. Huskisson in 1825, in order to trace the effect
of those measures on the important interests of silk,
linen, and wool. The first of these received a considerable development in France at a period when
it was scarcely introduced into this country. The
settlement among us of 70,000 French exiles, in
consequence of the revocation of the edict of Nantes,
inflicted a heavy blow upon the silk manufactures of
France, while it gave an additional stimulus to its
growth in this country. From that time, a peculiar
degree of favour was shown to it. National honour
and hospitality, nay even Protestant faith, were ad-
jured to protect the weavers of Spitalfields, and, with
them, the manufacturers of silk generally. At the
peace of Utrecht, an attempt was made to establish
our trade with France on moderate *ad valorem* duties,

---

* "Finances and Trade of the United Kingdom at the beginning
of 1852," p. 29.

but it encountered a successful resistance from our own manufacturers, who represented that our " black and coloured silks, gold and silver stuffs, and ribands,' were equal to those of France, that black silk for scarfs, &c., were now made annually to the value of £300,000, whereas it used all to be imported. A child would smile at such reasoning, if it were employed with reference to private individuals. If a person can manufacture better than his neighbours, why should he fear their competition, and if he cannot, why does he not turn his attention to something else? If the articles in question could be produced at a cheaper rate in England than in France, why not throw the market open to the French? But if they could not be produced cheaper, how puerile to allege, as an advantage, that they were at least produced at home; as if it would be better to make our tables and chairs at home, even though we could purchase them at the nearest cabinet-maker's at half the price for which we could construct them ourselves. But the fallacies of common life often become imposing when they are applied to national affairs; the English manufacturer found his arguments convincing, and continued to receive protection against his French rivals. In 1765, a law was passed, strictly prohibiting the importation of French goods, and this remained in force till 1826, a period of more than sixty years.

This long period of protection must have sufficed to bring out whatever latent influence a protective system can exert in favour of native industry, and it is not surprising, if, guaranteed the undisputed possession of the home market, our silk manufacturers made considerable progress. Taking for our guide

the quantity of raw material imported, which, owing
to our entire dependence for this article upon foreign
countries, is one of perfect precision, and comparing
the average annual imports of the first three years of
prohibition with those of the last three, we find that
the quantity of silk manufactured in this country increased, during fifty-eight years of the period, nearly
336 per cent., which gives an annual average increase
per cent. of 5·79.   Still, the existence of complete
protection did not ensure uninterrupted prosperity;
on the contrary, by the encouragement it gave to
smuggling, it was the direct cause of much embarrassment and distress.   In 1818, several petitions were
presented to Parliament from Spitalfields and Coventry, complaining that, in consequence of this illegal
competition, "the demand for manufactured goods
had for a long time so decreased, as to afford serious
ground of alarm to our manufacturers, and to threaten
the existence of the silk manufacture of this country."
Since more than fifty years' protection had not been
found sufficient to raise our silk manufactures above so
precarious a position, it was deemed high time to
adopt a different system; accordingly, in 1824, an entire
change was introduced.   The duty of five shillings
and six pence per pound on raw silk was reduced to
three pence, and ultimately to one penny.   The duty
on thrown silk, previously fourteen shillings and
eight pence per pound, was reduced to seven shillings
and six pence, and ultimately to three shillings and
six pence per pound, and a drawback to the amount
of this duty was allowed on exportation.   It was also
enacted that, after the fifth of July, 1826, the prohi-
bitiou of silk manufactures, the product of foreign

countries, should cease, and that such articles should thenceforth be admitted on the payment of a maximum duty, *ad valorem*, of 30 per cent.

Great was the consternation excited by the prospect of these changes. Experienced men declared their conviction that our silk manufactures would not survive their effects. Spitalfields, Norwich, Coventry, Macclesfield raised one cry of terror. It was asserted that the minister by whose influence these measures were introduced was deliberately consigning thousands of industrious operatives to ruin, and deserved to be impeached as a traitor to his country. Yet seven years had scarcely elapsed from the utterance of these gloomy forebodings, when the weavers of Macclesfield harnessed themselves to the carriage of Mr. Huskisson, and drew him through their town in triumph. He had saved their trade. So far from his measures having proved its destruction, but for these, to quote the language of a distinguished manufacturer, "we should have had no silk trade to talk of." On the passing of these measures the progress of the silk trade was immediate and rapid, yet, at the same time, of that steady character which promised permanence. We have seen that the aggregate increase in the quantity of raw material imported amounted, during fifty-eight years of absolute protection, to an aggregate of 336 per cent., or an average amount of 5·79 per cent. During the twenty-one years immediately following the step which was to prove so ruinous, the aggregate increase in the quantity of silk imported was nearly 247 per cent., or an annual average of 11·76 per cent., more than double the amount of the previous period. During the ten years preceding 1824, the quantity of silk "used by our manufacturers amounted to 18,823,117 pounds, being an average of 1,882,311 pounds per annum;" while, "in the ten years immediately following the change of system, the quantity used was 36,780,009 ℔s., or 3,678,001 ℔s. per annum, being an increase over the average of the former period of 95 per cent.;" and, "in the eleven years ending with 1844, the consumption was 43,588,386 ℔s., or 3,962,580 ℔s. per annum, being an increase of 110 per cent. upon the quantity used under the restrictive system."* These results will appear still more decisive, if we examine the kinds of silk which constituted our imports during the periods of protection, and comparative Free Trade. Under the restrictive system, the duty upon thrown silk was nearly three times the amount of that upon raw silk. This enormous duty was regarded as the palladium of that part of the British manufacture which consisted in spinning the raw material into thread, and it was confidently asserted that any considerable reduction of duty would at once throw thousands of our operative population into idleness. The actual result, however, proved exactly the reverse of what had been predicted. Notwithstanding the reduction of the duty on thrown silk to less than a fourth of its previous amount, the quantity imported steadily decreased, showing that the larger quantity required to meet the wants of our growing trade was the produce of our own spindles. Taking the average of the first three years of prohibition, the thrown silk imported

---

* Porter's "Progress of the Nation," sec. ii. ch. 2.

amounted to one-half the entire quantity consumed; at the end of sixty years' protection it still amounted to a seventh of the whole, but twenty years of comparative free trade reduced it to less than a fourteenth. If, in 1844, after twenty years of partial free trade, when the low rate of duty upon foreign thrown silk was so tempting to the manufacturer, we had imported only the same proportion of that article as we did under the protective system, the quantity so imported would have amounted to 2,727,011 ℔s., instead of which it was only 333,602 ℔s., and on an average of the ten years ending with 1844 was not more than 264,854 ℔s.; showing that our industrial interests, so far from having suffered in consequence of exposure to foreign competition, had immeasurably increased, and in proportion as we threw open our markets to the foreign manufacturer the better able were we to cope with him. Self-reliance had awakened energy, stimulated invention, supplied motives to economy, and thus enabled us to exchange the imperfect protection of unjust laws for that which is afforded by the more profitable application of our own faculties.

Let us note, in passing, a few of the social benefits which sprang from this prosperity. In the first place, the means of remunerative labour were greatly extended. Factories were multiplied, and the manufacture rapidly spread into new districts. The number of silk looms in Manchester in 1823 was 5,500; in five years they had increased to 12,000, and in 1832 to 14,000. Immediately on the reduction of the duty, the number of throwing mills in various parts of the country rose from 175 to 266, and the number of spindles from 780,000 to 1,180,000. Besides main-

taining their position in the home market, our manufactures pushed their sales abroad, and from 1830 a
gratifying increase is perceptible in the value of our
silk exports; their total value for the ten years ending
with 1839 having been £7,042,619, while during
the preceding decade their aggregate value had
amounted to no more than £3,149,618. In Germany
and the United States our fabrics came into successful
competition with the products of the French loom, and
in 1844 nearly three-fifths of the manufactured silk
exported to the whole of ·Europe were shipped to
France itself. The secret of this extending trade is
found in the greater excellence which has marked our
silk manufactures since 1824. During the era of
Protection, English goods could bear no comparison
with those of France.—Now, however, as regards
texture, they are fully equal, and even in figured silks,
in which the contest was thought to be almost hopeless, considerable orders have been executed for
American markets. The same causes which have
thus extended our silk trade abroad, have created a
still greater demand at home. Silk, instead of being
regarded as a luxury, has come to be regarded as an
ordinary article of female attire. The factory girl dresses
now in her silk gown, and the proportion of females
who on holiday occasions pass thus attired through the
streets of our manufacturing towns, is not immeasurably less than on the promenades of the metropolis.
The moral benefit which results from this extended
use of a more elegant material of dress is by no means
to be lightly valued, since every thing which tends to
refine the taste, and introduce a higher standard of
living, deserves a place among the agencies of civilisa-

tion; but it has a recommendation of a more utilitarian character, it establishes the manufacture itself on a broader basis, and guards it against those alternations of distress which were formerly incidental to every change of fashion. The progress of new designs from the highest to the lowest class of customers, is sufficiently slow to prevent the manufacturer from being surprised by any caprice of taste on the part of the public. Styles which have fallen into neglect in the fashionable *purlieus* of the West End, instead of being thrown as formerly, upon the owners' hands, find a ready purchase elsewhere. Hence business is conducted with less risk, and that uncertainty of employment is prevented which is, to some extent, more injurious to the operative than low wages

IV. The LINEN MANUFACTURE is another of our important interests whose history demonstrates the utility of Mr. Huskisson's measures. This branch of industry presents us, in its earlier annals, with a truly notable instance of legislative interference. About the end of the seventeenth century the progress of the woollen manufacture of Ireland excited the jealousy of those in this country who were engaged in the same trade, and who, instead of honestly endeavouring to beat their Irish rivals by superior skill, cowardly sought the protection of Parliament. In reply to an address of both Houses, King William III. acceded to their request for protection in the following terms:—" I shall do all that in me lies to discourage the woollen manufacture in Ireland, and to encourage the linen manufacture." Through the exertion of Royal influence, the Irish House of Commons passed a Bill forbidding the exportation of Irish woollens, except to

England, and the value of this exception was destroyed by the existence of prohibitory duties against its admission to this country. Repaying one injustice by the perpetration of another, the Government did its utmost to promote the linen trade in Ireland ; partly by the imposition of heavy duties on dressed flax, and partly by offering considerable bounties on the exportation of manufactured linen. The latter ceased only in 1830, and, though much reduced, amounted in the previous year to £300,000, or nearly a seventh part of the value of the linen exported. In the opinion of Mr. McCulloch, if all the money expended by Government in encouraging the linen manufactures had been put out at simple interest, it would have yielded more than the profit of the entire quantity exported.

Notwithstanding this liberal patronage on the part of Government, it is only during the present century that the linen trade has obtained a healthy footing in the United Kingdom. Its previous progress exhibited all the symptoms of a protected interest, while its unparalleled advance in Scotland since 1815, in consequence of which the exports of linen from Dundee alone equalled, in 1833, the entire shipments made in the same year from all Ireland, demonstrates that private ingenuity and enterprise constitute the true hope of commerce. In 1825 the duty on dressed flax was reduced from the enormous amount of £10 14s. 6d. per cwt., and on undressed flax from five pence per lb. —rates equivalent to *ad valorem* duties ranging from 40 to 180 per cent.—to a uniform rate of four pence per cwt. ; which was still further reduced in the course of the three following years to the nominal rate of one penny per cwt. The effect of these reductions was at once seen in a rapid augmentation of our imports. Taking the five years immediately preceding the change, we find the average amount of flax imported to have been 533,708 cwt., while the average quantity for the five years commencing with 1825 amounted to 881,042 cwt., and for a similar period ending with 1844 to 1,346,233 cwt. Moreover, the stimulus given to the manufacture by the greater cheapness of the raw material is seen during the same period in the progress of inventive skill, and the more than proportional cheapness of the manufactured article. In 1813 the length of a pound of linen yarn of average fineness was only 3,330 yards, in 1824 it was only 5,220 yards, while in 1833 it was 11,130 yards. " During that time the price of such average yarn had fallen from twenty-nine shillings and five pence to ten shillings and nine pence per bundle, so that, taking quantity into account, the price of yarn fell, in twenty years, to one-ninth of the price which it bore at the close of the war; the price of the raw material having fallen in the meantime about one-half. The improvements made in the operation of flax spinning in England are rendered apparent by the fact that we are now (1844) large exporters of linen yarn to Ireland and even to France. The earliest shipments to the latter country were made in 1833, and amounted to only 76,512 lbs., but the quantity rapidly increased until 1842, when it reached 22,202,292 lbs. This exportation of linen yarn is a new branch of trade, for which we are entirely dependent on the perfection of our spinning machinery. This country had previously been a constant importer of linen yarn, but there is at present (1844), every appearance of this state of things being entirely changed. So recently as 1827 our weavers used nearly 4,000,000 lbs. of foreign yarn, but each subsequent year the quantity has been diminished, until in 1834 it amounted to only about one and a half million of pounds, and in 1844 hardly exceeded one million of pounds."* In the meantime our exportation of linen fabrics had steadily increased; its declared value having risen from two millions and a half in 1834, to more than four millions in 1844; a rate of increase which throws into the shade the greatest ever attained under the shield of Protection.

V. A position, first in historical dignity, and only second in point of national importance, must be as-·signed to our WOOLLEN MANUFACTURE, and, at the same time, none affords us a better illustration of the mischievous effects of Protection, or the invigorating influence of Free Trade. This, perhaps, of all the branches of our native industry, has been most warmly cherished by the legislature, though the manufacturer has had to pay the heavy cost of protection in the shape of duties on the raw material. Our legislation on the woollen trade has evidently tended to the benefit of the wool-grower rather than the manufacturer. The chief boon professedly bestowed upon the latter was a prohibition directed against the export of home-grown wool, which, it was supposed, would ensure to him a monopoly in the fabrics made from that article. This prohibition lasted from 1660 to 1825, when it was entirely repealed, along with the other restrictive statutes already noticed. While

* "Progress of the Nation."

the exportation of British wool had thus been strictly forbidden, the importation of foreign wool had been left quite free till 1802, when it was subjected to a duty of five shillings and three pence per cwt. This was raised in 1813 to six shillings and eight pence, and in 1819 Mr. Vansittart raised it to the enormous rate of fifty-six shillings per cwt., or sixpence per lb. In 1825 Mr. Huskisson reduced the duty from six pence to one penny per lb., and, since that period, the manufacture has been permitted to develop its resources comparatively untrammelled by legislative aid.

The quantities of foreign wool imported into this country have been subjected to excessive fluctuations, but grounding our observations on averages of five years, we find an unmistakable increase during the period which has elapsed since the commencement of partial Free Trade. Thus, if we take the five years immediately preceding the reduction of the import duty in 1825, we find the annual amount to have been 17,477,492 lbs. Taking the same number of years, commencing with 1825, the annual amount was 28,134,825 lbs. Taking again the five years terminating with 1844, the annual amount was 51,238,457 lbs, being an increase upon the first period of nearly 200 per cent. At the same time, it is probable that a considerable increase had taken place during the same period in the quantity of home-grown wool. Assuming as correct the statement made in 1828 before the committee of the House of Commons, appointed to inquire into the state of the woollen trade, it would appear that the produce of the British fleece amounted in 1810 to 94,376,640 lbs.;

that in 1844, it had probably become 145,721,880 lbs.; and that the entire consumption of wool had increased by more than 100 per cent. since the beginning of the century. Large as was the increase in British wool during this period, the increase in foreign wool was proportionally much larger, having risen from nine per cent. upon the entire quantity of the former in 1800 to forty-three per cent. in 1844. And yet the price of British wool, which had often been the subject of loud complaints on the part of the agricultural interest, on the reduction of the duty on foreign wool in 1825, gradually recovered from its depression, and reached a higher range than it had ever been able to command under the protective system. But the most decisive advantage resulting from Free Trade in wool was the stimulus it gave to invention, and the greater excellence we were very soon able to realise in our manufactures when brought fairly into competition with other nations. The merinos which the French manufacturers were enabled to produce from English wool were at first superior to any article of a similar kind which had been made in this country. Our manufacturers, however, were not disposed at once to surrender the palm, and in a " few years produced merinos and other stuffs in every way equal to the fabrics of France. By this means the stuff manufacture received an important impetus. In the five years from 1820 to 1824, while the prohibition to export English wool was still in force, a prohibition which it was thought ensured the market in finer fabrics to our own producers, the average annual shipments of that description of woollen goods amounted to 1,064,441 pieces. In the five years following, during which the restrictions on exportation were taken away, the average annual shipments of the same description of goods amounted to 1,228,239 pieces, and in the next quinqueninal period, viz., from 1830 to 1834, the average rose to 1,505,993 pieces. Between 1835 and 1839, the average exportation somewhat declined, having been 1,429,057 pieces, but during the five years 1840 to 1844, it reached 2,128,212 pieces, being exactly double the quantity exported during the last five years, in which the prohibition existed." Such facts triumphantly prove that open competition is the proper element of industry, and that if one branch is weaker than the rest, no better method can be taken to invigorate it than that of exposing it unprotected to the rivalry of the world.

VI. Thus far we have considered the effects of Free Trade as applied to the reduction or abolition of protective duties; we shall now glance at a few of its consequences when applied to the reduction of duties which were imposed with an immediate view to revenue, selecting as illustrations an interesting department of domestic industry and the leading articles of tropical produce. The progress of the GLASS MANUFACTURE during the last sixty years, supplies us with many instructive lessons relating to the effect of excise duties and regulations in retarding the growth of trade, and diminishing the comforts of the people. In 1794 the previous rates of duty were increased by fifty per cent. What was the effect of this step? Examining the quantity retained for home consumption in each of the three years immediately preceding the change, we find that it amounted to an average of 373,782 cwt., while the average quantity similarly

retained during the three years immediately following
the change, was only 299,560 cwt., showing a diminution of one-fifth, and nine years elapsed before the
consumption of flint and plate glass reached the point
at which it stood in 1794.   In the year 1812 the rate
of duty was still further raised 100 per cent., and the
consumption at once fell from an average for the
three years preceding of 417,911 cwt., to an average
for the three following of 264,931 cwt., a decrease of
36 per cent.   It is scarcely necessary to say that the
effect of these changes on the revenue completely
disappointed the expectations of Government.   The
first enhancement of the duties by one-half, instead
of raising the net revenue in the same proportion,
produced an immediate increase of a very trifling
amount, and four years afterwards the produce was
actually less than they had yielded at the old rates.
In 1812, when the next and greater rise took place,
the amount of the revenue raised on glass, which, in
the previous year, had been £360,989, ought to have
been nearly doubled, or £729,372 in 1813, instead
of which it amounted only to £509,623; and four
years after, so much had consumption fallen below
its former amount, that it was no more than £325,963,
a sum considerably less than that which had been
raised in 1811.   Thus the public had been burdened,
in the one case by an addition of one-half to the
existing amount of taxation, and in the other by
doubling it, without the slightest compensatory benefit
accruing to any party, or any other result save that of
an exchequer still more impoverished than before,
and a vast amount of inconvenience and privation to
the nation at large.   It is true that, in both cases,

after the lapse of some years, the revenue equalled, and at length surpassed, its former amount, but this is due exclusively to the efforts of our manufacturers, who were obliged to tax their ingenuity in inventing more economical processes. How infinitely better would it have been if, by reducing duties, the manufacturers had been plied with the same motive from an opposite quarter? Increased consumption would have awakened a rivalry of skill, the effect of which would have been to extend the conveniences of life to a much greater number of individuals, and the exchequer would have recruited itself by the comforts, instead of the privations, of the people.

This is the precise effect which was produced by a partial appplication of Free Trade principles in 1819 and 1835. At the former date the duty on plate glass was reduced from ninety-eight shillings per cwt. to sixty shillings per cwt. What was the consequence of this reduction to the revenue? The quantity of plate glass manufactured during the three years immediately preceding 1819, amounted to an annual average of 4,905 cwt., the duty on which was £24,035 ; on the other hand the quantity manufactured during the three years which followed the reduction of the duty reached an annual average of 9,415 cwt., and the duty amounted to £28,244. Since that period the manufacture of plate glass has steadily increased, so that, during the five years previous to 1844, the quantity annually retained for consumption was 24,000 cwt., and the sum annually paid on its behalf into the exchequer upwards of £75,000. In 1835 a reduction to the extent of two-thirds was made in the rate of excise duty on flint glass, the effect of which was an immediate increase of revenue; the net annual amount having been, on an average of the five years immediately preceding 1835, £587,252, while the annual average for the five years immediately following the alteration was £685,367. But though the quantity of all kinds of glass retained for home consumption increased very considerably during the nine years following the reduction of the duty in 1835, yet so mischievous had been the effects of legislation, that from 1789 to 1844, an interval of fifty-six years, the consumption of most kinds of British glass had diminished rather than increased, though the population had increased during the interval by more than eighty per cent.; and the reason of this is seen in the fact that more than five times the amount of duty was raised on glass in 1834 than in 1789, though the quantity consumed was positively less at the first mentioned period than at the latter.

In the case of most of the articles which are subject to excise duties, the injury sustained by the manufacturer does not arise simply from the pecuniary amount of the impost, but from the vexatious character of the regulations which are deemed necessary in order to secure the Government from fraud. No interest has suffered more from this cause than the manufacture of glass. Common green bottle glass composed a few years since one-half of the entire glass manufacture of the United Kingdom. This being an inferior kind of glass, it was charged with a lower duty, and a lower sum was consequently charged as a drawback upon exportation. The use of cheaper materials, and the adoption of more scientific methods, enabled our manufacturers greatly to improve the quality of this article, and so to obtain an increased command over the foreign market. But, by such an exercise of skill, it was possible for bottle glass to be so improved in point of quality as to be mistaken for flint glass, and thus, on being exported, to obtain a larger drawback which was due upon those superior kinds which paid a heavier duty. Here, then, the excise officer interposed. Such improvements could not be allowed; the manufacture must remain stationary; the swaddling bands of government were adapted to a state of pupilage, and further it must not be permitted to advance. Such regulations were tantamount to a prohibition of the foreign part of the trade. Manufacturers abroad, prevented by no such obstacles from applying the discoveries of science to their profession, not only competed successfully with our produce in their own markets, but were enabled to underbid us at home. Hence the reduction of the excise duty gave our manufacturers only partial relief, and the era of Free Trade in glass can date worthily only from their entire abolition in 1845.

VII. We proceed now to consider the fiscal effect of low duties on the chief articles of tropical produce. These articles are necessaries of life chiefly in consequence of habit, and their consumption depends, to a great extent, upon the degree of ease with which the bulk of the people can furnish themselves with those kinds of food which are absolutely requisite to subsistence. In any given circumstances, however, the amount of consumption is largely regulated by the price of the article. This is the case, not only because the cheaper it is the greater the quantity which can be obtained in exchange for the same sum of money, or because the use of it strengthens habit, which is sure to seek indulgence except it is impeded by an insuperably high price; but because sugar, tea, and coffee are adapted to become regular elements of diet, they seem like the natural coadjutors of corn and animal food in the work of sustaining life. They are not absolute necessaries, but they are such luxuries as few persons would willingly dispense with. Even when introduced into every house as a part of daily diet, the limit of consumption in these articles is not soon reached. The difference, simple as it seems, between the watery infusion which sometimes passes under the name of *tea*, and the strength and flavour which would satisfy the taste of a connoisseur is equal to the fourfold increase or diminution of our entire imports of that article. The same may be said of coffee and sugar; and hence their consumption depends, within certain limits, entirely on the price, and the lower the rate of taxation with which its consumption is chargeable, the greater will be its productiveness to the revenue.

During the period to which we confine this first section of our inquiries, sugar presents us with comparatively few opportunities for illustrating these remarks by an appeal to facts. The quantity imported has always, until lately, sustained a pretty uniform proportion to the wants of the people; hence the price did not undergo any excessive fluctuations, and the duty, though altered several times, never rose higher than an addition of one-third to its minimum amount. It is remarkable, however, that, with one exception, which may be readily explained, every change occurring from year to year in the price of sugar has been attended by a corresponding change in the quantity consumed. Still, with sugar as with glass, the effects of Free Trade have been fully displayed only since the unreserved application of its principles subsequent to 1844. With tea, but especially with coffee, the case is different. These have been exposed to great variations in the rates of duty, and afford us the best means of estimating the effect of low duties on the enjoyments of the people and the prosperity of the exchequer.

In the year 1784, the duty on tea amounted to sixty-seven per cent. on its value, and the quantity then consumed was less than 5,000,000 lbs. The following year, this rate of duty was lowered to twelve and a-half per cent., and the consumption rose during the next three years to ten, twelve, and seventeen millions of pounds respectively. A still earlier experiment exhibits a similar result. In 1746, the duty was reduced by about two shillings per pound, and the very next year the quantity consumed increased threefold. In 1768, the duty on black tea was reduced by one shilling per pound, and the consumption forthwith rose as much as eighty per cent., and on this part of the duty being reimposed, a few years afterwards, consumption at once sank to its former limit. Since the opening of the China trade, in 1833, a considerable reduction has been made in the import price of tea, the effect of which has been a very great extension of its use. Two years before the trade became free, the quantity consumed was less than thirty millions of pounds, but in 1844, only eleven years afterwards, it amounted to more than forty-one millions, an increase of thirty-seven per cent.

In 1801, the rate of duty on British plantation ˙coffee was one shilling and sixpence per pound.   The effect of this was to confine the use of that article to the wealthier classes ; the average consumption per head was little more than one ounce a year on the whole population, and the sum contributed to the revenue in like manner by each individual was just five farthings. In 1811, the rate of duty was only sevenpence per pound, and consumption had increased in consequence as much as 750 per cent., being more than eight ounces per head, while the revenue had increased threefold.   In 1825, the duty was again reduced by one-half, and in six years, notwithstanding the immense increase just noticed, there occurred a further increase in the quantity consumed equal to more than fourteen millions of pounds, or nearly 200 per cent., averaging one pound four ounces per head, while the sum contributed to the revenue was one-third greater than that produced by the higher rates of duty in 1821, and exactly double its amount in 1811.   Thus far the reduction of duty had been confined to coffee, the growth of British plantations, but the increased consumption soon exhausted the supplies which could be obtained from that source, and raised the market price sufficiently high to allow of the introduction of coffee from the British possessions in India, although subject to the payment of heavy differential duties. This enhancement of the price rendered the consumption stationary for several years, but in 1835 the partial monopoly hitherto granted to the West Indian planters having proved insufficient to protect them, it was given up, and East Indian coffee allowed to be imported on the same terms.   Accordingly, the rate of consumption again started, and gained six millions of pounds in the next six years. Even the concession of Free Trade in East Indian coffee was soon found insufficient to meet the increased demand, and the rise of prices which ensued enabled the merchant to bring foreign coffee into the market, though subject to the payment of a discriminating duty of twenty-eight shillings per cwt., and burdened with the additional expense of sending it first to the Cape of Good Hope, in order to escape the prohibitory duty imposed on coffee of foreign growth. The loss sustained by the revenue and the country through these successive checks, this paying of justice by instalments, must have been very great. Mr. Porter estimates that if the change which was made in 1835, instead of merely reducing the duty on East Indian produce, had permitted the importation of all kinds of coffee on equal terms, the public would have had the means of spending additionally in its purchase the sum of £533,227; this sum would have bought nearly twelve millions of pounds, and thus have added forty per cent. to the consumption, and nearly £100,000 to the revenue.

VIII. Let us now briefly review the facts to which we have directed the attention of the reader, and consider their combined result with respect to the expediency or inexpediency of Free Trade. We have carefully examined a considerable number of instances in which the principles of commercial and industrial freedom have been applied; but the application was made with a timid hand; with many inconsistent enactments still in force tending to neutralize their effects; and the result is that, *in every case, the experiment succeeded.* The breaking up of monopolies was invariably followed by a great extension of commerce. Protective duties were in no case thoroughly abandoned, but the interests previously protected started at once on a new and more vigorous career; duties were never reduced but consumption immediately increased, and the exchequer became richer. Such were the uniform results of Free Trade principles in whatever department they were applied; in the most important as well as the least considerable branches of industry. The sickliest branches of national enterprise became strong as soon as exposed to its freshening gales, and were soon laden with luxuriant fruits. The combined effect of these successive relaxations of our restrictive system is strikingly seen in the aggregate amount of our exports at different periods. We will not speak of an earlier date than 1819, since, previous to that era, it may be supposed that the state of the currency gave a false magnitude to the estimated value of our exports; but, taking that year as one point of comparison, and 1826 as another, we find scarcely a single quarter of the world to which the amount of our exports had not fallen. The extent of this decline will be best appreciated by figures. In 1819 our exports were valued as follows :—to European states, in round numbers, £16,000,000; to Africa, £316,294; to the United States of America, £4,929,845 ; to British North America and the West Indies, £6,861,314 ; to foreign settlements in the West Indies, £892,306; while the total amount was £34,881,727. Let us now look at the year 1826. At this date the declared value of our exports to the same parts of the world was as follows :—To Europe, £13,000,000 ; to Africa, £295,768; to the United States of America, £4,659,018; to our colonies in North America and the West Indies, £4,601,072; to the foreign settlements in the West Indies, £570,409; making a total of £31,536,724. This was the result of the trial of unmixed protection during the earliest period, for many years, at which the trial could be fairly made. The only parts of the world with which our commerce experienced any increase during this epoch were Asia, to which Free Trade had been partially conceded in 1815, and the southern states of America, just recovering from the effects of the revolutions which had torn them from their European rulers. Carrying our eye forward to 1844, over a period during which the various modifications of our restrictive system to which we have directed the attention of the reader were gradually working out their results, we find the progress of our commerce indicated at that date as follows :—To Northern Europe our exports had nearly doubled ; to Southern Europe they had experienced an advance of almost 90 per cent; our exports to Africa had increased fivefold ; to Asia, 150 per cent. ; to the United States, 80 per cent. ; to British America and the West Indies, 25 per cent. ; to the foreign West Indies more than 100 per cent. ; to South America more than 75 per cent. ; and the total amount to £58,484,292, being an advance of no less than 86 per cent. upon the value of our exports in 1826. What can explain this change ? Why have we in the one case a decrease of three millions, and in the other an increase of twenty-seven millions ? No great discoveries had been made during the interval; no

K

considerable markets had been supplied then for the first time; the amelioration took place in those very branches of traffic which had previously shown the greatest tendency to decay. To what, therefore, can it be ascribed that the downward movement indicated prior to 1826 did not go on, and end in the ruin of our trade? We are shut up to one conclusion; the problem is clearly solved by the facts which have been brought before us. The partial change of policy in 1825; the commencement of a more rational system in managing our commercial interests; the removal of prohibitions which had hitherto prevented us from coming into healthful rivalry with other lands; and the repeal of those imposts which had hitherto rested as an incubus on the industrial energies of the people; this is the true cause of that steady rise in the value of our foreign trade which was afterwards observable. But however plentiful the harvest which we have reaped in consequence of this happy change in legislation, we should have seen far greater results if the same principles had been more fearlessly applied. As it is, in reviewing this period, our attention is arrested as powerfully by the obstructive influence of protection in those departments where it was still maintained, as by the creative energies of Free Trade, and we can only imagine the unexampled blessings which would have accrued to the nation from an anticipation by twenty years of the measures of 1846.

The effects of the Free Trade relaxations of this period were not wholly fiscal. The increase of our foreign commerce is always a fact which teems with the most cheering inferences relative to the condition of the people. When viewed as the exponents of social progress, figures lose their dryness; they become more poetic than the most inspired effusions of genius; they bring before us scenes of cheerful industry and plenty, a glorious panorama of well-being—the crowded factory, sending its wild notes of spindle and shuttle across the moor; thousands of cottages, with their crowds of healthy occupants; thriving towns, throwing out their arms on every side, and covering the land with human dwellings; they tell us of contentment, patriotism, education, morality, religion. In our crowded ports we see another of the many signs of the strong vitality which is stirring in the nation's breast; the ships unlading there seem freighted with abundance to our teeming millions. True, the state of our operative population affords but slight ground for boasting; although, with the self-complacency peculiar to Englishmen when thinking of their country, we sometimes speak of the social condition of other nations as if our own were faultless, yet it must be allowed that evils have been allowed to accumulate in our midst which it will take a long succession of prosperous years, together with all the efforts of enlightened philanthropy, to remove. The condition of our population, whether we regard it in a moral, intellectual, or religious point of view, is not yet what it should be, not to speak of what it was a very few years ago. But when we call to mind the state of the population during the ten years which followed the conclusion of the war; when we remember the privations which were then endured, the discontent which pervaded the working classes, and the terrible excesses which then broke out both in the rural and manufacturing districts; the rick burning, the conspiracies, the depredatory habits and revolutionary recklessness which, like the living ashes of the crater, indicated the furious elements which warred within, we cannot but feel that a great improvement had taken place in the physical and moral condition of the people even prior to the era of complete Free Trade. Mr. Huskisson's reforms were more potent in allaying the agitations of 1819 than the suspension of the Habeas Corpus act or the vigour of government prosecutions. As soon as the people obtained work and, through that, the means of purchasing with tolerable ease the necessaries of life, they thought no more of blanketeering expeditions, or annual conferences at Peterloo. If our commerce had continued to decline, and the partial application of Free Trade principles been much longer delayed, insurrection and pauperism must have been our lot, and the state would probably have been wrecked on those dangerous shoals which encompassed the question of parliamentary reform. It was the timely enunciation of enlightened measures, based upon the principles of Free Trade, which not only afforded us temporary relief from perils then pressing, and enabled us to await with safety the time when Free Trade should be fully embodied in legislation, but afforded us an opportunity of ascertaining beforehand, by unanswerable experience, that an opposite policy is necessarily suicidal to the morality, the happiness, and the prosperity of nations.

CHAPTER II.

EFFECTS OF THE MORE COMPLETE RECOGNITION OF FREE
TRADE PRINCIPLES SINCE 1840.

WE proceed from the past to the present; having witnessed the justification of Free Trade principles which was afforded by their partial application prior to the abolition of the corn laws, we are the better prepared to appreciate the results which have subsequently flowed from their more complete recognition since 1842. It must, however, be borne in mind that the circumstances in which the experiment of complete Free Trade was tried, were not favourable to its immediate success. The advocate of commercial freedom, taking his stand on the facts we have adduced, might indeed look forward with confidence to the ultimate effects of the new system, but he nevertheless had reason to fear that the unfounded and ignorant forebodings of its adversaries would be able, in the meantime, to boast of an apparent realization. He had no reason to expect, at once, an unanswerable demonstration of the soundness of his principles. At the moment the corn laws were repealed, the country was not enjoying an average amount of prosperity; on the contrary, the measure was precipitated by adverse events, which exerted a depressing effect upon trade. A deficient corn-harvest and the entire failure of the potato crop, reduced a large portion of the population of these islands to a state of starvation, while the railway mania had locked up every penny of disengaged capital. Instead of rising forthwith under the influence of Free Trade, the nation had first to be supported through a crisis. If this had been satisfactorily accomplished, if the nation had only been raised to an average height of prosperity, every reasonable expectation of those who abetted the change in our commercial system would have been fulfilled, and all, therefore, which has been done in addition, the unprecedented advance which has been made in our commerce, our manufactures, and the general well-being of the people, proves so much the more completely the utility of Free Trade.

It is evident that whatever benefits may accrue to a state from the adoption of a Free Trade policy, they must be conferred primarily through the medium of its exchanges with foreign nations. Free Trade embodies a commercial principle ;—its first effects, therefore, will necessarily be produced on the condition of commerce. A code of prohibitory laws no doubt affects every branch of inland trade, since, in a manufacturing community like ours, the national industry is entirely dependent on the state of our intercourse with foreign markets. The draper, clothier, or cabinet-maker, has as strong an interest in Free Trade as the largest firms of Manchester and Liverpool. But the influence of protective laws in depressing these branches of labour, and increasing the privations of the workman, must first be experienced by our foreign trade; on its way to our market-towns and villages, it must light first on our docks, our warehouses, and our ships. Fewer merchantmen will whiten the sea between Liverpool and New York, fewer piles of goods will encumber our landing-places, and the custom-house will record in numbers of diminished value the transactions of our dealers with foreign states. If the influence of protective laws make itself felt through these channels, so also will the influence which springs from their repeal. It will impart prosperity to our manufactures, raise the wages of our operatives, give an impetus to the minor handicrafts, and elevate the condition of the people, chiefly by extending our commerce. It is emphatically a *sea breeze* which sets our mills in motion, and spreads vigour, industry, and contentment throughout the land. This *rationale* of the influence of Free Trade determines the order in which its various effects on our industry must be considered. We shall naturally examine first, the comparative state of our foreign trade, which will lead us to a review of our leading manufactures as the source whence we derive the materials of commerce. From our manufactures we shall pass to a few of the less important branches of industry, with the view of ascertaining the effects of Free Trade on the minuter ramifications of society. It will be proper then to glance at those interests which are said to have been specially injured by Free Trade, in order to determine how far such a complaint is well founded, and finally we shall consider how far the facts which shall have been adduced under the foregoing heads are confirmed or weakened by an appeal to a few obvious tests of social progress or retrogression.

SECTION I.

EFFECTS OF FREE TRADE ON THE COMMERCE OF THE UNITED KINGDOM.

I. The first point to which we propose to advert, is the influence of Free Trade legislation on our FOREIGN COMMERCE. The most direct way of ascertaining this is to examine the Returns which are annually published by the Board of Trade, and compare the amount of our exports and imports year by year. Adopting this method, we find the following as the declared value of the exports of British and Irish produce and manufactures in each year from 1842 to 1853:—

1842	£47,381,023		1848	£52,849,445
1843	52,279,709		1849	63,596,025
1844	58,584,292		1850	71,367,885
1845	60,111,082		1851	74,448,722
1846	57,786,876		1852	78,076,854
1847	58,842,377		1853	93,357,306*

This statement speaks for itself. The facts of which it is the succinct expression cannot be explained in any way without assuming the existence of an amount of prosperity altogether without parallel in the history of the country. Our exports in the year 1853 were no less than 97 per cent. greater than they were in 1842. In this latter year the Free Trade measures of Sir Robert Peel received the sanction of the legislature, and in 1843 the value of our

---

* The total for 1853 is estimated by adding £6,000,000 for unenumerated articles. It appears from more recent returns that the value of our exports, as above, for 1853, actually reached the enormous sum of £100,000,000.

exports rose as much as five millions sterling. During the following year the advance was still greater, more than six millions sterling being then added to the value of our exports, and in 1845 their aggregate value exceeded sixty millions. During the three following years, the nation suffered from the effects of the railway mania and the Irish famine, and the result was a diminution of our foreign trade; yet the average value of our-exports during those three years exceeded by more than three millions sterling the highest point they had ever reached prior to 1842. In 1846 the corn laws were repealed, and in the course of the two following years a great reduction was effected in the tariff. On the subsidence of the famine and the railway panic, the effects of these measures were soon apparent. In 1849 our exports showed an increase of value over the previous year of more than ten millions, a rate which was almost equalled in 1850, while, notwithstanding such rapid progress, the exports of 1851 exhibited a further advance of more than three millions. This was sustained in 1852, but in 1853 the most sanguine expectations were outdone, the declared value of the principal articles for that year having been no less than £87,357,306, an increase of more than nine millions, or allowing 6,000,000 for unenumerated articles, the total value for the year was £93,357,306.

It will enable us the better to estimate the value of this rate of progress as a proof of the expediency of Free Trade, if we compare in this respect the last ten years for which we have complete returns, with a similar period under the protective *régime*. There are peculiar reasons why we should choose as our stand-point for this purpose the year 1832. That year falls about midway between the consolidation of our protective system at the close of the war, and the present era of Free Trade, and the value of our exports for that year sustains a suggestive relation to their present value. On referring to Mr. Porter's tables we find that, in 1832, the declared value of British and Irish produce and manufactures exported from the United Kingdom was £36,450,594, a sum less by three quarters of a million than the half of the value of the same kind of exports in 1851; our foreign trade having thus increased more than 100 per cent. in twenty years, during a considerable part of which period the maxims of commercial freedom have been recognised by the legislature. Let us now take up our position at an equal distance on the protective side of 1832. This conducts us to the year 1812; what then was the value of our foreign trade in that year, as shown by official returns? During the greater part of this period our merchants and manufacturers enjoyed the full advantages accruing from a protective policy, and we have therefore a right to expect that 1832 will be found to have been at least as superior to 1812, in the extent of our foreign trade, as 1851 was to the former year. If this ratio holds good, then the value of our exports in 1812 must have been something more than eighteen millions sterling. Instead of this, however, the value of our exports in 1812 exceeded forty-one millions, being more than 127 per cent. above its proper amount, and 14 per cent. above the amount of 1832. We have observed the progress of our commerce from 1842 to 1852; it will be instructive to compare its progress from 1812 to 1822, being a period of equal length, and situated at the same distance from the point of survey :—

Declared value of British and Irish Produce and Manufactures Exported in each year from 1812 to 1822 inclusive.

1812	...... £41,716,964		1818	...... £46,603,249
*1814	 45,494,219		1819	 35,208,321
1815	 51,603,028		1820	 36,424,652
1816	 41,657,873		1821	 36,659,630
1817	 41,761,132		1822	 36,968,964

On examining the above statement, it will be found that the annual average of our exports during the first five years of the series was £44,446,643, while the annual average of the same during the next five years was only £38,372,963, exhibiting an aggregate decline of six millions, or more than 13 per cent. If we were to continue our examination through the next series of ten years, till we reached 1832, we should find the annual average still lower. The case therefore stands thus:—Dividing the period of Protection into so many annular series, the average yearly value of our exports is highest under the first; from that starting point it becomes continually less; and dividing the period of Free Trade into an equal number of series, the average value of our exports is least under the first; from that starting point it becomes continually greater. Results thus uniform can have their origin in no accidental conjuncture of circumstances; they point to the operation of a fixed law. Free Trade invigorates and expands our commerce, as truly as Protection weakens and contracts it.

Such have been our exports in the aggregate, let us now look at the articles of which they chiefly consist,

* Records of 1813 destroyed by a fire at the custom-house.

The following figures will exhibit the declared value of the principal articles of British and Irish produce and manufactures for 1840, and each of the last seven years :—

ARTICLES.	1840.	1847.	1848.	1849.
Apparel, Haberdashery, and Millinery	1,208,687	1,824,529	1,512,271	1,905,006
Brass and Copper Manufactures	1,450,464	1,541,868	1,257,944	1,875,865
Coals, Coke, and Culm ..	576,519	968,502	1,088,221	1,087,122
Cotton Manufactures....	17,567,310	17,375,245	16,753,369	20,071,046
Cotton Yarn	7,101,308	5,957,980	5,927,831	6,704,089
Earthenware	573,184	834,357	722,012	807,395
Hardwares and Cutlery..	1,340,137	2,341,981	1,860,150	2,201,315
Leather & Leather wares	417,074	465,527	372,256	501,298
Linen Manufactures	3,306,088	2,958,851	2,802,789	3,493,829
Linen Yarn	822,876	649,893	493,449	732,065
Machinery	593,064	1,263,016	817,656	700,631
Iron and Steel	2,524,859	5,265,779	437,966	4,986,508
Silk, Thrown, Twist, and Silk Manufactures ..	792,648	985,026	588,117	908,334
Tin Plates, Tin and Pewter ware	360,816	485,073	553,175	727,825
Woollen Manufactures ..	5,327,853	6,896,038	5,733,828	7,342,723
Woollen Yarn	452,957	1,001,364	776,975	1,090,223

ARTICLES.	1850.	1851.	1852.	1853.
Apparel, Haberdashery, and Millinery	2,379,800	2,725,318	3,320,857	6,923,190
Brass and Copper Manufactures	1,978,196	1,639,156	1,704,083	1,851,689
Coals, Coke, and Culm ..	1,284,224	1,302,473	1,372,114	1,607,743
Cotton Manufactures....	21,873,697	23,454,810	23,223,432	25,813,931
Cotton Yarn	6,383,704	6,634,026	6,654,655	6,895,454
Earthenware	999,448	1,121,104	1,151,897	1,337,265
Hardwares and Cutlery..	2,641,432	2,827,011	2,691,697	3,663,856
Leather & Leather wares	608,865	598,159	844,759	1,579,309
Linen Manufactures	3,947,682	4,107,396	4,231,786	4,761,252
Linen Yarn	881,312	951,426	1,140,565	1,149,103
Machinery	1,042,167	1,168,611	1,251,360	1,976,502
Iron and Steel	5,350,056	5,830,370	6,684,276	10,848,080
Silk, Thrown, Twist, and Silk Manufactures ..	1,255,641	1,326,778	1,551,866	2,044,912
Tin Plates, Tin and Pewter ware	944,940	1,041,204	1,088,725	1,213,630
Woollen Manufactures ..	8,588,690	8,377,183	8,730,934	10,171,263
Woollen Yarn	1,451,642	1,484,544	1,430,140	1,454,457

A glance at these figures assures us of two facts; first our commercial prosperity, as indicated by the sum total of our annual exports, is general, not partial; it has not been produced by the undue develop- ment of any one branch, but has been felt pretty equally through all our industrial ramifications. Secondly, our commercial prosperity is not more un- precedented in its extent, than it has been natural and gradual in its growth. Ever since the commence- ment of Sir Robert Peel's policy in 1842, a change for the better has been apparent. The advance has not been without interruption, fluctuations have occurred, but as these fluctuations are capable of being satis- factorily explained, they furnish valuable proof of the healthiness of the movement, and afford a guarantee of its continuance. Step by step with the application of Free Trade principles, our commercial and manu- facturing interests have risen from their previous depression; gradually one interest after another has shared in the beneficent change, till at length the entire system of industry seems to be animated with preternatural life. Yet, in the midst of boundless activity, there is comparatively little speculation; the increase of trade has arisen from a new development of the wants and resources of the people, and not from any artificial stimulus administered to those which were previously in existence. In the quickened energy of our commercial and manufacturing opera- tions, we have experienced effects like those which usually spring from the highest degree of febrile excitement, yet without anything like that forced and unnatural tension of the faculties which is the sign of speedy exhaustion. There is nothing whatever to indicate that our prosperity is transient; it has within it the seeds of growth, and seems destined to indefinite expansion.

II. Let us now turn to the other side of our foreign trade; that which consists of imports. The articles imported into the United Kingdom are divisible into two great classes; articles of subsistence, and articles of manufacture. This division is not quite exhaustive, but the exceptions are of minor value, and the wide extent to which it holds good is very suggestive. It would not be difficult for the historian of future times to deduce from the single fact, that nearly the whole of our vast imports consists either of food or raw materials for the operative, the peculiar position of the population of these lands. When ninety-three millions' worth of exported articles is returned to us in raw materials for labour and the staple commodities of food, what more is requisite to tell us of multitudes dependent for their daily bread on their daily toil, and to whom successful competition in the markets of the world can furnish the only means of preserving themselves and their families from actual want; or what can more vividly pourtray the madness of doubly taxing the means of living, at once in labour and in food? A nation of manufacturers can only subsist as they sell their produce, and they can sell their produce only as they sell it cheap. But the ability to sell their produce cheaply implies a cheap command of the raw material, and of the workman's food; to tax these is to decree the nation's ruin, and involve all classes alike in bankruptcy and pauperism.

In attempting to ascertain the amount of our imports, it is useless to have recourse to their official values as furnished in the Returns of the Board of Trade. The scale of prices according to which those values are determined was fixed in 1694, and since then many circumstances have occurred to affect its accuracy. The difference between the real and official value of our exports is still greater, on account of the economy which has been introduced into most of our manufacturing processes during the last century, but in this branch of our foreign trade, the difficulty is met by a regulation which compels the merchant to state, at the time of shipment, the value of the articles he sends abroad. Hence the best general guide to the magnitude of our foreign trade is furnished by the declared value of our exports, since it is certain that, on an average, all the goods we send abroad will bring back an equivalent, together with the merchant's profit. If circumstances prevent a shopkeeper from knowing the exact amount of his cash receipts for the week, he turns to his list of sales, and by finding their aggregate amount, and adding his usual profits, he ascertains very nearly the amount of money or other articles of exchangeable value he has received. In the same way we may form a tolerably correct estimate of the extent of our foreign trade, by casting up the value of those articles which we have sent abroad, and inferring thence the value of those which have been received in exchange. This has already been done, but it will give us a more vivid impression of our commercial progress, and of the benefits which Free Trade has conferred on all classes of the community, if we glance at the *quantities* of the chief articles of foreign and colonial produce which have been received in exchange for our manufactures since 1840.

The most interesting division of our imports at the present juncture, comprises those articles which are used as food, and among these the first place is due to corn. The importance of this article is proved by the prominent place it occupied in the struggle which broke the fetters of monopoly. The corn laws were the Thermopylæ of Protection, and the strenuousness with which they were assailed by the nation, proves the solemn importance which attaches to the people's bread. The following statement shows the quantities of grain of all kinds imported into the United Kingdom from 1840 to 1853 inclusive:—

Years.	Wheat and Wheat Flour. Imp. Qrs	Other kinds of Grain and Meal. Imp. Qrs.	Total of Grain and Meal. Imp. Qrs.	Years.	Wheat and Wheat Flour. Imp. Qrs.	Other kinds of Grain and Meal. Imp. Qrs	Total of Grain and Meal Imp. Qrs.
1840	2,432,766	1,487,248	3,920,014	1847	4,464,757	7,448,107*	11,912,864
1841	2,770,647	856,915	3,627,562	1848	3,082,230	4,446,242	7,528,472
1842	3,040,269	657,010	3,697,279	1849	4,802,475	5,867,186	10,669,661
1843	1,064,942	368,949	1,433,891	1850	4,830,263	4,189,327	9,019,590
1844	1,379,262	1,651,419	3,030,681	1851	5,330,412	4,287,614	9,618,026
1845	1,141,957	1,287,959	2,429,916	1852	4,164,603	3,582,066	7,746,669
1846	2,344,142	2,408,032	4,752,174	1853	6,235,860	3,937,275	10,173,135

This is not the place to advert to the social effects of Free Trade, and though we would not for a moment entirely sacrifice to logic the social suggestiveness of the above figures, yet it is under a purely commercial aspect that we wish now to regard them. Let us look at our imports with respect to another important

* Under the head of "other kinds of grain and meal," is included an immense quantity of maize or Indian corn, introduced as a substitute for wheat during the Irish famine.

article of food. Previous to 1842, the British farmer was protected in the rearing and feeding of cattle, by a prohibition directed against their importation from abroad. In that year Sir Robert Peel changed the prohibition into protective duties, varying from one pound sterling to five shillings per head, and in 1846 their importation was permitted duty free. Since that time a considerable traffic ˙has sprung up with the neighbouring parts of the continent, the extent of which will be shown by the following figures:—

	1843.	1844.	1845.	1846.	1847.	1848.	1849.	1850.	1851.	1852.
Oxen & Bulls .	3,156	1,114	3,682	9,743	17,191	27,381	24,390	21,884	28,951	37,624
Cows....	1,038	368	1,154	6,503	25,349	35,480	22,506	17,920	17,757	24,026
Calves ..	70	39	53	587	2,503	12,406	15,642	13,645	19,754	24,870
Sheep & Lambs	644	217	2,817	15,957	94,624	142,720	130,583	129,266	143,498	201,859
Swine & Hogs	410	361	265	1,590	3,856	1,242	2,119	2,653	7,287	15,868

The productions of our colonies enter very largely into the subsistence of the people, and are scarcely inferior in importance to corn itself. In a mercantile view they are of even greater moment, on account of the vast amount of capital they put in motion, and the extensive market they furnish for the sale of our domestic produce. The following statement will show the great increase which has taken place in this part of our commerce, including a few articles of minor interest which have been affected by the fiscal changes of 1842 and 1846:—

ARTICLES.		1842.	1850.	1851.	1852.	1853.
Butter,	cwt.	175,197	330,579	353,718	285,497	404,194
Cheese,	,,	179,748	347,803	338,659	298,458	398,982
Cocoa,	lbs.	3,172,255	4,478,252	6,773,960	6,269,434	8,283,910
Coffee,	,,	41,444,414	50,803,152	53,110,660	54,935,510	55,454,884
Eggs,	No.	89,548,747	105,689,060	115,526,245	108,281,233	123,618,020
Pepper,	lbs.	6,021,290	8,082,310	3,996,295	6,631,700	5,496,886
Potatoes,	cwt.	11,202	1,348,883	636,771	773,619	1,133,609
Rice,	,,	511,414	785,451	744,847	987,813	1,505,118
Sugar,	,,	4,756,011	6,291,535	7,932,534	6,896,761	7,284,382
Tea,	,,	40,742,128	50,512,384	71,466,421	66,360,535	70,735,552

The other great class of imports to which we have alluded consists of those which supply our manufacturers with raw materials. It is impossible to overrate the importance of this branch of our foreign trade. If our population depend for cheap food upon the importation of foreign corn, they depend upon their labour for the means of purchasing it. Without work, and consequently without wages, of what use would well-stored granaries be to them? But the quantity of labour for which there exists a remunerative demand, is evidenced by the quantity of raw material imported, since it is by labour alone that this can acquire any value. Hence, if we find that an additional million pounds' weight of cotton has entered our warehouses, and that a similar increase has occurred in every other branch of our rude imports, we have an indubitable proof that the demand for labour is on the increase. But apart from the fact that the quantity of raw material consumed is a sure sign of the quantity of labour which has been employed, the importation of the raw material is a matter of the first moment, since it is only as we are able to import it in abundance, and at a moderate price, that we can extend our market for the finished produce. If the price of cotton, hemp, or hides, were to attain three times its present amount, our sales of the manufactured article would be diminished in almost an equal proportion. In reference to the element of material, as well as labour, it may be said that cheapness commands the world. Probably millions are now purchasing the manufactures of this country who would be completely disabled from becoming our customers by a general rise of fifty per cent. It is gratifying therefore to find that this department of our commerce has kept pace with the rest: that the demand for the raw material of our various manufactures has been large, and that the supply has been commensurate with it:—

		1842.	1850.	1851.	1852.	1853.
Cotton, raw,	lbs.	531,750,086	663,576,861	757,379,749	929,782,448	895,266,780
Flax, dressed & undressed	cwts.	1,145,759	1,822,918	1,194,184	1,408,714	1,883,374
Hemp, undresd.	„	585,905	1,048,635	1,293,412	1,068,155	1,237,872
Hides, tanned & untanned	„	613,800	608,850	692,078	569,034	815,368
Silk, raw	lbs.	3,951,773	4,942,407	4,608,336	5,832,551	6,480,724
„ thrown	„	397,407	469,527	412,636	426,463	828,493
Wool—Sheep, Lamb, & Alpaca	„	45,881,639	74,320,778	83,311,075	93,761,458	119,396,445
Timber,	lds.	*	794,178	1,009,708	1,118,350	1,344,020

III. In our view of British commerce we have so far confined our attention to the United Kingdom, as the proximate seat of exchange; it will be interesting to glance at some of the countries with which this

* The imports of timber cannot be specified by the *Load* previously to 1843; the total number of loads for that year is 609,693.

increased intercourse has been carried on. The first
remark which strikes us on thus extending our survey,
is the general evenness with which the increase has
been distributed. The sudden growth of our commerce has not been owing to a vast increase of business with any particular nation, but to a considerable
addition with nearly all. Some states have been
placed, by the special bearings of our Free Trade
policy, on an entirely new footing, and in these instances our commercial transactions have multiplied
at an unusually rapid rate. Of these we may particularise the ports of the Baltic, which have been chiefly
affected by the repeal of our timber duties; those of
the Black Sea, which have shared largely in the new
demand for wheat, as well as Brazil and Cuba, which
reaped the chief advantages resulting to foreign interests from our equalisation of the sugar duties;
but there is scarcely a name on the list of exports
which does not show some increase. These facts
convey to us the pleasing impression that our commercial prosperity springs from causes which we have
ourselves created. It is not to the legislation of
foreign states in our favour, nor to special concessions
gained by diplomatic agency, that we must ascribe
it, but to our own enlightened policy, and the energy
which it has evoked on the part of the entire nation.
This is the true basis of trade; on this foundation
we may assure ourselves of permanent success. No
temporary gleam of sunlight will our present prosperity prove to be, but the gradual breaking of a
summer's day, whose close, after the lapse of ages, will
be without clouds, the peaceful inauguration of one
still brighter.

The example of Great Britain in breaking down its tariff, and staking its commercial existence on the intrinsic excellence of its productions, has not been without a salutary influence on the conduct of those states with which our foreign trade is chiefly carried on. We cannot yet congratulate ourselves upon the adoption by them of a policy entirely conformed to our own, but we may rejoice in the existence of no feeble indications that, with all countries professing to be civilised, Free Trade principles will soon form a part of international law. Since the year 1846 a great change has taken place in the tariffs of the chief commercial nations, and, in the majority of instances, in the right direction. The chief exceptions to the latter part of this statement are the Zollverein, Belgium, and Portugal ; in Switzerland also a slight change of a retrogressive character has occurred. In 1846 the duties levied by the Swiss tariff were only nominal in effect, and the new duties are extremely slight when compared with those levied in other countries. The duties levied by the Zollverein, which represents most of the German States, have unhappily been increased since 1846. The increase is, on cotton yarn as much as 50 per cent., on linen yarn 200 per cent., some species of linen manufacture 100 per cent., and thread lace $9\frac{1}{4}$ per cent. ; coffee being the only article on which a reduction, amounting to $54\frac{1}{2}$ per cent., has taken place. In Belgium unbleached linen has to contend against duties $166\frac{1}{2}$ per cent. higher, while the increase on woollen yarn is 122 per cent., and on woollen coatings and deffels, and other similar thick stuffs, 164 per cent. A reduction however has taken place in all sorts of plain silk stuffs of

50 per cent., in copper of 95 per cent., while raw tin, raw lead and earthenware are now admitted free. In Portugal a small increase has taken place in the duties levied on cotton yarn and manufactures, woollen yarn, carpets, and merinos, while a considerable reduction has been effected in those falling upon metals, hardwares, and cutlery.

The above cases are the most unfavourable of the fifteen principal countries in which any alteration of the tariff has taken place. In the remaining eleven the changes have been altogether in harmony with the principles on which we have acted ourselves. Russia has conceded very considerable reductions, for the most part from 30 to 80 per cent., on the chief articles belonging to the cotton, linen, woollen and silk manufactures, as well as on all kind of metal, cutlery, *fire-arms*, glass, earthenware, leather manufactures, porter and spirits. Sweden has lowered the rate of duty upon nine articles, including cocoa, iron anchors, cast steel, ships and ships' stores, raising them however upon all kind of woollen manufactures, except flannel. In Norway a reduction of from 21 to 50 per cent, has been made upon several descriptions of the cotton, linen, and woollen manufactures, bar iron and coals, while no heavier duties are levied upon machinery than upon the raw material of which it is made. In Denmark a general reduction of duties has taken place upon all the products of the loom, as well as hardwares, cutlery, and coals. The changes which have been made in the Dutch tariff are, without exception, in favour of unrestricted commerce, though the range of articles is rather limited. The duty on iron, whether raw or in the simpler stages of manufacture, has been reduced by 50 per cent., that on anchors, cables, machinery, &c., 83¼ per cent., on copper 75 per cent., in rope work, in which a considerable and lucrative trade is now carried on, 66¾ per cent., and on sugar 80 per cent., while coals and salt are admitted free. The most important alterations which have been made in the French tariff relate to iron and coals. Coal, when imported by sea through any port from Dunkirk to Sables d'Olonne, in the department of La Vendée, formerly paid a duty of 4s. 7d. a ton; this has been reduced to 2s. 9d. When imported between Sables d'Olonne and Bayonne the old duty was 2s. 9d. a ton, and 1s. 4½d. when imported by any of the Mediterranean ports; these duties have been consolidated at the lower amount. Coke formerly paid twice the duty on coal, now only half the rate of the reduced duty. The alterations in the duties affecting iron will be best understood by the following table:—

	Former Duties per Ton.			Duties per Ton till Jan, 1855.			After Jan. 1st, 1850.		
	£.	s.	d.	£.	s.	d.	£.	s.	d.
Pig Iron	2	16	8	2	4	0	1	15	4
Iron in bars according to { from	6	12	0	{ 5	5	10	{ 4	8	0
dimensions .... { to	8	4	10	{ 7	0	10	{ 6	3	4
Iron Plate..................	17	12	0	11	0	0	8	16	0
Steel in bars, cast	26	8	0	} 17	12	0	13	4	0
„ „ wrought	52	16	0						

The Spanish tariff has raised its duties since 1846 on seven descriptions of articles, the chief of which are raw iron, silk manufactures of all kinds, and coffee. On the other hand, previously existing rates have been considerably reduced on fourteen classes of goods, including several kinds of woollen fabrics, on which the reduction is as much as 80 per cent, copper, glass and glass-ware, cutlery, and figured thread-lace; while cotton manufactures, cotton yarns, harness, and raw wool, which were formerly prohibited, are now admitted at varying rates of duty. In the Sardinian tariff, alterations have been made since 1846 on no less than forty-four articles, and in every instance in the right direction, the average reduction being as much as 50 per cent. Austria has reduced its duties on twenty-three important articles from 50 to 90 per cent. All changes in the Turkish tariff, affecting chiefly cotton, wool, and iron manufactures, have been in favour of Free Trade. Mexico, the only other country whose tariff has undergone a change since 1846, has raised its previous duties on two articles, and reduced them on twenty-two, the general rate of reduction being 60 per cent.

While we rejoice in the changes we have just described, it is important to see clearly that our own policy is altogether independent of them. We cannot but do ourselves good by Free Trade, whether other nations reciprocate our friendly overtures, or choose still to stand aloof. To illustrate this point, we will refer to the state of our commerce with those two nations with which we are most closely connected; the one by proximity, the other by a common origin and language. France and the United States of America still remain under a protective *régime*. No change has taken place in the tariff of the latter country since 1846, and the favourable alterations in the French tariff, affecting only two articles, date as recently as November, 1853, and have as yet but slightly affected our commerce. The following table will show the annual value of our exports and imports to and from France, from 1842 to 1851 inclusive, the latest period to which the last return extends :—

YEARS.	EXPORTS TO FRANCE.				IMPORTS FROM FRANCE.
	Declared Value of British and Irish Produce and Manufactures	OFFICIAL VALUE.			OFFICIAL VALUE.
		British and Irish Produce and Manufactures.	Foreign and Colonial Merchandise.	TOTAL.	
	£.	£.	£.	£.	£.
1842	3,193,939	5,506,842	683,872	6,190,714	4,160,503
1843	2,534,898	4,305,616	765,187	5,070,803	3,387,741
1844	2,656,259	4,375,239	828,955	5,204,194	3,689,221
1845	2,791,238	4,188,845	846,451	5,035,296	4,097,050
1846	2,715,963	4,279,114	847,959	5,127,073	4,486,563
1847	2,554,283	3,400,770	970,677	4,371,447	4,792,663
1848	1,025,521	1,936,388	455,168	2,391,556	7,130,394
1849	1,951,269	3,014,349	1,144,909	4,159,258	8,177,075
1850	2,401,956	3,434,815	1,222,575	4,657,570	8,454,193
1851	2,028,463	2,985,170	1,511,028	4,496,198	8,083,112

The first column of figures in this table shows the effect of the protective laws which are still in force in France; in other words, the amount of privation which the government of that country has imposed upon its population for the sake of a few producers. The difference of £600,000 between the value of British manufactures exported to France in 1842 and 1843 neither proves that the French wanted less linen or less iron in the latter year than in the former, for, if their population and internal traffic experienced any increase, they would require more of our manufactures instead of less; nor yet that the French manufacturers had in the course of twelve months found out some secret which enabled them all at once to beat their English rivals. It simply proves that the French were compelled to buy their goods of their own countrymen, and to pay handsomely for the privilege of doing so. Additional restrictions brought down the value of our exports between 1842 and 1843 by the amount just stated, though an immediate improvement, starting from a lower point became apparent, and continued till the doubly-unfortunate era of 1847-1848, after which the tide of improvement once more set in. But while that branch of our trade with France which has been exposed to the protective policy of its own government has experienced such fluctuations, the value of our imports from that country exhibits a continuous and considerable increase. Starting from £4,160,503, their official value remained at that level for four or five years, influenced, no doubt, by the difficulties which, till 1847, were thrown in the way of the export trade. At that period our new policy was acted upon more boldly, and an increase began which almost doubled the value of our imports within four years. It is of no consequence to ask by what means we paid for these increased imports. Doubtless it was with some commodity which we prized less highly than the articles we obtained in exchange.

We will now turn to the United States. Our kinsmen there have not constructed their tariff with a special regard to British interests, yet still, our Free Trade policy has not made us losers. Our magnanimity has been as profitable to ourselves as to them. So immensely has our trade with that part of the world increased, that the value of our exports thither in 1852 was no less than 356 per cent. greater than in 1842. In 1842 our exports to the United States were equal, in point of value, to $7\frac{1}{2}$ per cent. on our total exports for the same year; in 1852 the proportion had risen to $20\frac{2}{3}$ per cent. In 1842 the articles exported from the United States to Great Britain were worth **41** per cent. of their total exports; in 1851 that proportion had become 53⅔ per cent.

Return of the Value of British Exports to the United States in each year from 1842 to 1852 inclusive, and also their Total Value in each of those years.

YEARS.	Exports to the United States.	TOTAL EXPORTS.
	£.	£.
1842	3,528,807	47,381,023
1843	5,013,514	52,279,709
1844	7,938,079	58,584,292
1845	7,142,839	60,111,082
1846	6,830,460	57,786,876
1847	10,974,161	58,842,377
1848	9,564,909	52,849,445
1849	11,971,028	63,596,025
1850	14,891,961	71,367,885
1851	14,362,976	74,448,722
1852	16,134,397	78,076,854

Return of the Value of United States Exports to the United Kingdom, exclusive of Foreign Re-exports, in each year from 1841-2 to 1850-1 inclusive, and also the Total Value of those Exports in each of those years.

FISCAL YEARS.	Exports to the United Kingdom.*	TOTAL EXPORTS.*
	Dollars.	Dollars.
1842	38,254,511	92,969,996
1843	39,720,950	77,793,783
1844	47,794,124	99,715,179
1845	44,234,279	99,299,776
1846	45,501,957	102,141,893
1847	86,266,935	150,637,464
1848	67,762,741	132,904,121
1849	76,628,294	132,666,955
1850	68,733,730	136,946,912
1851	109,531,612	196,689,718

Nothing can be more gratifying than the facts

* This includes specie.

which are embodied in the foregoing figures. Notwithstanding the unfavourable position in which we are placed with the two countries to which they refer, our intercourse with both has advanced under our Free Trade policy, at a rate far exceeding our most sanguine expectations. The following table will show the value of our exports in the years named to some other of the more important of our foreign and colonial markets :—

Declared Value of British and Irish Produce Exported from the United Kingdom to various Foreign Countries and British Possessions.

COUNTRIES.	1842.	1849.	1850.	1851.	1852.
Russia	1,885,953	1,566,175	1,454,771	1,289,704	1,099,917
Sweden and Norway ..	334,017	367,363	362,947	447,133	430,010
Denmark	194,304	353,599	454,304	445,500	452,436
Prussia, Hanover, and Hanse Towns	6,579,351	5,965,921	7,411,911	7,650,897	7,820,480
Holland............	3,573,362	3,499,937	3,542,632	3,542,673	4,109,976
Spain and the Balearic Isles	322,614	623,136	864,997	1,015,493	1,253,957
Turkey, including Greece, Wallachia, and Moldavia	1,489,826	2,881,093	3,012,053	2,441,951	2,501,973
Cuba	711,938	1,036,153	849,278	1,164,177	1,033,396
Brazil	1,756,805	2,444,715	2,544,837	3,518,684	3,464,394
China..............	969,381	1,537,109	1,574,145	2,161,268	2,503,599
North American Colonies	2,333,525	2,280,386	3,235,051	3,813,707	3,065,364
West Indies	2,591,425	1,821,146	2,030,229	2,201,032	1,908,552
Cape of Good Hope....	369,076	520,896	796,600	752,393	1,064,283
East Indies	5,169,888	6,803,274	8,022,665	7,806,596	7,352,907
Australia	958,952	2,080,364	2,602,253	2,807,356	4,222,205

IV. Perhaps the most interesting feature of our commerce as influenced by Free Trade, is the increased intercourse to which it has given rise with parts of the world hitherto unknown, even by name, to the British merchant, and more especially with the wheat-growing countries which border the Mediterranean and Black Seas. In 1841 our total imports of wheat amounted to no more than 2,400,000 quarters, and of this quantity only 230,000 quarters, or less than one-tenth, were imported from those countries. In 1852, according to the careful estimate of Mr. Mongredien, the total quantity of grain, chiefly wheat and maize, or Indian corn, imported from abroad, was.6,750,000 quarters, of which 3,350,000 quarters, or more than one-half, reached us through the Straits of Gibraltar; more than fourteen times the quantity imported from the same part of the world ten years ago. The following figures will show the rapid growth of this part of our trade during the last few years, and the cheering prospect of new and enlarged fields of enterprise which it opens before us. For the sake of comparison we enumerate all the countries from which grain was imported during the years specified.

Statement showing the Total Quantity of Grain and Meal Imported into the United Kingdom from various Countries, in Imperial Quarters.

COUNTRIES.	1842.	1850.	1851.	1852.	1853.
Russia, Northern Ports .	98,216	363,779	572,257	343,949	634,404
„ Ports on the Black Sea	260,480	589,250	762,160	957,877	1,070,483
Denmark and the Duchies	152,164	1,077,735	843,007	770,194	947,116
Prussia	876,303	1,343,780	930,168	554,703	1,177,764
Hanse Towns	99,932	392,853	143,476	167,858	305,011
Other parts of Germany	194,225	·457,844	336,691	339,734	363,075
Holland.............	49,864	495,614	153,774	221,563	170,762
France	546,959	1,328,922	1,591,377	745,162	714,242
Italian States	644,825	210,249	555,905	193,974	237,755
Wallachia and Moldavia		217,505	624,242	713,876	665,106
Turkish Dominions not otherwise specified ..	15,789	276,528	474,937	200,021	744,084
Egypt	105,372	558,063	958,955	777,745	643,129
British North America .	214,919	95,860	143,378	126,240	189,357
United States	139,422	1,082,755	1,211,365	1,400,420	1,821,484
Other Countries	298,809	528,853	316,294	233,353	489,363

In perusing these figures the reader will observe the prodigious increase of our imports from Egypt, Wallachia, Moldavia, Turkey, and the Russian ports of the Black Sea. This may be taken as a specimen of a traffic which has scarcely made its appearance in the custom-house returns, and for which we are altogether indebted to Free Trade. The inhabitants of the rich vallies which are watered by the Danube and the Nile, those who dwell on the Vistula and the Sea of Azov, the peasants of Syria and Armenia, take their place for the first time among the customers of England, and are henceforth connected, by ties of interest, with the factory operatives of Lancashire. At this moment cargoes of grain are shipping or on their way from Bourgas, Anchialos, Rodostov, Larnaka, names which, in spite of their uncouth orthography, discourse " eloquent music" to the ear of the merchant and philanthropist. We hear now of " Ghirka wheats, shipped at Marianople, Berdiansky, Taganrog," &c., " Danube wheats from Galatz and Ibraila," " Roumelian wheats, shipped chiefly at Varna and Constantinople," and the entire quantity of wheat alone imported from these parts of the world, in 1852, is estimated at 1,700,000 quarters, being nearly twice the quantity imported from the same places in 1849. It thus appears that a branch of commerce which had no existence prior to the repeal of the corn laws, enabled us, in 1851, to dispose of commodities to the value of three millions and a half sterling, and is now advancing at a rate which promises to double it in the course of two or three years. It has, moreover, introduced amongst us an entirely new article of food, which will hold an important place in future statistics. Maize, or Indian corn, was first brought over in small quantities at the period of the Irish famine, and great repugnance was manifested to its use by the ignorant peasantry. It has, however, maintained its ground; we imported last year 1,550,000 quarters of this article, of which quantity 1,100,000 quarters arrived in vessels from the Mediterranean. We are indebted to the enterprise of a body of Greek merchants for this development of the grain trade, and their history, which may be given in a few words, furnishes a striking comment on our commercial progress. Their origin dates from 1820, when two or three Greek houses were established in London, for the purpose of trading with the Levant. At first their capital was small, but their plans proved eminently successful, and in a short time our trade with that part of the world passed entirely into their hands. From the neighbourhood of Constantinople and Smyrna, they extended their enterprises along the valley of the Danube, the shores of the Black Sea, to Egypt and the vast provinces of which Aleppo and Damascus may be considered the capitals. In 1820, the districts with which they trade took scarcely any of our manufactures, now they occupy among our customers the third or fourth rank. In 1822, the number of Greek firms in the United Kingdom was only five, and their joint capital not more than £50,000; now, in 1853, there are as many as 500 firms, and the yearly profits of one firm alone is fourfold the amount of their united capital in the former year. In 1846, the grain trade attracted their attention; their vast resources were instantly applied to its development, and with such success that the yearly amount of their transactions is estimated at £4,000,000 sterling, and their entire amount during the last seven years at little less than £30,000,000.

V. We have now taken a brief but comprehensive survey of our commerce, as it is placed before us in official records ; we have seen it rise from its previously depressed state, and advance in a few years as much as fifty per cent. ; we have seen it multiplying our relations with states which have been our customers from time immemorial, and at the same instant opening new channels in parts of the world which have hitherto scarcely echoed the British name, and bringing vast districts, which have lain for ages beneath the night of despotism, for the first time in modern history within the magic spell of civilisation. We have beheld the gladdening sight of plenty scattering the countless treasures of her golden horn around the thresholds and hearths of the labouring poor, and industry, sustained by comfort, lured back again to the silent loom, and sending her cheapened products to clothe millions in distant lands. It would require no ordinary measure of hardihood to withhold from Free Trade the credit of these facts. The connexion between the two is natural, obvious, and indisputable. If we plant a tree we forthwith expect to see it grow, and, at the proper season, bear fruit; and if this result follow we should as soon think of asserting, against the evidence of our senses, the non-existence of the tree, as of ascribing the result to any other cause than that of suitable culture. If a person chose to deny this, and to ascribe its fruitfulness to the colour of the garden wall, or the form of the garden-gate, or the appearance of some new star in the heavens, it would be difficult perhaps to prove him mistaken ;—we could carry him no higher than the demonstration of his senses. It is precisely so with our commerce. It was once fettered, it is now free. Ever since its fetters were knocked off it has progressed with unexampled rapidity, and there are some who venture to believe that it progresses the faster because it is free. If any one chooses to say that it moves faster than when its limbs were bound, not because they are unbound, but because an earthquake happened five months since, it is hopeless to attempt a mathematical demonstration to the contrary, but we can point to the facts as amply sufficient to obtain the verdict of all unprejudiced men. The repeal of the corn laws, and the abolition of the imposts previously laid on many hundred articles, occasioned an influx of those commodities which former regulations had kept out. But imports and exports are reciprocal. Protection to native industry says—" You shall not receive," and the corollary to this is " You shall not give." Once obtain permission to *import*, and the nation will forthwith begin to *export*. The cheapness which Free Trade produces expands all our markets. One of the heaviest burdens formerly sustained by our manufacturer was the necessity of competing with the lightly-taxed foreigner. The reduction which Free Trade has effected in the price of food and the raw material places him nearer to a position of equality, and helps to decide the battle of cheapness in his favour. But cheapness is the magic power of trade ; at its approach the market gives way on all sides, nation after nation crowds into it, and protec-

M

tive measures, adopted by enlightened communities in self-defence, are thrown up as gross anachronisms. Free Trade is, as we shall see, the means of introducing greater economy into our manufactures, and stimulating all engaged therein to the attainment of greater excellence. Protected interests invariably languish; those who engage in them resemble a number of well-salaried officials who are guaranteed the enjoyment of a fixed income whether they work or not, and who content themselves, in consequence, with the minimum of ingenuity and exertion. Once deprive them of this support, once leave them to take care of themselves, and their conduct will undergo an instant change. Like the man who is reported to have run away with great agility when a set of thieves plundered him of his crutches, they will be compelled to do their best, and will soon equal, if not beat, their rivals. These are all the inevitable results of Free Trade, and the one expression for the whole is just—increased exportation. The condition of our commerce is scarcely more flourishing than it was expected to be. All was foreseen. It blossomed in theory before it blossomed in fact. The Free-trader always said—" Only open your ports to the produce of other nations, and your factories will soon be in motion, and the sea will be covered with your shipping, conveying your merchandise to every clime." This was the prophecy again and again uttered; in the prosperous times which are passing over us we witness its fulfilment.

SECTION II.

EFFECTS OF FREE TRADE ON OUR STAPLE MANUFACTURES.

We proceed now another step in our inquiry—to consider the influence of Free Trade on the MANUFACTURES of the United Kingdom. Great as is the importance usually attached to our manufactures, it may be questioned whether they have ever had assigned to them their proper position in relation to our commerce. Whether this position has been clearly perceived or not, it is most certain that our legislation has been such as can only be reconciled with utter ignorance respecting it. The distinctive character of British commerce must be understood before we can fully comprehend the mischief which it has sustained in and through our recent prohibitory laws. Our commercial progress during the last century has been unprecedentedly rapid. The height we have reached is very lofty when compared with any which had been reached before, or is now occupied by other nations. Hence it has become the fashion with foreigners to eulogise indiscriminately everything which bears a visible connexion with the result. The maxim selected for eulogy may have been, in point of fact, detrimental to our commerce; but our commerce has succeeded, and, therefore, it has been argued, the maxim is good. This error is owing to the want of a correct insight into the nature of our trade. It has been regarded as the formal creation of the legislator, whereas it springs from the very genius of the British people. It is wrong to ascribe it wholly or even chiefly to our maritime position. Our seafaring

M 2

tastes have no doubt had much to do with its production, but they do not lie at its root.   Laws designed
to regulate exchanges between ourselves and other
nations, have tended to oppress, rather than encourage
it.   Not as mere merchants have we risen to affluence;
we do not obtain our wealth as the Venetians, the
Genoése, the Portuguese, the Dutch, and probably the
commercial states of the old world obtained theirs—
by mere barter, buying in one part of the world, to
sell with profit in another.   We do this to some
extent when we export to France, Germany, and
Russia the imported produce of our colonies, but a
glance at the Returns of the Board of Trade will show
how insignificant a part this traffic constitutes of the
whole of our commerce.   No,—the commerce of
Great Britain is fed by its manufactures ; the articles
we chiefly offer, are not the silks of China, or the
spices of India, but our own industry—the labour of
our hands, our inventive skill, our physical and moral
prowess.   There is an analogy between the character
of the articles and their origin.   They are not luxuries, such as can be laid aside without privation, but
articles of prime necessity to men of all ranks.   Hence
there is a vitality in British commerce which has enabled it to advance in spite of the egregious errors
and scandalous selfishness which have characterised
our past policy.   It has been so closely identified with
the very existence of the people, and has called into
such stern play at once their inventive and industrial
energies, that bad laws have been neutralised, and the
palm won in spite of obstacles which would have
check-mated for ever any of our predecessors in the
same path.   When Protectionists point us to our

commercial success as a proof of the excellence of a protective *régime*, we know not whether to wish them an increase of candour, or perspicacity. True, we have realized a certain measure of success, but with such vast advantages at our command, and such a mighty force pushing us on, why has it not been greater? If the elastic power is so strong, and the actual motion produced so small, how prodigious the incubus which has weighed it down!

Foremost in the rank of industrial occupations stand our TEXTILE MANUFACTURES, the raw materials of which are cotton, wool, flax, and silk. The total declared value of our exports in this department is upwards of fifty millions sterling, or four-sevenths of the value of the whole. The cotton manufacture alone employs 21,400,000 spindles, and furnishes subsistence to three millions and a half of the population of the United Kingdom; and assuming that the same proportion between the value of the manufactured produce, and the number of the workmen employed, exists in the rest of the above mentioned branches of the textile manufactures, they cannot afford the means of subsistence to fewer than five millions, or not much less than a fifth of the entire population. The territorial area required for the operation of the cotton trade does not exceed one-hundredth part of the entire surface of the United Kingdom, and yet the parties engaged in it contribute one-fourth of the entire amount of the national revenue, or more than £12,000,000 annually;* or,

---

* "Cotton, as an Element of Industry," by Thomas Bazley, Esq., p. 37.

assuming the same proportion for the woollen, flax, and silk trades, the entire contributions of those engaged in textile manufactures to the resources of the state, are not less than sixteen millions sterling. These facts prove to us the importance, in a national point of view, of this great department of industry, and make the question of its progress or decline one of the first importance both to the patriot and the legislator.

I. The *Cotton Manufacture*, to which we first turn, is of by far the greatest magnitude, its exports being twice or three times more valuable than those of our flax, woollen, and silk trades put together. We have already referred to some of the phenomena of its growth, the rapidity of which is unexampled in the annals of industry. It is only one hundred and twenty years since Wyatt, of Birmingham, invented the method of elongating cotton by means of rollers; only eighty-five years since Arkwright and Hargreaves first put in operation the water-frame and spinning-jenny; and scarcely fifty years since the adoption of the power-loom; yet this manufacture has already revolutionised the condition and prospects of the country. In the first five years of the eighteenth century the annual consumption of cotton was little more than one million of pounds weight; by the close of the century, the annual consumption had risen to fifty millions of pounds weight; and in 1851 it was seven hundred and sixty millions, or nearly seven hundred times the quantity used a century and a half before.

A complete analysis of the cotton trade, and a detailed inquiry into the state of its various branches, would fill a volume. Such a minute investigation is beyond the requirements of our present design, but it may still be desirable to preface the proofs we shall adduce of its prosperous condition with a brief outline of its leading ramifications. The two most extensive divisions of the cotton trade are spinning and weaving; the turning of cotton into thread and of thread into cloth. The production of the cotton thread is the chief triumph of manufacturing skill, and it is here that the greatest amount of ingenuity and novelty has been displayed. To such a state of perfection has spinning machinery been brought, that cotton can be spun into thread of a degree of fineness which will require 2000 hanks to weigh a single pound,* and 960 yards to weigh a single grain. The spinning-jenny, when first invented, had but twenty spindles, and these were as many as one person could manage; but now, one man, aided by a few children, will often have 200, or even 2000 spindles, and for some kinds of yarn nearly 4000 spindles, under his own control, each spindle producing a thread. In the days of hand-loom weaving, twenty-eight yards of good calico was considered a full week's work for one man; now, however, a single workman takes charge of four looms, and produces from them, in the same time and with less labour, twenty pieces of better cloth.† Looking at the woven fabric, we find it almost impossible to indicate its varieties. The most extensive subdivision is formed by regarding them as plain or printed; then, taking the former, we have sheetings, shirtings, fustians, ginghams, muslins, lace, quiltings, bed and

---

* A hank of cotton contains 860 yards.

† " Cotton, as an Element of Industry."

table covers, each of which constitutes virtually a distinct trade, with its peculiar "arts and mysteries." An interesting group of trades is comprehended under calico-printing. First we have the manufacturer of the copper cylinders, which are ultimately to impart the pattern and colours to the cloth; then we have the "pattern designer," whose business it is to sketch and colour suitable devices, which the engraver then transfers to the cylinder; and, finally, mechanics are required to construct machines for setting the cylinder to work. The cylindrical printing machine is one of the triumphs of art. Formerly, printing was done by blocks, which were impressed on the cloth by the workman, every colour in the pattern requiring a separate block, and a repetition of the entire process. By the cylindrical machine, this method is, to a great extent, superseded. By its aid, one workman can do as much work as would have required hundreds of men a few years ago, and, at the same instant, the pattern, together with eight colours, is impressed upon the cloth. " Preparations are making to increase the number of colours to fifteen, at the same time producing, as they doubtless will, six or seven hundred times as many pieces per day as if blocked separately."*

One of the chief tests of the progress of the cotton manufacture in all its branches, is the quantity of raw material which is imported annually for home consumption. The following figures will show the entire quantity of cotton brought into the United Kingdom, in each year from 1842 to 1852 inclusive, together

---

* "Lecture on Calico Printing," by Edmund Potter, Esq.

with the quantity exported in the same years for the use of other countries :—

Year.	Total Quantity Imported.	Total Quantity Exported.
1842 .... Bales..	1,398,136 .... Bales..	138,320
1843 .... ,, ..	1,743,618 .... ,, ..	121,410
1844 .... ,, ..	1,683,710 .... ,, ..	150,000
1845 .... ,, ..	1,856,860 .... ,, ..	133,900
1846 .... ,, ..	1,243,520 .... ,, ..	194,200
1847 .... ,, ..	1,234,010 .... ,, ..	221,850
1848 .... ,, ..	1,738,908 .... ,, ..	189,500
1849 .... ,, ..	1,905,616 .... ,, ..	256,300
1850 .... ,, ..	1,747,490 .... ,, ..	270,737
1851 .... ,, ..	1,903,475 .... ,, ..	268,617
1852 .... ,, ..	2,341,522 .... ,, ..	282,516

It appears from this that our imports of cotton have increased since 1842 by 943,386 bales, or by about seventy per cent., while our exports of the raw material have only increased by 144,196 bales, showing that this large increase has gone to augment our exports of manufactured cotton goods, or to multiply the comforts of our own population. It will be interesting to compare with this the following statement of the value of our cotton manufactures exported, on an average of three years from 1840 to 1851* inclusive:—

Average Years.	Declared Value of Cotton Man. Exported.
1840, 1841, 1842	£23,282,481
1843, 1844, 1845	25,124,217
1846, 1847, 1848	25,274,615
1849, 1850, 1851	27,762,645

This statement shows that the value of our exports of cotton manufactures, on an average of the three years ending with 1851, was twenty per cent. above the average of the three years ending 1842, and that the progress was chiefly due to the last triennial period, during

* Reports of the Manchester Chamber of Commerce.

which the influence of Free Trade began to be felt. The least progress was made in 1846 and 1847, owing partly to a depression, in other respects, at home, and a deficiency in the American cotton crop. The year 1850 was remarkable for the unprecedented amount of our exports, in the face of high prices for the raw material. The price of " fine Boweds," in 1850, was seven pence halfpenny per lb., in 1848 it was but four pence three farthings, yet the value of our cotton exports in 1850 was £28,252,818 against £22,681,200 in 1848, and amounted, in yards of manufactured produce, to 1,472,334,000, against 1,169,000,000 in 1848, while the excess for 1851 amounted to 175,000,000. The weekly consumption of cotton in the United Kingdom during the above years was as follows :—

1848 bales weekly..28,948	1851 bales weekly......32,011	
1849 „ „ ..30,534	1852 „ „ 39,596	
1850 „ „ ..29,096	Incr. of 1852 over 1848, 10,648 *	

Next to the quantity of cotton imported, and the value of our exports of cotton manufactures, the most valuable information respecting the present state of the cotton trade, as compared with the past, is to be derived from the reports of the inspectors of factories. There are four chief inspectors, whose labours are divided among as many districts, the first of which comprises Lancashire and the northern counties ; the second, the midland counties, Wales and Ireland; the third, Scotland; and the fourth, the eastern counties of England, including part of the West Riding of York. Thus the information contained in their reports, in addition to its being official, and therefore entirely reliable, gives us at once the

* Messrs. Littledale and Co.'s Circular.

state of our textile manufactures throughout the United Kingdom. In the second report of Leonard Horner, Esq., Inspector of the Lancashire and Northern District, for 1851, the following statement occurs: " In the year ending 31st of October last, no less than 81 new factories have been built or set to work (having been begun to be built in the preceding year) in my districts, having an aggregate power of 2,240 horses; of these 73, with 2,064 horse-power, are cotton mills. In addition to these, in 31 long-established cotton mills, the proprietors of which are men of thorough knowledge and long experience in the trade, additional engine power has been set up to the extent of 1,477 horses. The situation of these mills will be best understood from the following statement:—

	NEW FACTORIES.		ADDITIONAL POWER.	
	No.	Horse Power.	No.	Horse Power.
In Manchester, Salford, Bury, and part of Glossopdale	6	87	3	105
Preston, Blackburn, Accrington, Clitheroe, Chorley, Lancaster, Westmoreland, and Cumberland	22	663	5	200
Rochdale, Heywood, Shaw, Royton, Newchurch, Rawtenstall, and their neighbourhood	20	445	8	167
Bolton, Radcliffe, Burnley, Colne, Craven	19	265	5	192
Dukinfield, Staleybridge, Mossley, Oldham, &c.	14	780	10	813
	81	2,240	31	1,477
		1,477		
Total Horse Power	......	3,717		

The 3,717 horse-power will furnish employment to probably not less than 14,000 additional hands. To give you an idea of the magnitude of some of these new concerns I may mention that one of the cotton mills is 410 feet long, 76 feet wide, has six stories, a power of 150 horses, and will run 126,000 spindles. It was only partially at work at the end of June."

In his report for the year ending October 31, 1852, Mr. Horner says: "The increase of cotton mills (during the past year) has been very large. After deducting those that are at present unoccupied, and many of them will, in all probability, be soon again at work, especially those from which the machinery has not been removed, there have been set to work within the last two years 129 new mills, with an aggregate of 4,023 horse-power, and there have been 53 instances of addition to existing mills with an aggregate of 2,090 horse-power, so that there has been an increase of 6,113 horse-power, which must have given employment to not fewer than 24,000 additional hands in the cotton trade. Nor is this all, for many new mills are at present being built. In the limited area which includes the towns of Ashton, Staleybridge, Oldham, and Lees there are eleven, which it is estimated will have an aggregate power of 620 horses. The machine makers are said to be overwhelmed with orders, and a very intelligent and observant mill-owner told me lately that many of the buildings now going on would, in all probability, not be at work before 1854, from the impossibility to get machinery for them."

Similar accounts to that given by Mr. Horner are furnished by the inspectors for other parts of the kingdom. The following table will show the new factories, and additions made to existing factories in the cotton trade, and also the factories remaining unoccupied, for the year ending October 13st, 1852, in all the four districts :—

	NEW.		ADDITIONS.		UNOCCUPIED.	
	Factories	Horse Power.	Factories	Horse Power.	Factories	Horse Power
Spinning only	45	1,603	8	275	24	490
Spinning and Weaving	21	928	10	283	6	697
Weaving only	41	634	11	246	17	276
Doubling only	2	10			4	32
Total Cotton Factories	109	3,175	29	804	51	1,495

But the increase of factories is only one instalment of the facts requisite for gaining a real insight into the condition of the textile manufactures. Production has been greatly increased by the aid of superior machinery, without any additional moving power. This has been attained, partly, by allowing engines to work a greater number of feet per minute, the adoption of boilers having a greater steam-generating power, and the use of "high-steam," viz., raising, in properly constructed boilers, the pressure to the square inch from four, six, or eight lbs., to thirty, forty, or even seventy lbs. In a letter addressed to Mr. Horner, by Mr. Nasmyth, of the Bridgwater Foundry, Patricroft, the writer gives a full explanation of these various changes, and adds,—"I am confident that could we obtain an exact return (as to the increase of performance or work done by the identical engines to which some or all of these improvements have been applied) the result would show that, from the same weight of steam engine machinery, we are now obtaining at least 50 per cent. more duty or work performed on the average, and that, as before said, in many cases, the identical steam engines, which in the days of the restricted speed of 220 feet per minute, yielded fifty-horse power, are now yielding upwards of 100." This statement is practically corroborated by Mr. Redgrave, Inspector for the Eastern District, who says,—"I have before me a paper kindly prepared by a very intelligent juror in my district, showing the number of hands employed, their ages, the machines at work, and the wages paid from 1840 to the present time. In October, 1840, his firm employed 600 hands, of whom 200 were under thirteen years of age. In October last 350 hands were employed, of whom only sixty were under thirteen years; the same number of machines, within very few, were at work, and the same sum in wages was paid at both periods. I quote this to show that returns of power, of spindles or of looms, must be considered as indications, rather than as facts, and that there are many other circumstances which should be ascertained, and should accompany statistical tables, when the condition of the manufacturing industry of the country is under consideration."—It is evident that such other circumstances as those to which Mr. Redgrave refers, would all heighten the impression conveyed by the foregoing statements as to the present flourishing state of the cotton manufactures.

With regard to wages, scarcely any change has occurred within the last six years in the amount received in the various branches of the cotton trade. Notwithstanding the increased competition to which employers have recently been exposed, and the shortening of the hours of labour, the actual receipts of the workman have undergone no diminution. The following is communicated by a firm in the neighbourhood of Oldham, employing 600 hands: "Our spinners and piecers earn about the same amount of wages now as they did in 1846.

"The following is the quantity spun and the money earned in 1846 and 1852 :—

October, 1846—23,500 lbs., average counts, 30, £72 0 0
August, 1852—29,000 lbs.,   ,,   30, 72 0 0

Consequently, at the present time, we spin 5,500 lbs. of 30's more for the same amount of wages than we did in 1846. In winding and warping there has been no alteration. In reeling there has been a slight reduction, but operatives will earn the same amount now as they did before, by attending better to their work." The following averages, taken from the books of a weaving establishment in Manchester, employing in various branches nearly 1,000 hands, will show the wages paid in two great departments of weaving—that of plain calicoes, and that of "checks, ginghams, regattas, etc.":—

PLAIN CALICOES.	GINGHAMS, REGATTAS, ETC.
Warpers ...... 24s. to 25s. 0d.	Winders .... 10s. to 12s.
Drawers-in .... 18s. „ 26s. 0d.	Pin Winders .... 9s. „ 11s.
One helper .... 4s. 6d.	Warpers .... 11s. „ 12s.
Weavers 5s. 6d. per loom,	Drawers-in ...... 18s. „ 25s.
four looms........ 22s. 0d.	Weavers .... 10s. „ 16s.
One helper .... 4s. 6d.	Dressers .... 25s. „ 30s.
Overlookers .... 25s. 0d.	Makers-up ...... 20s.

These are the wages which have been paid in the same establishment for the last six years. It seems certain, however, that an advance will soon take place, since, although every workman of moderate abilities is in full employment, new factories are rising on all sides. We have been informed that in one district, where there are already no surplus hands, a new factory is just starting, and two others are about to be erected. In another district in the neighbourhood of Bolton, where employment is already good, no less than seven erections or alterations are going on at the present moment. Such facts seem to render a rise of wages inevitable, unless some further economical processes are discovered.

For the last two or three years the staple trade of Nottingham and the surrounding districts has experienced an unexampled measure of prosperity. A perusal of the weekly reports shows that a progressive and general improvement has taken place within that period. Its healthy and continuous character may be inferred from the fact, that the correspondent of the "Times" newspaper, in reviewing it at the commencement of 1853, uses the same strong language which he had already employed in describing the trade of 1851. On both occasions he says, " The (cotton) hosiery trade has been extended during the past twelve months beyond calculation, and bids fair to attain a degree of magnitude and importance deemed only a short time since to be beyond the bounds of possibility." This estimate is confirmed by the opinion of a gentleman, himself extensively engaged in the manufacture under review, William Felkin, Esq., of Nottingham: "I have not taken," says Mr. Felkin, "any actual census of the Nottingham trade since 1844, and therefore can only give the general impressions resulting from my intercourse with men of business, and my own experience as an employer of labour in this district. At the date just mentioned, the hosiery trade was and had been for many years in a very depressed state; wages were excessively low, and the condition of the stocking makers deplorable. Since then, the home consumption of stockings has much increased. The foreign trade has greatly extended; wages have doubled in the actual amount received by that class who are engaged in ' round' and ' cut up' work, and have risen 50 per cent. upon ' fashioned' work since 1844. The business is expanding rapidly, and flourishing in a degree unexampled for a century past. An invention has been discovered, and largely applied, whereby cheap hosiery can be made easily, and with astonishing rapidity, upon what is called the 'round frame.' Millions of feet will be clothed that never knew what a stocking was before. Some of the articles thus made are being exported at three shillings and six pence per dozen pairs, large enough for many women and girls' feet. Of course the price of provisions and all articles of artizans' use and clothing is now such that they may obtain comforts unknown to them for many years. There is a growing dearth of labour, especially of women and children, such having been too much, too early, and too long employed in the business of this district. I earnestly desire social improvement in this all-important matter."

Respecting the present state of the lace manufacture, Mr. Felkin says: "The wages of lace-makers employed at the looms are somewhat advanced, and labourers are scarce. The receipts of all women and children are advanced thirty or forty per cent., though nominally not increased in that proportion. But a thousand females and youths could find employment in a week, if imported into this district, so that the effect of present want of labour must be to raise the value of their labour. No material invention has been added to the lace frame during the last seven years, but we are continually changing from one point of the compass of fashion or use of material and design to another. For instance, the lace loom now furnishes curtains, window-blinds, anti-macassars, toilet covers, in the most elaborate designs, through the extended use of Jacquard machinery. A new branch of the trade has thus arisen. My remarks as to the effect of low-priced food apply to the working people of the lace and every other trade here, also to the improvement in their power of commanding social enjoyments."

The increased activity of the hosiery trade is no doubt owing in part to the increased ability of our own population to purchase its productions, but it has arisen in a great measure from an extension of the foreign market within the last two years, consequent upon the use of the " round frame." A few years since, our looms were unable to compete with those of the continent. Saxony, especially, became a formidable rival, and not only superseded us to a great extent in the American market, but exported largely to this country. In 1849, a deputation of Nottingham manufacturers visited Saxony, in order to find out the cause of this successful competition, and found that it was owing chiefly to the low rate of wages paid for labour there. The same amount of work which would cost an English manufacturer ten shillings, being done there for a thaler, or two shillings and ten pence of our money, and even this low rate would admit of a reduction by one-half if the state of business required it. On making this dis-covery, our manufacturers came home impressed with a conviction that the trade in low goods must be conceded to their rivals, and that they themselves could only hope to succeed in those higher branches in which

.capital and skill were necessary. At this moment a new invention saved them from despair. The Chevalier Claussen introduced his improved knitting frame to their notice. The principle of this machine had been discovered ten years before, by a Leicester-shire manufacturer, but the great amount of capital embarked in the old machines prevented its adoption; it was practised, however, by one house at Lough-borough, though with such extreme secrecy that few of the persons connected with the establishment knew how it was worked. Compelled at last to make some change, the manufacturers adopted M. Claussen's machine, and the result has been a degree of cheap-ness which leaves the manual labour of Saxony far behind. A few months since a deputation from Saxony visited Nottingham to inquire into the cause of our newly-acquired powers of competition, and an examination of our machinery convinced them of the hopelessness of competing with us, except by the use of the same means.

Our hosiery, like other branches of our cotton manufacture, will probably soon attain a position which will enable it to defy the competition of the world. During 1852, very large orders were received from the United States and Germany Unfortunately, the published returns of government do not distinguish the several branches of the hosiery trade, but the following facts will furnish us with a clue to the astonishing advance which has been made in our stocking manufacture within the last three years. In eleven months of 1850 the value of the cotton stockings exported amounted to £96,376; during the ·corresponding period of 1851 it was £179,606. A comparison of the *quantities* exported will place the increase in a still clearer light. The number of dozen pairs of stockings exported in the above named period of 1850 was 213,750, and in the corresponding period of 1851, 459,699; an advance of considerably more than 100 per cent. in twelve months. A similar increase has taken place in the export of woollen stockings, their value having risen from £65,048 in 1850 to £107,921 in 1851. The prospects of the lace trade are equally encouraging. Extensive changes are in progress, which are likely to double or triple the quantity of lace produced in the neighbourhood of Nottingham. Notwithstanding the perfection to which the bobbin-net manufacture has been brought within a comparatively short period, it is probable that much more important results will soon be developed, adapting the Nottingham manufacture to the wants of every nation and every clime. Besides those articles of general elegance already mentioned, an invention has recently been introduced by which fine qualities of wire can be worked in a similar way to cotton thread. Should this lead to a new branch of trade it will furnish additional proof of the valuable aid which the progress of science in one department of enterprise can render another, since the idea of it was first suggested in manufacturing a species of wire gauze, required by the Messrs. Elkington, of Birmingham, to carry out the invention of the electro-type.*

An advance of wages has recently taken place in most of the Nottingham trades. At the beginning of the year the principal manufacturers were waited

* "Times" Newspaper, Sept. 4, 1852.

upon by a deputation of workmen, in almost every branch of frame-work knitting, soliciting higher rates. The "drawer" hands asked an advance of nine pence a dozen, the silk-glove hands an advance of six pence a dozen; the Sutton hose hands an advance of from three pence to seven pence a dozen; the "cut up" and "selvage-heel" branches for an advance of from three halfpence to three pence a dozen.* Most of these demands have been acceded to. The workmen grounded their requests upon the sound and improved condition of the trade, and having preferred them in a respectful and temperate manner, they have been courteously listened to.

II. The past few years have been a season of general prosperity with our *Woollen Manufacturers.* The test derived from the quantity of raw material imported is not so decisive in this department as in the cotton trade, since a large portion of the wool consumed in the United Kingdom is furnished by our own farmers. It is certain, however, that the consumption of wool has been much greater during the last three or four years than at any former period. Since 1846 our farmers have directed their attention more especially to the rearing of sheep, and hence a much larger quantity of wool must now be derived from home sources. At the same time, as the figures we are about to give will show, our imports have increased at an amazing rate. Still, consumption has been in advance of supply. The price of wool in 1852 was two pence per pound, or ten per cent. higher than in 1851, and the stock of wool in hand on the first day of January, 1853, was many thousand bales less than on the corresponding day in 1852. The follow-

* " Times " Newspaper, Jan. 24, 1853.

ing table, taken by itself, is a sufficiently decisive proof of the extent of our recent prosperity in this important branch of national industry :—

Quantities of Wool (Sheep, Lamb, and Alpaca) Imported into the United Kingdom from various Countries.

Years.	Spain.	Germany: viz.—Mecklenburg, Hanover, Oldenburg, and the Hanse Towns.	Other Countries of Europe.	British Possessions in South Africa.	British Possessions in the East Indies.	British Settlements in Australia.	South America.	Other Countries.	Total.
1840	1,266,905	21,812,664	8,541,264	751,741	2,441,370	9,721,243	4,387,274	513,823	49,436,284
1841	1,088,200	20,059,375	8,305,994	1,079,910	3,008,664	12,399,362	9,174,249	155,220	56,170,974
1842	670,239	15,613,269	7,050,436	1,265,768	4,246,083	12,979,856	3,207,489	848,499	45,881,639
1843	597,091	16,805,448	5,877,538	1,728,453	1,916,129	17,433,780	4,588,987	295,667	49,243,093
1844	918,853	21,847,684	15,313,087	2,197,143	2,765,853	17,602,247	3,760,063	1,308,831	65,713,761
1845	1,074,540	18,484,736	17,606,515	3,512,924	3,975,866	24,177,317	6,468,338	1,513,619	76,813,855
1846	1,020,476	15,888,705	11,733,601	2,958,457	4,570,581	21,789,346	4,890,273	2,404,023	65,255,462
1847	424,408	12,673,814	7,935,697	3,477,392	3,063,142	26,056,815	7,295,550	1,665,780	62,592,508
1848	106,638	14,429,161	7,024,098	3,497,250	5,997,435	30,034,567	8,851,211	924,487	70,864,847
1849	127,559	12,750,011	11,432,354	5,377,495	4,182,853	35,879,171	6,014,525	1,004,679	76,768,647
1850	440,751	9,166,731	8,703,252	5,709,529	3,473,252	39,018,221	5,296,648	2,518,394	74,326,778
1851	383,150	8,219,236	14,263,156	5,816,591	4,549,520	41,810,117	4,850,048	3,420,157	83,311,975
1852	233,413	12,763,253	13,382,140	6,388,796	7,880,784	43,197,301	6,252,689	3,661,082	93,761,458
1853	154,146	11,584,800	26,861,166	7,221,448	12,400,869	47,075,812	9,740,032	4,358,172	119,396,445

A glance at the above table will show the vast importance of our colonial imports to our woollen manufacture. While we are indebted for nearly the whole of our raw cotton to foreign countries, a very large and rapidly increasing part of our woollen imports is from the various dependencies of the British Crown. We draw from Germany little more than one half the quantity for which we were indebted to that country twelve years ago. While Saxon wool is still chiefly used in the manufacture of the best cloths, and English wool, somewhat deteriorated by the rise of a new system of husbandry, is principally employed in the production of worsted fabrics, Australian wool supplies the manufacturer with raw material for the bulk of our woollen goods, including the beautiful fabrics known as challis, merinoes, and Indianas. The growth of this branch of trade has been singularly rapid. It is scarcely sixty-seven years since the "first fleet" landed, among other live-stock, 29 sheep on the shores of Australia; they were of the Bengal breed, rough, unsightly looking animals, and their wool was of little value. It is estimated that, including Western Australia and Tasmania, our colonists now possess upwards of twenty millions of sheep, while, by crossing with South Downs and Leicesters, obtained from the mother country, the breed has vastly improved. The first importation of wool from Australia took place in 1807, and amounted to 245 lbs. It was the produce of Mr. John Mc Arthur, a gentleman to whose intelligence and foresight, together with the encouragement received from the manufacturers and government of this country, we are indebted for one of the most profitable and promising branches of British commerce.

The great progress which has been made in our woollen manufactures during the period of Free Trade, will receive additional proof from the following state-ment, which gives the average value of our woollen manufactures exported during successive periods of three years, from 1840 to 1851 inclusive. It will be seen, on comparing the average for the three years ending with 1851 with the average for the same period ending with 1842, that the increase in point of value was as much as fifty-seven per cent., a greater rate of increase than was realized in any other branch of manufacture, or in the whole of our exports collec-tively; a proof that the manufacturers of the West Riding of Yorkshire have enjoyed a fair share in the prosperity occasioned by Free Trade.

1840, 1841, 1842	£5,817,008
1843, 1844, 1845	8,452,072
1846, 1847, 1848	7,196,326
1849, 1850, 1851	9,141,129
Excess of 1849-1851 over 1840-1841	3,324,121

The number of new woollen factories, and additions to existing factories, and factories become unoccu-pied in the year ended Oct. 31, 1852, is as follows:—

	NEW.		ADDITIONS.		UNOCCUPIED.	
	Factories	Horse Power.	Factories	Horse Power.	Factories	Horse Power.
Wool Spinning only	16	174	12	89	13	292
Spinning and Weaving ..	15	325	2	40	7	156
Weaving only	4	94	6	29	2	66
Dressing only	1	80	4	4	2	20
Total	36	673	24	162	24	534

Though the above table shows an increase of twelve factories, and 139 horse power in the year ending with October, 1852, it fails to give an adequate impression of the increased machinery which is now employed in the production of woollen fabrics, as compared with a few years ago. During 1851, there was an increase of no less than sixty-nine new factories in the neighbourhood of Leeds, Bradford, Bingley, Calverly, Guiseley, and Otley alone, exclusive of cotton mills. A large proportion of these new erections belonged to the woollen trade. In reviewing the business done throughout 1852, the "Leeds Mercury," of January 1st, 1853, says, "There never was a period when the trade of this district was so good as it has been this year. There has been no overtrading; in some cases the supply has not been equal to the demand. Now, when stocks generally accumulate, the White Cloth Hall is nearly empty. The mills and workshops are all fully employed. Fewer persons able and willing to work were never out of employ; the industrial classes were never better able to command a fair share of the comforts of life than at present." In corroboration of the latter part of this statement, more especially, we quote the testimony of persons actually engaged in the woollen manufacture, and large employers of labour. A manufacturer of Wellington, Somersetshire, writes thus: "The condition of the working classes here is much better than it was before the repeal of the corn laws. Though the general rate of wages is lower in this part of the kingdom than in the manufacturing districts of Lancashire and Yorkshire, the actual receipts of our factory operatives are in no case less, and in many cases more, than they were five or six years ago." The following is from a gentleman of great intelligence connected with the woollen trade in the Yorkshire district, himself a juror for woollen fabrics for the Exhibition of 1851: "We employ about 700 persons in our factory, &c.; the wages we are now paying, and have paid for the last year, are about the same for sixty hours' labour as we paid in 1846 for sixty-nine hours'; which is equivalent to an advance of fifteen per cent. They have this advantage besides the reduced prices of provisions, and are in good circumstances generally. At the close of 1849, our workmen had about £1,200 in the Savings Bank. This sum we believe is now considerably increased. Several live in their own very good cottages, thus being rent free, besides having one, two, or more to let, all from their own savings, and chiefly of late years. This description applies relatively to most of the district, though, perhaps, our work-people are in rather better circumstances than the average."

III. The *Flax Manufacture* is now in a very important transition state. Some temporary confusion exists in it at present, owing in part to its prosperity, combined with an unequal development of its various branches, and the changes which have occurred, and are still occurring, in the population and proprietary of Ireland. Everything indicates, however, that this important department of industry is just starting upon a new career, and that its future history will be fraught with the most beneficent results to the sister country. It may be truly said that its actual condition was never more prosperous, while it holds out the promise of a degree of success which will render its past progress altogether insignificant by comparison. Hitherto the position of the flax manufacture in the North of Ireland has resembled the position of the cotton manufacture previous to the adoption of the power-loom, or, earlier still, when calico weavers used to go from cottage to cottage in search of " weft." With linen the case is reversed; steam-power has been applied to the production of yarn, while weaving has been left in the hands of small farmers, who have pursued it at odd intervals as a supplement to agriculture. Thus one part of the manufacture has been dependent on mechanical arrangements, requiring corresponding regularity and energy in all connected with it, while the other part has been left to hand-labour. This system was always productive of inconvenience, but it is specially so now, when the effects of the late famine have driven so many of the small farmers from the kingdom. Those who remain do less work than formerly; their wages having advanced twenty or thirty per cent. in consequence of the scarcity of labour, they are comparatively opulent, and do not care about working more than three or four days in the week. Hence a crisis was inevitable. The system of cottage weaving is barbarous; a new system is necessary, not merely for the prosperity, but for the existence of the flax manufacture. One of the blessings of the unrestricted competition occasioned by Free Trade is that every industrial interest must be based on a sound footing, and this is the effect it is now exerting on the staple trade of Ireland. The Belfast Linen Trade Circular of 27th October, 1852, announces, " That at present four Irish firms are preparing to establish power-loom weaving. An enterprising Leeds machine-making firm have taken premises in Belfast for the purpose of carrying on the manufacture of power-looms, and it is not unlikely that, before long, power-loom weaving will be in proportion as extensively applied in Ireland to linens, as it is in England and Scotland to cottons."

We learn, on the authority of the same Circular of January 7th, 1853, that the aspects of the flax manufacture are most encouraging as compared with the same period of last year. In the spinning department, the increase of machinery, which has been so great during the last ten years, has been fully maintained. In 1841 there were about 240,000 spindles employed, in 1850 the number amounted to 326,000. With the great addition made in 1851 and 1852, the figure now stands at 506,000. A novel feature of the trade in 1852 is its extension into new districts, remote from the province to which it has hitherto been chiefly confined. Two new mills are now in course of erection, one at Limerick, another at Ballyshannon; the former is to hold 12,000, and the latter 6000 spindles.

The imports of foreign flax into the United Kingdom for the years 1840, 1841, and 1842, amounted to an annual average of 62,500 tons; in 1848, 1849, 1850, the average was 84,800 tons, an increase of 22,300 tons. The average for the three years 1851, 1852, and 1853, has somewhat diminished, but the quantity imported in 1853, taken by itself, is the largest on record. Notwithstanding this great increase in the quantity of flax imported, a greater breadth of land in Ireland is continually being brought under flax culture. The following statement, received by the Royal Flax Society from the census commissioners, will show the number of acres under flax culture in each of the four years 1849-1852 :—

	Acres.			Acres.
1849	 53,863		1851	 140,536
1850	 60,314		1852	 136,009

Since a greater quantity of flax has been imported and grown, a greater quantity must have passed into the hands of our manufacturers. The following averages for successive triennial periods since 1840, will show the value of that part of the manufactured produce which has been sent abroad :—

1840, 1841, 1842	....	£3,666,136
1843, 1844, 1845	....	3,958,155
1846, 1847, 1848	....	3,537,065
1849, 1850, 1851	....	4,627,760

Excess of value for 1849-1851 over 1840-1842, £961,624, or 26 per cent.

IV. The *Silk Trade* has hitherto been confessedly the least prosperous branch of our textile manufactures. It is that which has enjoyed, and still enjoys, most protection, and at the same time it is the least satisfactory to those engaged in it. A Norwich manufacturer writes : " Trade is not generally better here than it was five or six years ago. Upon the whole, there is about the same number of operatives employed. The wages for most fabrics are the same now as in 1846, but for two the rate was reduced in November, 1852 from fifteen to thirty per cent. Our operatives suffer much by stopping for employment four or five weeks twice in the year, when the summer and autumn trades finish, and before the spring trade commences. We want a branch of trade that would keep our people employed during those dull seasons, and thus prevent them from seeking, as they now too often do, parochial relief."—A shade gives reality

and life to a picture ; but before the Norwich manufacturer despairs, let him insist upon the application
of Free Trade to the entire length and breadth of the
silk manufacture; let every rampart be pulled down,
and the rival be fairly met.   Unrestricted competition
is a sovereign specific for weakness.   The spirit of
enterprise, which can be kindled only by entire self-
dependence, would soon discover some employment
for dull seasons.   From Coventry a highly intelligent
manufacturer writes :   " It is difficult to give any
statistical information regarding the wages and social
condition of our ribbon-weavers.   The mode of employment does not admit of it.   The most part (indeed
the very large majority) of our operatives work at
home, on piecework, and their wages therefore depend
upon their skill and diligence.   It is true, there is a
scale of prices, to which the manufacturers in the respective branches adhere.—I may say, 1st. The scale
has not been reduced since 1846.   2nd. With very
trifling exceptions there has been full employment
ever, since.   3rd. As regards the weavers, there has
been such an improvement in their looms during
the last two years, that those hands who have availed
themselves of them have earned, and still are earning, more than they have ever done within my recollection.   This refers to those only who work at home.
The factory workers, who, although they have greatly
increased during the period referred to, are still a
very small minority, are in the same circumstances as
to wages as they were seven years ago; *their* amelioration being the restricted hours of labour."

Turning to the reports of the factory inspectors,
we find ample proof that the silk manufacture is re-

garded as a profitable investment by those who have the best means of being informed respecting it. During the last year twenty new factories have been built and set in motion, eleven of which are intended for "throwing" only, four for spinning only, one for spinning and weaving, and four for weaving only. Our imports of raw silk, which, in 1842, amounted only to 3,856,867 lbs., were 4,385,107 lbs. in 1850, and the value of our exports last year showed an advance of more than half a million sterling upon that of 1842. Moreover, this increase is due in a great measure to the increased exportation of thrown silk. Speaking of 1852, Mr. H. W. Eaton, an eminent silk-broker, says: "The consumption of silk during this year has been the largest ever known, and exceeded that of 1851 by 606,003 lbs. The demand both for raw and thrown silk for exportation has exceeded that of any former period, that of the latter materially contributing to the advantage of the English throwsters, who, with their operatives, have for some time been fully employed, at an improved remuneration." Messrs. Perceval and Ludlow, in their annual circular, state, that the profits of throwsters, during the later months of 1852, were diminished by "a shortness in the supply of labour," a satisfactory proof of the general state of employment. They add, "One of the most remarkable features of the past year has been the greatly increased export of British thrown silk, opening fresh fields of operation, and extending others. It would appear that the supply in the several continental markets has not equalled the demand, and now that the foreign manufacturer has fully tested our 'throwers,' there is very little doubt but that the superior quality of

China silk, to which they have been hitherto but little accustomed, will eventually lead to a much larger consumption."

V. Leaving our textile manufactures, it is difficult to direct our footsteps anywhere without meeting with the most unequivocal signs of prosperity. The great interests we have been considering are most suitable, on account of their magnitude, to lay before us the industrial condition of the kingdom; but they are so far from having monopolised the prosperity afforded by Free Trade, that they have advanced in a less ratio than others; while, on a comparison of the averages for the three years ending with 1842, with those of the similar period ending with 1851, our exports of cottons have risen twenty per cent.; our linens twenty-six per cent.; and our woollens fifty-seven per cent.; the rest of the enumerated articles in the Returns of the Board of Trade have increased sixty-eight per cent. It is impossible, however, to traverse the entire circle, nor is it necessary; we will only pause for a moment before the important trades which are connected with Sheffield and Birmingham. Hardware and cutlery give employment to a numerous class of our population, and it is gratifying to find that this branch of trade has had a large share in the benefits resulting from recent legislation. The articles comprised under it are such as are least dependent upon civilisation for an active demand, and yet such as can only be furnished by a highly civilised people. The aggregate advance in the value of hardwares exported from 1832 to 1842, was twenty-nine per cent.; but during the Free Trade period the advance has been as much as sixty-one per cent.

The value of our iron and steel exports has been more than doubled during the same period.

A Sheffield manufacturer writes as follows, respecting the trades connected with that town, and the social condition of the workmen: " The trade of Sheffield is generally good, to a degree and for a length of time without parallel. There are exceptions in the smaller sections of the cutlery trade, but these do not affect the general report. There is abundance of work, wages are generally better, and without those drawbacks attendant on bad trade which render the actual receipts of the workman less than their nominal amount. Wages in several trades have considerably advanced, and that without any necessity for 'strikes ;' the demands were readily conceded."

To the same effect a gentleman who is intimately acquainted with the state of trade in Birmingham writes : "That all the principal trades in Birmingham are in a much better and more flourishing condition than they were six or seven years ago is a fact too evident to be denied. In the button-trade the work-people have had an advance of wages within the last six months, and are working more hours (at piecework) than usual. This is one of the most extensive trades in Birmingham, and there are constantly new inventions and designs secured by patent or registration. This frequently increases the demand in the department in which it occurs, while it causes a temporary stagnation in other branches of the trade, so that much of the prosperity of each branch depends on the ingenuity of the manufacturer. This remark applies to most of the trades here, so that several articles formerly in great demand are almost

entirely superseded by new inventions. This circumstance, while it occasions individual loss, tends to
increase the general prosperity of the trade.—The
jewellery trade has also many branches, all of which are
so flourishing at the present time that there are more
workmen wanted than can be obtained. A few years
since not half the workmen were employed.—The
manufacturers of japanned articles, tea-trays, work-
boxes, door plates, etc., commonly known as the
'Japan trade,' has increased the last two years;
skilled and tasteful workmen obtain a high rate of
wages.—Engineers and machinists are much more
fully employed than they were a few years since;
second-rate workmen are now receiving as much as
first-rate workmen could have secured five years since.
Brass founders have shared in the general prosperity,
—the trade is in a very healthful condition, notwithstanding a slight depression through the increased price
of the raw material.—The gun trade fluctuates much,
which, as an advocate of peace, I do not myself deplore.
At present, however, this also is full of activity. The
majority of work-people in the Birmingham trades are
paid so much per gross, or per hundred gross, for
work. The weekly amount of wages obtained by
girls is from two shillings to six shillings; women
from six shillings to ten shillings; jobbing-men from
twelve shillings to fifteen shillings; mechanics and
tool-makers from twenty shillings to thirty-five shillings. Those employed in particular trades requiring
great taste and skill, such as painters in the Japanese
trade, earn frequently from £3 to £4 a week."

SECTION III.

EFFECTS OF FREE TRADE AS SEEN IN THE CONDITION OF THE
MINOR BRANCHES OF INDUSTRY.

Having inquired into the condition of the more important branches of industry, it will assist us in forming a complete view of the state of labour, and the activity which generally prevails, if we glance at a few of the minor trades.

I.—CABINET MAKERS. In many respects, this trade furnishes a valuable test of the condition of the middle and working classes. Among our more intelligent operatives, and those who occupy the grades immediately above them, nothing so soon, or so surely, indicates increased means, as an improvement in the furniture of their dwellings. By carefully observing the fluctuation in this important item of expenditure between deal and rosewood, we might construct a social thermometer of considerable interest and accuracy. Our report on this branch of industry is derived from the communications of an intelligent manufacturer, who is well acquainted both with the wholesale and order departments of the business. The means of direct knowledge are more accessible with the wholesale department, since this is comprised within a comparatively few London houses, who supply all parts of the kingdom with ready made goods; and, at the same time, this department furnishes us with the more valuable social test, since goods of that description are purchased chiefly by the less affluent classes. It is believed, on accurate data, that the cabinet makers of the metropolis, residing in the districts of Finsbury and Tottenham Court Road, have done a third more business during the last two years than formerly, and this implies a similar increase in the dealings of their wholesale customers throughout the kingdom. During the same period, the order trade has been generally good, and payments punctual. The best proof of the accuracy of these statements is the advanced price of materials, in the face of greatly increased importations, and a considerable scarcity of labour. " Quebec pine," which was bought last year at one shilling and four pence per foot, now costs two shillings, and the superior article known as " St. John's pine " has risen twenty per cent. within the last three months. Wages, which averaged three or four years ago about twenty shillings a week, now average twenty-six shillings, and it is difficult to obtain a good workman at any price. Complaints are common among masters that their workmen have the game of employment almost entirely in their own hands. Instances of gross neglect are, unhappily, frequent, and yet the defaulter can scarcely be called to account, since the reply he would give would probably be the practical one of immediately quitting the shop, and obtaining an engagement elsewhere. The possibility of such conduct proves the excellent state of trade, but it is difficult to mention it without censure. It is painful to contemplate the improvidence and want of self-respect which it displays, and we can only hope that they who practise it will learn wisdom, without being compelled to learn it, when too late, by physical privations ; though, if such be the result, they will be indebted for it to the bounty of Providence, rather than their own deserts.

II.—The WATCH AND CLOCK TRADES. This branch of industry may also be regarded as affording, by its prosperous or adverse state, a sure sign of the general condition of the community, since articles of luxury and elegance are seldom bought, at least by Englishmen, while the ruder wants are unsupplied. Mr. Laing, in his "Notes" on the present state of the continent, remarks, that a foreigner will often make his appearance with an enormous gold chain, and a magnificent diamond ring, when his larder and wardrobe are destitute of articles of ordinary comfort; but the case is otherwise with ourselves. Here, whether wisely or not, the first thought is generally given to substantial comforts, the second or third to personal appearance, so that the extent to which articles of elegance are consumed in England indicates the prevalence of a much higher degree of social well-being, than consumption to the same extent abroad. Our watch manufacturers are not entirely dependent on the home market. A considerable trade is done in watches, or rather in the parts of which they are composed, with the United States and our colonies. Few trades, which are concerned only with the production of a single article, are divided into so many branches as the watch-trade. The dial, the pointers, the case, the springs, the chains, the brass-work, the glass, all constitute so many different departments, none of which can succeed without the rest. On these accounts, a virtual monopoly is given to those districts where the trade has long flourished. Only eighteen miles separate Birmingham and Coventry, yet the attempts which have been made to transplant the trade from the latter to the former place, have to some extent failed, and could not be accomplished without a very disproportionate outlay of capital. The superiority which one district thus acquires over another district in the same country, is acquired, for still stronger reasons, by a country in which the trade has long been established over another in which it is quite new. Unless fiscal regulations intervene, or time works a change, France and England will continue to be the watchmakers for the United States, since the cost of carriage per watch across the Atlantic is much less than would be requisite to pay a manufacturer for attempting its production. At the present moment, both the foreign and home branches of the trade are in a highly prosperous condition. Large orders for exportation are so abundant that orders of a smaller amount are executed with difficulty. We are assured by a Coventry manufacturer that masters cannot get their work done fast enough, and that skilful, industrious workmen were never doing better. No reduction whatever has taken place since food became cheaper; workmen are receiving the same nominal prices as they did seven years ago, while superior abundance of work makes a difference of probably one-third to their weekly income.

III.—ENGINEERING TRADES. This extensive and varied department of industry is one of peculiar interest, on account of the close relation it sustains to our general progress as a manufacturing and commercial people. It constitutes, in a very literal sense, the backbone and sinews of our national strength. To this source we owe the machines which keep fifty

or sixty thousand spindles in motion, which hurry
along our railway trains at the rate of sixty miles an
hour, or speed the " Great Britain," with its living
freight, across the Atlantic and Pacific Oceans in
eighty-four days. The great difference between the
present century and the past is expressed by this
single fact:—we have substituted mechanical for
human power; arms of iron instead of the bones and
sinews of men; and by this change we have crowded
upon our soil, the entire population of which does
not exceed eight-and-twenty millions, available force
equal to the combined energies of 600,000,000, or
two-thirds of the entire population of the globe.
This superiority over other nations in the mechanical arts, gives us the virtual monopoly we enjoy in
providing for the ruder wants of mankind. Our
mechanics, strictly so called, make the machinery
which makes our wealth; our manufacturers cannot
increase without additional orders being sent to their
workshops, and hence their condition is entitled to
considerable weight as a test of general prosperity.
As a proof that business in this department is plentiful, we need only point to the famous strike which
continued during the first four months of the year
1852, and which, though perhaps wisely precipitated
by the masters, who, seeing the battle was inevitable,
chose to fight on their own ground, was the direct
result of arbitrary demands on the part of the men;
demands which are never enforced in slack seasons.
During the whole of the past year business has been
accumulating; at many establishments the men are
working seven or eight days per week, and orders are
postponed without the prospect of being speedily

executed. Many cotton mills are standing idle,
or are delayed in completion owing to the difficulty
of getting them fitted up with the requisite machinery. The following are the rates of wages
which are paid at the present time by one of the
largest firms in Manchester. No change has taken
place in them for several years ; the wages which were
paid in dear times being paid still, when the necessaries of life are from ten to forty per cent. cheaper :—

WEEKLY.

		s.		s.				s.		.s.
Millwrights	from	30	to	34	Strikers	from	18	to	20
Moulders	,,	30	,,	34	Planers	,,	12	,,	24
Pattern Makers	,,	26	,,	36	Turners	,,	24	,,	32
Fitters .	,,	26	,,	32	Labourers	,,	15	,,	18
Smiths ·	,,	20	,,	32	Drillers	,,	5	,,	18

The above particulars are corroborated by a communication from another firm, employing upwards of
a thousand workmen, from which we give the following extract: " Five or six years ago our workmen
were receiving the same rate of wages as at present,
but then 'piecework' was general, while now that
mode of labour is the exception. In piecework a
man usually earned from fifteen to twenty per cent. in
addition to his weekly rate of wages, and the balance
so earned was paid him every ten weeks. The change
from piecework to day work was occasioned, to a
great extent, by the strike of last year. Nor is
this the only misfortune. which has been occasioned by that event. It caused the separation of
many men from masters whom they and their
families had served for years, so that the feeling of
unity, of sympathy and interest between the employer

and the employed, is much impaired, most of the workmen in our and similar establishments being known only to the foremen, and not to the masters. I trust, if agitations are avoided, we shall again become better known to each other, and by this means a more confidential feeling will spring up between us." We quote these remarks, chiefly, because they are very suggestive of the kind of relationship which subsists between the employer and the employed in our large towns, and on this account we commend them to the special attention of those persons who, in their ignorant abuse of the factory system, denounce the former as heartless task-masters, and the latter as imbruted slaves. Such a state of things exists only in their fervid imagination. Ask any one who can give an answer from the results of his own observation, what is the comparative quality of the tie which connects master and workman in the manufacturing and non-manufacturing districts of the kingdom, and he will at once declare that, omitting exceptions on both sides, it is, on the whole, more liberal and just in the former than in the latter. It has been vaunted as the peculiar excellence of agricultural employment that it produces a beneficial dependence of the workman on the employer, which often continues in the same families for many generations. We pass over much which might be said respecting the influence of such connexion ; we refer not to the degradation which almost always exists on the one side, and the arrogance which is too often manifested on the other; we wish merely to indicate the. fact that here among the masses of Manchester, and in respect to a thousand workmen, a number representing an amount of farm-

labour equal to the cultivation of some thirty thousand
acres, an employer speaks with paternal kindness of
men who, with their families, have served him for years;
of " mutual feelings of sympathy and interest," and
recognises the cultivation of a personal acquaintance
with them as a master's privilege and duty.

IV.—The BUILDING PROFESSION includes within it
an important fraternity of trades, whose prosperity not
only serves as an accurate social test, but directly
influences the welfare of a large portion of the population. The erection of new buildings can never go
on to any great extent, unless sustained by the
improving condition of the people. In adverse times
no tradesman thinks of increasing his expenditure;
the house which has been tenanted for years past,
which was entered upon when life and business were
young, and subsistence had to be won by rigid
economy, is still retained; the tempting idea of a
residence outside the town, where quietness and fresh
air might make up for the day's exhaustion, is
abandoned to better times. But let business revive,
let his shop be crowded with customers, his annual
profits double themselves, and the builder is soon put
in requisition to carry out the plans so long held in
abeyance. It is so with the mill-owner and capitalist.
We saw few factories in course of erection twelve
years ago; *that* was not the time to give the rein to
enterprise; our manufacturers were then guiltless of
the heinous offence which has recently been described
in the parodied language of Holy Writ as that of
" adding mill to mill." We saw then few quarries
opening on our hill tops, and sending their disinterred
strata to the erection of villages rising, as if by magic;

in the valley below: such sights are the heritage of better times. It is so, also, with the working-man. To him as to all others food is the first requisite, then clothing; but when plenty of work enables him easily to purchase these, a better house is his next desideratum, and it is pleasing to observe how, in this respect, a gradual improvement goes on in prosperous years. Hence the trades to which we have referred furnish us with an important indication of the general condition of the community; when other classes of society are prosperous *they* are prosperous, but when the nation is depressed they are depressed too.

One of the tests of prosperity in the building trades is *the quantity of timber consumed.* A most extraordinary advance has taken place, since the reduction of the duties on foreign timber, in the quantity imported for consumption into this country. In 1843 the quantity of unsawn timber and deals amounted to 1,317,615 loads, the following year it was 1,481,357 loads; during 1845 and 1846 the railway mania gave an unnatural impetus to consumption, and in the latter of those two years we imported no less than 2,024,939 loads. Subsequently, the quantity diminished, till it was acted upon by the more genial influence of Free Trade. In 1851 our consumption exceeded by 12,000 loads the exaggerated imports of 1846, and the following extract from the yearly circular of Messrs. Churchill and Sim, extensive timber-merchants, will show that the prosperity which this indicates has gone on increasing: " The wood trade has largely partaken of the general prosperity of the country during 1852. In 1851 its sudden extension in London might be ascribed to local causes, peculiar to, and centering in, the metropolis; in 1852, without these local influences, more business has been done, with more spirit and energy, with better prices and on an extended area, so that the indications of a successful year are strongly marked here (in London) as well as the other great ports of the United Kingdom, in all branches of the wood trade." We learn on the same authority that the importation of timber into London during 1852 exceeded 1200 cargoes, an amount closely parallel to 1851, both years showing an increase of 50 per cent. on those preceding, the average of which was 800 cargoes. Deals, battens, and other kinds of sawn wood, have taken an immense start during 1852, the number of pieces imported having been 6,800,000, in place of the previous average of 4,900,000. The extent of our obligations to Free Trade for this increased consumption of timber is proved by the large proportion which has been drawn from foreign countries, with which we were formerly forbidden to do any business by heavy differential duties. The greater part of our increased importation of sawn timber is from the Baltic ports of Sweden, which sent us, in 1852, 985,000 pieces of deals, and 86,000 battens, more than the average of the previous five years.

But timber forms only a part of the materials used in building; besides this, there are brick, stone, slate, iron, lead, glass, etc., almost each of which points as to a different trade. The repeal of the duties on *bricks* and *glass* has contributed, in a great measure, to the activity of building operations. It is more difficult than formerly to estimate the quantity of bricks consumed within the United Kingdom, but from the preparations which were extensively made to supply the increased demand which was anticipated from the repeal of the duty, and the high prices which have since been maintained, it must have exceeded, during the last two years, by a very high figure, its former amount. The extensive brick yards which have been opened near most of our large towns, but especially in the neighbourhoods of London, Birmingham, and Manchester, together with the improved methods in which the manufacture is carried on, and the higher rate of wages paid to the workmen, indicate the beneficial impulse which our Free Trade policy has communicated even to the lowest grades of labour. In one respect the glazing business has sustained an injury by the repeal of the duty on glass. The light thin glass formerly in use for the windows of houses and shops is rapidly being superseded by an article of a thicker and more expensive quality, but less liable to break. This change, however, is an advantage to the consumer, and the glazier is amply compensated by the new uses to which glass is now applied. We have a general type of these in the Crystal Palace. The adaptations to which that structure has given rise are already numerous; the frontage of shops no longer consists of broad blank walls relieved by a series of lantern-lights; combinations of iron and glass have fairly supplanted wood and brick. For strictly domestic objects glass is entering upon a new career of utility; flooring, roofing, partitioning, may now be executed in glass, and the time seems not far distant when the communistic wishes of M. Sue's hero will be realized, and every good citizen live within walls of the same material.

An inference of some interest may be drawn from the comparative state of wages among BRICKLAYERS AND MASONS, as given below. It cannot be thought that the latter have occasion for less skill than the former. The bricklayer finds his materials fashioned ready to his hands; the brickmaker's mould has given to them their requisite form, and his chief business is to raise them regularly upon each other; while the mason has to fashion his materials for himself, and that not by a mould, but by the dexterous use of the chisel, and according to a given pattern. It may safely be asserted that the stonemason's art requires more skilled labour than the bricklayer's, while it makes at least an equal demand upon the merely physical energies. Yet the bricklayer receives, at the present time, higher wages than the stonemason; while the stonemason's remain as they were six years ago, the bricklayer's have risen five per cent. We may carry the observation a step lower. While none of the occupations connected with building have suffered any reduction of wages, two only, viz., those of the bricklayer and the *labourer*, have experienced a positive advance. The labourer now earns only six pence a day less than the stonemason, the carpenter, the plumber, and glazier; only four pence a day less than the painter, and the same money as the slater. Perhaps the proper explanation of this circumstance is, that Free Trade has given a powerful impetus to the erection of dwellings for the middle and working classes which are chiefly built of brick, and that thus demand has got the better of skill. But the circumstance itself seems to have a deeper import;

we recognise here, in another shape, the leading feature of the present industrial movement—it is emphatically one for the masses; it is one in which, while all classes are the better for it, the largest share of benefit falls to the lot of the working man.

We subjoin the rates of wages actually paid at the present time by one of the largest building firms in Lancashire, premising that no reduction has taken place through the advent of cheaper times, while in the instances just referred to an advance of about five per cent. has been experienced.

WEEKLY.

		s.		s.			s.		s.
Excavators	from	18	to	21	Carpenters	from	27	to	30
Bricklayers	,,	30	,,	32	Plumbers & Glaziers	27	,,	30
Labourers	,,	21	,,	24	Painters	,,	26	,,	29
Masons	,,	27	,,	30	Slaters	,,	24	,,	27

V.—We will now briefly notice two important members of the fraternity of minor trades which are closely connected with the social and physical condition of the working classes. The BOOT AND SHOE MANUFACTURE affords the means of livelihood to a considerable section of the population, and stands on a level with hosiery in point of accuracy as a test of physical well-being. Applying to this branch of industry the same rule as that which has been applied in those already considered, viz., the price of materials and labour, we infer that its condition during the last year has been one of unusual prosperity, an inference which is sustained by the testimony of persons of long experience in connexion with it. The Messrs. Pownall, extensive leather brokers, say in their annual circular for 1853 : "The year which has just closed has doubtless been a favourable one for leather manufactures in almost every department. Raw goods at the commencement of the year were at low rates, and circumstances have taken place which have given to leather an increased value in a greater degree than for several years past. Among the causes of this advance in the price of leather, none is more apparent than the increased prosperity of the working classes, who are the great consumers of leather." In this account we trace the usual process by which trade is invigorated; cheap material, arising from abundant imports; ability, through cheap food, to purchase on the part of the people, and a consumption resulting from these causes which at length reacts upon the price both of the material and the labour expended upon it, giving to both a higher, though still a legitimate, value. During the last six months orders have poured into Northampton at a rate which has left the supply of labour far behind. Not one-half of the orders in hand can be executed for a considerable period. The workmen have seized a time of prosperity in order to demand an advance of wages, with which the manufacturers have generally complied, and they are now paid at higher rates than were ever known in the annals of the wholesale trade. In those districts where the workmen depend upon retail orders, no advance of wages has taken place for the past ten years, but at the same time no reduction whatever has been made during the era of cheap food, so that the greater abundance of employment and provisions renders them incomparably better off than they have been at any moment within that period. It may not be inappropriate to repeat here the observation we have had occasion to make respecting some other trades as to the injurious effects of " strikes " upon the condition of the workman. Fourteen years ago the " masters " in our large towns were in reality what they still designate themselves, " manufacturers " of boots and shoes. They kept twenty, thirty, or forty workmen, according to the demands of their business, giving them the work to execute on the premises. About that time " strikes " became prevalent. The " union " insisted upon the work being done at home, where the master's direct oversight could not be exercised. This gave rise to serious misunderstandings, which so affected the interests of the employers, that they gradually transferred their business to the manufacturing districts of the trade, and, instead of employing a corps of workmen of their own, sent wholesale orders to Daventry and Northampton. This change, which owed its origin entirely to the obstinacy of the workmen, turned out altogether to their disadvantage. The work was done at greatly reduced prices ; various small articles used in the trade, technically termed " finding," such as hemp and wax, and costing about a shilling per week, instead of being " found " by the master, as in former times, were left to the expense of the workman, and, when a considerable number worked together, he often had to pay for the space occupied while at work, as the Nottingham operative pays for his loom. Such changes may have been inevitable, but they were at least introduced by the *protective* organization of the trade. If no " union " had interfered on its behalf those changes could not have occurred ; the natural demand for labour would have prevented them, and

P

the trade would probably have been in a much better state. It will be well indeed if past experience teach our operatives, in a season of prosperity, the virtues of justice and moderation.

VI. The condition of JOURNEYMEN TAILORS AND CLOTHIERS has of late years attracted much attention. The testimony of medical men respecting the insalubrity of their employment, has extensively enlisted public sympathy on their behalf. In point of fact no class of workmen are more injured by long hours, badly-ventilated rooms, and other evils springing from the covetous negligence of employers. The trade itself has suffered from a variety of causes, which must be considered if we would properly appreciate its present state. It is entered without difficulty, requiring only an inexpensive outfit; it is one of those which suggest themselves most readily to the parents and guardians of the poor, as lying sufficiently proximate to their condition, and yet offering something better than a pauper's maintenance. The cause which has exerted the most powerful influence in depressing wages is, that its "mysteries" are not, like the hardier trade of the smith or the bricklayer, placed by their own nature beyond the province of women and children. In consequence of these circumstances the market has been inundated with cheap labour, a large proportion of the work has been executed away from the premises of the employer, and probably the larger half of the trade has fallen into the hands of "sloppers." Various attempts have been made to bolster up wages; in several of the more important strikes the tailors have borne a conspicuous part, and more than once they have petitioned for the interference of the legislature. It is an ungrateful task to speak slightingly of the efforts by which any body of operatives seek to prolong the value of their labour, since labour, in some form or other, constitutes their only means of subsistence; but, at the same time, it must be confessed that such efforts are false in theory and dishonest in morals, since they attempt what is impracticable, and, in doing so, withhold from others, as far as their own labour is concerned, the right they claim for themselves, that of supplying their wants as cheaply as they can. Those efforts have failed, the law of cheapness has maintained itself, and establishments in which it would have been deemed a degradation, some years ago, to be connected, in the remotest way, with the " slop" trade, now regularly entrust their lighter work to the hands of women. The efforts of Mr. Kingsley, and his associates in the cause of co-operation, have established several societies. on that principle, which, by the aid of special appeals; and special funds, have been enabled to maintain their ground. But the fault is that the trade is overstocked for the ordinary demand, and the sooner a few thousands find employment in some other line the better. Yet Free Trade has brought even here a temporary relief. The present demand for labour is barely equalled by the supply. The population requires more clothing. Free Trade has cheapened materials, increased the means of purchase, and raised the standard of personal attire. All this is beneficial to the tailor; employment is more plentiful than it has been for years; wages are firm or on the advance; the number of " tramps" at the chief club houses considerably diminished; and at the present moment the wholesale clothiers of Bradford, Leeds, and Manchester are zealously advertising for a large number of workmen, to whom they promise constant employment and good wages.

SECTION IV.

EFFECTS OF FREE TRADE ON INTERESTS FORMERLY PROTECTED.

We have so far considered the effects of Free Trade as they are manifested in the present state of the commerce and manufactures of the United Kingdom, and hitherto we have met with nothing which can invalidate the general conclusion, that those interests upon which the manufacturing classes depend for subsistence were never in a more satisfactory condition. We have seen the value of our exports advance more than eighty per cent. since 1842, and our imports augment in an equal ratio; cargoes of foreign corn, sufficient to support a fourth part of our population, have been consigned to our warehouses; our shambles have been replenished with more than a million head of cattle imported from abroad; we use half as much more tea, and two-thirds as much more sugar, as we did ten years ago; and the means of temporal well-being are now possessed by the working man to a greater extent than at any past period in our history. We have seen every branch of industry, from the gigantic cotton manufacture to the humblest species of handicraft, flourishing in unwonted vigour, shedding its fruits at the feet of the capitalist, only that they may be distributed, as by the hand of a benignant Providence, among those whose labour is their all. It is, however, incumbent upon us, having undertaken to delineate the effects of Free Trade, to include in our observation the entire landscape. Our object is not to portray the ideal, but the actual; our pole-star is not beauty, but truth. The blasted oak, the up-heaved granite, the burning lava, the desolated valley, must, if they really lie before us, be coloured by the pencil as faithfully as the peaceful river and the verdant lawn. From the cheerful neighbourhood of the factory we must visit our farmsteads, and those distant possessions which boast the protection of Great Britain; we must honestly contemplate, if such scenes exist, extensive domains, once smiling with fertility, given back to nature; famous cities, at one time the queens of commerce, with docks and warehouses which were the admiration of the world, fast becoming, like Tyre of old, a place where the fishermen will spread their nets; and imperial dependencies, once regarded as the brightest jewels in our regal diadem, now sinking in decay. Free Trade has unquestionably benefited our commerce and manufactures; let us see, therefore, whether it has destroyed our agriculture, our shipping, and our colonies.

· I. AGRICULTURE, as represented by the body of British landowners and farmers, is the most important interest which is said to have suffered from Free Trade, and therefore demands our first consideration. In order to appreciate the correctness and the value of the complaints which have been raised, it will be necessary to glance at its relative magnitude as compared with the other industrial interests of the country, and inquire into its present, as compared with its past, condition.   We must here at once distinguish between the different elements involved in the question.   The most important of these relates to the cultivation of the land, without any reference to either its owners or its occupiers, as the source from which our population must always derive its largest supply of food; the next is the condition of those who are actually engaged in agricultural labour, since they still constitute one of the largest sections of the population, and their welfare ought, on this account, to weigh much, both with the philanthropist and legislator ; the third element consists of the interests of the owners and occupiers of the land, who, though numerically a very inconsiderable part of the community, are yet, apart from all considerations of equity, entitled to high regard on the ground of their intelligence, patriotism, and general influence in the social scale.   These elements, which are all mixed up in the vague phrase " Agricultural interest,' are related to each other, though not identical.   There is logic in justice, but not in injustice.   When agriculture is in a prosperous state, when land is being enclosed; draining, manuring, and other improvements rapidly progressing, and every acre is made, by dint of science, to yield the maximum amount of produce, then none of its dependent interests can fail of being prosperous also.   The people will be in the enjoyment of cheap food, the labourer will be well employed, and the farmer and landlord will be in receipt of a fair revenue.   But it is possible that the class which consists of the proprietors and chief occupants of the soil may, by virtue of unjust laws, enjoy large profits, while the land is miserably cultivated, and the labourer barely sustaining existence. In estimating, therefore, the influence of Free Trade upon the "agricultural interest," we must analyse the general question into its several parts, and decide upon an impartial examination of the whole.

1. With regard to the proper cultivation of the land, it is impossible to exaggerate its importance to the nation at large. Viewing it only as a question of capital and profits, its magnitude places it in the very first rank among those which now occupy the public mind. What a vast quantity of *manufacturing material* is presented in the soil of England! How immense the sums of money which, in one way or other, have been employed upon it! It is surely an important matter to work up this material to the best advantage. If there were just reasons for thinking that twenty-five per cent. of the whole was annually lost through imperfect management, it would be worth the cousideration of the choicest intellects of the nation by what means the loss might be prevented for the future. Our sense of the economical importance of this question is increased when we reflect that it relates to the subsistence of the people, for which we are dependent to a great extent upon home produce. The ships of Great Britain would be insufficient to supply us with wheat from abroad commensurate with the wants of the population, even if other nations could furnish us with it in such vast quantities. Thus the cheapness of food, together with the consequent cheapness of our manufactures, depends upon the state of our agriculture. This question is no party one; we will not

yield it up to farmers and landlords; the land is a trust committed to their care, and though we have no wish to disturb those rights which, however doubtful in their origin, have been confirmed by time, yet self-interest prompts us to see that they do their duty, or at least to be assured that no legislative enactments offer a premium upon neglect. It may be said, that we have a guarantee that the greatest possible amount of produce will be obtained from the soil, because of the pecuniary interests of the occupier: We have such a guarantee *now*, but we had it not formerly. While the corn laws existed the farmer had no motive to increased production, since this, if carried beyond the point required by the natural increase of the population, would have issued in a fall of prices, and proved injurious to his interests. He had then no motive to undersell his neighbours; on the contrary, he had every possible motive to keep the price of grain only just below that at which the ports would be open to the foreigner, since this enabled him to realize the highest amount of profit on the lowest amount of capital and skill. Accordingly, under a protective *régime*, our agriculture advanced but slowly. All ideas of increased production were confined to the enclosing of more land;—a rude expedient when compared with the increased productiveness of the same number of acres by means of more scientific culture. Our farmers were, for the most part, men of tradition and routine; they tilled the soil and managed their stock as their fathers had done two centuries before them. Their farm-buildings seemed as if they had been raised by chance, without any order or visible adaptation; fences were suffered to attain a luxuriance of growth which would suggest the idea that they were regarded as the chief source of agricultural profit, instead of being simply designed for demarcation and division; while the large plots of ground which lay uncultivated, the number of broad, useless ditches, and the practice of long fallows, harmonised with the supposition that agriculture was taken up as a mere amusement, rather than that it opened a field of stern competition, where success was to be won only by intelligence, enterprise, economy, and well-directed toil. It is estimated that if all England were cultivated as well as the counties of Northumberland and Lincoln, it would be easy to raise from the soil twice the amount of produce which is now obtained. Here, then, is a loss, traceable to sheer neglect, not of twenty-five per cent., but of one hundred per cent., on the raw material of agriculture. In this way, the national trust has hitherto been abused; the estates of the landed proprietors have not been permitted to yield their proper quota to the sum of national well-being; where we ought to have had two quarters of wheat we have only had one, and the abuse was perpetuated by laws which secured to the farmer for his one quarter the same sum of money which should have sufficed for two.

2. In order to make out the beneficial influence of Free Trade on our agricultural interests, it is by no means necessary to prove that agriculture is at the present moment as profitable to those who are engaged in it as it was under our protective system. The permanent utility of the change to agriculture itself, may render inevitable a temporary diminution of profits. Measures which are in the highest degree

beneficial to the bulk of a population may *for a time* be anything but beneficial to particular sections of it. The immediate effect of Free Trade upon interests formerly protected, is to test their real value to the nation, to ascertain whether they can profitably support themselves without receiving their accustomed subsidy from the pockets of the people. As soon as they are exposed to competition, the persons engaged in them are obliged to task their utmost resources, and apply to their development the highest amount of skill and energy. For a time the struggle may be hard, and less profits may be realized than on the old system, but if, in a national point of view, such interests are worth cultivating, the foreigner will soon be driven from the market. If they are not worth cultivating they will soon become extinct, nor is there any reason, in such circumstances, to wish their perpetuation. Our agriculture is just now undergoing this wholesome ordeal; after ages of prescriptive right, our farmers have to contend for existence; that command of the British market which they have hitherto secured by unjust laws, they must now secure by superior energy, or abandon it to their rivals. But Free Trade is not to be blamed for this struggle. If smaller profits are for a time the result, it is not to be imputed as a fault to the change which has been brought about in our commercial system. The blame, if any exists, must be ascribed to protection alone. It was this system which enfeebled the resources of agriculture, nursed it into sickliness, kept the farmers, as a body, behind the age, and made such a crisis as the present necessary, whenever the nation should insist on doing justice to itself.

Nothing is plainer than the course which all who are directly concerned in the success of agriculture ought at once to pursue. The path is no new one; it has been trodden already by all the great producing interests of the country. Our cotton, silk, woollen, and flax manufactures have all had the same season of peril, when the only alternative was a fresh development of industrial skill, or ruin. This was very recently the case, as we have seen, with one great branch of the hosiery business. Our stocking frames would have been silent by this time, and a lucrative trade have left our shores for ever, if the manufacturers of Leicester and Nottingham had folded their arms in despair as soon as they experienced the impossibility of competing on the old system with the cheap labour of Saxony. But, instead of adopting such a course, they invented new machinery, set to work again with greater zeal than ever, and in two years completely defeated their rivals. Our agriculturalists must do the same. There is no reason why we should not have as great a superiority in agriculture as in manufactures. The farmer must become a man of science; mere manual dexterity, hereditary maxims, or even individual experience, will not suffice for the exigencies of the times. He must be familiar with chemistry, an intelligent student of the writings of Liebig and Faraday. By dint of scientific knowledge, combined with practical skill, our manufacturers have achieved success; our farmers must use the same weapons. Our leading manufacturers send their sons to the universities and public schools in order that they may be the better fitted to succeed them in carrying on their business; why should not our farmers do the same with those of their sons whom they intend devoting to agriculture? Why should not agricultural colleges, such as the Royal Agricultural College of Cirencester, of which his Royal Highness, Prince Albert, is President, be established by the public spirit of our landed proprietary in every part of England? In the United Kingdom there are upwards of four hundred " Agricultural Societies" and more than two hundred " Farmers' Clubs ;"—let these extensive organizations be at once turned to some practical end, by providing suitable institutions, where farmers' sons, on leaving school, may pass a year or two in learning the principles of the business in which they are to spend their life. Much more care is bestowed upon this subject in France and the United States than in this country. Scientific catechisms, in which agriculture is developed as a system, are there introduced into the primary and secondary schools. The pupil of twelve years of age is instructed in vegetable anatomy and physiology, the physical properties of soils, the action of ameliorators, stimulants, and manures, so that by the time he engages in farm work he has acquired a thorough mastery of the principles of his profession, and is enabled to estimate at their true value the traditions which may have descended to him with his paternal estate. France and the United States are the chief rivals with whom our own farmers will have to contend. Let the latter enter the contest with the same intellectual weapons : *Fas est ab hoste doceri.*

3. We rank among the chief benefits which Free Trade has so far conferred upon our agricultural interests, the diffusion of more enlightened senti-

ments among those who are directly engaged in them. With true English mettle, the farmer has already recovered from his depression, and is resolutely bent upon beating his opponents. The National Society for the Protection of Agriculture has just become defunct, and the Duke of Richmond, who presided at its obsequies, accepted on the part of the landed interest the new era which has commenced. There is a calm, but steady, movement going on; a determined effort at self-regeneration which cannot fail of success. While intelligent landowners are pointing out new kinds of crops, the practical farmer embodies the results of his experience in elaborate essays; and lectures which, ten years ago, would have been delivered to bare walls, are now listened to with eagerness. One of the most enterprising of the agricultural body, Mr. Mechi, whose model farm has been familiarised to thousands through the medium of the "Illustrated London News," recently delivered a lecture before the Chelmsford Literary Institute, in which he speaks without reserve of the present condition of agriculture, and the course which the farmer must pursue: "Our great manufacturing prosperity," he says, "has arisen from a diminution of price, and an enormously increased consumption, and I have a right to censure our national agriculture if it has not availed itself of similar advantages to produce similar results. Has the land yielded its maximum of fertility? Oh no! Has science or mechanical skill done its utmost? Most certainly not. Has agriculture been treated as a business? As certainly not, and our landed proprietors have yet to learn the fullest development of the trade of agriculture." The spread of such views will soon revolutionize the whole province of farming. The " trade sentiment," thoroughly applied, is all that is requisite to place it on a firm basis. Manures will be better adapted to the nature of different soils, the necessity of long fallows will be superseded by a new rotation of crops, greater economy will be introduced in the making of manure, and the maintenance of stock, as well as the distribution of the land; useless hedges will be destroyed, the corners of fields, and the large spaces now occupied by unnecessary ponds and ditches, will be brought into cultivation. Probably, also, the parks of our aristocracy will concede a portion of their wide area to the sternly economical spirit of the age, and instead of supporting, as in times gone by, herds of deer, as if to furnish a contrast to the bespent and care-worn labourer at his comfortless home, contribute a larger quota to the income of their owners, and the sustenance of the community. If capital should do for England what hand-labour and the subdivision of land have done for Belgium—convert it into a garden, in which every inch of ground is covered with some kind of produce, our landowners need not be afraid of low prices ; increased production will more than make up for any deficiency in that respect, while their interests will be removed from a shifting and artificial to a solid and natural foundation.

4. Since any great change in the general condition of agriculture must necessarily occupy a considerable space of time, it is not to be expected that the beneficial effects of Free Trade have as yet been fully developed, but still there are abundant facts to show us that the tide of improvement has set in, and that

the immense capital which is represented by the soil will, in future, be more thoroughly worked. The evidence of well-informed persons is unanimous on this point. A few months since, at the opening of the present parliament, Lord Grey demanded, without eliciting any denial, whether "from one end of the country to the other, drainage and similar improvements were not going on faster than could ever have been imagined?" To the same effect is the testimony of Lord Panmure, whom all will recognise as an authority in reference to Scotland. In a speech delivered at Arbroath, September 30th, 1852, his lordship says, " Whether it be to the increased energy of the tenant farmers, or whether it be to better devised means for the culture of the soil, this I know, that, to all appearance at least, agriculture is as much sought after by the people of this country as a means of earning their bread as ever, for at present *there is no land in the market*. There has been no land vacant throughout Scotland where the remark has not been made that, if it were taken, higher prices would be given for it than have been received for the last four or five years."* All the information we have been able to obtain from private sources corresponds with these facts. The existence of strikes among the farm labourers in many districts affords unequivocal proof, as far as they are concerned, of a better state of things. The wages to which they submitted when provisions were thirty or forty per cent. dearer they now find out to be too small, and exact an advance which their employers do not think it expedient to refuse. A gentleman and magistrate,

* "Times," October 4th, 1852.

who, from his position, is well acquainted with the agricultural districts of Wiltshire and Somersetshire, writes thus : " The agricultural labourers in the parish where I live have had their wages raised during the last year from eight shillings per week to nine shillings. Many of the same class in South Wilts have struck for an advance from seven shillings a week, which was, and I believe is at present, the rate of wages, to nine shillings a week. The farmers are willing to give eight shillings, but this the men will not accept. From the rise which has occurred in the price of produce, it is my opinion that the farmers will be obliged to give nine shillings. The price of most kinds of agricultural produce has much advanced, that of cheese, especially, is considerably higher ; mutton, which five or six years ago was from four pence to five pence a pound, is now from seven pence halfpenny to eight pence. The scarcity of labourers begins to be felt, partly from the great emigration which has taken place, and partly from their being able to get work in towns and manufactories. My own opinion is that the present prosperity of the country is based on a secure foundation." To the same effect is the testimony of a gentleman residing in North Devon. He says, " The improvement which has taken place in these districts is evidenced by the great diminution of pauperism. The number of paupers receiving relief from our union, which comprises about thirty parishes, in the last quarter of the years 1848, 1850, and 1852, respectively, is as follows :—

Last quarter of 1848 .... 174 Paupers
Ditto   1850 .... 132 Ditto
Ditto   1852 .... 109 Ditto

"I have not been able to get the exact numbers for the Torrington Union, but believe there is diminution on about the same scale. The condition of the agricultural population in the north of Devon is decidedly better than it was six or seven years ago. Land is letting, and letting on terms equally high as it did under the corn laws, and in many cases the wages paid to labourers are higher. Not much improvement has been made in my immediate neighbourhood in drainage, as most of the farms are small, and the farmers destitute of capital, but on the larger farms it is being carried out on an extensive scale. Lord Clinton and Lord Ashburton are draining very extensively on their estates, and on many of the smaller farms the subsoil plough is used as a substitute for draining." We add the following from a gentleman residing in Buckinghamshire, who has been intimately acquainted with the state of agriculture in that county for upward of forty years: " So far as my observations have extended, I am fully satisfied that our agricultural poor are as well, and I believe better off, than under any former regulations. Our farmers in Bucks, generally speaking, repudiate the propriety or the utility of returning to Protection. Pauperism is decreasing; there are fewer paupers in our union houses now than there have been for the last five years. Farms sell dearer, and rents advance, except in some deep, cold, clay lands. Facts to illustrate this assertion are daily coming before us in Bucks. If anything like a good piece of land is to be sold or let, numbers are ready to embrace the offer. Improvements are seen everywhere, and satisfaction with things as they are pretty generally prevails."

The following extract from a Belfast paper will show that the actual state and prospects of agriculture in the sister island are not inferior to those which prevail in other parts of the United Kingdom. " The present state of the markets," says the " Northern Whig," " is striking and singular; after a highly favourable and abundant cereal harvest, with a potato crop, although relatively deficient, considering the great extent of ground under it, but which has now, at all events for some months, been more than sufficient to sustain an enormous consumption; with ports invitingly open to the unrestricted importation of the universe, and in a time of profound peace, we find prices steadily advancing. Instead of our often expressed anxieties for the proper remuneration of the farmer, the fear now is that the meal of the humble operative may become too dear."* " There is a strong tendency in all the markets," says another influential Irish journal, " to rise at the present moment. All consumable commodities are on the advance. Bread-stuffs are rising. The price of the four-pound loaf in Dublin is seven pence halfpenny, and there is a prospect of another advance before Easter. For the present there seems to be no class of men having so much reason to be well pleased as the farmers. We seldom under Protection paid a higher price for bread, and had that system continued we must have been paying famine rates. Besides, the rise in bread-stuffs, bacon is on the advance, and so is mutton and beef, while the price of wool is steadily rising. All who are interested in agricultural produce, whether as growers or dealers, are doing well, and to

* Dec. 18, 1852.

all present appearance are likely to continue in that happy state."*

5. The remuneration of the farmer depends to a considerable extent on the price of animal food. During the reign of Protection it was thought absolutely necessary to guard this section of his interests against the competition of the foreigner, and the most gloomy forebodings were entertained from the free importation of live animals which was conceded in 1846. Since that period this branch of traffic has acquired some importance, every year a larger number have been brought from abroad, and the British grazier finds his stock offered for sale side by side with the produce of the Continent. What has been the effect of this change on our own producers? Have they been driven from the market? Far otherwise. "It is more than probable," says the "Farmers' Almanac" for 1852, "that still more attention than heretofore will be paid to the increase of the live stock of the farm, as it is the best paying portion, and will probably continue so." For three years past we have witnessed increased importation, increased production at home, and yet a continual tendency in prices to ascend, pointing us to a greatly increased consumption of animal food, consequent upon our manufacturing prosperity, as the only true explanation of so unexpected a result. It will be interesting to examine, as confirmatory of this statement, the following account of the number of cattle at Smithfield market, in corresponding weeks of 1850, 1851, 1852 and 1853, together with the prices of the different kinds of meat at the same periods :—

* "Limerick Examiner," January 8th, 1853.

Comparative Statement of Prices and Supply of Cattle at Smithfield Market.

Week ending December 23, 1850.

	s. d.	s. d.	s. d.		
Beef........	2 4	3 4	3 10	Beasts ..	979
Mutton......	3 0	3 10	4 4	Sheep ..	9,110
Veal	2 8	3 8		Calves ..	320
Pork	3 0	3 10		Pigs	180

Week ending December 22, 1851.

	s. d.	s. d.	s. d.		
Beef........	2 6	3 6	3 10	Beasts ..	1,230
Mutton......	3 2	4 0	4 4	Sheep ..	12,206
Veal	2 8	3 8		Calves ..	160
Pork	3 0	3 8		Pigs	340

Week ending December 20, 1852.

	s. d.	s. d.	s. d.		
Beef	3 0	3 10	4 4	Beasts ..	2,770
Mutton......	3 8	4 4	4 10	Sheep ..	15,152
Veal	3 2	4 8		Calves ..	190
Pork	2 10	4 0		Pigs	250

Week ending December 19, 1853.

	s. d.	s. d.	s. d.		
Beef........	3 4	4 4	4 8	Beasts ..	3,581
Mutton......	3 10	5 0	5 4	Sheep ..	15,951
Veal		4 6	5 6	Calves ..	70
Pork		3 8	4 4	Pigs	286

In connexion with the advance which has taken place in the price of animal food, and the prospect of remunerative enterprise which this affords, we may instance the Smithfield annual cattle show, which was held in December last. Here, if anywhere, we might have expected that the signs of agricultural depression consequent upon Free Trade would have been apparent, since the success of such exhibitions depends entirely on the degree of competition which they inspire. The existence of a first-rate cattle show cannot be explained, without assuming that farmers have not abandoned all hope, and that capital is still drawn to the soil by the expectation of fair profits. But it is admitted on all sides, that the last exhibition in Baker Street was remarkably good; altogether in advance of its predecessors. Not only was the number of entries greater than in former years, but there was a marked improvement in the character of all classes of stock. The animals were superior to those exhibited on former occasions in point of breeding and symmetry, as well as flesh. A growing attention has been displayed, for several years past, to the former qualities; mere bulk is disregarded, as a title to successful competition; a proof that more scientific views are beginning to prevail among the agricultural body. It is interesting to observe, also, that successful competition in reference to the higher qualities of stock was not confined to amateur agriculturalists, such as Prince Albert, or the Duke of Richmond, and the Earl of Leicester, but was very largely shared by the practical farmer, who has to make up for the inferiority of his resources by superior skill. These remarks will apply equally to the last great cattle show for the midland counties, held in Birmingham, the stock then exhibited showing the same general superiority as compared with former occasions. A phenomenon of some interest, as an illustration of the increased activity of agriculture, is the enormous increase of poultry sales in connexion with recent exhibitions. The number of pens at Birmingham was 200 greater than in any former year, and the value of the business done in this very minor department amounted to £1,000. We recognise here another of the numberless blessings of Free Trade, in restoring to the farmer, through an abundance of cheap grain, an interesting and profitable species of production.

6. It would occupy more space than can be afforded in these pages to enumerate all the proofs which might be given of the beneficial influence which Free Trade has already exerted on agriculture, and which assure us that a career of sound prosperity lies before it. Two general facts, however, require a brief notice; viz., the great variety of useful inventions which are now being applied to agricultural operations, and the new kinds of produce which are now, for the first time, attracting the attention of the British farmer. On glancing at the advertising columns of any agricultural journal, it is impossible to avoid being struck with the adaptation of machinery to all the leading processes of farm-labour. Manuring, ploughing, harrowing, sowing, drilling, reaping, threshing, winnowing, mowing, hay-making, all are being performed by methods which the last generation of farmers knew nothing of. There are now machines for crushing, cutting, boiling, or otherwise preparing food, and even for making hurdles. The steam-engine is being substituted for horse power, farm-buildings are so arranged that machinery can be employed in conveying materials from one part to another, the same as in the cotton-mill; and cast iron is supplanting wood as the material of which farm utensils are composed. This inventive movement is of recent date, and is becoming stronger every year. An eager desire to obtain the very best implements,

and to adopt the newest improvements, stimulates competition, and scarcely an agricultural meeting passes without some new candidate for public favour. A distinct branch of mechanics is being developed, which will not only constitute in itself a valuable addition to our national industry, but will give to our farmers a share in the benefits which spring from our national superiority in the mechanical arts. Ere long, the industrial application of the steam-engine will cease to remind us particularly of Manchester, with its palatial factories, and countless spindles; its associations will become rural; we shall see it under the farm-shed, its not ungrateful dissonance will chime in with the village bell, and Vulcan will lay the proudest trophy of his toils at the feet of "mighty Pan." We hail this mechanical activity as a sure sign of progress, but probably a still greater change will be effected in agriculture as a branch of remunerative industry, by the cultivation of articles which have hitherto been regarded as beyond the province of the British farmer. The beet-root has already been extensively introduced into the West of Ireland, with a view to the manufacture of sugar, and the facts which have been collected by Mr. William Digby Seymour,* seem to afford much ground for encouragement in reference to this novel species of enterprise. Still more sanguine expectations may be entertained of the culture of flax. There is already a large demand for this article; we are obliged every year to import large quantities from abroad, and our farmers would find a ready sale to almost any extent. Mr. Brisco, an eminent agriculturist of Cumberland, says,—

* "How to employ Capital in Western Ireland."

"Of all crops, flax is the one to save us. We must make an exchange with the foreigner, and as he has taken our wheat crops from us, because he can grow wheat cheaper, so we must take his flax crops, because we can grow flax cheaper." Mr. Long, one of the members of Parliament for North Wiltshire, has tried the cultivation of flax with considerable success. Sir James Graham, also, has applied his practical mind to this subject, and his sense of its importance may be inferred from the fact, that at the beginning of 1852 he summoned a special meeting of his tenants at Netherby, for the purpose of directing their attention to it. Sir James strongly advises the cultivation of flax, and expresses his confident belief that it will hold an important place among the products of the farm.* With such signs of progress, such indications of wider views and energetic adaptation to new circumstances on the part of our landowners, we cannot think that agriculture is on the point of becoming extinct. On the contrary, it is most evident that recent legislation has been the means of inspiring it with fresh life. Its energies have long been dormant; the farmer has been ignorant of the means of success which lie virtually within his grasp; Free Trade has roused him from his lethargy, and summoned him to a new career. We do not doubt that the British plough is destined to surpass its ancient fame, and though time has raised up other agencies, which we are bound to recognise as fellow workers along with it in promoting our national well-being, yet every British heart will now, as of yore, cry, "God speed it!"

II. We now proceed to consider another of the

* " Economist " Newspaper.

great interests which were specially affected by the recognition of a Free Trade policy by our legislature, viz.:—SHIPPING AND SHIP-BUILDING ; and the only question we have to ask respecting it is, has it been affected beneficially, or otherwise, by the repeal of the Navigation Act in 1849 ? We have already seen the results which followed from a partial application of Free Trade principles to this department of national industry in 1824, and were led to infer from them that a great boon would be conferred upon our mercantile interests by an entire repeal of the restrictive laws which related to shipping, and that a benefit, rather than an injury, would accrue to those engaged in the building and sale of ships. Still, the magnitude of the change awoke anxieties, and its consequences were anticipated with a considerable measure of alarm. We are now in a position to judge accurately of the effects of the repeal of the Navigation Act, and we are only echoing the verdict of those who are most competent to understand the question, when we say, that they are in the highest degree satisfactory.

1. Before entering upon an investigation of facts, it is necessary to premise, that the utility of Free Trade to the nation at large depends to a very trifling extent upon the influence it has exerted on the shipping interest in particular. We again repeat, that in all economical questions, the highest law is cheapness. This is the only law which connects the shipping with the other producing interests of the country, and by this alone the effects of Free Trade ought in strictness to be judged. It is evidently a gain to the nation when its productions can be

transported from place to place at a reduced cost. The expense of transit is to the profit of the manu. facturer what friction is to machinery, and it is an object of no mean usefulness to reduce both to the lowest possible point. Twenty years ago canals were the chief means of inland traffic: a cheaper method was proposed; individuals whose capital was sunk in canals opposed the change, but the nation decided that the cheaper mode of transit should be preferred, even though the canals might become less profitable. The case would not have been materially altered if the rivalry on which the legislature was called upon to decide had related to different canals; the same principle would have been applied—*cheapness.* When steam vessels were first introduced, a similar rivalry sprang up between them and the old sailing vessels, the nation however decided on the former as the cheaper, because quicker, mode of transit. These cases are the same, in an economical point of view, as that which arose in consequence of Free Trade, between our own and foreign ships. To the ship-owner and shipbuilder, as with the shareholder in canals when railways were introduced, it was a personal matter, but to the public it was simply one of cheapness. So that our trade increased and our profits became greater, what could it matter to the Manchester manufacturer or the Liverpool merchant, whether the ship in which he freighted his goods was made at New York or at Dumbarton? If the returns of the Board of Trade made it evident that our own ships were losing employment, and that Russian and American ships were attracting more and more of the carrying trade of this country, this would show us that we had hitherto employed our capital most unprofitably, and that the industry of the nation had been taxed for the benefit of the shipowner, who might, by turning his resources into a different channel, have gained equal and more honourable profits.   Thus the general expediency of Free Trade is altogether independent of its effects upon our shipping interests, and if it shall appear that they have sustained no injury from the change, it will only furnish us with an additional theme of congratulation, as demonstrating the solid foundation on which our industry is based, and the invigorating influence of unrestricted competition.

2. There are several obvious tests by which we may judge of the state of our shipping interests, as affected by Free Trade.   The first is found in the general prosperity of our commerce.   We have already seen that our foreign trade has increased in value about eighty per cent. during the last ten years, and that a considerable proportion of this has taken place since the passing of the Navigation Bill in 1849. This increase in money value does not adequately represent the increase in quantity which has taken place during that period.   In several branches of our manufactures the increased exportation has been owing to cheapening processes, which enabled the manufacturer to sell considerably more of the same article for the same money.   Taking this circumstance into account, the quantity of our exports, as requiring ship-space, has probably augmented more than eighty per cent. But an increase of traffic necessarily supposes an increase in the means of transit.   It is impossible for our foreign trade to have increased eighty

per cent. without a proportionate increase having taken place in the tonnage employed. But it may be said, —the repeal of the Navigation Act deprived the British shipowner of the benefits accruing from this augmented commerce. If, as in the good old times, the British flag alone were permitted to wave over the freights of British industry, we should indeed reap a golden harvest from the growing activity of trade ; but the case is quite different when the native has no preference over the foreigner, and Swedish, Russian, or American vessels can bid for customers on the same footing as ourselves. The proper reply to this objection is, that our Free Trade policy must be considered as a whole, and that the question at issue is not whether our shipowners are reaping profits as large as they might have reaped under any conceivable circumstances, but, whether they are as prosperous, or are likely soon to be so, as they probably would have been, if the system of protection had remained in force? The repeal of the Navigation Act was a corollary to the repeal of the corn laws. To have admitted foreign ships to equal competition with British ships, without, at the same time, setting our commerce free, would have been in a high degree detrimental to our own shipowners, since unrestricted competition would in that case have been allowed in a restricted trade. But to have set our commerce free, without, at the same time, allowing free trade in ships, would have been, in practice, to cheat our merchants with a semblance of freedom, to have given commerce, not liberty, but a new set of fetters. Unrestricted trade would have been nugatory with restricted means of transit, the rise of freights would have been so enormous as to have rendered it impossible to carry our intercourse with foreign states much beyond its old limits, and in the meanwhile a monopoly, in itself unjust, would have been rendered doubly lucrative at the public expense. Free Trade in corn and Free Trade in ships were reciprocally necessary, and if the shipowner imagines he has suffered from one of these measures, he. must place against it the undoubted benefit which he has received from the other, and he is bound to regard Free Trade as an absolute gain, if, on such a balancing of interests, he believes that his position is, on the whole, better than it would have been on the old system.

But in an anxiety to do justice to the British shipowner, we must not omit to state fairly the limits of the question at issue. The repeal of the Navigation Act in 1849 was the breaking down of a monopoly; it was the cancelling of an old piece of injustice, and, unless the eternal laws of retribution are quite extinct, it was to be expected that a temporary penalty would be exacted. No one ever anticipated that the position of our shipowners would be quite untouched by the change, at least our shipowners did not, else why their anxiety to retain the old system? For a long. series of years the ships of all nations had hovered round our ports, asking in vain for friendly admission. The superiority of British skill in every other department of enterprise might have taught them that if they were permitted to compete with our own ships on equal terms the struggle would be of short duration, but, unfortunately, this lesson was counteracted by the outcries of our shipowners, who pleaded so pathetically for protection that the foreigner might be forgiven for imagining that he had nothing to do but bring his vessels alongside our quays, to consign our ships to the dry dock. Accordingly, this circumstance was to be taken into account in anticipating the immediate effects of Free Trade upon our shipping interests, and constituted another reason for expecting a season of depression. Another circumstance also must be duly weighed, as tending to moderate our expectations of immediate triumph. ⁣ The ships of foreign states were built while our Navigation Act remained in force, and the energies of our own shipowners were kept dormant by legislative enactments in their favour. If the latter had been left to their own enterprise, with the advantage of Free Trade in all the materials required in the construction of ships, they might, by the magic of cheapness, have prevented the rise of these competing fleets, and the traffic of Europe might have passed quietly into British bottoms. Now, however, those ships were in the market, determined to find employment at some price or other ; a stronger sense of pecuniary loss being required to induce their owners to give them up than would have sufficed to prevent their being built. Hence the full effects of Free Trade on the employment of British shipping will be developed only in the course of years, and any benefit which may now be apparent may be regarded as the promise of a still greater benefit in the future.

3. Guided by these observations, let us now look at the facts of the case. Surveying a period of nearly half a century, we find that the quantity of shipping which has been built in the various ports of the British Empire has fluctuated considerably every few years. An interval of prosperity has soon been followed by one of depression. Thus, the total amount

of tonnage built and registered in 1820, was 112,173 tons; whereas, in 1823, it was only 67,144 tons. Again, in 1827, it had risen to 207,088 tons, while in 1831, it was only 110,130 tons. The largest quantity ever built and registered in one year was in 1841, when it amounted to 363,352 tons, but in 1845 it had sunk to 166,733 tons. Hence, the frequent complaints of our shipowners under the old *régime*. They experienced then the usual inconveniences of a protected interest; the Navigation Act not only proved itself powerless to secure them the enjoyment of uninterrupted prosperity, but was the direct cause of frequent adversity. It is easy to see how this effect was produced. The Navigation Act gave our shipowners, so far as it operated, a monopoly of the means of transport; British trade could only be carried on in British bottoms. Hence, if circumstances rendered our trade for a year or two unusually prosperous, a large number of ships were built, which, when trade declined, were thrown upon the market, bringing down the price of freights, and occasioning immediate stagnation in the ship-yard. If our merchants had been left to themselves, they would have made use of foreign vessels for a part of their redundant trade in seasons of prosperity, throwing them off when trade declined. Our own shipowners would have experienced a moderate rise of freights, without being exposed to a sudden reaction. The supply of home-made ships would have been limited to the average wants of commerce, and thus, the advance would have been steady and probably permanent. The following table will show the condition of the ship-building interest in the various parts of the British Empire for the ten years ending with 1853 :—

An Account of the Total Number of Vessels, with the Amount of their Tonnage, that were built and registered in the several ports of the British Empire in each year ending 5th January, 1844, to 1853, inclusive.

Years	United Kingdom.		Channel Islands.		British Plantations.		Total.	
	Vessels.	Tonnage.	Vessels.	Tonnage.	Vessels	Tonnage.	Vessels	Tonnage.
1844	698	83,007	38	2,276	494	55,904	1,230	141,277
1845	689	94,995	42	1,881	525	69,857	1,256	166,733
1846	853	123,230	37	1,689	638	90,696	1,528	215,615
1847	809	125,350	32	2,148	745	113,558	1,586	241,056
1848	933	145,834	48	4,090	756	155,313	1,737	305,237
1849	847	122,552	31	3,388	655	101,988	1,533	227,928
1850	730	117,953	41	3,313	691	123,864	1,462	245,130
1851	689	133,695	36	3,835	714	124,953	1,439	262,483
1852	672	149,637	30	2,926	680	141,116	1,382	293,679
1853	712	167,401	30	2,933	Re	turns	inco	mplete.

In 1814, the number of vessels belonging to British Ports was 24,418; the tonnage of which amounted to 2,616,965 tons. In 1833, the number of such vessels was 24,385, and the tonnage 2,634,577; or, during twenty years of peace, the mercantile marine of Great Britain could boast an increase of only 17,612 tons, or some nine good sized vessels. In 1814, the number of men and boys employed in the navigation of the above vessels was 172,780; in 1833, the number was 164,000, showing a positive decrease during twenty years of no less than 8,780 sailors. Nor have we given extreme figures. For eleven out of the twenty years specified, the quantity of shipping belonging to British ports was less than the amount last given; while, in 1827, the number of persons employed in the mercantile marine was as much as 25,000 less than it was in 1815. So much for the effect of the Navigation Act, that boasted palladium of British freedom, upon the interests of shipping and the means of manning the royal navy. Let us now look

at the steady increase in the number both of ships
and men during the period of Free Trade.

An Account of the Number of Vessels, and the Amount of their
Tonnage, and the Number of Men and Boys usually employed in navigating the same, that belonged to the several
Ports of the British Empire on the 31st day of December
in each year, from 1843 to 1852 inclusive.

Years ending	Vessels.	Tonnage.	Men.
31st December, 1843	30,983	3,588,387	213,977
„ 1844	31,320	3,637,231	216,350
„ 1845	31,817	3,714,061	224,900
„ 1846	32,499	3,817,112	229,276
„ 1847	32,988	3,952,524	232,890
„ 1848	33,672	4,052,160	236,069
„ 1849	34,090	4,144,115	237,971
„ 1850	34,288	4,232,962	239,283
„ 1851	34,244	4,332,085	240,928
„ 1852	34,402	4,424,392	243,512

4. We will now turn to the amount of shipping
employed in our foreign trade, and ascertain in what
proportions it is composed of home-built and foreign-
built ships.

A Return of the Tonnage of Vessels, distinguishing British and
Foreign, which entered Inwards and cleared Outwards in the
Foreign Trade of the United Kingdom, stated exclusive of
Vessels in Ballast, in each year, from 1843 to 1852 inclusive.

Year.	Tonnage Inwards.			Tonnage Outwards.		
	British.	Foreign.	TOTAL.	British.	Foreign.	TOTAL.
1843	2,919,528	1,005,894	3,925,422	2,727,306	1,026,063	3,753,369
1844	3,087,437	1,143,897	4,231,334	2,604,243	1,075,823	3,680,066
1845	3,669,853	1,353,735	5,023,588	2,947,257	1,361,940	4,309,197
1846	3,622,808	1,407,963	5,030,771	3,091,348	1,377,777	4,469,125
1847	4,238,956	1,852,096	6,091,052	3,205,794	1,513,447	4,719,241
1848	4,020,415	1,559,046	5,579,461	3,553,777	1,497,460	5,051,237
1849	4,390,375	1,680,894	6,071,269	3,762,182	1,667,726	5,429,908
1850	4,078,544	2,035,152	6,113,696	3,960,764	1,946,214	5,906,978
1851	4,388,245	2,599,988	6,988,233	4,147,007	2,336,137	6,483,584
1852	4,267,815	2,462,354	6,730,169	4,459,321	2,413,260	6,872,141

These figures unquestionably prove that we are now employing a much larger quantity of foreign shipping than we formerly did. The tonnage of foreign vessels engaged in our foreign trade in 1852 exceeded considerably the tonnage of British vessels thus engaged in 1837, and has almost quadrupled itself since that time. But it is also true that the quantity of British shipping engaged in our foreign trade is twice as large as it was in 1837. In that year the tonnage of British vessels, inwards and outwards, was 4,207,421 tons, whereas in 1852 it was 8,727,136 tons. Confining our view to the years comprised in the above return, the increased tonnage of British shipping since 1843 is a third more than the tonnage of all the foreign shipping in 1843. Still, in one single item, the tonnage of ships entering inwards, the foregoing statement shows a falling off in 1850, as compared with 1849. The appearance of this diminution was hailed by Protectionists as a confirmation of the truth of their predictions, but, when fairly examined, it is far from being so. Setting aside the circumstances which would have entitled us to expect a much larger diminution, the returns for 1850, when considered in connexion with other results of the new system, afford us by themselves a verification of its complete success. The number of ships which left our ports with cargo in 1850, was larger, as was also their aggregate tonnage, than in any previous year; the apparent diminution in that year, as compared with 1849, is owing solely to the smaller number of vessels entering inwards. We naturally ask why a smaller number of vessels than usual should have entered our ports, when a larger number than usual left them; and we find the reason in the greater opportunity of profitable employment which was afforded to our shipping at foreign ports. While our Navigation Act remained in force, retaliatory enactments prevented us from competing with the shipping of foreign states in their own trade. It might have been profitable for the English shipowner to carry freights from Rotterdam, St. Petersburg, Trieste, or Havanna to New York, but from such a branch of traffic he was altogether excluded. It would doubtless have been much to his advantage if he could have laden his ships to the United States with mixed cargoes of European produce, but the law of the United States, the faithful counterpart of our own, obliged him to send in British ships no articles which were not the produce of the United Kingdom. But the repeal of our Navigation Act caused a similar change in the system of the United States, and ships which sailed in cargo from this country were under less temptation to return. Their owners found themselves no longer aliens at New York, but in the midst of a most profitable field of enterprise, of which they were at full liberty to take as much as they could secure. It was optional with them to accept the best offers, and, instead of returning with a home cargo, to carry American produce to some other foreign port. This is not a merely theoretic explanation; the following facts will prove that it is the actual one. During the first six months of 1850 there entered into the ports of the United States from foreign countries 214 British vessels, measuring 618,127 tons, and during the same period there left the same ports, in direct and successful competition with the ships of the United States, with cargoes to various foreign countries, 204 such vessels, measuring 76,039 tons.* At the same time, as the following figures will indicate, our shipping found profitable employment in other parts of the world, from which the policy of our Navigation Act would have excluded them:—

Statement showing the Number and Tonnage of British Ships that entered and cleared from the undermentioned Foreign Ports on voyages from and to other Foreign Ports in the year 1850.

Ports.	Entered from Foreign Ports.		Cleared for Foreign Ports.	
	Ships.	Tons.	Ships.	Tons.
Havanna	48	9,170	99	22,712
Rotterdam.	16	2,984	5	889
Hamburg	82	16,148	52	10,326
Trieste	55	14,117	101	23,059
Antwerp	55	11,604	18	3,872
St. Petersburg..	72	13,318	154	34,762
Cadiz	179	29,679	173	32,093
Total	507	97,020	602	127,713

5. These facts completely prove the fallaciousness of the impression so prevalent among our shipowners before the act of 1849 came into operation. It was said that our own would be beaten by foreign shipping, that the latter would compete successfully with it even in our own ports; but instead of this being the case we see the exact reverse; our own ships are attracted from our shores by the opportunities of successful competition which are offered elsewhere. It must be borne in mind that the employment of shipping is now merely a question of

* "Finances and Trade of the United Kingdom at the beginning of the year 1852."

cheapness; in discarding antiquated prejudices the shipping interests of Great Britain and the United States obey economy alone. If our vessels have been engaged in American ports in preference to American vessels, it proves that their owners can afford to let them at a cheaper rate, and, as far as our shipping interests are concerned, proves the expediency of the recent change. If we can contend with the foreigner successfully in his own ports and with his own customers, there is surely no cause to apprehend that he will ever be able to disturb us here. The coasting trade of Great Britain, having hitherto been guarded from foreign competition, lies beyond the compass of our present remarks; still the following figures will be perused with interest, as showing the vast amount of business which is done in this department, and its recent progress. It will be seen that the tonnage of our coasting trade in 1852 was double that of our foreign trade. The same proportion however does not exist with reference to the shipping. In the coasting trade voyages are always short, and the same vessel may be entered a dozen or more times in the same year.

An Account of the Amount of Tonnage employed in the Coasting Trade, including that between Great Britain and Ireland in each year, from 1832 to 1852, inclusive.

	Tonnage Inwards.	Tonnage Outwards.	Year.	Tonnage Inwards.	Tonnage Outwards.	Year.	Tonnage Inwards.	Tonnage Outwards.
1832	9,588,004	10,026,297	1839	10,610,404	11,266,073	1846	11,985,409	12,981,456
1833	9,434,232	10,023,614	1840	10,766,056	11,417,991	1847	12,219,796	13,265,625
1834	9,875,647	10,290,173	1841	10,869,071	11,650,252	1848	12,523,872	13,315,350
1835	10,188,916	10,660,330	1842	10,785,450	11,302,657	1849	11,967,473	12,915,584
1836	10,337,545	10,762,690	1843	10,822,176	11,321,138	1850	12,564,631	13,640,520
1837	10,409,370	10,901,187	1844	10,964,707	11,694,861	1851	12,394,902	13,466,115
1838	10,491,752	10,825,523	1845	12,485,854	13,114,104	1852	12,475,401	13,441,815

6. We have explained in a previous chapter the leading provisions of the Navigation Act, and it will be remembered that, among other vexatious restrictions, they rendered it unlawful to import articles the growth, produce, or manufacture of Asia, Africa, or America into the United Kingdom from any port in Europe. Those provisions are now repealed; our commerce is freed from such arbitrary intermeddling with its natural course, and the ships of any nation are permitted to enter our ports with any description of cargo. It is evident that this change necessarily improves the position of our shipowners, since every measure which gives to capital greater freedom, increases its value. For example, the price of tea, sugar, indigo, or some other article of tropical produce, in this country, might render it advantageous for an individual making up a cargo at Antwerp to purchase a quantity for importation. The transaction might, in such circumstances, be attended with considerable profit to himself, and it would unquestionably be a public benefit, but on the old system it would have been illegal. From the 1st January, 1850, such importations have been lawful, and the following statement of those which occurred during that year, will convey some idea of the value of the concession.*

Articles.	Countries whence Imported.
Peruvian Bark ..	Hanse Towns, Holland, France, Sardinia, Austrian Italy.
Cassia Lignea	Holland, France, Spain.
Cinnamon........	Hanse Towns, Holland, France, Spain.
Cochineal........	Hanse Towns, Holland, France, Spain.
Cocoa	Hanse Towns, Holland, France, Portugal.

* "Finances and Trade of the United Kingdom."

Articles.	Countries whence Imported.
Coffee	Russia, Denmark, Prussia, Hanse Towns, Holland, Belgium, France, Portugal, Spain, Italian States.
Indigo	Russia, Hanse Towns, Holland, Belgium, Spain, Italian States.
Logwood	Belgium.
Mahogany	Hanse Towns, Holland, Belgium, France.
Nutmegs	Holland, Belgium, France.
Palm Oil	Hanse Towns, Holland, Portugal, Spain.
Pepper	Hanse Towns, Holland, France, Portugal.
Pimento	Hanse Towns, Holland.
Raw Sugar	Russia, Sweden, Prussia, Hanse Towns, Holland, France, Portugal.
Tea	Russia, Sweden, Norway, Prussia, Hanover, Hanse Towns, Holland, Belgium, France, Portugal, Spain.

7. The increased demand for shipping which is inseparable from the extension of our commerce, would lead us to expect that our shipbuilders have been busily engaged. The amount of tonnage built and registered in the United Kingdom in 1851, was 149,599 tons, against 137,530 in 1850, and 121,266 in 1849, from which it appears that the demand for British vessels has continuously advanced since the repeal of the Navigation Act. Accounts from the leading ports where shipbuilding is carried on, all agree in stating that it is experiencing at the present time an unprecedented degree of activity. During the past year, 142 new vessels, of an average tonnage of 398 tons, and an aggregate of 56,645 tons, have been launched from the building-yards on the Wear, showing an increase over the year 1851 of 4,822 tons and a decrease of four vessels. The destination of these vessels to the foreign trade is proved by their

size, the average of which is greater by one-third than the average measurement of the vessels built at the same port in 1849, having increased from 286 tons to 398 tons. There are at present fitting out in the port of Sunderland twenty new vessels, the aggregate tonnage of which amounts to 8,661 tons, and upon the stocks in the building yards about the same number and tonnage. While the building of timber-ships' is so active on the Wear, iron shipbuilding is equally brisk on the Tyne. One firm in the neighbourhood of Newcastle is launching, on an average, one iron vessel every month; another is executing a large order for the Austrian Lloyds, and the builders of the " W. S. Lindsay" have a vessel of 1800 tons burden ready for launching. Messrs. Tongue and Curry, eminent ship-brokers of Liverpool, in their annual circular for 1853, say, " On no occasion were we ever able to report so favourably for the year past of the sale of ships at this port, both with respect to the amount of tonnage sold, and the prices which have been obtained. The prices of colonial ships have advanced fully seventeen per cent., with a continual tendency upwards, while stocks have been reduced to forty-eight sail, against seventy-six in 1852, and eighty-two in 1851, without any immediate supplies being expected. The number of new vessels which have come into Liverpool within the year, and been sold, is 120, measuring in the aggregate 50,000 tons; the number of ships launched or in course of erection is thirty-nine, with a capacity of 15,000 tons, against twenty-three of 9,200 tons in 1851. The number of steamers built, and in course of erection, at Liverpool, amounts to thirteen, with an aggregate of 4,050 tons.

The number of foreign vessels which have changed hands, at the same port, since the Navigation Act came into operation, amounts to eleven, measuring altogether 5,000 tons." The effect of Free Trade upon the shipping interests of Liverpool, will be placed in a more striking light by the following figures. The facts they disclose are requisite to bring out all the gracefulness of that condemnation of a Free Trade policy, which emanated from its poll booths during the past year. In 1844, the shipping which paid dock duties amounted to 2,632,712 tons, in 1852 it was 3,737,666 tons, an increase of upwards of 1,100,000 tons in eight years. The increase during the previous eight years, though large, was far from being equal to this, having been from 1,947,615 tons to 2,445,278 tons, an increase of less than one half that which has been realized under Free Trade. Taking a still earlier period of eight years, the aggregate increase was still less; while if we go back to the time prior to Mr. Huskisson's measures, times which are still lauded as the golden age of shipowners, the greatest increase ever known during a period of eight years was from 709,849 tons to 892,902 tons, an increase of 183,053 tons, not more than a sixth part of that which has taken place during the last eight years. Passing from Liverpool to the ship-yards on the Leven, we find the same activity prevailing. The number of screw steamers launched at Dumbarton and the Clyde is very great. These steamers already monopolise the trade of the Mediterranean, they are extending along the coasts of North and South America and Africa, and are destined ere long to supersede sailing vessels on all voyages of moderate length, or where coaling facilities can be secured. The men employed in the neighbourhood of Dumbarton have received an advance of wages, and all the hands are fully employed. As an illustration of the general activity of shipbuilding on the Leven, we give the following statement, with which we have been furnished by Messrs. W. Denny and Brothers, one of the principal firms in that district, relating to the rate of wages paid, the number of vessels launched during 1852, and those ordered or on the stocks on the 1st January, 1853, premising that all are stated to be equally busy with themselves.

Iron Shipwrights, or Plate Setters...... 28s. per week.
Rivetters .... 24s.   ,,
Ship Carpenters .... 24s.   ,,
   ,,   Joiners .... 22s.   ,,
   ,,   Blacksmiths .... 23s.   ,,
Labourers .... 10s. to 11s.   ,,
Boys from 9 years .... 2s. 6d. to 4s.   ,,

Except labourers and boys, the advance of wages to all the hands employed has averaged about fifteen per cent.

The number and power of ships launched during the past year are as follows :—

	Tons.	Horse power.
The Australian (screw)	1450	 300
,, Sydney..................	1450	 300
,, Andes	1500	 300
,, Alps....................	1500	 300
,, Balbec	900	 170

The following are partly built, or are ordered to be gone on with immediately :—

	Tons.	Horse power.
The Thames (screw)	1200	 200
,, Teneriffe	1200	 200
,, Karnac..................	900	 170

	Tons.	Horse power.
The Persia (paddle)	3000	900
„ Elk	550	250
„ Stag	550	250
„ Lynx	550	250
„	300	100

With the exception of the last small paddle-steamer, intended for the Glasgow and Dumbarton trade, the whole of the above, both launched and on hand, are orders from one house, viz., the Messrs. Burns, of Glasgow.

. 8. It is unnecessary to multiply facts; we trust that those which have been adduced are amply sufficient to carry the verdict of any unprejudiced individual. We would simply add, with respect to the value of freight, the testimony of Messrs. Offor and Gamman, as given in their annual trade circular for 1853. They say, " The outward freight of goods to Australia is now £5 per ton, and £6 has been given for small parcels which pressed for shipment. In the Baltic trade freights were in many instances double at the close what they were at the commencement of the year, both for timber and grain. From the North American ports also very high rates were paid for fall ships, forty to forty-one shillings being given for the last vessels taken. Outward freights for coal have for the most part ruled high during the year to nearly all parts of the globe, and there seems every probability of their being maintained during 1853." Mr. W. S. Lindsay recently stated at Southampton, that freights of all kinds had risen during 1852 as much as 100 per cent. It is frivolous to say that the prosperity which is indicated by these figures springs from emigration. Granting the truth of the assertion to its fullest extent, it only demonstrates the wisdom of the legislature in repealing the Navigation Laws. If those laws had remained in force there would have been no emigration movement in this country, and the benefit of the gold discoveries would have been conceded to our rivals across the Atlantic. The colonisation of Australia, gold discoveries, and steam navigation, are the offspring of the present age, to whose genius the Navigation Laws were diametrically opposed. The repeal of those laws was demanded on the ground that they were an anachronism and absurdity in the nineteenth century; that they fettered the soul of a mighty people who were stirring themselves to fill the earth. These arguments have been justified by the result; it is proved that they who urged them were the true seers, the true co-workers with Almighty Providence. While these arguments have been justified, every prediction with which they were combated has proved false. The repeal of the Navigation Laws, while conferring a great boon upon the nation, has been of the highest service to our shipowners. Never were they better off; never was the ship-yard the scene of more vigorous activity. From the facts which we have passed in review, we turn to the future with pride and hope. Never were more glorious prospects dawning upon the world; never did the star of civilisation shine with so genial a lustre as at the present hour. It would argue a total want of sympathy with human progress if we could look forward to so many precursors of a better age without enthusiasm. The Anglo-Saxon race has taken up the precept which God gave at the outset of man's career; its hardy children are replenishing and possessing the earth. After reconnoitering it for ages, pushing their discoveries among tropical islands and polar seas, till every cape and bay is defined on the geographer's chart as clearly as the counties of their native land, they are choosing their homes, some by the broad waters of the Mississippi, and others within sight of the snowy peaks of the Himalayah, some on that part of the soil of Africa over which, to the fancy of Vasco de Gama, hovered the spirit of storms, as if to guard the passage from the western to the eastern world, and others in that vast continent of flocks and gold which lies far off among the blue waves of the Pacific. The brothers and the sons of Englishmen are found everywhere. What will hold them together? What will cement the living stones of this world-wide fabric? By what agency shall love and friendship hold converse over half the globe? How shall the productions of our factories be carried to the future homes of our emigrating multitudes, and the fruit of their toil be brought hither to fill our poor with bread? Our ships! our ships must be the bridges of our ocean empire. Railways have already taught us to substitute time and cheapness for geographical distance in the measurement of space. The steam-ship must do for the ocean what the rail has done for the land, and by means of rapid intercourse bind together by ties of virtual proximity every "nook" throughout the world that has furnished an abode to the "minds and manners" of Britain.

III. OUR COLONIES form the third great producing interest of the United Kingdom, which, according to the predictions of its friends, was to have been

ruined ere this by the effects of Free Trade.   Before
inquiring whether, and to what extent, this result
has been produced, it will be proper to remind the
reader, as we have done already in reference to agriculture and shipping, that the general expediency of
Free Trade is to a great extent independent of our
decision on this particular question.   In legislation,
the only object to be aimed at is the greatest good of
the greatest number, with which rule the dictates of
justice will never fail to coincide.   It is no sufficient
reason why any measure should be discarded by the
state that it will occasion inconvenience to a section
of the people; on the contrary, local inconvenience is
one of the necessary accidents of human laws.   A
very numerous class of persons in London and other
large towns, are daily experiencing the inconveniences
of legislation ; they would gladly dispense with the
system of Police Courts and Houses of Correction,
but it is expedient for the country that they continue
to suffer this inconvenience, and be allowed to prosper
only when they conform their lives to the rules of
justice.   All monopoly rests, in the last analysis, on
the same basis as simple fraud, the only difference
being, that in the latter case law and custom recognise
its true character, and in the former case agree to
call it something else.   The progress of equitable
legislation consists in pointing out such impostures,
expunging them from the statute book, and gradually
making public law conform, in every respect, to the
dictates of essential morality.   Hence the progress of
all just reforms necessarily brings inconvenience
upon those who, however pure and high-minded in
private life, have, as all monopolists must have done,

drawn profit from injustice. The monopoly which, till within the last seven years, was enjoyed by the West Indian colonies, was on a gigantic scale; it abstracted, year by year, millions of money from the pockets of the British public. The system of industry in operation there had grown up under the influence of that monopoly; its capital, profits, modes of labour, and social machinery, were all harmonised with the idea that this country would continue to tax itself for the benefit of the planter. Hence, no one could expect that the withdrawal of past privileges would be attended with no struggle; on the contrary, it was to be expected that our colonists would have to bestir themselves, and win, by means of superior skill and energy, the position which had hitherto, most unjustly, been guaranteed to them without effort. They are now in the position of persons who find themselves all at once deprived of a comfortable sinecure, and the result has been, first, a moment's consternation, a sense of utter ruin; secondly, a resolve, the very offspring of such circumstances, that they *will not* be ruined, if any resource within the reach of science and labour can save them.

1. Whether our sugar colonies are, or are not, able to sustain the change produced by Free Trade, one thing is certain, that our new policy is one of justice and widely extended benefit. Even if, as some said, we might as well have sunk them in the sea as abolish the differential duties on foreign sugar, still, even in such an extreme case, Free Trade would remain unimpeached, not only on the ground of equity, but of usefulness also. In 1846, West Indian sugar, the growth of our own colonies, was admitted to consump-

tion on paying a duty of rather more than twenty-five shillings per cwt., while the produce of Cuba and Brazil was kept out by a duty of sixty shillings per cwt. The cost of the quantity of sugar retained for consumption that year, exclusive of duty, was £9,156,872. The cost of a like quantity of Brazil or Cuba sugar, of the same quality, would have been £4,141,181. For the benefit of our colonial planters this cheaper sugar was kept out by law, and we had to pay £5,015,691 more than any other nation in Europe would have had to pay for the same quantity. In 1851, we consumed 382,000 tons of sugar, in 1845 sugar was £60 per ton, and the quantity consumed cost us £12,420,000. If the quantity we consumed in 1851 had been purchased on the same terms, it would have cost us £22,920,000, whereas its actual cost was less than that sum by £10,000,000, the price which, with the same amount of comfort we now enjoy, we should have had to pay as a subsidy to the West Indian planter, had the protective system been still in force. For a long series of years the West Indies were a positive drain upon the industrial resources of this country; the manufactures they purchased were less in point of aggregate value than the sum of which we were annually robbed for their maintenance; if all the goods which left our ports for the West Indies had been carted to the edge of Dover Cliffs and sunk in the Channel, the nation would have sustained no loss, if, as a compensation, it had merely received permission to purchase its sugar in the cheapest market. And for whom were those sacrifices made? The population of our West Indian colonies at the last returns was only

820,792; scarcely more than a third of the population of the metropolis and its suburbs, while no comparison could be instituted between them in point of moral and political importance. It would be deemed an excessive wrong if all England were taxed for the sole benefit of the inhabitants of London; and if, when it was proposed to repeal the tax, the proposal were met by the plea that the interests of the metropolis would suffer, public indignation would know no bounds. But even protection failed to secure prosperity to our West India planters; a period of five years hardly ever passed without dismal tidings reaching us of their approaching ruin. The outcries elicited by Free Trade are not greater than have been heard on many an occasion, even when immense duties gave them a monopoly of thirty millions of customers. These facts prove that the protection they enjoyed was merely a premium on ignorance and idleness, and while they might have led us to expect that the commencement of the new policy would be followed by a season of real depression, they also suggest the alleviating thought that our colonists needed a period of suffering in order to prepare them for one of sound prosperity.

2. Let us now look at facts. Are the predictions, so loudly uttered, in 1846, by persons connected with the colonial interest, verified?—Quite the contrary. Have the moderate expectations of temporary depression been fulfilled?—Even this can hardly be affirmed. Careful inquiries will show that our colonies were never in a more healthy state, that they have recovered already from the effects of the Act of 1846, and have made healthier progress since then than

during any former period. For thirty-five years previous
to 1846, the consumption of sugar made no progress
in this country. Population multiplied at a rapid
rate, yet the quantity of sugar used rather diminished
than increased. In 1810 it was 196,000 tons, but in
no subsequent year, up to 1830, was this point again
reached. In 1830 it amounted to 202,000 tons, and
then remained almost stationary for fourteen years,
having been little more than 206,000 tons in 1844.
After the change in the sugar duties in 1846, the
quantity consumed showed a rapid and steady increase,
till, in 1852, it was 382,000 tons. This enormous
extension of the sugar market suggests the possibility
of the grower making up for smaller profits by larger
sales, and that it must be the fault of our own planters
if they do not obtain a large share of this increased
business.

Hitherto, as was to be expected, this greatly increased importation has been supplied chiefly from
Brazil and Cuba, but, recently, the quantity furnished
by our own colonies has steadily advanced, while that
from foreign countries has experienced some decline.
We may apply here a remark similar to one which
we have made with respect to agriculture and shipping, viz., that if our planters have not been driven
from the market; if, in the face of unrestricted competition, they sell increasing quantities of sugar, it
proves that their interests are safe. If they are not
beaten they have virtually conquered, and the victory
will become every day more apparent. Starting from the
same point, there can be no doubt that British capital
and free labour will, if intelligently applied, compete
successfully with Brazilian or Cuban capital with

slave labour. Has, then, the West Indian planter maintained his ground?. Taking three years prior to 1846, viz., 1812-1844, we find that the average annual consumption of colonial sugar during that period was 127,000 tons, and in three years subsequent to 1846, viz., 1849-1851, the average annual consumption was 147,000 tons. During the first period, the average annual consumption of foreign sugar was 30,000 tons, during the second 48,000 tons ; while the average annual importation of East Indian sugar was during the first period, 49,000 tons, during the second, 68,000 tons. Taking the whole of our colonial sugar, its average consumption during the three years which preceded 1846 was 209,000 tons, and during the first three years of Free Trade 264,000 tons, showing an increase of 50,000 tons. The consumption of British colonial sugar in 1842 was 216,000 tons, in 1851 it was 309,000 tons, having increased in the interval as much as 93,000 tons, a far greater increase than had been experienced during thirty-five years of Protection.

3. It has been alleged, in reply to these figures, that the increased production which they indicate is confined chiefly to the East Indies and the Mauritius, and does not prove anything with regard to our older colonies. The best rejoinder to this assertion will be found in the following statement, which shows the quantity of sugar produced in our principal colonies on an average of five years before and after 1846 :—

	First Period, 1841-5.	Second Period, 1847-51.
East Indies	58,000 tons	71,000 tons
Mauritius	32,000 ,,	50,000 ,,
British Guiana	24,000 ,,	30,000 ,,

Trinidad	16,000 tons	20,000 tons
Jamaica	32,000 ,,	32,100 ,,
Barbadoes	16,500 ,,	24,600 ,,

From the above statement it appears that, while the largest increase in production has occurred in the East Indies and the Mauritius, there is no considerable colony in which some improvement may not be noticed, and, excluding Jamaica, the rate of increase in all is large, having amounted in British Guiana and Trinidad to twenty-five per cent., and in Barbadoes to nearly fifty per cent. It is true Jamaica is almost stationary, nor can this excite any surprise, when we remember the distressing events by which that island has been visited. First, the cholera swept away its thousands. Scarcely had it disappeared when the small pox followed, as if to complete its ravages. In a single year 40,000 labourers were carried off, while famine, and the social disorganization resulting from these afflictive visitations, rendered a still larger number unfit for their usual work. Considering these events, it must be regarded as no slight proof of the ability of our planters to cope with their altered circumstances, that, on an average of five years, the quantity of sugar produced sustained no diminution. It must be borne in mind also, that in Jamaica the abuses of our plantation system took the deepest root; slavery there existed in a worse form, and brought forth in the slave population, to a greater extent than in our other colonies, the natural fruits of disaffection and indolence. But even going back to a period before the abolition of slavery, and comparing it with the period of Free Trade, we find a difference in the quantity of sugar produced in the

West Indies greatly in favour of the latter period. The average quantity produced annually in the five years 1831-5 having been 221,000 tons; while during the five years 1847-51 it was 266,000 tons.*

4. Having glanced at these statistics, which prove undeniably that the present state of our West Indian colonies is one of progress, it will be satisfactory to let the colonists speak for themselves. Let us hear the sentiments of Mr. George Gordon, an eminent planter, who appeared before Lord George Bentinck's committee in 1848 to plead for a renewal of Protection; four years have wrought a great change in them :—" I think, if we separate the general effects of the bill of 1846 from its effects on certain individuals, you will find that, on the whole, it has been rather beneficial than otherwise. It has no doubt been the means of causing distress to a great many parties in the colony who had invested money under the protective system. I myself invested money on a fictitious calculation as to the value of property, but, if allowance is made for such cases, I hold that the bill of 1846 has been of great service to the community, and will work still greater. We can never get any prosperity in this country till we know the worst. When we come to the worst, and know all we have to contend with, we will, by means of improvement in cultivation and manufacturing economy, so reduce the cost of production, as, with our natural advantages, will enable us to compete with other countries. †" We learn from the "Commercial Gazette" of

---

* Speech of Mr. J. Wilson, in the House of Commons, on the effect of the new Sugar Duties.

† "Economist," Feb. 21, 1852.

St. Louis that, at the commencement of 1852, the
growth and manufacture of sugar were being carried
on in the Mauritius with unusual vigour.   Instead of
property being abandoned, fresh capital was being
invested in the soil.   Numerous improvements had
been introduced, and prospects were more cheering
than they had been for a long period.   Welzell's
new method of squeezing the juice from canes, by
which a much larger proportion of sugar is obtained
from the same quantity of canes, was being brought
into extensive use ; a centrifugal machine was at
work on one of the estates, and others were expected
from England.   This notice of new inventions and
" improved methods " is characteristic of the influence of Free Trade upon every manufacture to
which it is applied.   In the palmy days of Protection
all is smooth and dull,—we hear of few novelties.
Hitherto, from seven to eight per cent. has been regarded as a tolerable yield of sugar ; we hear now of
its reaching sixteen or eighteen per cent.   Taking
the highest figure in the one case, and the lowest in
the other, it thus appears, that, without an acre more
of land being cultivated, by mere economy, the produce of our sugar plantations may be soon doubled,
and doubled too at a trifling additional expense.
The effect of these improvements is seen in the increased cheapness of sugar.   It was stated in 1848,
that the cost of producing sugar in the Mauritius
was twenty shillings per cwt.; we are now informed,
on the authority of the largest planter in Trinidad,
that it is produced there at thirteen shillings per cwt.;
and a witness who expressed his conviction before
the committee of 1848 that the Mauritius would be

ruined without protection, believes that the present crops will not average ten shillings per cwt.

Barbadoes, which, next to Jamaica is the most important of our West Indian colonies, exhibits the same activity as the Mauritius. A sugar refinery has been established there, and its produce is coming into use throughout the West Indian Archipelago. The "Guiana Chronicle" says, "We have seen both the loaf and the crushed, and have no hesitation in saying that it is equal to any imported from England; in fact we give them the preference, especially the lump, which is much cleaner than the same description imported from home. The establishment is in complete operation, large orders are being received from the neighbouring islands, and we hope that, as soon as the present stock diminishes, our mercantile friends will send their orders to Barbadoes." The "Royal Gazette" of British Guiana says, "The crop of 1851 greatly exceeded that of 1850. It is true that, for this excess, we are in a great measure indebted to the favourable season with which it has pleased the Almighty to bless the land, yet cautious observers, competent to form a judgment in matters of agriculture, have not failed to note that various decided improvements have been introduced of late in the practice of husbandry by our planters, and that returns from the soil which would have been quite satisfactory a few years ago, are far from satisfactory to the planters of the present day. Should this opinion be sound, it leads to another gratifying conclusion, viz., that the work now done by our labouring (free) population is of a better quality than it used to be. It would be erroneous, however, to suppose that the demand for labour has at all diminished during the past year among persons connected with the management of estates. With these the cry for emigrants continues unabated, notwithstanding the arrival of several vessels from Madeira and the Azores with Portuguese immigrants; that of the 'Brandon,' a fine ship of from 1,100 to 1,200 tons burden, with 452 Africans from Sierra Leone, and the 'Zenobia' and 'John Gibson,' both from Calcutta, with Coolies, 524 in all."[*]

5. While our planters have reason to congratulate themselves upon the results of the last four or five years, it must not be thought that they have reached their ultimate position. Our West Indian colonies, Jamaica especially, are still in a transition state, and the facts which the above extracts bring before us, are cheering only in reference to the past. The planter has yet to prove himself fully equal to the demands of the age. He must employ more capital, and import more machinery, if he would long maintain his ground. He has hitherto pointed to the ability to employ slave-labour as a circumstance favourable to his rivals. It might easily be shown, from admissions made by planters themselves, that this is an error, and that slave-labour is more expensive than free-labour; but other facts are at hand to prove that Cuba and Brazil owe the superior cheapness of their produce to honourable enterprise, rather than to the supposed advantage of possessing slaves. In 1846, the quantity of sugar produced in Porto Rico, Cuba, and Brazil was 342,000 tons, and in 1851, 406,000 tons, being an increase of eighteen per cent.; but, in 1846, the number of slaves imported into Brazil was 53,324, and

* "Economist," Feb. 21. 1852.

in 1851 only 3,287. Thus, while the quantity of sugar had considerably increased, the number of slaves employed at the latter date was much less than at the former. The cause of this increased production under such circumstances, is found in larger imports of machinery. In 1845, the value of copper, iron, and machinery exported from this country to Cuba and Brazil, was £50,324, in 1851 it was £158,771. The value of machinery exported to our own West Indian colonies, at the same date, was, in 1845, £220,000, and in 1851, £138,000; while the total produce of sugar increased, as we have seen, from 220,000 tons in 1845, to 305,000, in 1851. It appears from these figures, that while with the fancied advantage of slave-labour, together with machinery to the amount of three times its former value, the sugar produce of Brazil and Cuba advanced only eighteen per cent., our own colonists, with free-labour and a diminished use of machinery, raised the aggregate amount of their produce in the same period by thirty-eight per cent. The only uncertain element in this comparison is labour; machinery, it is admitted, tends to increase production, and yet the larger increase is found on the side where machinery was least used. The conclusion seems fair that, instrumentally, our planters owe their comparative success to free-labour; and if so, how much greater might it have been if their enterprise had been equal to that displayed by their rivals!·

6. As with our agriculture and shipping, so also with our colonies, the future is one of kindly promise. They have weathered the two storms which successively darkened their horizon, and which were inevi-

table at some period or other; they have weathered them bravely; the rigging is not torn, the helm still works freely, and, with smooth seas and a clear sky, they may expect a prosperous voyage. Having more than survived the two events which were to have crushed them, and at length attained to a position which is both politically and economically just, without any other revolutions to anticipate, there is no reason why they should not be as flourishing as any part of the British Empire. Their resources are not as yet half developed. Demerara and Trinidad, alone, possess abundance of land, richer than either Cuba or Brazil, and only need labour and capital to become the sugar producers of the world. Much may be done by introducing new articles of cultivation. The West Indies could grow cotton, for example, as well as the United States, and they formerly supplied no small proportion of that consumed by the British manufacturer. Why should it not be restored to its old place among their exports ? The geographical position of the West Indies is making them more and more an entrepot for our western traffic, and the railways of Central America will place them ere long on the high road to the Pacific. A few years spent as freemen under the discipline of British law, together with the educational agencies now at work, will soon raise their population to a higher state of intelligence, and give their labour a higher value ; while social improvement, by attracting more capital and a portion of the stream of emigration now pouring from our shores, will bind them to the mother country by ties a thousandfold stronger, because more just and beneficent, than those which the legislature has wisely severed

SECTION V.

COLLATERAL PROOFS OF THE INDUSTRIAL ACTIVITY CREATED BY FREE TRADE.

Having endeavoured, so far, to estimate the effects of Free Trade by a specific inquiry into the present state of each of the great industrial interests which are affected by it, we cannot, perhaps, more appropriately close this part of our investigations than by an appeal to a few tests which are common to them all.

I. Among the more general tests of prosperity, an important place is doubtless due to that portion of the returns connected with the INCOME TAX which relates to the profits of trades and professions. It is the more necessary to advert to this subject, on account of the fallacious statements which have been made respecting it by the Protectionist party. During the late elections it was re-echoed from platform to platform throughout the kingdom, that the profits arising from the above-mentioned source were less by ten millions sterling in 1850 than in 1843. The assertion could hardly be believed, statistics seemed here to be at issue with the evidence of the senses, which assured us that business had been more active, and the aggregate amount of profits greater, at the former than at the latter period. It is true that, owing to the abundance of capital during the last few years, the *rate* of profit has been smaller, but this has also occasioned an increased consumption which, it was presumed, would restore the balance. On the whole, it was anticipated that the profits of persons in business, though representing a less degree of improvement than had been realized by the labouring classes, would prove much greater under Free Trade than under Protection. Fair inquiry will show that this has been the case, and turn the argument of the Protectionists into one against them. The following figures show the amount of the various assessments on which the income tax was levied from 1843 to 1851 inclusive :—

England and Wales.

1843	. . . £63,021,904		1848	. . . . £60,068,090
1844	. . . 56,627,161		1849	 56,701,896
1845	. . . 55,505,733		1850	 54,977,566
1846	. . . 60,888,094		1851	 55,587,248
1847	. . . 60,867,494			

The high value of the figures for 1843 is probably due to inaccuracies incident to the first returns, since no two years near that time were sufficiently different, in a commercial point of view, to explain a difference in profits of nearly £7,000,000. Without pursuing this explanation, however, let us ascertain the precise years represented by the series of assessments. The assessment to the income tax is made on the average profits of three years, and the statement of average profits which is given in any one year, serves as the basis of taxation for the next. Thus, the statement on which the income tax was levied in 1843 was made in 1842, and since persons in trade usually balance their accounts at Christmas, it represented the average profits of the three years ending with the Christmas of 1841; viz., 1839, 1840, 1841. In the same way the assessment which is placed in the above columns opposite 1851 represents the profits, not of that year, but of the years 1847, 1848, 1849. Applying this rule to the rest, we obtain a result which fully harmonises with our anticipation. Passing over the first column, as obviously incorrect, we find in the assessment on which the tax was levied in 1844 and 1845, a tolerably accurate index to the state of trade in 1840, 1841, and 1842. In this last year the amended tariff came into operation, and this, with a series of good harvests, which brought down the price of wheat from an average of seventy shillings and eight pence per quarter in 1839, to an average of fifty shillings in 1843, produced an unusual measure of prosperity. Accordingly, we find a considerable increase in the assessments on which the income tax was collected in 1846, 1847, and 1848, which correspond, in the manner explained, with the period 1842-1846. This season of prosperity was followed by the railway mania and potato famine, the combined effect of which was to cripple capital, and almost put a stop to trade; accordingly, we find a difference of £5,000,000 between the average profits of business during the triennial period 1846-1848, as represented by the assessment on which the tax was collected in 1850. In 1848, capital began to recover the shock, the Free Trade measures of 1846 were making themselves felt, and in 1851, the latest year for which complete returns have yet been made public, the assessment representing the average profits of 1847-1849 exhibited an advance in round numbers from fifty-four to fifty-five millions. But even this assessment includes the unfortunate year 1847, and the slowly improving one of 1848, so that the profits of 1849, exhibited by themselves, would have shown a much greater advance. With reference, therefore, to the effects of Free Trade, the income tax returns teach us this lesson :—During the years 1847-1849, when the nation was still labouring under the effects of a most severe crisis, such was the invigorating effect of Free Trade that it enabled us to cope with our difficulties, and rendered the average profits of those years scarcely less than the like average of 1840-1842, when no unusual causes of depression existed. We must wait till the returns for 1854 are published, ere we can draw a complete inference, from this source, as to the general condition of trade during the last three years, but, considering that the profits of 1849 were sufficient, when incorporated with those of the two indifferent years preceding, to raise the average by a considerable sum, we have reason confidently to expect that future returns will only serve to strengthen the demonstration already given of the utility of Free Trade.

II. The state of the MONEY MARKET affords another means of testing the general prosperity and soundness of trade. On this subject an author to whom we have already referred, writing in January, 1852, says, " The quantity of bullion in the Bank of England is extraordinarily large ; it has risen from £13,817,000 on the 26th of July, to £17,320,000 on the 27th of December, 1851. All the predictions as to the drain of bullion to be caused by the repeal of the corn laws, have been falsified." Since this was penned some changes have occurred. The amount of bullion in the Bank continued to increase, till, on

July 3rd, 1852, it was £22,197,000, having augmented at the rate of more than eight millions in twelve months, while the securities in the hands of the Bank showed an actual decrease during the first three months of 1852. At this date the tide began to turn. The Bank returns for the first week in July showed a slight increase in the amount of securities; during the next three months they advanced from £25,094,000 to £26,110,000, and from October 1st, 1852, to January 1st, 1853, their amount rose to £29,284,000. While the value of securities had advanced the amount of bullion had declined, having fallen from £22,197,000 in July, to £21,553,000 in October, £20,527,000 on the 1st of January, 1853, and to £19,765,621 by the 15th of the same month. The consequence of this change was a rise in the rate of discount on the part of the Bank, at first from two to two and a half, and soon afterwards to three per cent. An event like this was sure to attract the attention of Protectionists, already suffering from a dearth of argument, and attempts have been made to connect it with Free Trade. Let us understand the nature of that connexion, if it really exists. The only kind of connexion which Protectionists are anxious to establish is that the decrease of bullion in the Bank was caused by a drain upon this country for gold, in consequence of the disproportion between our exports and imports. Facts are fatal to such an attempt. No large payments had been made in specie. We had received during the previous year a considerable quantity of gold from the United States, a proof that none was required to balance our imports. The only real connexion which exists between the decrease of bullion in the Bank and Free Trade, is that the latter had created a legitimate demand for capital which tended to an exchange of securities for gold.   Half as much more business was being done throughout the country than formerly, and hence more money was needed to carry it on.   But this would not of itself have created so sudden a change in the rate of discount if it had not been for peculiar circumstances in the financial condition of France. The accession of Louis Napoleon to the Imperial throne was soon followed by a greater amount of public confidence than had for some time animated the French people.   Whatever might be the abstract merits of the republican *régime*, no one had faith in it as the form of government which was to give repose to the nation.   Behind the factions of the National Assembly, the instincts of the middle classes beheld a tumultuous crowd of possible revolutions.   Whether legitimacy or socialism would succeed, few ventured to predict, though many saw in the triumphs of either the ruin of the state.   Hence capital was excessively shy; great enterprises were held in abeyance; no person who had money to spend was willing to stake it upon what the morrow might bring forth.   When Napoleon laid his firm grasp on the reins of power, those feelings vanished, and confidence returned. Industrial movements were now rife; commercial schemes and social improvements became again the order of the day.   In consequence of this increased activity, money, which had previously been cheap, became dear, and while bullion went to Paris for employment, securities came to London for discount. Allowing for this circumstance, the quantity of gold in the Bank of England at the present time is a proof of the healthy state of our own trade. No commercial crashes have followed the rise of interest, and money is still abundant for every object which gives a reasonable hope of profit.

The most complete refutation of the old notion that Free Trade would empty the country of gold, is furnished by a glance at the weekly liabilities and assets of the Bank of England. In order not to encumber ourselves with unnecessary figures, we will confine our extracts to the last quarter in each of the years referred to.

Quarterly Averages of the Weekly Liabilities and Assets of the Bank of England.						
	Liabilities.			Assets.		
Quarter ending	Notes in Circulation	Deposits.	TOTAL.	Securities.	Bullion.	TOTAL.
	£.	£.	£.	£.	£.	£.
Dec. 8, 1840	16,446,000	6,337,000	22,783,000	22,078,000	3,511,000	25,589,000
7, 1841	16,972,000	7,369,000	24,341,000	22,768,000	4,486,000	27,254,000
31, 1842	19,230,000	9,063,000	28,293,000	20,560,000	10,330,000	30,890,000
30, 1843	19,098,000	11,751,000	30,849,000	21,067,000	12,855,000	33,922,000
28, 1844	21,156,000	13,661,000	34,817,000	23,500,000	14,466,000	37,966,000
27, 1845	22,151,000	16,112,000	38,263,000	27,770,000	13,742,000	41,512,000
26, 1846	21,386,000	15,993,000	37,379,000	25,771,000	15,090,000	40,861,000
24, 1847	20,058,000	15,574,000	35,632,000	29,492,000	9,798,000	39,290,000
23, 1848	18,744,000	15,310,000	34,054,000	23,636,000	13,886,000	37,516,000
29, 1849	19,391,000	17,548,000	36,939,000	24,059,000	16,045,000	40,104,000
28, 1850	20,386,000	18,391,000	38,777,000	25,968,000	15,951,000	41,919,000
27, 1851	20,752,000	17,085,000	37,837,000	25,103,000	15,915,000	41,018,000
24, 1852	24,295,000	19,461,000	43,756,000	25,562,000	21,367,000	46,929,000
24, 1853	23,369,000	18,232,000	41,601,000	29,402,000	15,462,000	44,864,000

The average price of wheat during the last quarter of 1840, was sixty-one shillings and three pence; during the last quarter of 1853, it was sixty-nine shillings and eleven pence. In 1840 we imported and paid for only 2,432,766 qrs. of wheat and flour; in 1853 we imported and paid for 6,235,860 qrs., yet the amount of bullion in the Bank of England was more than four times greater in 1853 than in 1840. During the interval between those years our industrial activity increased, as we have seen, at an enormous rate; a vast amount of capital has been permanently invested; a greater quantity of gold has been required to meet the daily wants of business, while our imports have been on a gigantic scale; yet still, with the additional pressure of a harvest more than a fourth below the average, the Bank of England retained, in December, 1853, bullion to the amount of £15,462,000 in its coffers.

III. The state of INLAND TRAFFIC is a sure test of commercial prosperity. It belongs, in fact, to the same class of evidence as our shipping returns. A very small portion indeed of the imports and exports of the United Kingdom is consumed or produced at our seaport towns; the raw material has to be conveyed to the place of manufacture, and carried back again for export when changed into the finished article. Increased consumption of what kind soever involves the transit from place to place of a greater quantity of goods, as well as a greater number of buyers and sellers. The centralisation of the means of conveyance in the hands of a few railway companies, enables us to estimate the amount of traffic which is carried on throughout the kingdom much more easily than could have been done a few years since. The following figures show the receipts of the principal railways for the third week in January, 1853, and for the preceding six months, as compared with similar periods in 1852:—

	Week, 1853.	Week, 1852.	Half Year ending Dec., 1852.	Half Year 1851.
Aberdeen......................	1,589	1,251	38,603	34,689
Caledonian	9,146	6,950	218,477	197,283
East Lancashire................	4,517	4,125	14,112	12,390
Great Northern	12,508	9,745	25,228	19,148
Great Western	17,938	13,907	49,774	42,384
Lancashire and Yorkshire	16,568	15,315	59,514	45,120
London and North Western......	44,128	39,204	132,719	117,841
Midland	22,191	19,911	67,919	60,013
Newcastle and Carlisle	2,211	1,866	4,316	3,946
South Eastern and Dover........	13,751	10,733	388,111	370,176
York, Newcastle, and Berwick	13,363	12,719	40,706	38,694

IV. The number of persons who succeed in business is greater in prosperous than in adverse times. Exceptions may occasionally occur, since prosperity is apt to excite a spirit of speculation; when capital is abundant, schemes of a doubtful character are often taken up, and hence more failures may happen than in times of steady depression. If, however, from other proofs we infer the existence of great industrial activity, then the smallness of the bankruptcy list is a sure sign that the movement is healthy; that it represents a corresponding increase in the wealth of the community. The following is the number of BANKRUPTCIES for the first three months of 1849, 1851, 1852, and for the first three weeks of 1853 :—

	Number of Bankruptcies.	Number per Week.
Quarter ending 25th March, 1849 ..	382	32
,, ,, 1851 ..	167	14
,, ,, 1852 ..	240	20
First three Weeks of Jan. 1853 ..	27	9

V. An INVENTIVE EPOCH must be one of general prosperity. The object of all inventions is either to provide the public with new articles of convenience

T 2

or luxury, or else to economise labour in the production of those which are already in use. When all classes are bent upon retrenchment, and business, however capable of improvement, must for the want of capital remain stationary, there is nothing to stimulate an inventor; he waits till plenty of capital provokes competition, and compels everybody to adopt the most economical processes of manufacture. It seems a heartless thing to abridge labour, by inventing new machines, when thousands are scrambling for the barest means of subsistence; but when labour is scarce and "union men" talk high, then the inventor reaps his harvest. If we apply this test to the present time, it gives us a result in perfect harmony with those which have been obtained already. We hear of inventions in every branch of manufacture, from patent spoons and ladles, revolving heels for boots and shoes, and improved bricks, to the construction of ploughs, better methods of combing and manufacturing flax, of producing colours on textile fabrics, of economising steam-power, of glazing pottery, etc.; indeed a lengthy analysis alone could give any aggregate impression of the variety of interests which are being affected by new inventions. Birmingham is especially prolific, confirming the remark that the question of profits in most departments of manufacture in that town is mainly a question of ingenuity. A recent alteration in the law of patents has given great encouragement to this kind of competition. By the old law a patent could only be obtained for a term of fourteen years, and for this a payment was demanded of £72 17s. for England, £70 for Scotland, and £120 for Ireland. This regulation entailed great hardship on an inventor, since it compelled him either to obtain a patent, at a considerable cost, before he could fully ascertain the value of his invention, or else, by giving it a fair trial before applying for his patent, to run the risk of its being appropriated by others. By the present law an inventor can obtain complete protection for six months at a cost of five pounds, and has the option then of purchasing a patent for three, seven, or fourteen years. We may justly claim this law as one of the incidental effects of Free Trade, since it was rendered absolutely necessary by the stimulus given to every branch of enterprise in consequence of that policy. Some idea will be conveyed of the mental energy which is being thrown into our manufacturing pursuits, by the following figures, which show the number of inventions which appear as provisionally registered in the " London Gazette" at the dates given. We may add that a large proportion of these inventions will be fully patented.

Date of Ap. in Gaz.	No. of Inventions.	Date of Ap. in Gaz.	No. of Inventions.
Dec. 3rd, 1852	59	Jan. 14th, 1853	23
,, 10th, ,,	71	,, 21st, ,,	39
,, 17th, ,,	88	,, 28th, ,,	54
,, 24th, ,,	56	Feb. 4th, ,,	58
,, 31st, ,,	69	,, 11th, ,,	86
Jan. 7th, 1853	81		

VI. The most general test of the prosperity of all classes, as well as of the expediency of Free Trade, is found in the state of the NATIONAL FINANCES. A large proportion of the public income is derived from the customs and excise duties, and as these consist, almost exclusively, of taxes levied on consumption, and necessarily yield a greater or less amount according to the quantity of taxed articles consumed, we could not have a better means of ascertaining the circumstances of the population as evidenced by their ability to purchase the necessaries of life. Since 1842, our financial system has undergone a great change; the first step has been taken towards the substitution of direct for indirect taxation, and the success which has attended it demonstrates the soundness of the leading principle of Free Trade, viz., that the burdens of the state ought not to be laid on consumption, but on profits. Taxes on food raise the value of labour as a means of subsistence, while they tend to depress its value as a marketable commodity, thus occasioning severe privations to the working classes; while, by limiting consumption, they fail to replenish the exchequer. Taxes on raw material increase the cost of production, narrow our markets, and prevent the growth of public wealth. Taxes on food and raw material constitute a drain at the spring-head, which will soon leave the channel dry; whereas, a drain to the same extent, after the river has run its course, drawing supplies from all sides, and is about to empty itself into the ocean, makes no perceptible difference to its volume. We are indebted, as we have seen, to Mr. Huskisson for the first recognition of this principle in legislation, but the boldness with which it was applied in 1842 will associate it with another name, and commenced a new era in our financial policy. The principle of Sir Robert Peel's system was to take away the pressure of taxation from the *process* of exchange, and place it on the *profits* of exchange, or, expressing the same principle in other terms, to relieve industry at the expense of property, and that with reference to all classes.

The best illustration of the wisdom of this measure

is seen in its results. To appreciate these we must remember that the starting-point was a deficiency in the national income, as compared with the expenditure, which amounted, in 1842, to £3,979,539. Instead of meeting this deficiency in the old way, by fresh taxes on consumption, it was proposed to lay a tax on all incomes above a certain amount, which would yield, as it was estimated, about £5,000,000; and at the same time to repeal, as far as possible, the taxes which pressed most heavily on industry. Accordingly, in 1842, taxes were remitted to the amount of £1,596,366, of which no less than £1,500,000 consisted of customs' duties. In 1843 other reductions were made in the customs and excise, amounting to £411,821. The process was continued in 1844 by a further reduction of £458,810, and in 1845, when the income tax was renewed, duties were repealed to the amount of £4,546,306, of which no less than £3,617,306 consisted of customs' duties, and the excise duties on one article alone, viz., glass, which were entirely repealed, amounted to £624,000. In 1846 still further reductions were effected, and the net amount of taxes reduced or repealed in ten years, amounts to between ten and eleven millions. The effect of these measures was soon visible. In 1844 the deficit of £3,979,539 was changed into a surplus of £3,356,105, and in the following year, £3,817,641, sums amounting to nearly three-fourths of the entire proceeds of the property tax for the same years. The present state of our finances will be shown most readily by placing side by side our income and expenditure for 1842, and the last four years.

Net Amount of the several Branches of the Revenue of the United Kingdom paid into the Exchequer.

Branches of Income.	1842.	1850.	1851.	1852.	1853.
	£.	£.	£.	£.	£.
Customs	21,025,145	20,442,170	20,615,338	20,551,542	20,902,734
Excise	12,517,646	14,316,084	14,442,081	14,835,073	15,337,724
Stamps	6,982,952	6,558,332	6,385,082	6,761,634	6,975,416
Taxes	4,273,593	4,360,179	3,563,962	3,377,843	3,153,867
Property Tax	571,055	5,383,037	5,304,923	5,509,637	5,588,172
Post Office	608,000	820,000	1,069,000	1,022,000	1,104,000
Duties on Pensions, Offices, &c.........	5,311	4,762	4,424	4,423	4,635
Small Branches and Hereditary Revenue	520,356	16,331	25,826	14,851	16,670
Surplus Fees, Suppressed Offices	63,830	116,246	108,916	110,097	105,071
Crown Lands........	133,000	160,000	150,000	260,000	402,888
Old Stores, Unclaimed Dividends	264,740	633,539	563,454	762,971	830,166
TOTAL	46,965,630	52,810,680	52,233,006	53,210,071	54,430,344

Amount of the various Branches of the Expenditure of the United Kingdom out of Revenue paid into the Exchequer.

Branches of Expenditure.	1842.	1850.	1851.	1852.	1853.
	£.	£.	£.	£.	£.
Permanent Funded Debt	24,631,580	23,950,559	23,829,749	23,708,025	23,623,757
Terminable Annuities	4,071,530	3,737,325	3,784,664	3,822,856	3,812,437
Total Funded	28,703,110	27,687,884	27,614,413	27,530,881	27,436,194
Unfunded and Exchequer Bills	725,010	403,706	402,714	403,652	368,651
Civil List	390,120	396,481	397,730	398,589	399,573
Annuities & Pensions, except Diplomatic..	610,346	384,694	378,342	353,709	352,435
Salaries & Allowances, except Diplomatic..	248,639	284,663	273,526	279,409	268,710
Diplomatic Salaries & Pensions	212,184	159,285	152,799	151,655	149,777
Courts of Justice	724,760	1,089,894	1,090,227	1,089,878	1,107,094
Miscellaneous Charges on Consol. Fund ..	182,416	549,443	295,056	281,014	233,226
Army	5,987,921	6,401,883	6,485,498	7,018,164	7,023,488
Navy	6,640,163	6,437,883	5,849,917	6,625,944	6,640,596
Ordnance	2,174,673	2,553,178	2,238,442	2,491,798	2,661,591
Miscellaneous, chargeable on Annual Grants of Parliament, &c.	4,345,826	3,882,880	4,327,946	4,167,819	4,533,504
TOTAL	50,945,169	50,231,874	49,506,610	50,792,512	51,174,839

(Note: the left margin of the expenditure table is labelled vertically "Acct. of Natl. Debt" grouping the Permanent Funded Debt, Terminable Annuities, Total Funded, and Unfunded and Exchequer Bills rows.)

In order to appreciate the preceding figures, it is absolutely necessary to bear in mind the great reductions which we made in taxation, and the new principle of taxation which was applied, during the period to which they refer. An experiment of equal magnitude, and crowned with equal success, was probably never tried in the fiscal history of any nation. It opens a new lesson in political economy, one which other states would do well to ponder. On this ground we beg here to present, in a tabular form, the whole of the changes which have occurred from 1842 to 1853.

	Amount of Taxes Repealed, Reduced, or Imposed.			
	Repealed or Reduced.		Imposed.	
YEARS.	Nature.	Estimated Amount.	Nature.	Estimated Amount.
		£.		£.
1842	Coffee	201,113	Property Tax	5,100,000
	Timber and Wood	608,414	Export Duty on Coals	141,930
	Export Duties'	109,778	Spirits, Ireland	240,000
	Other Customs' Duties	579,639	Stamps, Ireland......	121,745
	Stage Coaches	77,779	Other Taxes	26,314
	Other Taxes	19,643		
	Total......	1,596,366	Total......	5,629,989
1843	Timber and Wood	126,453		
	Spirits, Ireland	240,000		
	Other Taxes	45,368		
	Total......	411,821		
1844	Coffee	86,174		
	Currants	95,816		
	Wool	97,140		
	Marine Insurances ..	101,959		
	Glass	45,000		
	Other Taxes	32,721		
	Total......	458,810		

Years.	Repealed or Reduced.		Imposed.	
	Nature.	Estimated Amount.	Nature.	Estimated Amount.
		£.		£.
1845	Sugar	2,309,857	Auctioneers' and Appraisers' Licences ..	53,720
	Molasses............	129,183		
	Cotton, Raw	682,042		
	Coals, Export Duty ..	115,438		
	Other Customs' Duties	380,786		
	Auctions	305,000		
	Glass	624,000		
	Total......	4,546,306		
1846	Butter and Cheese ..	205,437	Meal and Flour	2,000
	Silk Manufactures....	162,985		
	Spirits	482,286		
	Tallow.............	101,966		
	Woollen Manufactures.	27,970		
	Seed, Clover	36,077		
	Other Customs' Duties	135,069		
	Total......	1,151,790		
1847	Woods from Foreign Countries	243,085		
	Sugar and Molasses ..	53,152		
	Rum	46,974		
	Other Taxes	1,675		
	Total.....	344,886		
1848	Copper Ore	35,745	....	84
	Rum, British Possess.	69,353		
	Sugar and Molasses ..	258,854		
	Wood, Foreign	215,028		
	Other Taxes	6,988		
	Total......	585,968		
1849	Sugar and Molasses .	355,257		
	Oil and Sperm	29,327		
	Other Taxes	4,214		
	Total......	388,798		
1850	Sugar and Molasses ..	331,073		
	Stamps	520,000		
	Bricks	456,000		
	Other Taxes	3,078		
	Total......	1,310,151		

Years.	Repealed or Reduced.		Imposed.	
	Nature.	Estimated Amount.	Nature.	Estimated Amount.
		£.		£.
1851	Window Duty........	1,878,800	Inhabited House Duty	600,000
	Coffee	149,161		
	Sugar and Molasses ..	359,804		
	Wood and Timber, Foreign	292,099		
	Total......	2,679,864		
1852	Sugar and Molasses ..	95,928		
1853	Tea	968,877	Customs	16,383
	Butter and Cheese....	106,535	Excise (Spirits)	590,000
	Sugar and Molasses ..	78,793	Stamps (Succession	
	Raisins	65,659	Tax)	2,000,000
	Other Articles	279,610	Property Tax........	750,000
	Excise, Soap, &c.	1,171,000		
	Stamps	277,000		
	Taxes, Assessed......	300,000		
	Total......	3,247,474	Total......	3,356,383
	Total Repealed or Reduced since 1842 ..	16,818,162	Total Imposed since 1842.............	9,642,176
	Clear Reduction of Taxation since 1842	7,175,986		
	Gain to the Revenue since 1842	7,464,714		
	Financial Effects of Free Trade since 1842	14,640,700		

The lesson to be drawn from the foregoing statements is as simple as it is striking. The amount yielded by the customs and excise duties in 1853, was only £122,411 less than in 1842, although taxes had been reduced during the interval in this department alone, of more than £10,000,000. Moreover, in 1850-1 £520,000 was abandoned on the stamp duties, and £1,200,000 on the substitution of a house for a window tax, and yet the entire income of 1853 exceeded that of 1842 by £6,862,779. The chief additional source of revenue acquired during the interval was the income tax. The amount of this in 1853 was £5,588,172, or a million and a quarter less than the excess of the revenue of 1853 over that of 1842. On the whole it appears that, by laying on £9,000,000 of direct taxation, we have been enabled to add more than £6,000,000 to the revenue, and remit £16,000,000 to the pockets of the people. In other words, through the application of the Free Trade principle, which bids us set free the process of exchange, we have not only attained a sound financial footing, committed to the Chancellor of the Exchequer the task of dealing with surplusses instead of deficits, but have presented ourselves with a clear gain of more than £7,000,000 sterling annually. It is this which has given life to trade; this amount of capital has been silently diffused over the whole kingdom, finding its way into the factory, the cottage, the shop of the retail dealer, and the savings' bank, everywhere tempting and rewarding enterprise. When we reflect that the very same measures which freed us from this load of taxes, also created a demand for labour; that the greater consumption to which cheapness gave rise, rendered necessary a larger quantity of manufactured goods wherewith to repay the foreigner; when we remember that, in a few years, and from one quarter of the world alone, £30,000,000 worth of corn has been paid for by British manufactures; we cannot wonder that our exports have so prodigiously increased, and that the nation has been thrown into such a ferment of industrial activity. Let us not forget the cause of the change. It was Free Trade finance, which gave the magic touch to our commerce and manufactures; the influence under which they have bloomed with such vigour, and produced such unexpected fruits, came forth from the Treasury chambers. This is the chief lesson which the foregoing statements teach us, and it is one which the nation will see applied.

VII. We have now passed in review the effects of Free Trade upon the commercial and manufacturing interests of the United Kingdom, as far as they can be gathered from public documents, or inferred from unquestioned facts; it only remains for us now to sum up the evidence which has been adduced, and show its bearing on the question at issue. We have not confined our view to a recent period, when it might possibly have been urged that peculiar circumstances modified the result of the experiment; nor yet to one or two species of industry which might be thought capable of deriving, from special causes, advantages from unrestricted competition not likely to be shared by others; on the contrary, we have taken in a series of nearly forty years, and have marked the effects of the same principles when applied by men of the most dissimilar opinions, and with respect to interests of the most opposite nature. The idea which we have thus sought to put to the test of experience, embodies no partial, one-sided maxim.; it asserts the right of unfettered exchange, and, in denouncing all duties which are levied for the purpose of protection, questions the justice or utility of all which fall upon consumption. We now confidently ask the reader to record his verdict; on economical grounds, judging it by no higher standard than expediency, waiving for a moment what we can never forget, the absolute claims of RIGHT, and viewing it as a matter of mere utility, we ask, is Free Trade a failure? Has it proved a delusion and a snare? Is the nation the better for it, or the worse? In deciding this question he will take into account, first, the negative element of proof; he will remember that a protective policy completely failed, on the fairest trial, to secure prosperity; that under its influence our commerce retrograded, our manufactures languished, employment grew scarce, food rose frequently to famine prices, and a spirit of political disaffection spread rampant throughout the land. He will then turn to the application of Free Trade principles, and consider how every department of industry affected by the measures of Mr. Huskisson, our woollen, flax, and silk manufactures, recovered at once from their lengthened depression; successfully competing with foreign rivals, extending our trade, giving employment to our work people, and spreading through districts, once the hotbeds of sedition, the blessings of contentment and social order. After witnessing the gratifying effects of Free Trade principles when applied on this narrow scale, he will pass to the time when the physical wants of our population, together with the increase of our manufacturing resources, rendered necessary their wider application. He will observe the phenomena of 1818,—dear food, scarcity of employment, stagnant trade, a discontented population, demanding, in 1840, the like remedies, and under them totally disappear. Passing forward to 1852, he sees the marvels of our past history eclipsed by the astonishing progress which has been made during the last ten years, and which is still going forward on every side; he is overwhelmed by displays of activity and enterprise such as our fathers never witnessed even in that heroic age of British manufactures which gave us the water-frame, the spinning-jenny, and the steam-engine. Not in Lancashire only, the land of the loom, but in every district of the kingdom, among the furnaces of Stafford-shire and Lanark, the mines of Derbyshire and Corn-wall, the cutlers of Sheffield, the plate-workers, tool-makers, and machinists of Birmingham, the stockingers and lace-manufacturers of Leicester and Nottingham, and even the sequestered villages of Suffolk and Devon, a consciousness of well-being seems to inhabit every bosom, and in the hum of countless factories, the noise of the forge, the wilful shriek of the steam-engine, and the jubilant shouts of merry workmen, songs of gratitude too big for lips to utter seem borne to the gates of heaven.

But has the picture no shadows? Look, and reply. The farmer is draining, fencing, and manuring his land; the farm-yard, undisturbed for two or three centuries, is yielding at last to an improving age; steam whistles there; corn, cattle, horses, poultry, are no longer regarded as the mere ornaments and accidents of rural life, but as *manufacture* to supply the wants of men, as much so as a dozen pair of stockings or a web of cloth, and requiring the same economy and science in order to produce them. A new spirit is pervading agriculture; the landlord receives his former rents, but grants longer leases, and allows a freer choice of crops; the farmer be-comes a member of the nearest literary institute, opens long-neglected journals, attends lectures, and occasionally delivers one himself, and lends a docile ear to the scientific opinions which are gaining ground; even the plough-boy is conscious of having recently passed through some great change, and has caught the salutary impression that, for some reason or other, he must henceforth live faster. Across the Atlantic, the colonist is following the example set at home, he is improving his mode of culture, practising more rigid economy, raising and selling more produce, and is already rejoicing in the prospect of greater prosperity than he enjoyed in the palmiest days of Protection. Granting that the farmer and colonist both exhibit more of the stretch of mind which bespeaks difficulty, and that stern, indomitable resolution which suggests the nearness of despair, than characterised them in former days—this is no hardship; it is to them a rescue from degradation and helplessness. The effort to render our personal well-being compatible with justice is surely the first duty of self-respect. Elsewhere, not even the semblance of privation can be descried. Our ports are filled with shipping; ship-builders, ship-owners, and seamen are all doing well, happy in the profitable falsification of their own predictions. Keeping, then, within our view all the interests which can be affected by Free Trade, what is the verdict that must be given? There can be but one reply:—Through the mercy of God a greater blessing has been bestowed upon this land in the legislative recognition of Free Trade than was ever vouchsafed to it before; it has saved us from.ruin; it has given us food, contentment, wealth; it closes a shifting,. precarious ·past, and opens to us a glorious future.

PART III.

RESULTS AND TENDENCIES OF FREE TRADE—SOCIAL, POLITICAL, AND RELIGIOUS.

FROM the effects of Free Trade, as they are seen in the state of our industrial interests, we pass now to consider those remoter influences which it has exerted, and will hereafter exert, on the condition of our country and the world. The effects to which we refer are less definite than those we have so far examined; they are less capable of being reduced to the simple test of figures; but they are equally real, equally certain to ensue, and far more valuable. Popular well-being is so closely connected with commercial prosperity as to have formed with it one inseparable idea; but, if we *could* separate them we should have to acknowledge that the latter is valueless, except as a means of realizing the former. The welfare of the people is the supreme end of government; it is, therefore, still more the touchstone of every economical system which claims our adoption. To fill our coffers with gold, to crowd our palaces with luxury, to pour

U

into our lap the riches of all lands, is a barbarous enterprise; and if our commerce were merely adding to aristocratic pomp, or augmenting our national treasures, the philanthropist might see it decline without pity. As a theoretic economist, he might still advocate the principles of Free Trade, but they could have no alliance with his heart. Commerce is a divine gift, because it enriches *all*, because it passes, like a visitant angel, to the cottage of the poor man, stirs the dying embers on his hearth, and empties the horn of plenty on his humble board.

In that part of our inquiry upon which we now enter, we propose, first, to consider the effects which Free Trade has *actually* produced, as they are visible in the physical, social, political, and religious condition of the community, and then to extend our survey to the *prospective* effects of Free Trade upon the general development of Great Britain and the world.

CHAPTER I.

ACTUAL RESULTS OF FREE TRADE.

FIRST, then, we have to consider the results of Free Trade, so far as they have been already realized in the condition of the people. In order to remind the reader of the organic completeness of this part of the subject, we need only point to the connexion which exists between the lowest and highest forms of well-being. The lowest consist in the ability to supply with ease those wants which belong to the animal nature. This, however, is but the stepping-stone to enjoyments of a higher grade. The absence of pressing anxieties gives scope for the development of the intellect. A starving man cannot read books. When a person is pinched by want he is reckless and extravagant; give him the means of supplying himself and family with a fair share of the comforts of life, and you supply him with the strongest motives to carefulness and economy. Hence, social well-being is the direct offspring of physical well-being; abundance of food and clothing has a moral power; slowly but surely it leads to the acquisition of those home duties which are the proper foundation of every other. But even social well-being is not the highest kind of human culture; the social leads to the political, and lastly, to the religious; that, in which the affections are ripened toward the Creator and toward man. In the delicate texture and bright colours of the expanded petal we see the choicest product of the vegetable juices extracted from the soil; and so in religion, the mind's blossoming, we trace the effect in no small measure of those influences which temporal abundance yields. Hence moral well-being is the remoter offspring of physical well-being; plenty is clothed with a religious, as well as a social power, it tends to make our sentiments more genial and correct both towards our fellow-men and towards God.

In considering the effects of Free Trade under this threefold aspect, it is requisite to bear in mind, at the outset, the law which governs the progress of that which we call *influence*. The law to which we refer is that, in acting on the condition and character of individuals, influences of all kinds become slower in their operations in proportion as they become more spiritual. Adopting the well-known axiom in mechanics, we may affirm that what is gained in velocity is lost in power. The physical effects of Free Trade, for example, are all but instantaneous; a greater demand for labour, higher wages, and cheaper food, change in a few days the workman's home from a scene of privation to one of plenty; his larder is well stocked, his hearth is blazing with abundant fuel, and before many months have passed by he and his family have laid aside their ragged attire. The social effects of Free Trade, starting from the same point, are longer in showing themselves. The improvident habits contracted in the time of poverty are, perhaps continued till experience or reflection suggest the necessity of reform. The desire to escape from degrading dependence upon charity is not felt at once in all its power; the sense of self-respect has to be developed till it is strong enough to inspire a loathing of the bread which is not earned by the sweat of the brow. The means of providing for the future do not disclose themselves immediately to the mind. Thousands never avail themselves of savings' banks and other provident institutions, though they might easily do so, simply because they have not yet attained the moral power. The mind cannot be clothed and furnished as easily as the body; intellectual improvement is of slow growth; some years must elapse before the man whose average reading has hitherto risen no higher than the Sunday newspaper, will be able to derive interest from the pages of Bacon or Macaulay. Thus the social benefits which may fairly be ascribed to Free Trade, nay, which must infallibly flow from it, will develope themselves much more slowly than those which begin and end with the physical condition of the individual. For similar reasons the same remark will apply with still greater force to those higher influences which physical and social amelioration never fail to exert. It is with the human heart, in this respect, as with the advance of spring. We do not see the snow disappear, the rivulets begin to flow, the meadows resume their verdure, and the wood re-peopled with summer birds, in the course of a few hours. The undoing of winter's chains is gradual;

wreath after wreath is woven in nature's fairy garland, till at length it is thrown finished on the breast of May. The heart, frost bound with vice and ignorance, yields not at first to the softening beams of truth. Stubborn passions, deeply rooted habits, gross and sensual sentiments, have to be broken, eradicated, and dispelled, before it can be adorned with summer beauty. Religious influences, considered solely so far as they flow from natural causes, being more subtle and powerful in their effects, are also slower in action than the rest. Guided by these thoughts we shall expect to see the effects of Free Trade most evident in the physical condition of the people; developed less perfectly in their social improvement; and giving the promise, rather than the realization, of benefits in what specially relates to religion. In each successive department, however, the indications of progress will bear a higher value, and furnish, as a whole, a pledge of progress throughout the entire extent of our national condition.

SECTION I.

EFFECTS OF FREE TRADE AS SEEN IN THE PHYSICAL WELL-BEING OF THE PEOPLE.

We glance, first, at the effects of Free Trade on the physical condition of the people. The limits within which we may expect these effects to be apparent are at once obvious. The middle and upper classes have unquestionably derived great advantage from Free

Trade, but the majority of persons belonging to these sections of the community were able, even in the worst times, to provide, with comparative ease, for themselves and their families. Whether trade is prosperous or otherwise makes but little difference to the dwelling of a wealthy man; it is in the poor man's abode that the change is wrought. Hence we are justified in looking primarily to the working classes as those whose outward condition is chiefly affected by Free Trade measures. It would be difficult to exaggerate the importance of this part of our population. It is by far the most *numerous*, and this fact alone is full of suggestiveness. Granting that it represents but half the intelligence and wealth possessed by the ranks above, it represents in an equal ratio all that is sterling in humanity; the largest mass of the raw material of which the greatest minds are made. The eye of the beneficent Creator regards us chiefly in those capacities which constitute us His intelligent offspring; as possessing deathless powers, endowed with the kindling eye of fancy, the constructive aptitudes of genius, the keen glance of judgment, and the clear, calm, open intuitions of reason, points in which wealth interferes but little, and compared with which all conventional distinctions are but as a film of gossamer round the features of a marble statue. Philanthropy only reckons numbers; her eye never distinguishes diamonds, crosses, and coronets, but *men*, and true patriotism does the same. The comfort and elevation of the masses are characteristic themes of the present age, the nation has lent to them its ear, and a greater number of ameliorative agencies are now in operation than at any past period. We are bound to contemplate the effects of Free Trade on the assumption that, whatever multiplies the conveniences of the humbler portion of our fellow citizens, is a boon deserving the gratitude of the entire nation.

There are two agencies through which our commercial prosperity benefits our operative population—wages, and the price of food. We are aware that, on scientific "grounds, there is no room for such a distinction. Wages and the price of food are equivalents given in exchange for other articles. Labour is as much a marketable commodity as bread, and wages indicate its current value in the same way as any list of prices indicates the current value of provisions. Moreover, if the price of labour and the price of food always maintained the same ratio, never rising or falling but in the same degree, then they need not be considered separately, since the same amount of wages would always purchase the same amount of food, and a glance at the price paid for labour would at once show the whole extent of improvement realized. Before Free Trade was tried its opponents assured us that this would happen. They told the working man that it was no question of his ; that, if provisions fell, his wages would fall too ; that, in fact, it was the operation of the corn laws alone which prevented such a decline. It was asserted, in reply to these statements, that no such connexion existed between the price of labour and other commodities; that the price of labour was, in reality, as independent of the price of corn, as the price of currants was independent of the price of bricks; both being guided solely by the relation of supply and demand. But it was also shown that the cheapness of provisions, so far from bringing down the rate of wages, would tend very powerfully to raise it. The free trader, when told that lower food prices would reduce the rate of wages, pointed to our millions of ill-clad labourers and their comfortless homes, bidding his opponents tell him whether, if those millions had to spend on food only two-thirds of what they then spent, they would not buy furniture and clothing with the remainder, and whether this would not at once create more work, and raise the rate of wages? Such arguments were scouted then, but experience has demonstrated their truth.

I. The subject of WAGES has been already noticed in our review of the leading departments of industry, and the result of our observations may be stated thus:—In hardly any instance has the rate of wages declined; in many it has experienced a considerable advance. This statement applies, so far as our inquiries have extended, to every important branch of industry in the kingdom; the only exceptions which exist are to be found in subdivisions of particular trades which have been exposed to the influence of new inventions. Here, of course, both master and workman are subjected to inconvenience; to such the present times are much less prosperous than eight or ten years ago, when the country was not half so flourishing as it is now. These cases, however, are quite exceptional. In many instances the rate of wages, understanding by this phrase the sum of money given per piece or per yard, is lower than formerly; as we have seen in an instance already quoted, 5,500 lbs. more yarn could be spun, for the same sum of money, in 1852 than in 1846, but this is due entirely to improvements in machinery, which enable the workman to get through a greater quantity of work with the same physical effort and in the same space of time. It does not follow, in such cases, that the profits of the employer are greater, on the contrary, they may be less, than when the higher rate was paid per piece or per pound, and the sole advantage resulting from the mechanical improvement is that he is enabled, by offering his goods at a lower price, to keep possession of the market, and thus to find employment and wages for his work-people. The true test of wages is the amount actually received in exchange for the same amount of physical effort, and, adopting this definition, it may be safely affirmed that, with the exceptions already mentioned, no reduction has taken place. Where no increase has occurred in the sum paid for the same duration of labour, a great difference has been made in the receipts of the workman by more abundant employment. Thousands who in 1840 worked but thirty hours per week now work sixty, and thus receive double the amount of wages they received then. It is true that for this they perform more work, but full employment at the factory for sixty hours per week does not express a difference, in point of physical wear and tear, of one-half over employment for thirty hours per week. The un-employed workman cannot rest; day after day he goes to the workshop, though he may have no hope of finding employment; anxiety prevents him from seeking alleviation, and at evening he is more fatigued, and has really expended more bodily and mental energy, than he would have done in the course of ten hours' regular toil.   Hence an increase of wages, though it results only from increased employment, may be regarded as an absolute benefit.

It is rather instructive to observe that the rise of wages in different trades has been altogether independent of the amount of protection they enjoyed. Almost every branch of the stocking trade has experienced an advance of wages, though its long-depressed condition had rendered any effectual combination among the workmen impossible.   The mechanics, whose perfect organization enabled them to hold out against their employers for four or five months at the beginning of 1852, are now receiving the same wages as they received six years ago, while the cabinet makers, who have long been, as it is wrongly deemed, at the mercy of their employers, and among whom it has not been uncommon to find more apprentices than men, have received an advance of from 15 to 20 per cent.

It is a fact, therefore, that under Free Trade wages have not declined; the workman is not remunerated now less liberally than under the old system, but quite the reverse.   Wages have advanced under Free Trade, and are still advancing.   We are sorry to add that " strikes" are beginning to occur more frequently, though we fervently trust that on this point the working classes will take counsel from experience.   It is certain that we have not reached the ultimate effect of Free Trade on wages.   The surplus of workmen existing in former years has been gradually absorbed, and the investment of any more capital in manufactures will infallibly lead to a general advance in the price of labour.   We will not weaken the value of this fact by any reference to the position of the employer. The Protectionist said Free Trade would bring down wages:—Has it done so?—The workman laughs its confutation from Caithness to Cornwall. If then the price of provisions were precisely what it was ten years ago, the working classes would be much better off than they were then. But prices have notoriously fallen to a very great extent. There is hardly an article of common consumption which is not purchaseable at a much lower rate than formerly, and in some the difference is as much as 40 or 50 per cent. Flour, which cost a few years since half-a-crown per dozen lbs., can now be bought for twenty pence; tea, which cost five shillings per lb., is now reduced to four shillings; coffee, candles, soap, currants, bacon, cheese, have all fallen in the same proportion. Adding together the increased means which are furnished to the working man by the rise of wages and the cheapness of provisions, we may infer, without exaggeration, that his command over the necessaries of life is twice as extensive as it was ten years ago. Such an inference as this opens to us a wide prospect of improvement. The working classes, with twice the means at their disposal, have not consumed twice the quantity of the same articles as formerly; no, the range of their enjoyments has been extended; they are now acquainted with a greater *variety* of the elements of well-being. The first series of physical wants has not exhausted their pecuniary resources,—they have been enabled to assign a portion to the second; well entrenched in the possession of necessaries, they have advanced to comforts and luxuries.

II. We have alluded, in a commercial point of view, to the VAST IMPORTATION OF FOOD which has taken place during the epoch of Free Trade; we refer to it for a moment in this place as bearing on the physical condition of the people. We have seen that, taking the last five years for which, up to the moment of which we write, complete returns have been given, the quantity of grain and meal of all kinds imported into the United Kingdom has amounted to an average of almost ten millions of quarters annually. This may be truly termed " a great fact,"—it is impossible to contemplate it without a certain mixture of pleasure and pain, since it reminds us as much of past suffering as of future well-being. Bread is that article of food which is most necessary to subsistence, and least likely to be wasted by extravagance. A person may easily abstain from luxuries, or indulge in them to excess, but if he is able to purchase bread to a boundless extent, he will never consume much more or much less than he requires. The consumption of bread ought not to vary with the price; if, when flour is half-a-crown per dozen lbs., the people buy as much of it as they can eat, they will buy no more though it be reduced to one shilling per dozen. Taking these considerations into account, the fact is startling, that, for five successive years, three of which were years of average crops, ten million quarters of grain touched our shores only to be absorbed by the population. It has been said that our own farmers have grown less corn since the importation of such quantities from abroad; but granting the truth of this to some extent, no one will seriously assert that it offers even an approximately correct explanation of the importation of a quantity of grain equal to the produce of several of our largest counties. There is no way of escaping the conclusion that our population has consumed during the last five years much more of the first necessary of life than formerly.

Next to a cheap supply of bread the most important requisite to the working man is abundance of animal food. Since 1846 more than a million head of live animals have been imported and sold in the British market. This is another fact which gages the power of consumption in a prime necessary of life, and proves the existence of previous privation. When we point the Protectionist to the vast quantities of corn which have been imported from abroad, he tells us that the British farmer has grown less; what then will he say to this large importation of animal food? If the growth of corn has been discontinued, it certainly is not that the ground may be idle, else why the continued competition for farms? But the increased production of other crops points us to the breeding and rearing of greater numbers of live stock, which would not pay if meat did not fetch good price in the market. We infer, therefore, that the number of live animals imported does not fully indicate the increased consumption of animal food among the working classes, since, notwithstanding this large importation, and the increased supply furnished by our own agriculturists, no proportionate fall has taken place in the price of meat. But this implies a great change in the power of the working classes to purchase domestic comforts. In the times of Protection, thousands seldom ate a full meal of animal food.   That so large an addition of this necessary article of subsistence has gone to their table within the last few years is a grateful fact, and we confidently hazard the belief that no Englishman, be he farmer, grazier, landowner, or aught besides, would wish, for any amount of pecuniary gain, to deprive them of this blessing, which has been conferred upon them by Free Trade.

Bread and meat, though the chief, are not the only necessary articles of food ; thanks to the progress of civilisation, much more than this is requisite to render even a working man contented.   He must now have his tea, his sugar, and his tobacco.   Beyond a certain point, the more essential articles cease to indicate the progressive ability of the people to supply their physical wants, and we are obliged to fall back upon luxuries.   Applying this test to the period of Free Trade, the result is in every way satisfactory.   During the last ten years the consumption of sugar has increased by three millions of hundredweights, or sixty-nine per cent., that of tea by sixteen millions of pounds, that of coffee by more than four millions of pounds, that of tobacco by more than six millions of pounds.   During the same period the importation of rice has increased fifty per cent., that of cheese and butter has been more than doubled, while bacon, hams, and various descriptions of salted meats, have been introduced in much larger quantities.   A glance at the returns of our trade with France furnishes the most gratifying proofs of increased well-being. In 1849 we imported porcelain and chinaware to the value of £16,000, in 1851 to the value of £20,000. In 1851 we imported 9,000 more clocks than in

1848; a greater number of musical instruments, to the additional value of £11,000; 70,000 more prints and drawings, and between two and three thousand pounds' worth more toys. Proceeding to eatables, which suggested this enumeration, we find that in 1851 we imported three thousand pounds' worth more *cherries* than in 1848, 30,000 bushels more chestnuts, fruits of various kinds to the additional value of £8,000, and eggs to an equal additional amount. Most of these articles are trifling in point of intrinsic worth; neither the political prospects of England nor yet the substantial comforts of our operatives, depend upon the quantity of cherries sold in our streets, or the number of toys in our nurseries; but precisely because they are trifling are they important as tests of well-being. They prove that the middle and working classes have more money to spare than formerly, for it is among these portions of the community that this excess of imports has been distributed. The wealthy man consumed in 1842, as now, his forty pounds of sugar per annum; the additional 300,000,000 of pounds imported since then have found their way to those whose consumption was limited before to nine pounds per annum, and who now, thanks to Free Trade! can purchase twenty-three pounds. So, also, with lesser luxuries; they have been bought by those who formerly could not afford to buy them. In this light the most trivial articles, yes, the purchase, by a working man, of a child's toy or a pound of cherries, is of infinitely greater interest to the eye of the philanthropist and politician than the Arab horse or Sévres porcelain on which a nobleman expends his thousands.

Cheapness of provisions is one of the causes of the flourishing state of trade and the high rate of wages. The extent to which it operates will be seen by considering the saving which it enables the nation to make in money. At the commencement of the present year the price of wheat was about forty shillings per quarter, and even this was an advance upon its previous price. But, under Protection, sixty shillings per quarter was not thought an extraordinarily high rate; its average price from the commencement of the century down to 1844 having been sixty-eight shillings. Assuming, therefore, for the sake of comparison, sixty shillings and forty shillings as the prices of wheat under the old and new systems, Free Trade enables us to save twenty shillings upon every quarter of wheat which passes into consumption. During the last five years, we may assume the average importation of wheat, including Indian corn, to have been about 5,000,000 quarters, and this has, probably, constituted about one-fifth of the entire quantity consumed. This gives us £25,000,000 sterling as the annual sum saved in one article alone, or an aggregate in five years of £125,000,000. In sugar, a great reduction has taken place. We are under the mark in stating that sugar of the quality for which seven pence per pound was paid in 1845, can now be purchased for five pence. This has led to a greatly increased consumption, amounting, in 1851, to 6,884,189 cwt., and showing a still greater increase for 1852. The difference between seven pence and five pence per pound, amounts to a saving of more than six millions annually; and if the consumption of sugar had

X

been equally large. during the whole of the last five years, the aggregate saving would have been more than £32,000,000. During the time that these reductions have been going on, a reduction of one shilling per pound has been made in the price of tea. In 1851 the quantity of tea consumed in the United Kingdom was 53,965,112 lbs., the saving upon which, at one shilling per pound, would amount to £2,698,000, and, in five years, to an aggregate of £13,491,000. A similar reduction has been experienced in the price of other articles of daily use, such as soap, candles, rice, tobacco, etc., which must amount, collectively, to a very considerable sum. Proceeding no further, however, than the three important commodities of wheat, sugar, and tea, the nation saves annually on their purchase, as one of the effects of Free Trade, no less than £34,000,000, or an aggregate amounting in five years to £170,000,000; a saving equal in a quarter of a century to the extinction of the national debt. What becomes of this surplus? That it is actually produced is certain from the continuance of the same scale of profits in business, and the advance of wages. How, then, is it disposed of? We cannot hesitate as to the reply which must be given. During the period in which this saving has been effected we have seen universal activity prevail; not only our staple trades, but every branch of handicraft has seemed to grow with fresh vigour; the smallest towns and villages, equally with our most populous cities, have enjoyed unusual prosperity; the blacksmith, the carpenter, the tailor, the shoemaker, has found him-self overwhelmed with orders; his labour has suddenly acquired a new value, and become for him a more efficient instrument of physical well-being. This change has been effected with so little noise that it resembles a spontaneous movement of nature, the silent development of hitherto latent capacities, rather than the product of human agency. We recognise in it, nevertheless, the indubitable effects of recent legislation—it is the creation of Free Trade. The genius of cheapness has passed from village to village, and from town to town, distributing some forty or fifty millions annually among the people, and they, instinctively guided by their wants, have exchanged it for the productions of the artizan.

SECTION II.

SOCIAL INFLUENCES OF FREE TRADE AS ILLUSTRATED BY STATISTICS.

Having considered the means by which our commercial and manufacturing prosperity reaches the bulk of the people, viz., through the twofold avenue of high wages and cheap provisions, we must now glance at some of the social results of the improvement thus effected in their physical condition. Among these the first place is due to those which admit of being verified by statistics and public documents.

I. PAUPERISM.—This gigantic evil, to the growth

of which our laws have given too much encouragement, has of late years steadily diminished. The highest point of pauper expenditure since the commencement of our Free Trade policy, was reached in 1848, when it amounted to £6,180,764. Since that year it has continued to decline till, in 1851, it amounted to only £4,962,704. Comparing the half-year which closed with Michaelmas, 1852, with the corresponding period in 1851, a still further reduction is apparent; the total expenditure for the half year, in 607 unions and single parishes in England and Wales, having fallen from £1,609,761 to £1,583,130, or a clear decrease of £26,631, or £53,262 upon the year. To appreciate this fully, it must be borne in mind, that great reductions had taken place in previous years. The diminution for the six months ending with Michaelmas, 1851, as compared with the same period of 1850, was £40,824, or £81,648 on the year, and during the previous year the reduction had amounted to £405,000. It must also be borne in mind, that during the last year provisions were generally dearer than during 1851, and that therefore the diminished expenditure indicates a more than proportionate decrease of actual pauperism. The following list of English counties, showing the increase or decrease per cent. in point of expenditure during six months of 1852, as compared with six months in 1851, will enable us to form a correct estimate of the relative extent and causes of existing pauperism in different parts of the kingdom :—

	Per Cent.			Per Cent.	
	Increase.	Decrease.		Increase.	Decrease.
Bedford	2·3	..	Monmouth	..	0·4
Berks	0·6	..	Norfolk	1·9	..
Buckingham	..	0·3	Northampton ..	..	1·4
Cambridge......	..	0·6	Northumberland	..	2.3
Chester	1·9	..	Nottingham	..	2·7
Cornwall	..	0·8	Oxford	..	3·6
Cumberland	..	4·3	Rutland	4·4	..
Derby..........	..	5·3	Salop	..	4·2
Devon..........	..	2·4	Somerset	..	2·8
Dorset	..	2·0	Southampton....	..	2·6
Durham........	..	3·4	Stafford	..	2·2
Essex..........	..	1·4	Suffolk	0·6	..
Gloucester	..	1·7	Surrey	..	2·6
Hereford	..	3·8	Sussex	..	1·0
Hertford	3·4	..	Warwick........	..	3·3
Huntingdon	..	3·6	Westmoreland ..	..	7·2
Kent	1·4	..	Wilts	..	0·7
Lancaster	..	7·7	Worcester	..	3·8
Leicester	..	6·0	York, E. Riding .	..	..
Lincoln	1·5	..	York, N. Riding .	..	2·2
Middlesex	0·4	..	York, W. Riding.	..	0.6

It appears from this statement that the increased expenditure has taken place in agricultural districts, remote from large towns, and, consequently, where the effects of our revived trade have been but slightly felt. This is no more than might have been expected. The state of a large proportion of the rural population has long been so bad, that years must elapse before it can be placed on a healthy footing. Early in the present year a clergyman sent a letter to the "Times" newspaper, in which he compared the wages received by the agricultural labourer in his district with the cost of necessary articles of subsistence, from which it appeared that, after meeting them, he had nothing left for obtaining such necessaries as tea and sugar.

A correspondent from Buckinghamshire complains of
the hard condition in which farm labourers with large
families are placed; a man with ten children getting
no more money than he can earn himself. The strike
of the Wiltshire labourers, now going on, discloses a sad
fact; hundreds of families forced to maintain themselves
on seven shillings per week, less than half the sum
which thousands of factory operatives in Lancashire,
not yet out of their teens, carry home weekly. Assuredly, if Protection did much for the farmer and
landowner, it also did much for the labourer; if it
enabled them to live in ignorance and luxury, it
forced him to live in misery. If the blessings of the
corn law had been mercifully vouchsafed much longer.
to him, they would have placed him effectually beyond
the reach of injustice, in that common asylum of the
wretched, where " the wicked cease from troubling."
Mr. Caird, in his recent work on English Agriculture,
tells us, that, within the last eighty years, the average
price of arable land has risen 100 per cent.; that the
average produce of wheat has increased fourteen per
cent.; that the price of butter has increased 100 per
cent., meat seventy per cent., and wool 100 per cent.,
while the wages of the labourer have only advanced
thirty-four per cent. ; in other words, he was twice as
well off eighty years ago as he was immediately before
the repeal of the corn laws. In the counties visited
by Arthur Young, the rent of the labourer had increased in his time from seven pence halfpenny to
one shilling and five pence per week, 125 per cent.;
while his wages had only risen from seven shillings
and three pence to nine shillings and seven pence,

per week, or thirty-four per cent. Happily Free Trade has altered his condition, but still, with *seven shillings a week* for the maintenance of a family, how narrow is the space between independence and pauperism ! A slight increase in the price of provisions necessarily sends him for aid to the union-house. It may be asked, why do they not avail themselves of the state of trade in the manufacturing districts to obtain better wages ? We reply, that many have done so already, that it is no easy matter for persons accustomed all their life to farm labour, to adapt themselves all at once to the loom, and that those who have betaken themselves to the towns are chiefly young persons, unencumbered with families, leaving a larger proportion of married and aged persons behind them. Besides, the long continuance of low wages, joined to the attraction of ready parochial relief, has trained up in our agricultural districts a generation of paupers, who reckon the assistance of the Board of Guardians among the ordinary means of getting through the world. Still, with all these drawbacks, in more than twenty agricultural counties there has been a diminution of expenditure during the last six months, and, if we except Middlesex, the same has taken place in all the manufacturing counties.

The diminution of pauper expenditure leads us to expect a diminution of actual pauperism. The following statement will show the facts of the case on this important branch of the subject :—

Number of Paupers (exclusive of Vagrants) in Receipt of Relief in the several Unions and Parishes under Boards of Guardians in England and Wales, on the 1st of January in each year.

Year.	Number of Unions and Parishes.*	Adult Able-bodied.			All other Paupers.			TOTAL.		
		Indoor.	Outdoor.	TOTAL.	Indoor	Outdoor	TOTAL.	Indoor.	Outdoor	TOTAL.
1849	509	28,123	173,521	201,644	91,252	641,523	732,775	119,375	815,044	934,419
1850	600	26,151	155,008	151,159	92,408	646,976	739,384	118,559	801,984	920,543
1851	600	23,322	131,203	154,525	87,243	619,125	706,368	110,565	750,328	860,893
1852	608	19,752	117,566	137,318	86,661	610,445	697,106	106,413	728,011	834,424
1853	608	18,138	108,082	126,220	86,048	586,554	672,602	104,186	694,636	798,822
1854	618	21,964	114,085	136,049	91,573	590,693	682,266	113,537	704,778	818,315

These figures are exceedingly gratifying. They exhibit a continuous decrease in the numbers of paupers from 1849 to 1853, the difference in favour of the latter being no less than 135,597. As might have been expected from the higher price of bread, a slight increase has taken place during the present year. This however only furnishes an additional proof of the vastly improved condition of the people. In December, 1849, wheat was thirty-nine shillings per quarter, and the total number of paupers 934,419. In December, 1853, the price of wheat was seventy-one shillings per quarter, and the number of paupers 818,315, a diminution of 116,104. This fact speaks volumes. The following return for IRELAND is still more pleasing:—

* The population of these Unions and Parishes is, according to the last census, 16,250,861, being 1,676,748 short of the total population of England and Wales.

1st Week of January,	Adult Able-bodied.	All other Paupers.	Total.		
	Indoor.	Indoor.	Indoor.	Outdoor.	Total.
1849	74,534	122,858	197,392	423,355	620,747
1850	72,617	130,703	203,320	104,650	307,970
1851	71,936	134,532	306,468	2,719	209,187
1852	53,817	114,431	168,248	3,170	171,418
1853	43,939	94,825	138,764	3,058	141,822
1854	30,463	74,141	104,604	2,198	106,802

The general impression which these statistics give of the improved condition of the working classes, is strengthened when we inquire into the state of particular districts. The following statement, recently presented to the authorities of Manchester, by H. B. Farnell, Esq., Poor Law Inspector for the Manchester district, will speak for itself. Selecting February as the month which best represents the average relief of the year, Mr. Farnell states the number of paupers on the books within his district in the years 1847-1852 as follows :—

1847 13,744		1850 13,317
1848 23,000		1851 11,365
1849 15,858		1852 11,912

A difference of 11,088 appears from this statement between the number of paupers on the books in the Manchester district in February, 1852, and February, 1848, and in June, 1852, the number fell as low as 9,492. Mr. Farnell states that in Lancashire and the West Riding of Yorkshire alone, 79,388 paupers have been struck off the books since 1848. Passing into the Midland Counties, Mr. Hunt, Poor Law Auditor for the Warwickshire and Oxford districts, states, that the expense of pauper relief in his district was less by £12,231 in 1852 than 1848, having fallen from £44,108 to £31,777. To the same effect is the report of Mr. Corder, Clerk to the Guardians of Birmingham. According to this document, the number of persons receiving relief in the Birmingham Union January 1st, 1853, was 4,125, while on January 1st, 1849, the number was 11,554, showing a decrease of 7,429 persons. It is also stated in the "Economist" newspaper, that the Poor Law Guardians of Birmingham applied during the last year for permission to engage twenty independent labourers to repair walks, etc., and twenty needlewomen to do the sewing of the union-house.

II. The next statistical proof we shall adduce of the improvement which has taken place in the social condition of the community, is derived from the last report of the Registrar General, relative to the number of BIRTHS, DEATHS, and MARRIAGES, within England and Wales, for the quarter and year ending September, 1852, combined with more recent parliamentary returns. It is unnecessary to point out the value of these returns as a sign of social progress or retrogression. We might define a "prosperous year" to be one in which the circumstances of the bulk of the population are easy, and one of the surest results of this is, that a greater number than usual find themselves able to venture upon the responsibilities of marriage. Such a test is commensurate with the whole community, though applying, perhaps, with greater force to the middle than to the working classes, since the checks of prudence are felt most powerfully among the former. The rate of mortality at any given period depends chiefly upon two causes, the sanitary state of the population, and atmospheric phenomena over which we have no control. The latter will be found not to influence the average rate of mortality when taken on a series of years, since they constantly recur at intervals, though they may largely affect the returns of a single year. The sanitary condition of the population depends also upon two general causes—the state of the streets and dwellings where they reside, and the price of food and clothing. We see here the extent to which Free Trade exerts a direct influence on the health of the people. Ere long it will, we trust, by its indirect influence, completely revolutionize the dwellings of the humbler classes, pave and drain our streets, provide the means of healthful recreation for the people, and thus affect the public health through the other half of the circumstances on which it depends, but at present its influence is exerted chiefly through the superior comforts which it places within the reach of the hard-working operative.

The following table exhibits the number of Births, Deaths, and Marriages during each of the last five years, as compared with 1842 :—

Years.	Estimated Population.	Births.	Deaths.	Marriages.
1842	16,148,598	517,739	349,519	118,825
1849	17,571,744	578,159	440,853	141,883
1850	17,735,871	593,422	368,986	152,738
1851	} 18,004,551 {	615,865	395,174	154,206
1852		624,171	407,938	158,439
1853		612,341	421,775	162,135

The annual average rate of births is 3·282 per

cent. of the entire population, or nearly one in thirty. In 1852 it rose to 3·472, or one in twenty-nine; declining a little in 1853, though still higher than the average. The average annual rate of deaths is 2·242 per cent., or rather less than one in forty-five. In 1852 the rate of mortality was 2·269 per cent., or nearly one in forty-four; while in 1853 it rose to 2·342 per cent., or more than one in forty-three. The number of marriages in 1853 was 3,696 greater than in the preceding year, and no less than 43,310 beyond that of 1842. In the summer quarter of 1852, 38,291 marriages were solemnized in England and Wales, while the corresponding quarter of 1840, 1841, 1842, 1843, the number never exceeded 29,397, and in 1842 fell as low as 27,288. In the summer of 1844 there was a sudden increase, and in that of 1845 the number of marriages was 35,003. In 1847 and 1848, times of peculiar pressure, the number fell to 32,439. They rose slowly during the summer of 1849, but in each of the four following years the marriages during the summer quarters have not been less than 37,155. Mr. Farr adds to this statement, " Nothing probably indicates more accurately than these figures the condition of the people, or the view they took of their prospects in life during the last eleven summers." In looking over the districts where the increase has taken place, we find among them many parts of the country which were to have been ruined long ago through the pernicious influence of Free Trade. The increase is observable not only in London, but in the South-eastern Counties, and still more in Devonshire and

Somersetshire.   In the South Midland Counties the rate is nearly stationary, but it has increased in the North Midland, particularly in Shrewsbury, Dudley, Worcester, Birmingham, Coventry, Warwick, Leicester, and Nottingham, all districts in which manufactures are extensively carried on.   In Cheshire and Leicestershire marriages are much more numerous than in 1848.   In Manchester and Liverpool a decrease is observed as compared with 1851, perhaps, as the " Times" facetiously suggests, because those places are " married out," but assuredly not because they are less prosperous than others.

The only items in the above returns which can be considered at all unfavourable, is the decrease in the number of births, and the increase in the number of deaths, during 1853, as compared with the average of preceding years.   Probably the statistics of emigration should be weighed in connexion with both these changes.   During the last three years no fewer than 1,033,537 persons have left the United Kingdom to find a permanent home in the United States or the British colonies.   During the same interval the population has remained stationary, the decrease arising from emigration being about made up by the number of births.   But the rate of mortality is highest among children, while those whose places they fill up on the census tables were to a great extent married couples, many recently married with a view to immediate emigration.   The increase of deaths during 1852 and 1853 is susceptible of another explanation. The autumn and winter of 1852 were particularly unhealthy.   On October 30th a period of wet weather set in of a higher temperature than any on record. The mean temperature of November was 48·9°, being 6½ in excess of the average of eighty years. The mean temperature of December was 47·6°, or 8¾ in excess of the average. At the same time the fall of rain was unusually large, having attained a depth of 50 inches in Cornwall, 30 or 40 in most midland districts, and 58 at Stonyhurst and South Shields. The diseases, which show an increase for the last quarter of 1852, are just those which a warm and humid atmosphere would aggravate. Taking these circumstances into account, we may regard the trifling increase in the number of deaths in 1852 as a decisive indication of social well-being. The increase in the number of deaths in 1853 is due in a great measure to the partial return of cholera, the ravages of which at Newcastle and several other large towns were far more severe than on its previous visit. This is an enemy which cannot be conquered in a day. Its complete subjugation will reward nothing less than the toils of a century.

III. INDUSTRIAL INVESTMENTS.—A pleasing proof of the beneficial effects of Free Trade upon the condition of the working man is found in the new modes of investing his savings which have recently sprung into existence. Of the character of these, in an economical point of view, it is not necessary to speak. Probably those which are now attracting most attention among the working classes are, on the whole, safe; but whether they are so or not they furnish the same proof of the improved means and habits of the people. Much knowledge has of late years been diffused on this important subject. The friendly societies which were formed half a century ago have nearly all failed, and taught the working classes by bitter experience the necessity of having a scientific basis in any scheme for mutual help. Odd-Fellowship itself has received a blow from the calculations of Mr. Neison; its progress is much less rapid than formerly; partly from a suspicion of insecurity, and partly from the effect of its childish mummeries, its popularity is on the wane. It is probable that this circumstance is traceable to a still more gratifying cause. The economical views of the working classes are becoming more enlarged; they now look further than a mere provision for a time of sickness; they are bent upon a general improvement in their condition, and think that a cottage of their own, and as large a sum as they can afford in the savings' bank, are the best provisions they can make for future casualties.

1. The number of savings' banks throughout the kingdom, and the description of persons who usually avail themselves of their advantages, render them a very important test of the condition of the community. If we apply this test to the period of our Free Trade policy, the result is quite in unison with the other indications of prosperity already noticed. The following statement will show the number of depositors of all classes, and the aggregate amount deposited by each class, on the 20th November, 1845, and 20th November, 1850:—

Depositors.	Total, 1845.		Total, 1850.	
	Number Depositors	Amount.	Number Depositors.	Amount.
		£.		£.
Not exceeding £20	597,631	3,851,027	677,969	4,046,941
,, ,, £50	267,609	8,247,304	251,131	7,752,517
,, ,, £100	113,727	7,815,347	106,510	7,335,789
,, ,, £150	37,924	4,563,790	35,609	4,275,740
,, ,, £200	21,302	3,633,971	18,914	3,229,867
Exceeding £200	3,001	702,981	2,448	557,709
Number and Amount of Individual Depositors	1,041,194	28,814,420	1,092,581	27,198,563
Number and Amount of Charitable Institutions	11,695	630,898	12,912	655,093
Number and Amount of Friendly Societies	10,041	1,303,515	7,506	1,077,326
	1,062,930	30,748,833	1,112,999	28,930,982
Number and Amount of Friendly Societies in direct account with Commissioners	488	1,913,956	586	2,277,340
Total	1,063,418	32,662,789	1,113,585	31,208,322

The above statement is very instructive. Its chief
feature is the increase of small depositors by more
than 80,000 persons, and of the sum deposited by
nearly £200,000; while a decrease has taken place in
every other class of depositors and deposits. How
is this decrease to be accounted for? It cannot but
appear remarkable that the cause, whatever it may
have been, should only have influenced the larger
deposits. This circumstance points us to the true
explanation. The railway panic is still fresh in our
memories. We all remember how the insane fever
infected all classes, from the highest magnates of
the aristocracy, to the humblest clerk and artizan who
had a sum of money worth investing. While dukes
and marquises exchanged their thousands for scrip,

the industrious operative, fired by the accounts of enormous profits which reached his ears, hastened to draw his fifty or hundred pounds from the bank, where it was receiving its sober three per cent., to invest it in undertakings the profits of which would be reckoned by hundreds. We know many cases in which money was thus withdrawn, and in which, almost without an exception, it was swallowed up in the vortex which engulfed more than a hundred millions of British capital. This is, no doubt, one cause of the diminution of first class depositors in savings' banks; but there is also another which has probably had some share in the result. Where trade is active, an impetus is experienced by all industrial interests; there is then a general movement, as in heated water, towards the surface. Each individual seizes the opportunity of rising a step. The thrifty journeyman becomes master, a man accustomed hitherto to obtain a livelihood by manual exertions, opens a shop, or embarks in some other enterprise which requires capital. The persons who compose the second and third class of depositors in savings' banks are those who generally avail themselves of the opportunities afforded by good times. But in seasons of this kind there are also many who first begin to invest their savings, with the hope of similarly employing them at some future period. Hence, the rule we should expect to see hold good in reference to savings' banks is, that when times are prosperous the number of small depositors will increase, but that sums of sufficient magnitude to invest in trade will be withdrawn in a like ratio. This is precisely what has occurred.

The following table will show the total amount re-

ceived and paid by trustees of savings' banks; and of the
capital invested in each of the last four years, and in
1842, distinguishing the different parts of the United
Kingdom.   It will be seen that the amount of money
in savings' banks in 1853 was between four and five
millions greater than in 1850. The temporary depression arising from the railway losses of 1847 and
1848 has passed away, and though the briskness of
trade has no doubt led many a thrifty man to employ
his savings in profitable enterprise rather than place
them in the bank, and emigration has probably led
to the withdrawal of a great deal, yet there is above
a million and a half in the hands of the trustees of
savings' banks at the present time more than was
ever thus invested before.

Total Amount Received and Paid by Trustees of Savings' Banks
from and to Depositors, and of the Capital of Savings' Banks.*

		England.	Wales.	Scotland.	Ireland.	United Kingdom.
		£.	£.	£.	£.	£.
1842	Received	4,519,094	100,966	290,109	879,034	5,789,203
	Paid	4,475,133	113,881	179,336	887,810	5,656,160
	Capital ..	21,780,373	531,928	652,129	2,354,906	25,319,336
1850	Received	5,226,778	103,673	612,164	421,075	6,363,690
	Paid	5,755,550	151,620	477,197	375,961	6,760,328
	Capital ..	25,655,145	648,669	1,325,063	1,302,105	28,930,982
1851	Received	5,620,388	111,792	620,457	429,422	6,782,059
	Paid	5,276,875	123,537	497,160	407,994	6,305,566
	Capital ..	26,770,457	659,387	1,488,707	1,359,103	30,277,654
1852	Received	6,041,533	122,089	648,363	469,192	7,281,177
	Paid	5,624,231	118,471	536,259	405,945	6,684,906
	Capital ..	27,967,641	681,614	1,045,040	1,459,966	31,754,261
1853	Received	6,231,989	153,095	736,640	531,796	7,653,520
	Paid	5,985,281	112,155	582,882	436,012	7,116,330
	Capital ..	29,180,894	742,567	1,837,874	1,599,067	33,360,402

* Exclusive of Friendly Societies in direct account with the
commissioners.

The latest accounts from individual savings' banks in different parts of the kingdom, are of a very encouraging character. Thus, in the Birmingham Savings' Bank, the number of depositors in 1851 was 1,025 more than in 1850, and the aggregate increase in the sum deposited amounted to £20,000. The Provident Society in the same town, under the presidency of Lord Lyttleton, is also very flourishing, both in members and funds. The sums deposited in the Nottingham Savings' Bank during 1851 amounted to £5,000 more than during the preceding year, the entire amount being £49,000. Besides this, a single institute, known as the District Visiting Provident Society, received £2000 in small sums throughout the year. The Stourbridge and Dudley Savings' Bank, representing an extensive coal and iron district, showed a clear increase at the close of 1852 of more than £3,500 on the close of 1851, and the report adds that this represents but a small portion of the savings of the neighbourhood among the operative classes.

2. The investment of money in land or house property, through the medium of freehold land societies and building clubs, has been growing in popularity among the working classes during the last five years. It would be impossible to form an approximate estimate of the number of building clubs which are in operation throughout the kingdom, but it must be very large. In 1851 more than 1,300 houses were built in Birmingham, besides 700 which were in progress at the end of the year, and excluding 75 villas, of the largest class, erecting at Edgbaston. In Sheffield between 2,000 and 3,000 have been built within the last twelvemonths, and not less than 4,000

in Manchester. In this latter town scarcely a month
passes without some new building society coming
into operation, and the magnitude which some of the
older societies have attained may be judged from the
fact that in one of them, a short time since, no fewer
than 12,000 shares had been disposed of, which, reck-
oning £60 a share, are equivalent to a building capital
of nearly three quarters of a million sterling. It is
chiefly through the medium of these societies that
working men succeed in obtaining a cottage of their
own to live in. The freehold land movement is progressing on a very large scale, and the union which
exists among the various societies enables us to
ascertain, with complete accuracy, the amount of
savings invested in them. To take a single instance,
not less than £132,000 has been paid in four years
into one freehold land society in Birmingham. The
ordinary receipts for the year 1851 were £15,000, and
though the directors had advanced £20,000, not one
person was behind in his subscriptions. Of Coventry,
Sheffield, and other places, similar accounts might be
given, but the most complete view will be obtained
from the following statement, presented at the Freehold
Land Conference held in London, December 8th, 1852.
All the returns applied for by the secretary had not
been sent in, but, according to the most careful estimate, there were then, throughout the kingdom, 130
societies, containing 85,000 members, who held
among them 120,000 shares; 310 estates had been
bought, 19,500 allotments had been made, and the
sums actually received had amounted to £790,000.
These figures, compared with the previous year, show
an increase of thirty societies, 40,000 members, 55,000

shares, 174 estates, 5,500 allotments, and £480,000 in payments; estimating the shares at an average of £30 per share, the total sum subscribed for is not less than £3,600,000. These facts deserve to rank among the leading phenomena of the age. They bring before us tens of thousands, belonging almost exclusively to the working classes, who are silently rising to the position of landed proprietors. The soil of England, under the stimulating effects of Free Trade, is rapidly passing into the hands of its humblest sons, and that, not by revolutionary confiscations, but by the peaceful efforts of well-directed labour. Free Trade has a double connexion with the freehold land movement, since it not only produces the prosperity which is so essential to its progress among the working classes, but directly originated it. The suggestion to purchase estates and divide them into small freeholds, issued first from the chambers of the "League;" it was a weapon of war, beaten now into a ploughshare for the social advancement of the people.

3. As an illustration of the increased forethought, in itself the proof of a higher social condition, which now characterises the middle and industrial classes, as well as of the improved means which they now enjoy for carrying out its suggestions, we may mention the great increase which has recently taken place in the number of insurance companies. It is not necessary to touch upon the pending controversy respecting the prospects of these new institutions; their existence proves that an increasing number of the community are desirous of providing for future emergencies. The sums assured in the English and Scotch offices, that is to say, the amount of all the

life policies at present outstanding in the hands of
the public, are computed at £150,000,000. The
greater part of this vast sum, £116,000,000, is distributed among 152 English offices, of which 75, or
nearly one-half, have been founded since 1844.
Of the entire number ten were formed before 1800 ;
during the next ten years ten more originated; from
1810 to 1820, five; from 1820 to 1830, sixteen; from
1830 to 1844, thirty-six ; and from 1844 to 1850,
seventy-five. Thus the number established in the six
years ending with 1850, was twice as many as those
established during the preceding fifteen years ; or
the rate of progress was five times greater under the
Free Trade period than under any preceding one.

IV. In a country like Great Britain, where the
influences, both moral and physical, which act upon
its population, are so very similar, and its narrow
extent, combined with the cheap and easy means of
passing from place to place, prevents the growth of
local peculiarities, one large town may be regarded
as an average type of all the rest ; and Manchester,
Birmingham, Nottingham, or Glasgow, is a kind of
microcosm of the manufacturing districts. Glasgow
has the great advantage of undergoing a social analysis
yearly at the hands of its accomplished registrar, Dr.
Strang, and from the report of that gentleman, dated
January 11, 1853, we select a few facts which will
place in a striking point of view the progress which
has been made during the last five years in the commercial metropolis of Scotland, and the second city
in the empire. We may remark that in the report
for 1851, Dr. Strang stated that a great change had
transpired in Glasgow, during the five years preceding,

in reference to the food of the inhabitants; inferior grains, such as oats, being rapidly exchanged for wheat. Comparing 1852 with 1851, epidemic diseases had been less prevalent; pauper burials had diminished by 199 or 7·1 per cent.; there had been 359 more births, and 231 more marriages. The consumption of provisions of nearly all kinds had increased. There had been killed 1,669 more oxen, 7,616 more sheep, and 55 more pigs, and even these figures give a very imperfect view of the increased consumption of animal food, on account of the continually increasing weight of the oxen and sheep brought into the market. The quantity of tea brought out of bond at Leith and the ports of the Clyde during 1852, for home consumption, exceeded that of 1851 by 121,842 pounds; that of sugar exceeded the quantity of 1851 by 4,069 tons; that of molasses by 834 tons. In 1852, as compared with 1851, 10,380 tons more shipping were registered; upwards of 20,000 more letters passed through the post office in a single week than in the corresponding week of the previous year; 1,838 more money orders were issued and paid in a single quarter. In spite of all the emigration which had taken place, the increase of money at the credit of depositors at the National Savings' Bank on the 2nd of November, 1852, was £56,832 11s. 0d.; and although 7,477 old depositors closed accounts, there were 9,067 new ones to take their place. Notwithstanding an increasing population, pauperism had declined. The number of paupers receiving relief for the parish of Glasgow in 1850 was 5,929; in 1852, 5,432; for the parish of Gorbals in 1850, 290; in 1852, 78; for the parish of Barony in 1850, 4,186; in 1852,

3,587; and for the parish of Govan in 1850, 1,767; in 1852, 1,024; while during the last five years the cost of pauper maintenance has decreased by more than £34,000. In the factories of Glasgow the increase of cotton consumed in 1852, as compared with 1851, was 25,000 bales; the harbour dues increased by more than £7,000; the weekly traffic on three principal railways increased in value by £1,564; and, finally, the number of sequestrations, which in 1841 was 114; in 1851, 118; in 1852 was only 98. The facts we have adduced in reference to other parts of the United Kingdom render it probable that Glasgow is neither alone nor pre-eminent in point of social progress. As a healthy member of the body politic, it proves the soundness of the entire system. An analysis, equally detailed, of other towns would produce the same results, and we may safely say, *ex uno disce omnes.*

SECTION III.

COLLATERAL PROOFS OF THE SOCIAL BENEFITS OF FREE TRADE.

The statistics to which we have referred, though furnishing indisputable evidence that a great improvement has taken place in the social condition of the labouring classes, nevertheless fails to convey an adequate impression of its extent. Innumerable facts which cannot be registered by statistics, but which are evident to the most cursory observation, give us a more vivid picture of the change, and enable every person to verify its reality for himself. No one disputes that the times are better than they were; all are conscious of it, just as they are that the sun shines or that the wind blows. The Glasgow operative changes his oatmeal for wheaten bread ; the Englishman regales his children at Christmas with fare which would do no discredit to the table of a nobleman. The Nottingham weaver, who in 1840 was a walking skeleton, so that a man far gone in consumption was said to be "as thin as a stockinger," now " exhibits a degree of *embonpoint* that would do honour to any class of Her Majesty's subjects." During the last autumn serious inconvenience was felt in many rural districts from the scarcity of labourers, wages rose for a time to three or four shillings per day, and at an earlier period of the year, when harvest work was not pressing, the wages of farm labourers in the neighbourhood of Settle and Wakefield were fifteen shillings a week. From Buckinghamshire we hear that the "poor are better off than under any former regulations." A Birmingham manufacturer complains that he has been harassed all the summer by " the frequent absence of his men on excursions, either by rail or steamers," and mentions as a " serious evil" that they are able, by working two or three days in the week, to provide easily for the whole. Other accounts from the same district tell us of workpeople, as at Messrs. Elkington's electro-plate manufactory, forming themselves into societies for mutual help, and making considerable grants to charitable institutions. With respect to female labour, a great change has taken place ; Mr. Felkin, of Nottingham, says, "A thousand women and children would find instant employment in this neighbourhood." The Earl of Shaftesbury states that he recently offered 200 young women, of the class that a few years since could earn no more than four pence halfpenny during a day of fourteen hours, a permanent situation in the north of six shillings a week, including lodging, and that the offer was declined because they could do better for themselves in London. The embroidery of muslin is now offering to hundreds of young women in Glasgow the means of lightening their dependence on parental support, or even of procuring a tolerable maintenance. The general scarcity of female servants in large towns is a matter of common complaint; the register offices find a difficulty in obtaining an adequate supply, and the wages of those who combine a good character with ordinary skill have risen thirty per cent. during the last four years. " A Templar" complains that the old stock of laundresses, formerly so abundant near the Inns of Court, is dying out, and that none are eager, even with the prospect of a comfortable livelihood, to supply their place. Crossing the channel, we learn that the farmers in the neighbourhood of Belfast are in a state of unexampled comfort. With one or two sons engaged at the loom, and as many daughters at needlework, they live in opulence compared with their condition a few years ago. The increased activity of our foreign and coasting trade has attracted a large amount of unskilled labour to our ports. Not only those of the first class, as London, Liverpool, Glasgow, Hull, Bristol, but the entire chain of harbours round our coast, have given employment to additional hands. The same process has been going on in the neighbourhood of our large towns. We have seen that, in some cases, the wages of the labourer have been raised when those of the skilled workman remained stationary. Accordingly, the agricultural operative, previously earning his seven or eight shillings per week, has quitted his native parish, and located himself in the nearest town. Thus a process of exhalation has been going on with respect to the country districts, and the spur to agricultural improvement which has been given by the free importation of foreign corn, has been sharpened by the necessity of paying higher wages for work done. These are only a sample of the facts which hardly strike us, because they are so familiar, but they demonstrate none the less the happy change which, through the goodness of God, we have experienced—a change which has passed over us, like summer breezes over ripening corn, and turned the voice of wailing into joy.

Besides such isolated illustrations of social improvement, there are several *classes* of facts, having a more specific bearing upon the same point, to which we invite attention. They are furnished by unexceptionable witnesses, who have personally experienced what they relate.

I. The first class of facts relates to the superior kind of clothing which is now worn by our operative population. It has been well remarked, that good clothing is the first thing a poor man puts off, and the last thing he puts on. Food occupies his first cares, useless indulgences of various kinds, too often, come next, while dress ranks last in the scale. This is not equally true of the middle classes; per-

haps the very converse would be more applicable to
them; they are under the influence of different
motives, and " a respectable *appearance*" is often to
them the highest end of life.   There is, perhaps, no
more accurate or extensive test of the condition of
the working classes in Lancashire with respect to
dress, than that afforded by Sunday schools.   We
need not say that those institutions are eminently
popular; they have taken firm hold of the affections
of the people, and four-fifths of the entire juvenile
population of the districts to which we now refer are
under their tuition.   Hence they exhibit, on the
largest scale, that illustration of the pecuniary ability
and social *status* of the parent, which is always afforded
by the condition of his family.   We have taken pains
to ascertain the comparative condition of the children
in twenty of the largest schools, and are enabled to
report upon it as follows :—Six or seven years ago
the clothing of the scholars was generally of a very
scanty and inferior kind; many were not decent
enough to attend the school, and, as winter approached,
nothing could be more painful than to notice the
insufficiency of the clothing for the purpose of warmth
and comfort.   They were especially deficient in
under-garments; stockings and flannel were often
altogether wanting.   To remedy, as far as possible,
such a state of things, clothing clubs were established
in connexion with many schools, into which the
children paid a small sum weekly during the summer
months, the managers of the school adding a bounty
of two pence in the shilling, and the whole being laid
out in the purchase of materials at prime cost, which
were sold at the same rate to the parents.   By such

schemes, vigorously carried out, a large number of scholars were annually furnished with a suit of warm clothing, and the school became a valuable instrument of physical as well as moral amelioration. *Now*, however, the state of things is changed. It is an exception to find a boy destitute of warm and decent clothing, and the machinery of the club is laid by for worse times. In addition to this, which relates to the younger portion of the scholars, it is instructive to observe a similar process among the "senior classes," and more especially among those which consist of young women. Classes of this description are not common in similar institutions in the South of England, but in Lancashire and Yorkshire it is not unusual to find half-a-dozen in connexion with the same school, containing an aggregate of one hundred scholars, who earn, by their employment at the factory, an average of probably eleven shillings per week. Among young women of this description may be observed not only a great improvement in the general quality of dress, but actually a periodical change of fashion. As spring comes on the winter attire disappears ; lighter clothing, silks and ribbons of brighter colours, take its place ; artificial wreaths of ivy and snowdrops, the emblems of sterner seasons, give way to the violet and the rose. Nor must we omit to state a fact which is not without its significance as an index to social condition ;—with this increased expensiveness of dress there is, as far, at least, as our observation has extended, a superior neatness, a nearer approach to the " *simplex munditiis*" of the Roman poet, which indicates a greater refinement of taste among the female portion of the community. We can imagine that such statements will provoke censure from stern economists, who would regard it as a higher proof of civilisation if the increased earnings of our factory girls were taken to the savings' banks, instead of being spent on dress. Such a sentiment is probably correct, but its general recognition is destined to be a farther stage of social progress; the philanthropist must accept with gratitude instalments of improvement.

II. Another illustration of social progress, is the decline which has taken place in the pledging system. In bad times this is the first resource. Five years ago a very large proportion of the population, in the poorer districts of our large towns, were in the regular habit of resorting to it. It is otherwise now. On the concurrent testimony of intelligent persons, whose professions bring them into frequent contact with the working classes and their homes, we believe that the practice has considerably diminished. Mr. Felkin, of Nottingham, whose extensive acquaintance with a class of operatives who were once driven by privation to this expedient for relief, entitles his opinion to great weight, says, "As far as my researches on this subject have extended of late, I believe the working classes pawn less than formerly," adding, however, his belief, that the middle classes pawn more. It will be satisfactory, on the general question, to adduce the testimony of persons actually engaged in the trade. From inquiries we have made in several quarters, it appears that the number of articles pledged is about two-thirds of what it was formerly. One of our informants has been engaged in the business more than eighteen years; he says he never

knew the profits of pawnbroking less than they are
at the present time. A few years since, this person
registered as many as six or seven thousand articles a
month, giving an aggregate of eighty-four thousand
for the year; now it is about four thousand, or an
aggregate of fifty thousand a year. This smaller
aggregate unfolds, it must be confessed, a very
serious evil; we can congratulate ourselves only by
way of comparison; the absolute amount of pawning
which is still carried on, betrays the existence of
social phenomena which require to be met by prompt
and bold measures. At the same time, the decrease
which has taken place, if rightly weighed, speaks
most decisively of the improved condition of the
working classes. This decrease, it must be remembered, has been effected upon a section of the pawnbroker's customers. There are very many whom no
change in the price of provisions or labour can affect;
the dram-drinker, the indolent, the wilfully improvident, the prostitute, the thief; these are stated
visitants, not from necessity but from choice, or, at
least, a necessity which is self-made. An actual
instance, in verification of this remark, may not be
inappropriate. It relates to a family consisting of a
mother and four daughters; the daughters are employed in a cotton factory, and receive, pretty regularly,
thirteen shillings a week each, making a total of
£2 12s. for their joint support; and yet, almost every
Wednesday, they are compelled to pledge some articles
of clothing in order to obtain money till Friday, the
day when the wages are paid. The fatal curse, in
this, as in a multitude of similar cases, is drunkenness.
When we see the same number of such persons as
formerly enter the pawn-shop, we are forced to admit

that abundance of food, and the means of obtaining an honest livelihood, are not the sole requisites for making a nation virtuous, but this by no means proves the social inefficiency of Free Trade. It is not too much to assume that persons of this description constitute, even in adverse times, one-half of the frequenters of the pawn-shop, and as they pawn on a system, pledging and redeeming one week after another, it is probable that their articles constitute nearly three-fifths of the whole. This leaves but a small comparative number for industrious and honourable men of the working class, who are driven to the practice by sheer necessity, and it is on this number that the effects of Free Trade would chiefly operate.

III. Another gratifying proof of social progress among the working classes is the readiness they have shown to avail themselves of means of improvement, whether physical or mental, which have been provided for them by the more wealthy portion of the community. Perhaps no period has been more fruitful in the creation of such means than that which has elapsed since the commencement of Free Trade. With British merchants and manufacturers, prosperous seasons are not devoted wholly to selfish aggrandizement; no, the scale on which they receive, is also that on which they give; and scarcely any interval of prosperity passes by without leaving in our large towns some new memorial of their beneficence, to cheer the darker interval which may succeed. Humanity and Free Trade are closely allied; the age which demands the one is ready to exercise the other. The spirit of monopoly is freezing, harsh, contracted, suggestive of all crabbed and cold ideas, while that of Free Trade is warm, open, benignant, finding its nearest type in the sunbeam or the gushing fountain. The same year witnessed the introduction of the first Free Trade measures into the House of Commons, and the establishment of the first Mechanics' Institute in the United Kingdom. This was but natural; when industry asked for light, it also panted for freedom.

1. One of the homeliest, but not least important, provisions which have recently been made with a view to the social improvement of the masses, is the establishment of public baths and wash-houses. Some doubts were thrown upon the movement when it first began. It was said the people were in love with dirt, and the scheme of cleansing them was benevolent, but Quixotic. We have facts before us for a triumphant reply. The first establishment was opened in Whitechapel, in 1848, for bathers only, and in that year, no fewer than 48,637 persons availed themselves of its advantages. In 1849, the number of establishments was two, and arrangements were made for washing; the number of bathers during the year was 297,831; that of washers, 9,070. In 1850, three establishments were in operation; the number of bathers rose to 509,200, while that of washers was 60,154. In 1851, the number of establishments was increased to five, affording accommodation in the year to 647,242 bathers, and 132,251 washers; while in 1852, when there were seven establishments, the number of bathers was 800,163, and that of washers, 197,580, making a total of washers and bathers in five years of 3,000,000.

2. In the libraries and parks which have been opened there within the last few years, Manchester

z

and Salford have set an example which deserves to be
imitated by every city and town in the empire. The
public parks, with their flower gardens, grass-plots,
shrubberies, and gymnasiums, furnish the means of
healthful recreation to the working classes, and the
trifling damage accruing from unrestricted admission
is a proof of their growing habits of order and self-
respect. The public libraries present us with a
more intellectual test, and the result is very striking.
The Manchester Public Library had been opened
eighty-eight days on December 16, 1852. During
that period the number of books issued was, for the
purpose of reference, 24,816 volumes; for reading
at home, 26,408; total, 51,244, making an average
of 582 per day. At the same time, the number of
"vouchers," or recommendatory papers signed by
householders, was 3,413.—The public library at Peel
Park has been opened for a longer period, and a
classified statement of the *kind* of books lent for reading, during the month of May, 1850, 1851, 1852, is
very gratifying. The following is the statement
referred to; the number of books being purposely
confined to the first three thousands issued:—

YEAR.	Theology & Religious History.	Juris- prudence, Politics.	History, Voyages &c.	Sciences, and Arts.	Poetry, and Drama.	Works of Fiction.
May, 1850	60	27	432	300	250	1931
„ 1851	87	52	680	234	263	1684
„ 1852	107	51	616	256	784	1184

	1850.	1851.	1852.
Total works of all classes not fictitious	1069	1316	1816
Total of Fiction	1931	1684	1184
TOTAL.	3000	3000	3000

This statement, as illustrating the progress of the intellect, is a valuable contribution to psychology. "First that which is natural, and afterward that which is spiritual," is the invariable law of mind. First in order is the development of the senses, and the ripening of those passions which depend upon them; but even this inferior part of our nature cannot be profoundly affected without calling higher faculties into play; by degrees, reflection, taste, and sentiment are aroused, and ere long the sensual is dethroned. The opening of the reading-room, in 1850, attracted a class of readers, chiefly young men, who, having learned to read at school, had acquired facility in the art by the perusal of low works of fiction, such as issue in prodigious numbers from the London press. Suddenly obtaining command of a large library, these persons hastened at once to gratify their acquired tastes; but, having cloyed themselves with sweets, they soon felt an appetite for more substantial fare. In such circumstances, novels and romances may aid the progress of the intellect; they never kill a mind that is capable of higher studies, and he who once deliberately exchanges them for history and philosophy, is freed from their chains for ever.

IV. We are happy in referring, as another distinguished proof of social progress among the working classes, to "the Factory Workers' Exhibition and Bazaar," which was held at Bolton, in September and October, 1852. This pleasing industrial display originated in a suggestion of the Earl of Shaftesbury, and has recently been alluded to by his lordship, in a letter addressed to the *Times* newspaper, as helping to vindicate the present condition of British society from the severe criticisms which were made by an American writer in reply to the " Stafford House address.' We mention it with the same design, to show that the operatives of Lancashire were never more earnestly bent upon self-improvement than at this moment, and to repel those calumnies which brand the industrial development to which Free Trade has given rise, as a system little better than that of negro slavery.* The chief object of the " Exhibition " was to stimulate the working men of Bolton and its neighbourhood to a due improvement of the leisure secured to them by the " Ten Hours Bill." It is no part of our purpose to justify the expediency of that measure, but there will be but one opinion respecting the propriety of making its provisions as useful as possible to the classes chiefly affected by it. The " Exhibition" consisted of 6,000 articles, the work of 1,800 factory operatives, during the spare hours of evening. The nature of these articles, their thoroughly practical and *domestic* character, will be gathered best from the following enumeration of the materials purchased for the workers. These were, prints of all kinds for frocks and female dresses ; fine and coarse linen ; fine and coarse cotton for shirts and chemises ; fine diaper of all sorts, for baby pinafores ; fine linen for small shirts ; brown Holland for pinafores ; ginghams, for frocks and pinafores ; flannel and white muslin, for petticoats ; alpaca, coburg, and other stuffs, for frocks ; worsted for stockings and garters ; wool and white

* Witness the letter of the Marquis of Westmeath to the *Times* a few months since.

cotton for sampler work and knitted shawls ; cotton, for crochet work and fancy knitting, and many other things "difficult to enumerate ;" among which, however, we must not forget to mention, as characteristic of rural sentiments widely spread among our factory population, a stall of vegetables, plants, and flowers, decorated with garlands displaying exquisite taste, the work of three factory boys; and also specimens of writing and arithmetic. The raw materials cost, at wholesale price, £220, and the entire receipts of the exhibition, after continuing open nine days, including £52, the estimated value of the remaining articles, amounted to £802. It may be interesting to add, that in order to give full scope to competition in the department of "writing and arithmetic," masters were engaged to teach gratuitously all who chose to avail themselves of their aid ; their services being defrayed out of the profits of the exhibition. The value of the " demonstration," as a proof of social capability, may be gathered from the fact, that though it was devised and carried out entirely by working men, it was regarded as of sufficient importance to be formally opened by a procession of the town authorities, and to attract the leading manufacturers of the district, many of whom, together with the Bishop of Manchester and several members of parliament, were among its approving visitors. It is not too much to claim for this "Factory Workers' Exhibition" a humble place beside the proud structure in Hyde Park; if the latter gave us the poetry of labour, the former gives us its prose, and the intelligence and energy which it proves to exist among our factory operatives, constitute the best guarantee that we shall carry the palm in any future contest to which we may invite the rivalry of the world.

But, it may be said, by what link are these signs of social improvement connected with Free Trade? We reply, by one which is most obvious. Free Trade has given to the working man employment, good wages, decent clothing, and abundant food. Perhaps these are not, strictly speaking, the cause of in-tellectual and social progress, but they are the in-dispensable condition of it. Light is not the cause of seeing, but without light we cannot see; and though the friendly hand which uncloses the shutters of a gloomy dungeon, might be unable to construct the lenses, retina, and nerves, which constitute the organ of vision, yet the prisoner, long shut up in darkness, will bless the boon—the eye he had, the light was all he wanted. A man whose children cling to his knees and cry in vain for food, is in no humour for industrial exhibitions. Talk to him of self-improvement and he laughs in your face with bitter irony. The temper of his mind is moody despair. One of two things he *may* do in such circumstances; he may sit down by his cheerless hearth, and inwardly curse everything and everybody that seems to stand in the way of his well-being, or he may start up at the call of reckless crowds outside to " stop the engine" of the nearest factory, or force open the provision shops. We have witnessed such scenes; it is Free Trade which has made them vanish, and when we see the long tables of a Public Library bent over by the studious brows of factory workmen, who might otherwise have been surveying with defiant looks an array of jurymen at Lancaster, we cannot but ascribe the pleasing change to the repeal of that monstrous injustice which once denied them bread.

SECTION IV.

POLITICAL RESULTS OF FREE TRADE.

One of the chief advantages of a constitutional government is the self-directive power with which, in reference to all political matters, it invests the body of the people. The reforms which emanate from a despotic authority are, when once undertaken, effected more rapidly than those which transpire in a free commonwealth, but the former are much less permanent than the latter. In the one case the people are already ripe for the change; before it is effected they are already pervaded, so to speak, by its spirit, and are therefore quite able and ready to carry it out; but in the other case, the ideas of a few enlightened men are submitted on paper to multitudes, who neither understand them nor care to do so ; the change may be commenced, but it is at once neutralized by apathy and ignorance. A nation despotically ruled makes no political progress; it is nursed into a kind of political babyhood; it has never been suffered to think, speak, or act for itself, and its faculties have continued dormant. Such a nation is a stranger to those combined movements in which a free people become conscious of their power, and inherits none of those precious legacies which a truth, when fought for and won, bequeaths to future generations.

I. One of the important, though minor, effects of Free Trade is, the pacific spirit which it has breathed into the minds of the people. We no longer hear the rumours of civil war; our workmen no longer talk of the efficacy of pikes and bayonets; our rural police do not now encounter battalions of men a thousand strong on their way to some moonlight drill. In this respect, to what cause soever it may be ascribed, there is an undeniable change for the better. Let anyone peruse the numerous placards which cover the waste walls of our large towns; he will find there notices of auction as usual, puffing advertisements in abundance, programmes of lectures, soirées, temperance gatherings, all indicating an exuberance of public life; but he will find fewer political meetings, where reckless adventurers discuss the rights of man, and pour a vein of scurrility upon the dearest institutions of society. Some, perhaps, will think that the cessation of such meetings is a questionable advantage; it would be so if, in abandoning them, the people had sunk into apathy, and were ready to submit tamely to any government which might succeed in getting itself installed in power. Such is not the case; the people are as political as ever, but they are learners, not actors, and they sit at the feet of other masters. The people are not less political than formerly, but they are less destructive.

Perhaps the most significant feature of the political condition of the masses is the abeyance in which Socialism is held. We have mentioned this evil in its social aspect, but Socialism is a political power.

Its political tendencies are neither less strong nor less dangerous because they pass over details, and abut against the first principles of politics. Socialism is a protest against the rights of property; and Free Trade has repressed it by showing every man how he may acquire property for himself. The political influence of Socialism is as dangerous in its reflex as in its direct movement, as pernicious in the reaction which it excites in the public mind as in its own stealthy advances towards ascendancy. Its appearance in the community at once alarms everybody who has anything to lose; all such at once move off in an opposite direction; and, as we have seen in France, rather than expose themselves to the excesses of Socialism, will submit to the strong arm that puts it down. A few years since, the principles of Socialism were making rapid progress among our working people. It was a tempting thought to the victim of corn law oppression, that the corn fields which waved, as if in mockery, around his dwelling, were his own, and his, too, the broad lands of England, its mansions, its factories, its magazines of wealth; and that a sound principle of legislation would at once make him their actual possessor. It needed strength of intellect, indeed, to resist fallacies which were so grateful to the heart. All is changed now. Socialism, *soi-disant*, has vanished, and the true Socialism has come. The capital of the political agitator is gone; he has now to make bricks without straw, and finds it profitable to abandon the task. The people, instead of listening to incendiary harangues, are engaged in their workshops and homes discussing temperate measures of reform, and what is more, are fitting themselves for their reception. The people are contented now, not merely because their homes are the abode of plenty, much less because they have ceased to feel an interest in public questions, but because they feel that public men are interested in their welfare, and believe that justice at last is recognised as the basis of the state.

Beyond a doubt, the most cheering progress has been made during the Free Trade period in the fusion of all classes, nor is it easy to exaggerate the political importance of this fact. As a people we want unity, to feel that we are *one* by a better tie than mere geographical neighbourhood. Our economical position requires this. As a commercial people we are exposed to seasons of depression, when hardships have to be endured which can only be encountered by a strong development of the social virtues. Our political condition and prospects require this unity. In the great movements of the future, the whole people must walk abreast; every section of the community must find its place therein. Exaggeration, whether aristocratic or democratic, will prove destructive. The greatest popular victories which may be won, the widest possible extension of the franchise, must be harmonised with the retention of everything truly valuable in the bequests of our ancestors. In order to work out this destiny, we must be penetrated with the same vitality, and animated by the same pure and disinterested patriotism. For the first time in our history a pacific triumph inspires us with this unity of feeling. We possess at the present time, under the benignant effects of Free Trade, an intenser consciousness of political oneness than at any past period.   The flotilla and army of Napoleon I., when within sight of Dover cliffs, did not create in us a national sentiment half so strong as the public recognition of justice in the establishment of Free Trade.   If any division has been created by this policy, it is a division of the few in hostility to the many ; of 200,000 landed proprietors and tenants in chief, against 26,000,000.   Nay, even this division has not been caused by Free Trade; the division existed before ; all that Free Trade has done is, by a stroke of justice, to bring about a change of sides, to give contentment to the millions and dissatisfaction to the few.   Even this division is capable of being removed.   The former, having been based on injustice, warred with nature, and could never be healed by time ; but Free Trade has only asserted a principle which conscience approves, and every hour must hasten the correction of any accidental inconveniences or asperities.

II. Another important effect of Free Trade is the political knowledge it has communicated, and the political action to which it has roused the people   In these respects the consequences of the movement will be lasting.   In the influence of a disciplinary process there is a direct analogy between individuals and nations.   Whatever rouses the energies of an individual to the accomplishment of something great, confers on him a boon of far greater value than the particular object which called forth his exertions. That mental enlightenment, that consciousness of power which the struggle evoked, all this is abiding; he comes out of the contest a new man.   It is so with a nation.   Once let a great object engage the public mind, calling into unwonted activity its moral and intellectual powers, dispelling its prejudices, appealing to its sense of the just and beautiful, and rousing its energies into full play, firing it with sublimer heroism at every step, till at length the goal is won; in such a case the nation is great for ever. The object itself, though nothing less than a people's freedom, is trifling when compared with the intelligence and energy by which it was achieved. This is the true career of nations; the opportunity of acquiring self-discipline is the highest gift of liberty.

The Free Trade movement was one of those which stamp, in this way, a deathless character upon the age in which they occur. Some parts of its machinery, when first put in motion, produced an effect on the public mind as novel as it was strong. It is startling, even now, to think of anti-corn law lecturers taking their stand beneath the shadow of baronial castles, and expounding there, to crowds of farm labourers, the same principles that their masters had to contend against in the senate. We know something of the feudal tyranny which hides itself under the forms of modern procedure, in districts remote from the influences of large towns. It would shock a speculative admirer of our free constitution to find what absurd and extravagant notions of aristocratic prerogative abound there. The owner of the castle is still the lord of the middle ages, invested, to rustic fancy, with unlimited power; and defiance of his authority is something more than treason. What ideas must the harangue of the anti-corn law lecturer have communicated to the audiences which gathered round him in such places! His very appearance, as the representative of the cotton lord in yonder dreaded, hated Manchester, the ban of baron and bailiff notwithstanding, was a fact which could not but teach a few important political lessons. But how much more effective were the thoughts he uttered! The labourer then found that his bread was dear, because it was taxed for his landlord's benefit,—that, besides a heavy rental for his cottage, and wages which barely sufficed, even in good times, to keep him above parochial relief, in every mouthful of meal his children ate he paid something towards the maintenance of that grandeur before which he had hitherto trembled. This was a stirring fact, for a starving peasantry. No wonder that they met to talk over their grievances, and that the novel sight was presented, of labouring men wielding their honest vernacular before an audience of labouring men, and even women coming forward to recount with tears the sufferings they endured.

Better times have arrived, but is that impulse lost? Oh no! The labourer, by his cottage hearth, blesses the movement which gave him cheap bread, and looks with brotherly feelings towards those great cities, through whose efforts the boon was bestowed. Free Trade has loosened his local attachments, broken his feudal ties, and connected him with his country, not through the old medium of clannish devotion to hereditary chiefs, but by direct fellowship with millions of free men. Such sentiments are the first elements of political life, and are the forerunners of a day, when the electoral franchise may be safely confided to the rural population.

But the political impulse which has been given by Free Trade must not be estimated alone by its effects upon the lowest and least receptive class of our agricultural population. If it has kindled the first spark of political knowledge in the mind of the labourer, it has no doubt produced still more important effects elsewhere. The tenant farmers are an influential section of the community, whose relation to the state has been considerably modified by our present policy. The common features of this class have hitherto been a blind and slavish dependence on their superiors, a notion of prescriptive right as "the first producing interest," and an exaggerated idea of the public worth and influence of the landowner. There is no reason, in the nature of the case, why the tie which connects a tenantry with the landed proprietor should differ from that which connects the manufacturer with those who send him the raw material. The farmer is a manufacturer, and the landlord is the person of whom the raw material is bought. The connexion is thoroughly commercial; there is nothing political in it any more than there is in the tie which connects the woollen manufacturer with the wool grower. Hitherto the connexion existing between landlord and tenant has been of a feudal character. The latter has been looked upon as a dependent, an obliged party, rather than as one of two parties who are mutually obliged. Hence the tenant has been only a higher kind of serf, —one of the more favoured of his lord's retainers. Hence the tenure of the land was thought to carry with it a political obligation; all who rented under the same proprietor felt themselves bound to support his political interests, and he, in his legislative capacity, felt himself bound to promote theirs. The result of all this is that our county constituencies combine, with few exceptions, in a formidable phalanx, the objects of which are territorial, not national, and whose influence goes to make the House of Commons a mere echo of the House of Lords; the father often sitting in one place and the son in the other.

A state of things which has been the growth of many ages cannot be entirely changed in a few years. We may mark, however, the commencement of the process, and recognise the agency by which it has been produced. Free Trade has scattered in an hour many of the political delusions which have heretofore darkened the agricultural mind. The farmers are now awake; their prestige of political supremacy, so pernicious to themselves, is gone; in a stand-up fight they have been beaten; they can obtain no protection in return for political sub-serviency; and territorial influence, for its own aggrandizement is no more. What follows? The old tie is broken, and the farmer, vote in hand, will support whom he pleases. While private motives will henceforth lead the farmer more and more to maintain this right, it will become increasingly the interest of the landlord to accord it. Deprived by the repeal of the corn laws of the profitable expedient of artificial prices, he will be obliged to regard his land as an article of commerce, to be let to the person who can afford to pay him the highest rent. Science will become requisite to profitable tenantry, and we shall find ere long as familiar an acquaintance with the principles of chemistry in the farm-house as in the shed of a calico-printing establishment. When this end is reached, and Free

Trade will assuredly cause it to be reached, the
political ideas now associated with the tenure of the
soil will be extinct. "Bœotian dulness" will then have
given way to the fire of intellect, and the narrow
instincts of a class to sentiments of enlightened
nationality. We shall hear no more then " of rival
interests;" it will be recognised that the culture
of land is no more opposed to the weaving of calico,
than this is to the manufacture of glass, and capital
and labour, whether held by peer or peasant, will
flow without preference into the most profitable
channels. Mutual independence, or rather the equal
dependence of one class upon another, will purify our
political ideas. We shall legislate then for the
whole nation, and our conduct, freed from selfish
admixture, will recognise no other guide than justice.

But the permanent effects of Free Trade on the
political life of the people are not to be measured by
the knowledge which it has communicated, and the
altered relations which it has brought about; it has
reached the same end by a more direct channel, by
stirring the depths of the national mind. There is
a marvellous moral efficacy in events. The human
soul seems to gather more strength from experience
and history than from any other source. Life is
elaborated by action, and in attempting great achievements nations, as well as individuals, surpass themselves. Who does not recall with admiration the
conscious greatness which marked the people of
Greece, when they had chased the Persian invader
from their soil? After the heroism displayed at
Salamis and Marathon, a Greek believed himself equal
to anything; and colonisation, commerce, philosophy,

poetry, art, all which has rendered his country's name immortal in the domain of taste and letters, began at once to bloom. A similar effect was produced on the English mind by the overthrow of the Spanish Armada. The real danger which then threatened our liberties, coupled with the gigantic efforts which were made to avert it, and the complete success which was achieved, inspired the nation with exalted sentiments, not specially warlike, which exerted an important influence on its political development. We are far from comparing Free Trade with those events; but the mode of their achievement was nearly the same, and they were pregnant with the same results. In one respect it differs from those immortal struggles— it was pacific throughout; at its triumph no cannon boomed; no shrieks of dying men were heard; no blood-stained banners waved contempt in the loving face of heaven. But this, without rendering it less powerful, makes it more sublime. By purely moral means the nation has achieved a revolution in one of the most important departments of legislation; a revolution which was opposed by the prejudices and interests of the most powerful classes in the community, and which, only a few years ago, seemed altogether hopeless. What is the effect of this victory upon the victors? Self-reliance: *they know what they can do.* They know that when they are united in just demands no power in the state can long resist their concession—they know that the majorities of the Commons, the almost unanimous opposition of the Peers, and even, if that were ever to be encountered (which God forbid!) the hostility of the throne, would be scattered like chaff before the irresistible might of the people, roused in the name of justice, and controlled by inflexible adherence to law. How fruitful is this knowledge! The strength of the people is tranquil, because they know it is omnipotent. Bent upon carrying out the most searching reforms, they exhibit no fervid impatience to begin, knowing that, when the proper season comes, they will be equal to the emergency. This conscious power is the epitome of freedom, and the germ of all greatness; it is at once the surest pledge of progress, and the strongest safeguard against destructive change. The people who have demolished the corn laws, entrenched, as they once were, in the prejudices and imagined interests of the aristocracy of England ;— who demolished them without any other weapons than intellect and logic, and demolished them in seven years, will neither despair of any change, nor stoop to any species of violence to hasten it. Free Trade has solved the problem of the people's sovereignty, reduced it to a simple lesson, and placed it, in its own achievements, before the eye of the nation. The nation sees it, exults in it; under its influence becomes hopeful, tolerant, forgiving ; rests awhile on its laurels, but purposes ere long to start anew, like a waking giant, to the fulfilment of its glorious destiny.

III. Another important effect of Free Trade is, the change it has wrought in the maxims which guide the formation and conduct of political parties. This is no matter of indifference. We are ruled by parties, and the principles which control the conduct of public men exert an influence upon the laws themselves. The unwritten code of honour lies nearer our actions than formal legislation, and the welfare of the state requires that the code of honour coincide in every respect with the laws of morality. Hitherto this has been but imperfectly realized. There has been a discrepancy between the abstract morals of legislation, and the maxims which have been held binding upon the legislator. Obvious circumstances in British society led to the formation of two great political parties, supposed to be, and at one time really, the representatives of two opposite political principles. As the question on which they had divided was which of these two principles should rule the state, and there was no way of deciding this but by party triumphs in the House of Commons, patriotism and honour combined to fire the rival factions with one spirit, and drill them into unanimity in order to ensure success. So far as this arrangement sprang from individual conviction, and went hand in hand along with it, no fault could be found with it, but if, in any case, it drew an expression of opinion which did not accord with the individual's real views, or was supposed to lay any one under an obligation to give a partial vote merely to keep a political chief in power; so far, it was immoral, and therefore necessary only on false principles. Yet this is the abuse into which the arrangement fell; the heads of parties in the House of Commons resembled, at length, the Scottish chieftains of two centuries back; every honourable gentleman had his "laird," whose standard he followed, whose colours he wore; and any defection from the ranks, brought with it a charge of apostasy. Thus was inaugurated a new and most immoral principle for the guidance of public men—conscience and reason were to be silenced, and the mandates of a chief obeyed. Free Trade has broken through this false maxim. The very existence of the present ministry is, if nothing else, a legitimisation of honesty in the House of Commons. "Measures, not men," is now the popular cry. The way in which the change has been brought about is obvious. Free Trade was a measure of social justice, not necessarily Whig or Tory, and yet one which enlisted, on both sides, very powerful prejudices. Hence, when the crisis came, it produced an explosion of parties, and, in the resettlement which followed, the majority grouped themselves according to their convictions. In doing this, they were only imitating illustrious examples already set. The Free-traders had taken the lead in this manly course. Night after night they had been found in the lobby of the House of Commons, with those whose views they ordinarily opposed, following their principles whether they placed them in juxta-position with a Radical or a Tory. In this course they were at length followed by their opponents, and the accession of Sir Robert Peel to their ranks completed the canonisation of honesty and integrity in the British Senate.

IV. In conferring upon us this great benefit the Free Trade struggle has given us another of still greater value, in superseding, not only the maxims by which the conduct of political parties was guided, but the very principles on which they were based. Formerly they were merely political,—the doctrines of Whiggism and Toryism, originating in the civil contests which marked the era of the Stuarts, arrayed in genuine hostility by the dangers which attended a change of dynasty, forged into weapons of faction by the eloquence of Pitt and Fox, and, finally, rendered obsolete for ever by the passing of the Reform Bill. These distinctions ought then to have disappeared from the stage, but for stage purposes they were still retained. They were still allowed to walk across the scene, attract the attention of the spectators, and form the *dramatis personœ* of the political plot. It was high time to consign them to the tomb of " all the Capulets," and to bring on men of real flesh and blood. What were the great subjects of debate previous to the intro- duction of the Free Trade question? With a few great exceptions, they were miserably unimportant when compared with the real exigencies of the nation. The entire significance of existing party divisions was derived from old distinctions, possessing no longer any vital hold upon the people, while the great and pressing wants of the masses, often reduced to the brink of starvation by unjust laws, were the theme of scarcely one in a thousand of the discussions in the House of Commons. However it may fare with these old principles for the future, at present they do not form the basis of public parties, but a principle of mere justice and economy, deriving all its importance from the social condition of the people. The practical good of the people is now recognised as the end of legislation, and the first deliberative as- sembly in the world, discarding its old traditions, divides on a question which really amounts to this,— shall the nation be fully or scantily supplied with food? Such a state of things furnishes the happiest augury for the future; we may hope that the House of Commons will become more and more a people's committee for managing the people's affairs; that the intrigues, the frivolous discussions, the official stateliness, the laborious pedantry of the past, will give way to simplicity, straightforwardness, and common sense.   Such a change will destroy nothing which is worth preserving; it will not lessen the occasions, and need not detract from the qualities, of parliamentary eloquence; it will not diminish the dignity of statesmanship, which is conferred by capacity and integrity alone; it will not render a strong government less difficult of acquisition; but it will at the same time enforce, as the condition of existence to every government, the enacting of useful measures; it will scatter the prejudices which have been fostered in the popular mind by ages of partial legislation, and gather round our institutions that cheap and pure defence which is found in the affections of the people.

SECTION V.

THE INFLUENCE EXERTED BY FREE TRADE ON THE RELIGIOUS PROGRESS OF THE PEOPLE.

Having now passed in review a variety of facts which are adapted to convey a proper impression of the physical, social, and political effects of Free Trade, we may be permitted for a moment to advert to the religious aspects of the question.   We are aware that this is somewhat delicate ground, but we enter it with all boldness, sustained by a sense of honesty and candour.   Not as dogmatists of any particular school do we enter it;—indeed, to any thoughtful man, the subject is too sacred for dogmatism;—but guided simply by the dictates of humanity as applied to the highest part of human nature. There are few who do not admit that the religious element is the highest in human nature, and that its systematic culture is necessary in order to impart to man the highest degree of spiritual beauty; or who will not grant, especially with the facts which have been ascertained by the recent census before their eyes, that religious convictions exist in the minds of a majority of the population in a state of comparative crudeness and inefficiency. To those who make such admissions, we confine this section of our remarks. The religious influence of Free Trade arises from two sources, one general, the other specific; partly from the prosperity which Free Trade has produced, and partly from the particular principles of which it is the recognition.

The general influence of Free Trade on the interests of religion may be summed up in the assertion, that worldly prosperity is, on the whole, not irreligious in its tendency, but the reverse. This will, perhaps, be disputed by some persons, who, in scanning the ways of Providence, do not sufficiently distinguish between the *ordinary* and the *special* treatment which man receives from his Creator. We are aware that, in one sense, the whole of life is disciplinary, and sometimes most so when most prosperous; but now, taking our life to pieces, laying on the one side its bright, smooth, happy moments, and on the other its dark and rugged ones, may it not be asserted that the former are more religious in their tendency? The latter, are, doubtless, sometimes of the highest moral value, but they owe this, in a great measure, to their being exceptional. The discipline of a House of Correction is intended to be reformatory, and often is so, but it surely will not be contended that men, in general, would be more virtuous if they were to pass their life within the walls of a prison. The pinch of want may be occasionally useful in awakening wholesome reflections and resolves, but we cannot think that, if starvation were the ordinary lot of men, they would be morally better than when enjoying a moderate degree of plenty. A small section of the community contemplate with horror the rapid progress of national wealth, under a system of Free Trade, as likely to prove destructive to everything which they deem essential to national piety. They point us with fervid declamation to Babylon, Persia, and Rome, whose wealth, they tell us, proved their ruin;·and, absurd as it may appear, would rather advocate Protection, as putting a check on our prosperity, than advocate Free Trade, because it gives that prosperity the rein. Other persons are secretly hostile to Free Trade on similar, and equally mistaken, grounds. They are enthusiastic admirers of Spartan virtue; they would tolerate no metal but iron; they would banish all elegance, refinement, and the many fruits of opulence, and stereotype society, to all ages, on the plan of log-huts and linsey-woolsey. Effeminacy is their dread; we shall become enervated by wealth; we shall lose our ancient valour, and some day, like the luxurious Romans under the empire, fall before the conquering Sclave or Gaul. Whether entertained on grounds of patriotism or piety, such fears are happily absurd. It is not wealth, but the abuse of it, and chiefly those abuses which spring from the mode in which it is acquired, that causes the evils they dread. Wealth, wrung by conquest from down-trodden nations, prepares a just revenge by debauching the minds of the victors. Wealth, thus obtained, puts a stop to industry, draws off the energies of the people from the channels of peaceful toil—from tilling the earth, from planting the vine and the olive, from the civilising pursuits of commerce, and pours them along the path of insane ambition; it suppresses the sense of justice, the dictates of moderation, prudence, and economy, and fosters pride, revenge, reckless contempt for divine and human laws, and thus sows the seeds of decay in the heart of commonwealths. No instance can be given in which commerce has rendered a people effeminate; the change has often been advanced, we venture to challenge proof. It was not so with Tyre, whose hardy train-bands detained the conqueror of Persia so long before its walls, and forced him at last to enter the city over their dead bodies. It was not so with Carthage, whose very ashes were instinct with terror to the mistress of the world. It was not so with Genoa and Venice, and the other Italian republics of the middle ages; nor was it so with the Dutch and the English in more recent times. War is hateful; it is the foulest offspring of crime, the heaviest scourge with which depravity, in its most retributive excesses, ever lashed the world; but if any admire the physical energy and daring which it requires, and fear lest Free Trade should make us cowards, let them remember that commercial states, when forced into war, have always been among the most warlike.

Thus, the immoral and emasculating influence of prosperity is not its necessary result, but depends altogether upon the source from which that prosperity springs. If it springs from war, conquest, injustice, it is necessarily hurtful; if from peaceful and humanizing pursuits, it is favourable, rather than otherwise, to the development of the moral faculties, and the attainment of the highest degree of moral excellence. Successful labour supposes two things—vigorous application as the cause, and physical comfort as the result. But these are both invested with a strong moral power, which is in the highest degree favourable to religion. How many vices yield to no other specific than hard work! How true is the nursery maxim which instructs us from our infancy as to the sort of employment which is found for " idle hands !" Business is, strictly speaking, an intellectual occupation ; in business the hand and tongue only minister to the several mental operations. What is buying and selling, but a battle of judgment? Business, far more than literature and art, far more than any professional employment, keeps the sterner, drier, more matter-of-fact part of the intellect in constant and energetic action. The negative influence of this development is very valuable; if it produces no flowers, it tends effectually to kill all weeds. We do not say that constant employment will eradicate vicious habits, but we do say that it favours the acquisition of a moral mastery over self, which is a great ally to virtue. While successful labour is thus favourable to religion on the intellectual side, in the sentiments which it directly calls into exercise, it is the same on the moral side. Poverty is too often the parent of envy, malignity, peevishness, and despair; the proverb which makes the moment of love's exit identical with that of poverty's entrance, is of very wide application. Benevolence is a plant which rarely blooms amid the arctic snows of want and wretchedness.

But besides this general tendency of Free Trade to promote the religious development of the people, it possesses one which is more specific; it has removed a sense of injustice from their minds, and given them a pledge that nothing shall be withheld from them which fair dealing demands. While the corn laws were in force the working man could always point to an unquestionable grievance—the maintenance of regulations unfavourable to himself, for the good of a privileged few. When driven well-nigh to desperation through the double influence of scarce employment and dear food, he naturally asked, Why am I reduced to this condition? Am I not a man, with head and hands capable of supplying the wants of those for whom I have made myself responsible? Why do I live a pauper, self-degraded, when every sentiment of my soul urges me, with honest pride, to owe my bread to nothing but my own toil? The sole reply which could be given to such a question was, Your labour is rendered worthless by laws which shut our ports against the only commodities that could be offered in exchange for it. The wheat of the Wallachian peasant is rotting in his barn, because the government, towards the maintenance of which you pay in every mouthful of your scanty meal, prevents him from bringing it to you. But why this cruelty? If government in its corporate capacity has no conscience, ought it not at least to be destitute of sentiments which prompt to oppression? No man will commit injustice if he does not receive some price for it; why am I then deprived of my birthright, and forced, like a fool, to "beg" when I only plead for permission to "dig?" To this, also, the reply was obvious. You cannot be allowed to exchange your labour with the foreign wheat grower, because that would bring down the price of home grown wheat, and this would reduce the profits of our farmers and the incomes of our aristocracy; yes, your children must starve, in order that theirs may enjoy a few more luxuries. The sentiments which such a series of interrogations and replies is adapted to excite, we need not particularise; we ask simply, are they religious? If hatred of injustice, burning indignation at relentless tyranny, are religious, then are those sentiments religious too; but those are not the sentiments to purify and elevate our nature; love alone can mould man to perfection, can attune his bosom to harmony with his fellows and with God. Hence the corn laws were profoundly irreligious—incomparably more so than the vulgar kinds of vice and blasphemy. They were an outrage on eternal justice, a sin against the very goodness of the Creator. Their continuance helped to make the community godless, and their destruction has removed one of the most formidable barriers from the path of moral progress. Firmly relying ourselves in the specific doctrines and institutes of Christianity, we recognise their high position and supreme moral power. But Christianity itself is but a part of a system of moral means, and its greatest triumphs cannot be separated from preparatory processes carried on by other agencies. Hence we recognise in Free Trade an ally to the gospel. The conciliation of the people to religious truth will be aided by nothing more than by the recognition of justice in the recent enfranchisement of commerce, and the many schemes of popular improvement, which, in common with that measure, we rejoice to believe are the offspring of the loftier morality of the present age.

From the peculiar nature of religious principles and manifestations, it will not be expected that facts can as yet be adduced in support of the views above stated. All we can do, and this is amply sufficient, is to point to the prevalence of better *tendencies ;* the greater disposition which exists to let religious efforts take their course, and the greater prospect of definite results. We have been favoured with communications from two gentlemen possessing ample means of becoming acquainted with the feelings which prevail among the working classes on this subject—the Rev. John Garwood, M.A., Secretary to the London City Mission, whose agents paid last year no fewer than 1,176,055 visits among the poorer part of the population of the metropolis and its neighbourhood, and the Rev. Stephen J. Davis, Secretary of a denominational institute, the operations of which lie chiefly in the rural districts of the provinces. Both these gentlemen, while deploring the apathy which still prevails among the working classes on the subject of religion, nevertheless express their belief that, under the influence of improved circumstances, they are more friendly to religious sentiments, more accessible to persons engaged in a religious capacity, and in all respects more hopeful with respect to the future, than at any past period.   At the same time they express their conviction that, in connexion with other agencies, social and educational reforms must be pushed on with unceasing vigour, in order to draw the highest moral results from the prosperity with which we are favoured.

CHAPTER II.

PROSPECTIVE RESULTS OF FREE TRADE.

FROM the actual results of Free Trade, as they have been already realized, we turn now to the influences which it may be confidently expected to exert on the future condition of the world. Grouping them in the order of development, the earliest effects of our new policy will be experienced in the commercial relations which subsist between our own and foreign states; these will diffuse a higher class of political ideas, and these again will ultimately prepare the way for the universal triumph of truth and justice.

In entering this department of inquiry there is a general distinction, applicable throughout, which it will be important, for the sake of clearness, to keep in view. Some of the effects which may be anticipated from Free Trade are *logically involved* in it; they flow so obviously from the same principles, or are so necessary to its development, that the concession of Free Trade implies their concession too. Consequences of this class are numerous and valuable; their value consisting in this, that they demonstrate the magnitude of the achievement of Free Trade, as the triumph of a principle, the establishment of an axiom in political economy, which thus becomes a lever, by the aid of which we may carry all possible reforms. It is its logical fruitfulness which renders the acknowledgment of a principle momentous; the particular fact in which it is embodied may be of little consequence, but the admission it contains may constitute one of the world's best hopes. This is pre-eminently the case with Free Trade. But while Free Trade is so important in its recognition as a principle, it is scarcely less so in its tendencies as a fact. The ever-increasing measure of well-being to which it will give rise, the additional intercourse which it will soon establish with distant and now benighted parts of the world, the mental and physical energy which it will put in motion, the capital it will accumulate, the facilities for the propagation of sentiment which it will furnish, are all fraught with incalculable advantages to the human race. As a principle it is one of a constellation of stars, which will lend to it ere long their tributary splendour; as a fact it is itself one of the purest emanations from the Father of lights, given to bless His offspring and lead them on to a better day.

SECTION I.

LOGICAL DEMANDS OF FREE TRADE IN RELATION TO COMMERCE.

Taking up the prospective effects of Free Trade in the order just indicated, we consider, first, those which relate to commerce. An impression prevails to a very considerable extent, among persons who ought to be better informed, that the repeal of the laws relating to corn, sugar, and navigation left us with scarcely anything to desiderate. There are also others who, with something like the same views as led many persons, for a long time after the passing of the Reform Bill, to consider that act as final, and discourage all attempts to obtain a more comprehensive measure, think we have made sufficient concessions to the manufacturing and commercial interests, that Free Trade may be carried too far, and that, if we are not prepared to grant our farmers and colonists a compensation for the losses they have sustained, we ought, at least, to let our policy sleep awhile. Nothing could be more mistaken than the first impression, or more false than the second. The repeal of the corn laws and the navigation act, and the equalisation of the sugar duties, have laid the foundation of commercial freedom, but they have not finished the structure; while every Free Trade measure which has received the sanction of the legislature is, to a great extent, nugatory, and altogether unjust, if the principle embodied in them is not carried fully out, and every practicable step at once taken to secure their effective working. We will briefly enumerate some of the further measures which seem to be required in order to place our Free Trade policy on a thoroughly sound basis, and supply it with the means of successfully coping with that unrestricted competition to which it will hereafter be exposed.

I. Obviously, the first step to be taken is, the immediate repeal of all duties which are levied for protection.

Among the articles still protected are various descriptions of silk and linen manufacture. Of the former we may enumerate satins, satin ribbons, silk gauzes, silk velvets, and silk plush for covering hats, all of which we import from France, or other parts of Europe, as well as various kinds of silk handkerchiefs from India. The amount of duty received on silk manufactures is about £250,000. It will be remembered, in connexion with these duties, that the branches of the silk trade which are still protected are among the least prosperous. The duties on certain kinds of linen cloth, such as diapers, damasks, cambrics, lawns, &c., do not yield more than £5,000 annually; but the damage done to our trade, as well as the loss to the consumer, is not to be measured by this sum. The receipts from this source have greatly declined since 1846, showing that a greater quantity of our own goods have been used at home, and, consequently, the uselessness of this shred of protection. A more important section of traffic is that which relates to the wine trade. The policy we have pursued for a century and a half has been to favour the wines of Portugal at the expense of those of France. Previous to 1830 every gallon of French wine brought into this country paid seven shillings and three pence at the custom-house. In 1831 the duty was lowered to five shillings and six pence a-gallon, at which it still remains. The expediency of reducing this duty, or altogether repealing it, is proved by the effect on our trade with France of the reduction already made. In 1830 our whole exports to France amounted to no more than £475,884, while the average annual amount of our exports to that country for the ten years 1841-1850, was £2,472,643. The wine manufacture is one of the chief occupations of the French peasantry. Before the celebrated Methuen Treaty, French wines were favourites with us, and were consumed to a great extent. A reduction of the duty would, no doubt, be followed by a great increase of consumption, and a social tie would be created with a country which cannot be bound too closely in friendship to our own. Besides these duties, there are others, of the same protective character, on such manufactures of cotton, linen, silk, and wool as are "wholly or in part made up," on "embroidery and needlework," on certain kinds of glass, on lace, gloves, boots and shoes of all sorts and sizes, on copper in ore, "wrought or partly wrought;" on fruits, fresh pork, poultry, butter, cheese, eggs, hams, cloverseed, &c. While protective duties are allowed to remain on these articles, it cannot be said that we have consistently carried out the first principles of Free Trade, and their immediate repeal is demanded both by justice and expediency.

We say, the first principles of Free Trade require these changes, for it is questionable whether Free Trade, if consistently carried out, would not demand much more. Our present financial system has recently been assailed with great vigour, and methods have been proposed which would altogether do away with the customs and excise duties, and substitute in their stead a system of direct taxation. With the details of any proposed measure we have nothing to do; they leave the question as to the expediency of direct or indirect taxation to be decided on its own merits.

The question may be stated thus :—It is necessary to raise about £50,000,000 annually for national purposes, how shall we raise it? Shall we tax the people at once, by assessing their property and incomes, or shall we tax their food? Our present system is an amalgamation of both methods, though as much as £35,000,000 is derived from the customs and excise alone. By some this system has been lauded to the skies, as one of the grandest devices of political wisdom. Nay, one writer, who speaks with intelligence on most subjects, regards it as a species of birthright for the poor. In comparing the systems of taxation followed in this country and on the continent, Mr. Samuel Laing praises the indirect method because it allows everybody who chooses an opportunity of escaping taxation altogether, simply by abstaining from taxable articles, as though, granting that taxation is just, any citizen can have a right to escape it. The author of the " History of Europe " surpasses himself in eloquently eulogizing a scheme of taxation in which the tax-gatherer is *invisible*, in other words, a scheme in which executive extravagance can easily cajole the " ignorant impatience " of the people ; and pathetically deplores the successive inroads which have been made upon it. Such advocacy proceeds on an assumption which, happily, is becoming antiquated ; viz., that the people are something distinct from the state, to be systematically tricked and managed for objects of the expediency of which they are supposed to be incapable of judging. If these views are correct, then it is right for the directors of a joint stock company to form themselves into an interest distinct from the shareholders—to adopt stratagems for getting hold of their money, instead of openly asking for it on the strength of well-devised plans, in an honest, legal way. But is this right? If not right on the smaller scale it must be wrong on the larger. There is no difference in nature between an ounce and a pound of injustice. The theory of politics is simple:—The people constitute the state, the state is charged with its own maintenance, with the duty of promoting its own efficiency by methods of which itself must be the judge; the executive and legislative powers are but the organs of the state, and the individuals who wield them are its servants, not its masters. Hence, a proper scheme of taxation involves in it three things: first, a full and candid exposition of national wants; secondly, the recognition of these by the people; thirdly, a self-imposed contribution adapted to meet the case. This is already recognised in theory; the direct imposition of taxes alone agrees fully with the spirit of the British constitution.

It is unnecessary to press a heavier charge against a system of indirect taxation, than that it is thoroughly unbusiness-like and anti-commercial. What mercantile firm would ever think of adopting a like method to meet its expenses of management? The rule of such an establishment invariably is,—make the process of exchange as easy as possible, simplify business to the utmost, carry economy to the very point at which, if carried further, it would begin to trench on the most complete efficiency, and then let all expenses be defrayed out of profits. A nation ought to manage its affairs in the same way; any other opens a door to injustice and extravagance, besides tending to diminish the profits of exchange, on which the wealth of the community depends. But, acquitting the system on business considerations, it nevertheless seems unwise, to say the very least, in a commercial people, to lay the bulk of their taxation on the intercourse between themselves and foreigners. Granting that taxes fall none the less upon our own pockets, for this very reason it would be expedient to shift the point of incidence, while it is false in science to tax *international* relations for national burdens. Such a plan, moreover, is unfair. It necessarily favours one branch of industry at the expense of others. Are the colonies a constituent part of the empire? On what ground then is sugar made to pay four or five millions annually to the Exchequer, while our home grown wheat pays nothing? On what principle of justice are malt, spirits, and paper charged with burdens amounting to £16,000,000 annually, when so many other articles are free? Fairness, at all events, requires that *all* articles be taxed or *none*. If it be said that to tax all articles equally, or to tax them according to some uniform standard, is impossible, and that the government is obliged to cling to those imposts which have been found to pay best, we reply that it is time to inquire whether a great nation can devise no better method for meeting its expenses than one which is confessedly based on compromise and injustice. Taxes on food diminish the comforts of the people, without replenishing the exchequer. If all taxes on consumption were repealed, then, supposing that the people consumed no more foreign commodities than they did before, the great object of simplification woüld be gained. But we cannot think that, under such circumstances, consumption would remain at its present point. The ability to purchase coffee, tea, sugar, tobacco, &c., at a cheaper rate would lead to larger importations; this would call for larger exports of our manufactures, the profits on which would probably more than cover our increased expenditure, leaving the people, notwithstanding this addition to their well-being, equally able to meet the demands of the state as they were before.

II. Free Trade not only demands on behalf of our commerce the immediate repeal of all protective duties, and a complete revision of our system of taxation, it imperatively requires that the shipping interest shall be freed from its remaining trammels. Foremost among these is the monopoly of the Trinity House, by which, under the pretence of maintaining lights and beaconage, that corporation raises, at the expense of the shipping interest, a large revenue for their own use. The money expended by them on "lights" in the year 1845 was £141,000, a sum pronounced by experienced shipowners to be double what is necessary, but the surplus revenue amounted in the same year to twice that sum, so that we have here, including possible reductions, a tax of £300,000 levied annually on an important branch of industry, and that for no public benefit whatever. Of the same character is the practice of paying "passing tolls," for the maintenance of so called harbours of refuge. The ports which enjoy this monopoly are Ramsgate, Dover, Whitby, and Bridlington, ports which, on the authority of Mr. Lindsay, no ships would think of entering in case of a storm, and to all

intents useless. A still more vexatious part of existing shipping regulations, is that which relates to the
crews of merchant vessels. By one of those regulations a certain proportion of every crew manning a
British ship must be British sailors.* The effect of
this is to give the men a monopoly of labour which, in
some circumstances, may prove exceedingly annoying
to the masters. For instance, when one of our ships
is at a foreign port, the crew may act as they please,
knowing well that the captain cannot supply their
place. The repeal of this law would place seamen on
the same footing as other operatives, and furnish
their employers with a wholesome check against
insubordination. By another of these regulations
our ships of war in any part of the globe are permitted
to recruit from merchant vessels. On arriving on
one of our naval stations abroad, a merchant vessel
may all at once be disabled by the desertion of
the crew to the Queen's service, the crew having been
openly tempted to do so by such offers as are so
liberally plied in the neighbourhood of the Horse
Guards. The inconveniences and loss of money
which are entailed by such a procedure are immense.
Bad as these regulations are, they yield in point of
iniquity to those which relate to salvage. Our navy
costs us nearly six millions sterling annually; the
only pretence on which this vast expenditure is justified, is the necessity of protecting British interests
abroad, and it is supplied to a great extent from the
profits of commerce. Yet this same navy, thus
splendidly maintained at the cost of the British

---

* This has happily been repealed by a measure passed in the
session of 1853.

people, is not allowed to perform common acts of humanity without exacting exorbitant remuneration, amounting sometimes to the confiscation of the vessel requiring help. It is infamous that a British merchant ship, if stranded or otherwise disabled, may be compelled by our admiralty courts to pay £3,000 for being taken in tow by a British man of war; but salvage to that amount has been awarded when the only cause of disability in the ship requiring help was the desertion of her crew to the Queen's service. The process would be absurd, if it were not an outrage upon justice: a boat from some war-ship which may be cruising in the neighbourhood appears alongside a merchant vessel; a number of the crew forthwith desert; the ship, bereft of its hands, is disabled; the man of war gallantly comes to her aid, and finally demands £3,000 for the service of towing her into the nearest port. The law which permits this is an insult to commerce; if this is to be tolerated we had better disown our civilisation and go back to the days of black mail.

III. These acts of justice granted, Free Trade asks for commerce a better administration of commercial law; whereby the decision of questions pertaining to trade may be more promptly, economically, and equitably secured. This demand includes within it the codification of such statute-laws as relate to commerce. More than 20,000 statutes have been enacted by parliament since the time of Edward I., having no other arrangement than that of time, lying in ghastly confusion, like corpses in a catacomb. The codification of these statutes is a public necessity, and we rejoice to learn that it is forthwith to be attempted, so that in a few years an opportunity may be afforded of being able, by immediate reference, to ascertain on any point what is or is not English law. The administration of justice in commercial matters is a reform of a more practical kind, and one which is not so intimately connected with others as to necessitate much delay. Attention has already been drawn to the subject, chiefly through the efforts of Lords Wharncliffe and Beaumont, and the society for promoting its discussion which has been formed under their auspices. The necessity for legislation is established by very impressive facts. In a memorial presented to the Lord Mayor of London, in 1851, by a number of influential merchants and tradesmen, it is stated that " our present system for the administration of commercial law, is ruining many honest and well-intentioned men in the midst of their industry." A person, with but little to lose, finds himself involved, perhaps involuntarily, in a commercial dispute. If the question might be submitted to a number of gentlemen acquainted with the usages of trade, there is no reason why it might not be equitably settled in a few days. Instead of this, however, it is carried before the courts, subjected, for six months, to all the refinements of legal hair-splitting, and, after running up an enormous bill of costs, is perhaps referred to arbitration at the last moment; the only object gained being that of furnishing briefs to needy barristers, and ruining an honest man. The public at large have no idea of the extent to which such an expensive and useless course is pursued. The following facts will place the magnitude of the evil in a striking light. In 1849, out of 84,860 causes of action entered within the jurisdiction of the three superior courts of Westminster by issue of writ, to only 44,406 were appearances put in, while only 2,614 were actually brought to trial. A case has recently been mentioned, in which a leading mercantile firm are involved in a dispute, a stake of £50,000 depending on its issue, and during the last three years they have spent £3,500 in vain attempts to induce the opposing party to agree to a reference. In order to meet such evils, it has been proposed to establish " tribunals of commerce," to be composed chiefly of commercial men, where the point at issue might be canvassed on its own merits, and decided on grounds of equity alone. Similar institutions already exist in France, Belgium, Rhenish Prussia, Denmark, Spain, and even in Turkey; and it is said that during the three years immediately preceding their establishment in Den-mark, there came before the courts of law 25,512 causes, whereas during the following three years the number was only 9,658, making the astonishing difference of 15,854 lawsuits.* Before pronouncing, however, upon the propriety of adopting this or any similar scheme, it will be well to await the decision of the commission of inquiry which has recently been appointed to investigate the whole subject.

IV. The repeal of protective duties, the removal of existing restrictions on shipping, and the better administration of commercial law will only set our commerce free, and bring the great engine of competition into full play. These changes merely grant the prayer of Ajax, for light, the battle has after

---

* Report of the Executive Committee for establishing Tribunals of Commerce, December 20, 1852.

all to be won by address and bravery. Free Trade demands, for the sake of its own justification, that we fit ourselves for winning in the struggle to which it has introduced us. It was folly to leave the shield of protection if we are not now determined to keep the field. Our future success as a manufacturing and commercial people depends, for example, to a great extent upon an abundant supply of raw material. The importance of this is truly startling when we look at our staple manufacture. Three millions and a half of our fellow subjects are dependent upon the cotton manufacture, and this is sufficient to identify with it the welfare of the whole kingdom. Yet for three-fifths of the quantity of cotton imported we are dependent upon one country, and to a section of its population which cannot much longer remain in a state of slavery. By what means soever slavery may be abolished in the United States, we cannot but expect that its abolition will greatly influence the growth of cotton, and it is not improbable that for several years we should not be able to procure more than a third or a fourth of our present supply from that country. Since the case stands thus, we are the people whose interests are chiefly imperilled by the approaching abolition of slavery in the United States; that act of justice would be to America a less terrible blow than to Great Britain. Apathy on this all-important subject is doubly criminal, since we have the remedy in our own hands. India, the mother country of the cotton plant, is under our sway, and in order to obtain a supply from that quarter commensurate with any possible demand, it is only requisite that the government of

India do its duty. Free Trade has a deep stake in the measures which may be adopted on the India question in 1853.* Justice to the Hindoo, however, will coincide with expediency to ourselves. The two great obstacles to the growth of cotton in India are the system of rack-rents, and the total absence of good roads. Nominally, the land is in the possession of the natives, who cannot be dispossessed while they continue to pay the land tax; but practically the native rents the land from the government, the land tax being equivalent to the highest rent he could afford to pay. Still, this is not the gist of the evil, which lies here:—The maximum amount of the tax is so high that the proprietor is seldom either able to pay it, or expected to do so, and it is the business of the collector to remit the portion which seems to be beyond his means. This, which appears, at first sight, a humane arrangement, is, in fact, quite the reverse, and merely constitutes an efficient instrument for wringing from the unhappy native the last farthing beyond a bare subsistence. The practical effect of this merciful law is, that the government takes ALL, and would still take all, even if the profits of the estate proved a third or a half above the average. We are told of Hindoo indolence as the reason why cotton cannot be grown in India; rather let it be said it is the shameless rapacity of its rulers. The gross revenue of India is £29,000,000 sterling, yet, with

* Since the above was written the anticipated measure has become law. It is unnecessary here to point out its glaring defects; our duty is clear to obviate those defects, and render the measure as useful as possible, by the formation of an enlightened public opinion with regard to the affairs of our Indian Empire.

this vast income, scarcely a rupee is spent upon the public works which are absolutely essential to the development of its magnificent resources. Cotton grown within twenty or thirty miles of the coast, cannot be shipped because of the expense. In many parts of the country in order to travel twenty miles it is necessary to make the circuit of a hundred. In Guzerat, which is at present the principal cotton field, " there is not a single made road." On the Taptee and Nerbudda rivers, which furnish the only means of communication with the interior, there is not a single pier at all worthy of the name, the only semblance of one being no larger than the landing stage of a ferry-boat. " The cotton gets into the boat the best way it can, frequently getting soaked by the rising tide" before this simple process is complete. Indeed, a common method is to wait till the tide rises high enough to float the bales, which are then shoved alongside the boat, and hoisted in. These evils require a speedy remedy. However highly we may appreciate the enterprise of European gentlemen, such as the Messrs. Lees and Longshaw, who have gone out to promote the cultivation of cotton in India, it is not upon such efforts that we must rely. The best encouragement the immediate rulers of India can give to the growth of cotton is, to do justly, to employ their vast resources in developing the industry of the country for whose welfare we are responsible in the sight of God and man. This is all which is wanted in order to render India the cotton country of the world, and less than this ought not to be accepted by the British public at the hands of any government.

V. Along with a cheap supply of material we must

have the highest quality of labour, if we would successfully maintain our position under the Free Trade *régime*. The first thing requisite in labour, as in every other article of commerce, is that it be free, and Free Trade in labour is one of the principles which remain to be fully conceded by the workman and by the state. To some extent the concession has been made; the necessity for a seven years' apprenticeship is now dispensed with, and the ancient power of guilds is abolished. The " Ten Hours' Bill" was a retrogressive step. We see in this measure, however humane the motives which led to its adoption, an unjust interference with the rights at once of capital and labour. Notwithstanding the agitation which is recommencing in order to secure a more stringent application of the principle of the measure, it cannot stand against the force of prosperous times; the working man will not be and ought not to be, prevented from earning all the money he can. The great Protectionist of the present day is the workman. Enjoying the blessings of Free Trade in the greater cheapness of provisions and the enhanced value of his labour, he still repudiates Free Trade with reference to the only article over which he has direct control. He aims, with a spirit worthy of being incarnate in the most fervid advocate of the corn laws, to defend himself both against the capitalist and his fellow labourer. Let us for a moment examine the fallacies on which this conduct proceeds. Labour must defend itself against capital. The spirit of this aphorism is best illustrated by observing the tactics of two rival commanders, brought face to face on the field of battle. Napoleon at Austerlitz, or Radetzky on the plains of Lombardy, each seeking to circumvent his rival, and force him to a battle on unequal terms, furnishes an apt parallel to the chiefs of our " amalgamated societies," and the manœuvres by which labour and capital strive to outwit each other. With those generals, granting the morality of their vocation, there was nothing wrong; in the one case Frenchmen were opposed to Austrians, and in the other Austrians were pitted against Piedmontese. But if, in both cases, the opposing armies had belonged to the same nation, and carried the same banners, the tactics of the generals would have been absurd. But what is capital?—It is the instrument of labour. What is labour?—It is at once the root and the fruit of capital. Oxygen and nitrogen are not more essential to air, than capital and labour are essential to wealth. But the advocate of what are called " the rights of labour" arms himself, not only against the capitalist, but against his fellow workmen. He restricts the number of apprentices; that is, when Providence sends twenty labourers into the field, he says to ten of them, " go and lie you down yonder, and die;—all the work and wages and food within reach we intend keeping to ourselves." These enthusiastic advocates of the rights *of labour* have forgotten the right *to labour;* they have lost realities in abstractions. It is no greater act of dishonesty to seize a man's purse, and place it where he cannot reach it, than to deny him the honest use of his head and fingers, to provide for the temporal wants of himself and family. If labour has rights—a logical abstraction—the labourer assuredly has *his.*

Labour once set free, we must look at its technic and artistic qualities. This is a point demanding the serious attention of our manufacturers, and we cannot do better than quote, in reference to it, the opinion of Thomas Bazley, Esq., President of the Manchester Chamber of Commerce. Speaking of the Exhibition of 1851 he says, " Of the actual manufactures found in the cotton department, many articles were of great merit, while it would be difficult to determine from what precise country the most meritorious product was derived. It may be assumed, from good evidence, that, in many fancy fabrics, where beauty of design and of colour and fine taste appeared, the French and other continental nations took decidedly the highest position; whilst in useful goods, adapted rather for comfort than ornament, British manu- factures were pre-eminent, especially if the latter be associated with their cheapness. Here, however, a word of advice or of admonition may be offered to both British manufacturers and merchants. There is, unquestionably, a cheapening tendency pursued by them which, with its consequent deterioration, must inevitably lead to an ultimate diminution of business, and which, it is feared, is already damaging the national character, and giving to foreign rivals, for their superior productions, fame and credit superior to our own."* We are aware that the verdict of the jurors of the Great Exhibition has not been universally acquiesced in, but, granting its accuracy, there can be no reasons why our printed muslins, cambrics, and calicoes should be inferior in point of colours and good taste to the product of any foreign

* " Lecture upon Cotton," by Thomas Bazley, Esq., p. 61.

country. Whatever weight we attach to special criticisms, it is evident that a higher quality of labour would essentially tend to secure to us the markets of the world.

On this point two suggestions have been made, which deserve to be well weighed. One is from the pen of Dr. Lyon Playfair, and advocates the introduction, to a greater extent than heretofore, of physical studies into the curriculum of ordinary and collegiate education. Without any disparagement to classical literature, much less with any wish to remove it from the place it now occupies, as an auxiliary in the training of youth, it may be questioned whether the physical sciences have received in our schools that measure of attention which they ought to receive at the hands of a commercial and manufacturing people. How many schools can boast of a good collection of the ancient classics, which possess neither laboratory nor museum? Nay, is not even the estimation in which men of science themselves are popularly held, slightly tinged with ridicule? Is there not an unjust, an ignorant association of scientific experiments with the performances of Faustus or Dr. Dee? If current feelings were to interpret for us, would not the French *savant* be translated by the English wiseacre? Whatever room may exist for reform in this respect should at once be occupied; science must be brought down to our schools, and the minds of boys familiarised with its principles. The other suggestion to which we refer occurs in the last report of the Commissioners for the Great Exhibition, and recommends the establishment of schools where instruction may be specially given in the principles of science and art. The examples selected for our imitation are probably such as we should not choose in all respects to follow, since they agree with Continental, rather than with English, notions respecting the province of government; but they are useful, if only to show us the kind of competition which we must be prepared to meet. We learn from the report in question that, in Germany alone, 13,000 persons annually receive the "high technical and scientific" training of the Industrial Schools and Polytechnic Institutions; while more than 30,000 workmen are being systematically taught the elements of science and art in schools which communicate instruction to them during their leisure hours. Besides these there are important institutions, equivalent to industrial universities, in the capitals of nearly all the German states. The systems pursued in them vary in details, but agree in the common object of teaching the principles of science and art, on which production depends, explaining fully the nature of technical processes, and preparing them for actual practice in the workshop or factory. Even the little Duchy of Baden supports its industrial college, at a great expense. The institute at Carlsrhue has 330 pupils, with a staff of forty-one professors or teachers. In France the "Ecole Centrale des Arts et Manufactures" annually instructs 300 young men in the higher branches of applied science and art, and the councils general of twenty-nine departments have instituted exhibitions in connexion with it. At the present time 500 of the youths thus trained are occupying important positions in various parts of the world. Making due allowance for the more speculative habits of our neighbours, we discern here an array of intellectual force which it would be ignorance itself to despise. In manufactures, as in all things else, tact and energy may do much, but intellect, after all, will carry the day. We need not go to government for help. Let our manufacturers look after their own interests; they have wealth enough, and science can be had for money. In the establishment of Schools of Design, and the recent affiliation of Mechanics' Institutes, we see the type of what may be done, and it will be our fault if, in the struggle on which we have entered, our workmen do not acquire as high a reputation for taste and skill as they have already obtained for their industrial and moral virtues.

VI. If we suppose, now, that these reforms will be conceded, and that our manufactures will maintain the ascendant both for cheapness and excellence, what may we expect will be the effect upon our commerce of this universal application of the letter and spirit of Free Trade? Twelve years ago an impression was gaining ground that we had reached its limits ; we were to build no more factories, construct no more engines, import no more cotton, send our superfluous workmen into our colonies, and gradually accustom ourselves to quiet continental modes of living. The popularity of emigration schemes, long before the discovery of gold superseded all other motives, is an index to the true state of feeling which then prevailed. Those schemes for transporting our population to the antipodes were expressive of unbelief in the future destiny of England—a suspicion that we had reached well nigh the end of our commercial career. We need not confute the fallacy; its confutation may be read in the history of the last twelve years; in the increased value of our exports by more than forty millions sterling; in the unprecedented activity which has since prevailed in branches of industry which were thought to be completely ruined. What then are our prospects for the future? Standing on a pedestal of a hundred, instead of fifty millions, can we expect our exports to go on increasing? This question will receive a practical answer by comparing the amount of our foreign and our home trade. It is difficult to estimate the precise amount of the latter. Mr. Porter regarded it, in 1845, as equal to the whole of our foreign trade, including in the latter that which we carry on with our colonies and dependencies throughout the world. If this estimate was correct in 1845, it is so still, for our home trade has certainly kept pace with our foreign trade during the last five or six years. But if anything like such a proportion is correct, what a career does it not open to us! Our entire trade divisible into two equal parts, of which one part is carried on with 27,000,000 at home, and the other with 800,000,000 abroad! Hitherto, with all our vaunted progress, with our " world-wide commerce," with our colonial system devised on purpose to form a channel for our trade, we have only induced 800,000,000 to take as much of our produce as is consumed by 27,000,000. With these facts before us, to ask whether our commerce can be extended is simply absurd. There is no reason why we should not send ten times the quantity of goods abroad that we do now; there is no natural limit to our commerce but the wants of other countries and our ability to supply them.

The effect of the greater development of our commerce which may be expected from Free Trade will be greatly to enlarge the influence of our manufactures as a social agent. Their present vocation is chiefly to bring over to us in Britain the products of other climes, by enabling us to offer an acceptable equivalent. This is the first result of our manufacturing energy, and the progress which has been realized in social comfort during the last few years has been already considered. But in proportion as the wants of our own people are supplied, the further extension of our commerce, in both its branches, will be made abroad, and its civilising influence will be shared increasingly by other lands. So long as we retain our manufacturing position, our exports will go on increasing, and with them our wealth, while a single part of the world requires any of the productions of another. Our cotton and linen goods, our iron and hardware, will become a kind of current money throughout the globe, for which we shall receive in exchange the produce of every country, not, perhaps, to bring it to our own shores, but to transfer it wherever it may be saleable with profit. Thus Britain will become more and more the factor and negociator for the world, its vast capital rendering it an industrial agency for diffusing and equalising the collective affluence of mankind. The blessings which it has conferred upon this country it will also confer upon the semi-barbarous populations of Russia, the miserably clad races which inhabit the countries bordering on the Lower Danube, the fifty millions who are scattered over the vast plains of Africa from Morocco to the Cape, the inhabitants of the thousand islands of the Pacific, the savage tribes of Eastern Asia, and the half developed communities which are spread along the vast plains extending from the Gulf of Mexico to Cape Horn. As these states and communities rise in the scale of nations, their wants will increase; the produce of their own territory, which contented them in a barbarous state, will not meet one half of their acquired tastes; they will require in places thousands of miles apart the produce of each others' labour. What, then, will bridge over the intervening oceans? What will enable the different communities of the world to hold intercourse with each other? If existing maritime states resolve still to act on the maxims of protection, if wars arise to call antagonistic feelings into play, the mode of intercourse will be the creation of national fleets; cheapness will be slighted, the possession of comforts and luxuries be dispensed with, rather than incidentally minister to a rival's opulence. But England has discarded her protective policy, her shipping is offered to the world on the intelligible and just basis of mutual profit; and should peace continue, rising states, instead of building ships for themselves, will accept the more economical agencies which this country can supply. The prospect which such thoughts open to us is truly boundless. The patriot and the philanthropist alike may turn away from it with feelings of devout exultation, as they see the greatness of their country linked with the pacific progress of mankind. The star of England set? The star of intellect, peace, justice, never sets! The bloody lustre of ambition is already fading, and, as the opening day advances, it will totally disappear, but the lustre of righteousness is immortal, it is the day-star shining evermore.

SECTION II.

POLITICAL CONSEQUENCES WHICH MAY BE ANTICIPATED FROM THE TRIUMPH OF FREE TRADE.

We have already remarked that Free Trade, considered in itself, is an economical and social rather than a political principle. This is true, but at the same time the triumph of a Free Trade policy in the legislature is one of the most important political events which have distinguished the present century, and cannot fail of leading to equally important consequences. A measure acquires its character, not only by its own nature, but by the principles on which it is advocated or opposed. Until the very last stage of the struggle, Free Trade questions were never discussed in Parliament on purely economical grounds. A previous question had first to be decided, viz., whether, supposing Free Trade to be advantageous to the community at large, it ought not nevertheless to be deferred, out of regard to the interests of the aristocratical section of the community. Thus the question was practically a political one; it was a struggle for ascendancy between the landed proprietary and the nation. The decision which might be arrived at on such a question could not possibly stand alone; whether in favour of popular rights or against them, it could not help becoming a precedent for other decisions. Considering the political maturity to which the people had attained, the question of right, in opposition to class aseendancy, could only have one issue. The people were to conquer, and their conquest was to become a vantage ground from which other victories might be won.

I.　One of the political consequences which cannot fail to flow from the triumph of Free Trade, will be the gradual, but sure progress of constitutional reform. A victory so dear to the people has been won with difficulty, and hence the nation has been taught the peril as well as the absurdity of the present narrow basis on which the House of Commons is elected. What an anomalous spectacle was presented by the present House of Commons during the discussions which preceded the fall of the Derby Ministry! Nearly all the genius and administrative talent of the House was found on the opposition benches; there were the veterans of parliamentary warfare, whose wisdom had guided successive governments; there were found the representatives of nearly all the large towns in the kingdom, and every constituency which is entitled to a leading place in the guidance of public opinion; and on the same side also was arrayed the enthusiastic support of nine-tenths of the nation; yet so nicely were parties balanced, that a Protectionist government was driven from power by the slender majority of nineteen. The majority of nineteen, therefore, in the present state of the franchise, is the parliamentary basis on which the intelligence, wisdom, and above all, the industrial hopes, of the country rest. An opposition composed of all that is brilliant in talent, commanding in intellect, and elevated in public character, secured to no greater extent the senatorial confidence of the nation, and a cause on which the people outside would have polled ten to one in its favour, was saved from shipwreck by such an ignominious majority.   What is the truth which flashes broadly upon us from this fact?—It is that the country is not safe while the distribution of political power outside the House of Commons can allow of such a spectacle within.   What is the end of the House of Commons, if not to represent THE PEOPLE?— Is it not a constitutional maxim, that each member must be deemed to represent, not this or that constituency which had the privilege of choosing him, but the whole people?—Since the House of Commons is designed to represent the whole people, since any other design would be politically unjust, let the whole people choose the individuals that compose it.   The instability of the governments which have succeeded each other during the last six or seven years has been the theme of frequent remark.   Some have ventured to assert that we have reached that point in the history of the country, at which a constitutional government is impossible.   Free Trade has again and again been accused of having caused this dilemma.   It is indeed its glory to have caused it.   Truth and falsehood cannot work together.   A system must be of the same nature throughout, to work smoothly.   An error may co-operate well enough with an erroneous system, but substitute truth for error, and the system then falls into confusion,—all truth, or all error, this is the fundamental law of harmony. Our present restricted franchise worked well enough in the days of monopoly; but commercial freedom having been conceded, political freedom alone will quadrate with it. One act of justice thus necessitates another, and a course of amelioration once entered upon, becomes perpetual. Having obtained Free Trade, we must obtain for our large towns a weightier influence in public affairs. It must no longer be permitted that Manchester, with its 18,000 voters, 300,000 inhabitants, and vast moral influence throughout the world, should have no greater share in the deciding of parliamentary questions than some obscure Thetford, with its population of 4,000, and a constituency of 200. Or that Devonshire, with its assessment to the poor rate of £2,028,583, its 90,104 houses, and its 572,207 inhabitants, should send twenty-two members to the House of Commons, while Lancashire, with its poor rate assessment of £6,463,363, its 313,436 houses, and its 2,063,913 inhabitants, should send only twenty-six.

II. Free Trade will necessitate, sooner or later, a change in the tenure of landed property throughout the kingdom. It is impossible that the barbarous ideas and customs which now prevail respecting it should much longer exist; they must disappear before the civilisation of the present age. The statutes which regulate the transfer or transmission of real property carry us back to the feudal system. The fundamental principle of that system was the territorial sovereignty of the monarch; he was king, not of the French, but of France, not of the English, but of England. Nor was this designation, which our

neighbours changed on the remodelling of the
sovereign power in 1830, an empty phrase; every
inch of land was considered as belonging originally to
the king, and every title derived its validity, in some
way, from the throne.   In the first instance the land
was presented to the leading vassals in return for
services rendered in war, and on condition of rendering similar services.   Thus the land was not made
over to them in absolute right, it was a possession
granted upon conditions.   This first process was the
model of every other which occurred in the transfer
of land.   The great baron, who had received his ten
thousand acres in fief, parcelled them out among his
vassals on similar terms; they were to accompany
him to the field, and give to him a certain portion of
the produce.   Such is the outline of the system as it
was first practised, but time and political revolutions
soon broke in upon it.   Civil war soon arrayed vassals
and barons against each other.   The growth of a
middle class, possessing money, which they were often
willing to exchange for land, joined to the necessities of those who held the land, originated a new order
of proprietors and a new description of titles.   Probably, in many cases, long tenancy gained a right *de facto*
which at length became associated with right *de jure*.
Though the practice of entailing the ancestral estate
on the line of the eldest son perpetuated the leading
features of the feudal system, yet the claims of other
portions of the family could not be so far dissevered
from the paternal inheritance as to prevent large
portions of it from passing into other hands by
marriage.   By this means a large proportion of the
landed property of the kingdom has become alienated

from the nobility, and subject, in its transfer, from person to person, to the ordinary maxims of commerce. Yet still, though such a series of changes have occurred to break up the old principle of transfer, its analogy is rigidly pursued in all investigations respecting titles. The spirit of the feudal system has created existing laws, and given rise to customs which seriously interfere with the well-being of the country. One of the most pernicious of these is the practice of entailing estates, in virtue of which a vast extent of land passes from father to son, without any individual in the series being absolute possessor, or more than a trustee for those that are to follow. The aim of this arrangement is to maintain an hereditary nobility by preventing its pauperization. To this it is owing that no member of the aristocracy is ever found side by side with the plebeian operative, working like him for his daily bread. The title, being connected with the estate, carries along with it great nominal wealth. Here, however, another abuse comes to view. The law which permits entails, does not prohibit settlements; though the present holder of an entailed estate may not be able to devise it away from his heir, yet he may burden it with as many incumbrances as he chooses by way of provision for other members of the family. Hence it is not uncommon to find land, thus entailed, mortgaged so heavily that it is rather a dead weight to its nominal possessor than a source of revenue.

The entire question of the tenure of land demands an early and bold investigation. The principles of Free Trade must be applied to it; and applied without any narrow regard to customs which are probably honoured more in the breach than the observance. It is worth while asking whether even the maintenance of an hereditary nobility is a sufficient compensation to any class, or to the nation at large, for the heavy price which must be paid for it. The application of the Encumbered Estates Bill has brought to light a fearful state of things in reference to the proprietary of Ireland, and though we are better off in this country, yet the same evil exists to a serious extent. How often is the nominal holder of large estates utterly insolvent, burdened with mortgages and settlements, yet unable to alienate a single acre with the proceeds of which to render himself the actual owner of the rest. But the inconvenience of such an arrangement to the parties more immediately concerned is the least evil, it involves in addition a serious loss to the nation. A large proportion of the land is shamefully cultivated, broad domains lie in a state of semi-barrenness from year to year. The reason of such waste is, no doubt, the want of money; but why want money in a country overflowing with capital? Why not sell a part, and apply the remainder in draining, fencing, and other improvements? Or if the estate is so heavily burdened that the sale of a portion would be insufficient to redeem the rest, why not dissolve the figment of ownership, and let the estate pass altogether into the possession of persons who have money enough to buy and improve it? To these questions there is one simple reply,—the law will not allow of such a step.

All the changes which are necessary in order to release the land from such burdens, extricate the landowner from a most embarrassing position, and

greatly promote the agriculture of the United Kingdom, are comprised in one sentence:—Render land
rigidly and fully an article of commerce. Let there
be in no case any greater difficulty in the way of
disposing of land than of shares or bank notes.
What we plead for is not a compulsory partition of
landed property on the death of the owner, as in
France; with regard to testamentary arrangements,
a person might exercise his rights of proprietorship
in the same way as with his other property, it being
solely forbidden to exercise any power over the person
to whom he bequeaths it, so as to restrain him from
selling or otherwise disposing of it as he may see fit.
A simplification of titles is absolutely necessary to
greater ease in the transfer of land; the present
complication of titles constitutes a real burden and
grievance to the landed interest. A clean sweep
should be made at once of the old title deeds, reaching back to the compilation of Doomsday Book, as
serving no purpose beyond that of thickening the
mysteries of law, giving work to its needy scions, and
retaining the present in visible bondage to the past.
Possession is said to be nine points in law, let it for
once be made the tenth also. The establishment of
a court of registration, to which a statement of sale
in due form might be returned, would prevent confusion, and furnish a standard of appeal in case of
litigation. These measures are necessary to place
the landowner on the same advantageous footing as
the owner of other kinds of property, to release land
itself from the protection of absurd usage, and make
it a full sharer of the privileges of commerce.

III. Free Trade will not only break down the existing monopoly of political power by extending the franchise, and destroy the monopoly of land by rendering it an article of commerce ; these great changes conduct us to others which flow equally from the same principles, we refer to the removal of the intellectual and religious monopolies which disgrace our age. Far be it from us to dip our pens in gall ; we have no sympathy with sectarian bigotry ; we speak simply as Englishmen, who have a right to assail injustice wherever it is found. The destruction of these monopolies is logically included in Free Trade,—Free Trade permits the free development of commerce, destroys monopoly with respect to the ledger and the purse, and thus infuses new vigour into an important set of practical interests. But man is not merely an automaton of business ; he is intellectual and religious, and these qualities are clothed with importance not only to himself as an individual, but to the community of which he forms a part. Do we wish to ascertain the value of a citizen ? We ask whether he is ignorant or enlightened ; whether his mental faculties are untrained, or whether they have been disciplined by study ; whether he has walked from childhood round the narrow circle of his own ideas, or whether he has habitually conversed with the great men who have lived before him. We ask, whether he is selfish, sensual, unscrupulous ; or, whether the sentiment of rectitude is properly developed, and his bosom beats with love to God and man ; we ask, in a word, whether he is intelligent and religious, and from the nature of the reply we infer whether he is a good or a bad citizen. Thus the subject we have mooted has a national and secular aspect; in this, and in this alone our subject calls upon us to consider it.

1. In a healthy national development, of which commercial freedom is but a part, education holds a position of the first importance. Even in reference to the comparatively narrow interests which are strictly comprised in Free Trade, it is impossible to set too high a value upon it. We have abandoned ourselves to an open contest with other nations, a contest in which, other things being equal, the most intelligent will gain the prize. It is absolutely necessary to establish a system of national education, in which, without doing violence to the religious scruples of parents or guardians, our youthful population may be instructed in the knowledge which is necessary to enable them to perform their proper part in life. The expense of such a system might be fully met by an economical administration, under act of Parliament, of the monies left for distinctively educational purposes by our fathers. The great educational monopolies of the day are seen at Oxford and Cambridge. No nation under heaven can boast so many munificent endowments for public education as are attached to the two universities, and certainly nowhere do we find a similar instance of abuse. We cannot regard those institutions in any light without perceiving some feature of injustice. Many of the founders intended their benefactions for the use of _bonâ fide_ poor students; their object was to found charities for the needy, not splendid abodes for the opulent; but how far have these intentions been carried out? The founders in every instance

intended their bequests to go directly towards promoting education, and chiefly towards remunerating
qualified men for the work of teaching; but how
small is the portion so applied! The giving away of
rich fellowships as rewards for scholastic distinction
is very different from their being regarded as strictly
tutorial offices, upon which ought to devolve the work
of gratuitous instruction. At present the wealth of
the university is enjoyed by men who render no
equivalent in return, and who hold a fellowship as
a sort of *otium cum dignitate* till it suits them to
exchange it for something better, while the real work
of tuition devolves upon a class of persons who have
no recognised *status*, and who derive their support,
not from college funds, but the fees of their pupils.
Another monopoly is that of confining the dignity
and emoluments of the professorships almost exclusively to persons in " holy orders." This is, no doubt,
of ancient date; would that every other ancient regulation had been observed as well! But why should it
be so ? Is there any reason why the communication
of secular knowledge should be delegated to clerical
hands? The system is a relic of the dark ages, when
a baron could not sign a bill or indite a letter without
the aid of a clerk, and may be regarded as a symbol
of those mistaken views, elsewhere prevalent, by which
the development of the intellect is regarded as the
proper work of the theologian ; but where is the
wisdom of retaining in the nineteenth century the
prejudices of the age of Charlemagne ? Even this is
not the worst feature of monopoly which marks our
university system. In a country proverbially abound-
ing with religious sects, the academic advantages of

those institutions are confined to one. Dissenters of every grade are excluded from those munificent foundations which were laid by the piety of our common ancestors for the common benefit of the people of England. We might speak of the moral aspect of such an arrangement; we might point out how it sets a premium on dishonesty, and excludes those only who are too conscientious to practise a tenth part of the mental reservation which many have practised who have passed on to high honours. We waive these objections, however; we put in on a secular footing alone, and we ask, is it just? is it in harmony with the principles of Free Trade? Are we not bound by those principles to throw the national seminaries open to the nation?*

We recognise, then, in the reform of our educational institutions, another sphere in which the legislator will find ample scope. The spirit of that bold and just policy which has regenerated our commercial laws, must purify also those seats of learning where the national mind is trained. The matter has already been taken up, and the sentiments expressed by the Chancellor of the Exchequer on the occasion of his recent visit to Oxford encourages us to hope that it will be dealt with on truly enlightened principles, untrammelled by useless deference to moth-eaten statutes, and with an exclusive eye to the public good. Let idle placemen no longer live in academic state on funds which

---

* We gladly remind the reader that, thanks to Mr. James Heywood, M.P., these remarks are already antiquated. The Universities' Bill, which provides for the admission of Dissenters, passed triumphantly through both Houses, and now only awaits the Royal assent.

were intended to furnish the means of instruction to
our rising youth, nor superstition and blind faith be
permitted, beneath the cloak of mediæval darkness,
to emasculate the future mind of England. The
property enjoyed by our universities, amounting to
£741,000 annually, might, if economically applied,
bring the boon of a sound, practical, and cheap
university training within the means of the bulk of
the middle classes.

2. From academic we step into religious ground,
though still in our political character. Free Trade
is but a part of the unrestricted development of the
national mind; it implies the doing universally what
is just. We will not define the province of the legislature with regard to religious phenomena; we are
content to leave the subject unargued on this abstract
ground; but we cannot avoid pointing to the wastefulness and gross injustice which mark the ecclesiastical establishments of this kingdom. The agricul-
turalist complains of his inability to cope with
foreigners, and yet the agricultural interest pays, in
the shape of tithe commutation, an annual tax of
three millions sterling, representing, at twenty-five
years' purchase, a capital of £75,000,000. In addition
to this there are glebe lands, worth annually half a
million, episcopal and capitular revenues, valued at
an equal sum, *scholastic revenues*, valued by Lord
Brougham at £2,000,000 annually, besides various
other sources of income, valued at a million more.
Truly this enormous aggregate of seven millions sterling, annually drawn, in some way or other, from the
industry of Great Britain, constitutes a public right
to control its management. For the abuses con-

nected with the administration of these large sums, we need only refer to the discussions elicited in the House of Commons by the various motions of Mr. Horsman, the facts which have been brought to light by the Ecclesiastical Commissioners, and those which have so often received ignominious exposure in the *Times*. Granting the expediency of ecclesiastical establishments, we ask whether it is not possible so to economise this income as to leave a considerable surplus for educational, or other useful objects, in the benefit of which all could equally share? But are such establishments expedient? Considering their inevitable partiality to one sect, and the social evils which flow from this prolific source, none will regard them as expedient, except on the ground of their being absolutely necessary to the moral well-being of the nation.* But, in the face of facts, can it possibly be alleged that they are thus necessary? Across the Atlantic we behold a people as religious as ourselves, descended from the Puritans of the Commonwealth, with whom Christianity is a matter of profound conviction, among whom we find a much larger proportion of persons avowing personal faith in its principles, than in any other community; yet among them we find no established hierarchy, no sect fostered by the state, no public money paid for the maintenance of a Christian priesthood; religion is sustained by those who feel its worth, and the state, in its corporate capacity, takes no cognizance of it. Religion there does its own work; all that it enjoys or

---

* "When will the church, too, bow to that rule, which in a free and self-governing community will, first or last, make the common weal override every consideration?"—*Times*, Jan. 31, 1854.

asks at the hand of the civil power, is freedom; and this given, it throws itself, unarmed and unadorned, upon the convictions and affections of the people.*

IV. Free Trade clearly involves the necessity of a reform in the administration of our colonial system. In repealing the differential duties on timber, sugar, coffee, etc. which formerly protected the interests of our colonies, we recognise a new colonial principle, and it is necessary that our system should be brought into entire harmony with it. The idea which at first controlled the relation subsisting between this country and its colonies, was that of *paternity*. Perhaps, however, this designation expresses too favourably its real nature. The Home Government avowedly sustained a paternal relation to those of our countrymen who had planted themselves in various unoccupied portions of the globe; but the wisdom and disinterestedness proper to the paternal relation gave way, not unfrequently, to the most disreputable selfishness. Entrenching ourselves in an imaginary paternal right, we sought to make our colonies the means of our own aggrandisement. Instead of recognising them as federal parts of the state, having a claim to all the privileges which are enjoyed on British soil, and therefore to be invested, at the earliest possible moment, with the functions of self-government, we regarded them as a sort of national chattels, the personal *property* of Great Britain, subservient to home interests, both in politics and commerce, to be turned at pleasure into military posts or penal

* For an admirable statement of the argument furnished by Voluntaryism in the United States, the reader is referred to a small work by the Rev. J. H. Hinton, M.A., entitled "The Test of Experience."

settlements, to enrich us by their produce and to employ us by their wants. Nothing can exceed the iniquity of those monopolies, the last remnants of which have been destroyed by Free Trade. They constituted a gigantic system of wrong—the most subtle arrangement ever formed for inflicting injustice on one part of an empire or repressing the energies of another. In the first instance, our colonists were prohibited from buying or selling any article, save with our own merchants. Their tobacco, rice, rum, and cotton had to be brought here, and exchanged for our produce. The English manufacturer had the world for his market; the Jamaica or Canadian was confined to this country. But injustice cannot long be all on one side; the Canadian and Jamaica merchant had a right to ask for some recompense; it was given out of the pocket of the British consumer, in the shape of a law practically forbidding us to buy except from them. At first it was not intended that the colonists should be the chief gainers; it turned out so, however, and for fifty years they enjoyed a truly regal share of plunder. As an equivalent they have been treated as the vassals of Downing Street, and while their monopoly lasted, they had no wish to escape from their chains.

Free Trade has at length put an end to this absurd state of things. The paternal relation has vanished, and it only remains that our conduct be conformed to the fact. Our relation is now an intelligible one. Just the same tie subsists between the British Government and a resident in Jamaica, as between the same government and a resident in Yorkshire. Mutual justice is the bond which has succeeded the antiquated one of paternity, and around this, in time, all patriotic and national sentiments will cling. The Colonial Office must henceforth recognise the sovereignty of local opinion in all local matters; self-government must be conceded to the smallest community as well as the largest. We must aid them, not by sending out bulky constitutions for them to adopt, but by encouraging them to make constitutions for themselves. Away with the pedantry of statesmanship! There are not a dozen Englishmen in the world, who, if thrown together on the same spot, would not be able to frame most efficient regulations for their own protection. It is constitutional on our part to accept such self-made laws, and, so far as they are just, recognise them in our intercourse with the infant colony. By so doing how much would be gained; what bitterness should we escape abroad, and what vast labour should we save at home.

V. Another change which Free Trade demands is the application of the most economical principles to every department of public expenditure. We have already referred to this incidentally, but its importance claims for it more special notice. The history of the British exchequer presents us with a sad picture of rapacity, ignorance, and profusion. Formerly, abuses were chiefly displayed in the means which were adopted for replenishing it; in arbitrary exactions, forced loans, and absurd restrictions on the freedom of industry. In later times we seem to have made up for the greater degree of justice exhibited in the means by which the revenue of the state is raised, for the absence of royal and aristocratic extortion, such as was exercised under the Tudors and the Stuarts, by a growing wastefulness of expenditure. We are happy in being able to give some limitation to this remark with respect to recent years. Without asserting that our financial system has received the thorough revision which it requires, it will be admitted that a more economical spirit has prevailed in the legislature during the last ten years than at any previous period. The nation owes a debt of gratitude to its financial reformers; to the veteran perseverance of a Hume, the bold plans of a Cobden, and the manly denunciations of a Bright. Their united efforts have led the " People's House" through many a salutary ordeal, and at length succeeded in reconciling even aristocratic tastes to a sterner vigilance over the public purse. The doctrine of parliamentary stewardship has been placed in a clearer light; the wholesome truth has been expounded that the representatives of the people, in fixing the disbursements of the exchequer, are disposing, to a great extent, of the hardly-earned contributions of the labouring poor, and that every shilling extravagantly spent inflicts needless privation somewhere. Economy is one of the chief laws of wealth; it is one of the highest doctrines in political ethics. Free Trade itself is an economical doctrine; its vindication would be unanswerable on the ground that it seeks "to make the most" of temporal advantages; to encourage every nation and every individual to direct their labour to the department in which they will be likeliest to excel, and then exchange with each other as their wants may render necessary. The same principle should lead us to

retrench all superfluous expenditure; to bring the
salaries of public men, the maintenance of public
institutions, to the test of utility, since every farthing
saved leaves the energies of the people the freer to
increase the wealth of the state by adding to their
own.

VI. Perhaps the greatest political result of Free
Trade is the influence it will have in preparing for the
peaceful triumph of democracy. That the time will
come when the people everywhere will be invested
with the fullest political power, we hold to be among
the first inferences from the progressive character of
the human race, as evidenced in all history. We
have witnessed within the last five years a universal
uprising of the people. From Berlin to Palermo
the masses seized the sword, and strove to grasp
their freedom. We heard the movement from afar,
like the advancing roar of artillery, or the shock of
an earthquake. Happily the fierce convulsion broke
harmlessly against our shores, and too soon the
voices of impassioned millions were hushed in such
a death-like silence as succeeds to the tumult of
battle. But though the oppressor sits again in
triumph on his pile of chains, those fetters must be
broken, and the people rise again. The base of
despotism is rotten, it cannot stand against the ever-
advancing intelligence and energy of mankind. All
that was immortal in the middle ages, all which they
had to bequeath to human progress, has been infused, in the long course of years, into the spirit of
the present age; but all that sprang from the in-
firmities of human nature; their feudal scaffoldings,
their childish pomps and vanities, their iron des-

potisms, must fall. Sooner or later the incapacity of childhood, the warm and impetuous passions of youth, will be succeeded by the calm brow and firm resolve which bespeak the man. Europe will attain to political maturity. Finn and Sclave, Croat and Celt, Cossack and Magyar, will stand up side by side with the Anglo-Saxon, and from Cadiz to the Ural Mountains will be spread a family of friendly states, a vast confederation of free men.

While such are the prospects of Europe, democracy has speedy triumphs to win in Britain. In our own times very serious alterations have been made in the details of our constitution, but it is questionable whether far greater changes do not await us in the same path. The suffrage must be extended through wider and wider circles, till at length it comprises the whole people. Such a change, however great it may now appear, can scarcely be called organic, since it would be merely realizing the theory of the constitution ;—leaving untouched that threefold symbol of political perfection,—king, lords, and commons. But will the constitution remain always composed of these three elements ? On this point, who will dare to trespass beyond the poetic blissfulness of ignorance? One thought we will venture:—There is some ground for hereditary nobility. It may be a weakness, but it is one very closely bound up with human nature. Though we may well believe that every man, at some time or other, has had what is called a *noble* ancestor, yet if we were introduced into the presence of one whom we believed to have a direct descent from Cæsar, Alexander, or Alfred the Great, we should experience at least a slight effort to sup-

press a spontaneous feeling of admiration, or something akin to it.   So far this is natural.   But hereditary statesmanship—an hereditary legislator—has
no ground in nature; it is absurd.   Might not, then,
the quality and the function be released from their
artificial union, with advantage to all parties ?   Might
we not recognise, if so we choose, nobility of descent
in one person, and legislative capacity in another ?
Would not both parties be gainers by such a step ?
The nobleman be released from onerous duties, and
the legislator from awkward honours—leaving it to
electoral bodies to unite the two, as often as desirable, in the same person ?   But, however this may
be, the concession of Free Trade has given a permanent character to our political progress.   We may
confidently hope that there will be no asperities,
no violent revolutions.   Free Trade is the kiss of
charity; a sacred oath of friendship at the altar of
God.

SECTION III.

PROBABLE INFLUENCE OF FREE TRADE ON THE MORAL
RENOVATION OF THE WORLD.

From this point we may look abroad, and contemplate for a moment the effects of Free Trade,
thus socially, religiously, commercially, and politically
developed among ourselves, upon the rest of the
world.   For this purpose it will be requisite to form

a definite idea of the changes which may be expected in the future history of our race. The orator and the poet tell us of a " good time coming," a time which they depict in the warmest colouring of fancy. The inherent conviction and aspirations of the noblest minds point them onwards to a distant goal, at which humanity is to rest after the toils of centuries. What estimate may we calmly form of these hopes? How do we expect to see them fulfilled? By what particular tendencies will Free Trade hasten their fulfilment?

I. We own, at once, that, in assuming the certainty of a future political and moral "millennium," we take for granted what some deny. Many are thorough "infidels" with regard to man's destiny on earth. They have no confidence in his real progressiveness, or in the permanence of any moral results. The future presents to their mind's eye a scene of gloomy disorder; a dim vista of social and political earthquakes. It is to them a looking through the twilight of some inorganic world. They think that time will continue to re-enact his old horrors, play off his old impostures, and exercise, in new shapes, the tyrannies of king and priest:—that civil blood will still be shed; armies, scaffolds, and dungeons still raise their brute barriers against the holy march of peace, till, at length, the power which shall have borne with us too long will totally destroy a race which is proved at last to be unworthy of His protection. Such a faith as this is not enthusiasm, it is fanaticism in its most malignant form; it is itself the grim and faithless thing that throws so dark a shadow on the future. If such is life, of what use is it living?

If history has no better escutcheon to hold up to the universe than one which is crowded with follies and crimes, to what end have good men suffered, why have patriots and martyrs bled? Grant the views we oppose, and where is the moral of man's existence? The nobler spirits of the race, Plato, Dante, Luther, Shakspeare, Milton, Bacon, Descartes, Pascal, Howard, Washington,—have they lived in vain? Did He, who came to " save that which was lost," depart unsolaced by any hope that His bitter travail would some day be rewarded by the spread of love and justice throughout the world? If the history of man shows us nothing better than the utter failure of moral principle when brought into collision with injustice, it is a picture of hopelessness in reference to the moral destinies of the universe which we can but sorrowfully wish it. had been consistent with sovereign wisdom to withhold.

There is a disposition in some men, when two alternatives, equally probable, are offered, to .prefer the more terrific. .The fascination sometimes felt in circumstances of great danger, which almost tempts us to rush headlong into it, gives us a clue to the nature of such a disposition. They love to think that. the present age is the prelude to a tragedy, and the spice of misanthropy which mingles with the feeling only makes it the more palatable. There are, however, two opinions which influence the growth of this feeling: one of these we have just mentioned. It is that man is not really progressive; that revolutions bring on reactions; and that a season of freedom, by leading to wild democracy, brings back despotism—that man, instead of following an ever onward course, walks perpetually, like the mill-horse, round the same circle. An inference of this kind may be drawn from a contracted and partial study of history, but it disappears before reflection. Viewed aright, history rather represents an unfinished drama, with many acts and interludes, but all centering in one plot, and all contributing towards the same *dénouement*. In social and political changes action and reaction are not equal; what is true in mechanics is in this respect false in humanity. So far as human revolutions are mechanical, the maxim holds good; but, though they always spring, in part, from mechanical causes, they spring from a cause far deeper—from life; and the law of life is, not reaction, but progress. Experience proves this. Who will say that the prospects of mankind are no better now than they were when Xerxes filled the Persian throne, and kidnapped strangers were exposed for sale in the market of Athens?—or when the Roman Empire was sinking in collapse, and countless hordes of barbarians poured over the Danube into Italy and Gaul;—or when English troops were using their long knives at Cressy, when Europe was without any international law, and its populations, as well as its rulers, seemed animated with a common desire to rob and murder each other? Or, coming down to more recent times, is British liberty no more secure than it was under the Stuarts? Are the prospects of France less hopeful than they were under Louis XIV.? Has Germany made no advance in political knowledge, and aptitude for enjoying political freedom, since the close of the seven years' war? With states of Anglo-Saxon origin fringing the eastern coast of the

Pacific; with British settlements at Borneo, Hong Kong, New Zealand, Natal, and the Cape of Good Hope; with India under British rule; new communities rising in Australia; with Chinamen emigrating to California; a marvellous revolution rending in twain the Celestial Empire; a line of steamers from San Francisco to the Sandwich Isles; Turkey adopting the principles of Christian civilisation; canals and railroads connecting the Atlantic and Pacific; and the electric telegraph enabling us to converse over an extent of a thousand miles, who will say that the prospects of civilisation are no better than they were some centuries ago?

In estimating the probable influence of any moral agency, a very important element is time. There is an impression somewhat prevalent that the world is hastening to some crisis, and that the period allotted for its moral development will soon expire. Neither experience nor reason, nor, we may add, religion, gives ground for any such sentiment. Granting its truth, then, our faith in moral agencies, and especially in the effects of Free Trade, as a means of humanising the world, is shaken. Our own social development, the wealth, the knowledge, the fitness for political action, which we enjoy, is the growth of 1,500 or 2,000 years. It may be expected that, with better means of progress, other states will grow faster, but when we reflect on the condition of two-thirds of the population of the globe; when we think of their present ignorance, barbarism, superstition, and political incapacity, we cannot, consistently with known laws, expect that their elevation will be achieved in the course of one or two centuries.

Analogy supports this view. ·The works ·of Providence are slow; the universe is never in a hurry. If, as geologists tell us, the world occupied some millions of years in being fitted for man's abode, surely a few more thousands of years may have to pass before his destiny here is over.

II. Recognising, therefore, the reasonableness of the hope which all feel, that a future period of political and moral perfection is in reserve for the world, how will Free Trade influence its approach? We answer, in a threefold way:—

· Free Trade will elevate the physical and social condition of the world. The groundwork of civilisation is labour; a sense of its value, and an economising of its results. The effect of Free Trade on civilised communities with respect to the value of labour, is very plain,—it creates a demand for it, and gives the labourer a proportionably greater share in the enjoyments of life. But it will produce the same results, in some measure, upon barbarous communities too. It will induce the peasant to till more ground, to sow more wheat than he can consume himself and exchange with his neighbours, and, in return, it will bestow upon him comforts of which he before knew nothing. This reward will expand his views, and stimulate his exertions; gradually he will learn to invest capital, his wealth increasing, step by step, till at length he becomes an owner of estates and ships, and an extensive civiliser in his turn. One such individual cannot rise alone; others will be stimulated by his success, and, in time, national opulence will be the result. By stimulating a demand for labour, and conferring its rewards, commerce will build up mankind in that social well-being which affords the most favourable opportunity for the due development of every political and moral virtue.

Free Trade will tend to spread the knowledge and the practice of purer political sentiments.   On this subject there prevails much ill-judged enthusiasm.   Justly grateful for the freedom which we enjoy, assured that freedom is necessary to attain man's highest well-being, and, also, that it is his inalienable right, we are apt to forget the only condition on which it can be possessed.   We are ready to imagine that all which is necessary for the happiness of a people, is a constitution like ours; constitutional government is with us a recipe for every disease.   If the question at issue were merely one of political systems, our views would probably be correct; but the question is too often a social one.   Physical force is, in many cases, resorted to, as a means of obtaining political rights, and too often only to occasion a closer rivetting of the chain.   The sure mode of enfranchising mankind, is to raise them in social comfort and moral excellence.   Without these attainments, liberty could not be kept if it were won, but with these attainments liberty will come of its own accord.   Hence commerce is the emancipator of mankind—it creates wealth, it inspires with energy and self-respect, it fosters habits of justice and moderation, it strengthens the love of property, and thus opens so many sources of political power.   A commercial people almost necessarily become in time a free people.   We have been pointed, again and again, to the serfs of Russia,—with thousands Russia is a hateful name, the symbol of oppression and wrong.   How then might we best aid

the slave population of Russia in the work of emancipation? By sending our men of war into the
Baltic and Black Seas, and scattering eloquent mani-
festoes on liberty?—Nay, trade with them, and in
time they must be free. Commerce brings nations
together, unites communities by the ties of reciprocal
benefit, till at length, the people loving each other,
the wrath of princes falls as harmless as a spark on
granite rocks.

Free Trade will aid in spreading beliefs which
exalt and stimulate the faculties of those who receive
them, and thus lay the foundation of all political and
moral greatness. We need not say that the special
beliefs to which we refer are those of Christianity.
We waive here the higher aspects of Christianity, and
claim for it nothing but what the mere historical
student admits, on the ground of experience and fact.
It will not be denied that religion is the most influential element in moulding individual and national
character, and that on purely political grounds merely,
the choice of beliefs is no matter of indifference.
We find in Hindostan, for example, a religion which
developes the passive qualities; which favours con-
templation, endurance, mysticism, rather than vigorous exertion:—Hindostan has never been free from
a foreign yoke. We find in Turkey a faith which
inspires every man with the conviction that all things
are under a law of inevitable necessity; that it is an
act of impiety to attempt to arrest the progress of a
fire, or to escape from death, and which, at the same
time, calls the voluptuous passions into play by
visions of celestial houris:—Turkey is at this moment
at the mercy of Christian powers, and silence on the

part of France and England would seal its doom. In Britain and the United States we see a faith which tells us that man's destiny is practically in his own hands; which stimulates inquiry and independent thought, asserts the equality of all men in the sight of God, and bases all virtue on an intelligent appreciation of his will:—These two nations are now exerting a moral and political power, which we shall hardly exaggerate in pronouncing equal to that of all the world beside. This comparison might be carried into the minutest details, and exemplified in the largest variety of instances, and it would be found fully proved, as a matter of fact, that where the elements of Christian civilisation have been most vigorous, there the greatest triumphs of industry and political greatness have been achieved.

But what is Free Trade?—It is itself a Christian idea. It is the embodiment of the Christian thought that men are brothers. It takes the olive branch which Heaven in mercy sends to earth, and bears it to every land. Free Trade tells us that war is wicked; that the millions of armed men that cover Europe should beat their swords into ploughshares, and their spears into pruninghooks. In proportion as mankind accept the principles of Free Trade, they will admit the morals of Christianity, and may be the more easily led to adopt the doctrines from which they spring. But it exerts a still more direct tendency in the same direction. As our commercial connexions extend, so also will our moral power; with the prosperity occasioned by Free Trade, our population will increase, to be drafted off by thousands to our colonies in distant parts of the globe. Nothing will tend so much to people Australia, Southern Africa, and New Zealand, as the effects of Free Trade. By the life it will infuse into commerce, and the political freedom which it will give to our dependencies, it will tend to spread throughout the world, at a rate of which we have no conception, the language, manners, literature, and faith of Britain. But the colonisation of the Pacific will be its Christianisation too. Bring the shasters and the gospels together, as they are seen in the languor and servility, or the energetic independence of their professors, and the result will not be long doubtful. Free Trade says:—" Let men come together." We hail the bidding; such contact is vital for truth. The figments of superstition will then vanish, priestly sanctities and impostures will be scorned away, and man everywhere stand up erect, wearing the image, and blest with the liberty of God.

POSTSCRIPT.

1853—1854.

ALMOST a year having passed away since the preceding pages were written, it is necessary, before committing them to the press, to ask how far the events which have happened during that interval substantiate or contradict the conclusions we have endeavoured to establish.

If Free Trade were a merely party question, its advocates might allege the non-appearance of the defendants, and be satisfied with judgment by default. It must be confessed that the chiefs of the Protectionist party have maintained a remarkable silence. If they have not heartily bestowed their blessing upon our recent policy, they have at least refrained their lips from curses. After a career of persevering opposition, they lay down their arms, and acquiesce in the triumph of their foes. We cannot regard this conduct as an act of chivalrous submission to the decision of the legislature, since the duty of those to whom the nation entrusts its interests is in direct antagonism to such a step: To throw obstacles in the way of a law once passed is a very different thing from an exposure of its pernicious consequences. The one is inconsistent with a sense of honour; the other is not only perfectly consistent with it, but an imperative duty. If the legislature has unhappily fallen into a great error, it may not be right for those who opposed the step to avenge themselves by adopting an obstructive policy, but it is certainly wrong for them to suppress any additional circumstances which may have come to light, tending to expose that error. It is not for us to impeach the patriotism of any of the members of the legislature; we cheerfully credit the disposition of the leaders of the Protectionist party to risk in the service of their country the obloquy of calling attention to unpalatable but incontestable facts; especially when those facts would prove the unsoundness of measures they have always opposed, and to which all but themselves stand committed, and make it the duty of the nation to reinstate them in political power. But such considerations force us to impute their silence to another cause. It must be that their prognostications are unfulfilled; that the evils they foreshadowed have not been realized; that the nation has not been ruined, but greatly benefited, by Free Trade, and that the champions of that policy must be left to exult in their triumph because there are no facts on which it can be successfully disputed.

In matters that relate to the economical condition of a nation, a process which is natural is also usually slow. Exceptions occur to this rule, but very seldom, except through the removal of previous obstacles. When the energies of trade have long been repressed by artificial laws, an artificial degree of force is thereby generated; capital, hitherto held in check by protection, stands ready to seize upon those opportunities for the profitable employment of its resources from which it has been kept back. Hence, when obstacles are suddenly removed, trade rushes, with almost explosive vehemence, into the channels which are waiting to receive it, and whatever test we apply to the state of the nation proves that an immense change has taken place. This, however, is to a great extent reactionary; as soon as the barrier is broken through, the pent-up force is quickly exhausted, and progress again becomes subject to ordinary rules. After having witnessed the wonderful results of Free Trade during the five years which followed the repeal of the corn laws, we might expect the sixth to furnish but a trivial amount of additional proof, and if during the sixth year the previous rate of progress has not been kept up, it is no more than might have been anticipated. Hence, if the rate of increase is found, not only to have equalled that of previous years, but even surpassed it, we have the strongest possible proof that the movement is sound and permanent. When commercial activity springs from spurious causes it is sure to be followed, at no great distance, by a season of depression. Its golden hour lies nearest its commencement; its existence is a brilliant but brief episode, sudden in its rise, and certain in its fall. A course of uninterrupted progress continued through six or seven years cannot spring from mere excitement, but from causes which, if circumstances continue equally favourable, must always produce the same results.

Before we refer to the additional facts which have
been furnished up to the present moment in vindication of our Free Trade policy, we will briefly refer
to the progress which has been made in carrying out
its principles by the legislature.   There is much here
which deserves a grateful acknowledgement.   The
present ministry, though shrinking, as they might
have been expected to do, from the application of
Free Trade principles to some matters which the
nation will ultimately consent to see adjusted by no
other rule, have nevertheless taken several decided
steps in advance.   With reference to merchant shipping, they have broken down the monopoly hitherto
enjoyed by the British sailor, thus conceding to the
employer of capital on the ocean the liberty which
is enjoyed by the capitalist on land, of entering into
a contract with any workman who is able and willing
to serve him, in what part of the world soever he
happened to be born.   The throwing open of our
coasting trade to foreign vessels, as has been proposed
by government, will be a still more important change.
This step is demanded alike by justice and expediency.
No law exists to prevent the foreigner investing his
money in canals and railways within the kingdom,
on what principle, then, should he be prohibited from
furnishing us with the means of trafficking round its
shores?   Moreover, the vast increase of trade which
has taken place during the last ten years, an increase
which not only keeps our railways fully employed,
but has also rendered some of our old methods of
conveyance much more profitable than formerly, has
rendered the monopoly of the coasting traffic exceedingly injurious to the public.   The rise of freights, to

which we shall presently advert, has seriously interfered with trade, and exposed the public to much loss
and inconvenience ; so that it has become a clear
case of self-interest to accept from every available
quarter of additional means of transit. Our foreign
trade will reap considerable advantage from the
change, since other governments will, no doubt, follow
our example, and thus, in the case of the United States,
an immense seaboard, both on the Atlantic and Pacific,
fringed with some of the busiest ports in the world,
will be thrown open to the competition of British
ships. An assault, long needed, has also been made
upon the custom house, and though the constitution
of the board for the present remains unchanged,
several salutary alterations have been permitted in
other departments, all tending to give greater facilities
to trade. The power to transmit merchandise in
bond from port to port for transhipment, was an
important privilege already conceded, the value of
merchandise thus transhipped having amounted in
1853 to more than five millions. In the important
matter of taxation, the principles of Free Trade have
been consistently applied. The succession duty has
given the Chancellor of the Exchequer a lucrative
source of income, without the imposition of any
sensible burden upon the country, and another step
has been taken towards removing the unjust distinction which had hitherto been maintained between
real and personal estate. The increased expenditure
incident to war, instead of being met by taxes on
consumption, which would have entailed disabilities
on trade, has been provided for by an increased tax
on income, and thus another decision has been

recorded in favour of direct, in preference to indirect, taxation. In ecclesiastical affairs very cheering progress has been made. The Canadian "Clergy Reserves Bill" not only recognises the independence of colonial legislation, but marks an important step towards the establishment of entire religious equality in our colonies. On the university question a great and unexpected victory has been won. Dissenters are no longer to be excluded from our national seminaries because they cannot sign the articles of the Church of England. The measure has not gone to the length of altering the constitution and rules of colleges in their favour, but the concession it contains is, nevertheless, of immense value. In these changes we recognise a disposition to walk abreast with the convictions and wishes of the more enlightened sections of the community, but in other measures the same feeling has not been apparent. The reception which was given to the motion of Mr. Locke King, on the practice of entail, and the spirit which evidently presided at the framing of Lord John Russell's Parliamentary Reform Bill, evince a determination to maintain by artificial means-the territorial influence of the aristocracy. The principle on which the corn laws were repealed is opposed to the use of any artifice to prolong the ascendancy of any class or any system. Without any abstract antipathies, willing that everything which has vitality should live, it demands permission for that which is moribund to die. If an acre of land and a hundred guineas are commercial equivalents, let them be political equivalents also ; let them pay an equal amount of taxes, command as many votes at the hustings, and as much influence in the legislature. But the recognition of this equality supersedes the necessity for one-sidedness in legislation. Where right and might are identical the respective claimants may be left to themselves.

Glancing now at the commercial and social condition of the country, the first fact which arrests our attention is the high price of bread. In one respect this is very opportune. Whatever its social disadvantages may have been, it will at least have the effect of showing our farmers that open ports and low prices do not always go together, and that as yet there is no sufficient cause for despair. When a Protectionist chides Free Trade for raising the " people's loaf " to double its last year's price, we may at least enjoy the satisfaction of congratulating him on the result, and trust to find him henceforth somewhat less hostile to Free Trade. But it is said that the high price of wheat is the result of restricted cultivation ; that the farmer devotes his land to other crops, or suffers it to lie idle rather than grow corn. One of the members for North Warwickshire, when he informed his constituents of this circumstance, implied that it was admitted in Manchester, and stated that placards were posted up in that city throwing the blame of dear food, and he might have added, of the " strikes" now unhappily rife, upon the League. We are afraid we cannot acquit the League of some share in the matter of the second indictment, for it is unquestionably Free Trade, the work of the League, that occasioned such an abundance of employment as made the workman dissatisfied with his old rate of wages. In this the League is *particeps criminis*, just as much as the sun is when its light conducts the infatuated victim of misfortune to the river where he purposes to drown himself. But as for Free Trade having been the cause of dear bread, the only proof of this, so far as Manchester is concerned, is the placard in question, the genealogy of which may be reduced to two elements, the unscrupulousness of a defeated faction, and the liberty which is enjoyed by an English bill-sticker.

If the cause of the high price of wheat is really that which Mr. Newdegate assigns, it is at least curious that the price should have risen at all. It was not complimentary to an agricultural audience to suggest such an explanation, since, if true, it proved that the intelligence of the agricultural body was unequal to the emergencies of their new position; that they had, in fact, ruinously miscalculated the effects of Free Trade. But if foreign competition has really compelled our farmers to give up the cultivation of wheat, why has not foreign competition supplied the deficiency? Why did the foreign wheat-grower permit the price of wheat to rise as high as seventy shillings per quarter, and refuse to make his fortune by coming to the rescue of the British consumer? Another fact equally difficult to explain on this theory is, that while the price of wheat has been high at home, it has been equally high abroad, and that in December, when wheat was fetching seventy shillings per quarter in the English market, large purchases were made there for the still dearer markets of the continent. During the autumn we imported wheat from Belgium, and before the end of the year we exported wheat thither, a fact which clearly proves that the rise of prices was greater there than here. Moreover, a large quantity of the wheat shipped at Odessa, which in ordinary times would have found its way to this country, was drawn to the ports of Italy by the higher prices ruling there. With such facts before us, it is evident that the cause of scarcity at home was identical with the cause of scarcity abroad. We have mentioned in another place the unseasonable weather which prevailed at the close of 1852; high temperature and excessive rain. After a mild winter came a late and cold spring, with wet weather extending throughout the summer and autumn. Many farmers did not sow one half the usual breadth of land with wheat; a good deal of the seed perished in the ground, while the rain that fell, all but incessantly, during harvest, spoilt a large proportion of the grain which came to maturity. It was conjectured that the yield of wheat would be at least twenty-five per cent. below the average, and the official returns of the quantities of wheat sold in England and Wales, whatever opinion may be had of their value, would seem to indicate that even so low an estimate was under the mark; the quantity of wheat sold since the harvest of 1853 having been thirty per cent. less than the quantity sold during the corresponding period in the previous year. Over a great part of the continent, the season was equally unfavourable to farming operations. Countries which usually have a large surplus of wheat for exportation, were obliged to become buyers. We have here the true solution of the case. The sole reason why the price of wheat rose so high, is that we had a bad harvest, and that other countries experienced a similar calamity. It is not improbable that farmers in England have recently turned their attention to other crops as a substitute for wheat. If such is the fact, it is a matter for congratulation rather than regret. The high price of wheat, however, does not offer the slightest clue by which we might find out whether less is grown here than formerly. In the absence of agricultural statistics, we are as much entitled to conclude that Free Trade has had precisely the opposite effect.

The whole significance of the high price of bread during the last six months, in relation to the character of our Free Trade policy, is comprised in two facts : first, the price has been as low as, considering the state of the harvest in those countries which are commercially connected with us, it could possibly have been. Our ports have been open to the world ; no law has obliged us to send back a single quarter of wheat which other nations had to spare ; if it has gone elsewhere, it has been because prices were higher there than here, that is, because the population stood in greater need of it than we did ourselves. Thus the law of supply has been in accordance with the law of humanity, and the slight inconvenience we have suffered has been inflicted, not, as formerly, by human legislation, but by circumstances which man can neither foresee nor control. The second fact is, that the price of bread has been no higher than was once thought so salutary, that the legislature interposed to prevent it, if possible, from selling at a lower rate. The corn law of 1815 wholly prohibited the importation of wheat for home consumption, until its price in the home market reached eighty shillings per quarter, and even the sliding scale of Sir Robert

Peel, that vast concession to cheapness which was to ruin the farmer, was intended to render the importation of wheat profitable only when its price rose above sixty shillings per quarter. But the average price of wheat during 1853 was only fifty-three shillings and three pence, and during the three dear months of October, November, and December, when the character of the crops was fully known, it was under seventy shillings. We beg to suggest to those individuals who seize with such avidity the present occasion for throwing upon Free Trade the odium of dear food, that the facts to which we have now referred would form an admirable peroration to the harangues on the same subject with which they may propose hereafter to gratify the public.

The high price of food during the last six months has no doubt exerted an important influence upon the state of trade, and one which can hardly fail to make itself apparent in the commercial statistics of the year. It must have made a considerable difference to the weekly expenditure of families in bread, and proportionally limited their power to purchase other articles. The workman who ventures, when food is cheap, to expend a portion of his earnings with the cabinet-maker or draper, has no surplus fund to draw upon when the rising price of necessaries absorbs that small sum. He is driven to economize; to deny himself of this or that luxury, to leave an empty corner of his apartment unfurnished a little longer, and to make the dress which he or his wife has worn during the winter, suffice also for the spring. Two shillings per week is probably below the average sum which the enhanced price of bread alone has

F F

added to the former outlay of each family. This gives a weekly total of £431,238, or nearly twenty-three millions during the year, most of which is withdrawn from the ordinary channels of commerce. Nor is this a mere diversion of expenditure from one channel to another; it represents, on the contrary, a clear loss, which has been incurred by circumstances over which man has no control, and diminishes to its full extent, not the purchasing ability of one particular section of the community, but the common stock of the nation.

Though the dearness of food has contributed to the partial difficulties which have recently been felt in the commercial world, we must not overlook a variety of circumstances, at home and abroad, which have exerted an influence unfriendly to commerce. Among the latter we must reckon the civil war in China, which seems destined to work such vast changes in the commercial, political, and religious condition of the East. When we duly consider the character of that revolution; when we reflect that it aims at the subversion of a throne which has hitherto been recognised by more than three hundred millions of subjects; that, in pursuit of this object, numerous battles have been fought, vast provinces transferred to other hands, and a powerful army marched from the confines of the empire to the neighbourhood of the capital, we shall feel surprised that the foreign trade of the country has suffered so little derangement. If anything were necessary to prove the popularity of the movement, it would be found in a comparison between the wonderful measure of success which has attended it, and the slight interruption which has occurred to the pursuits of industry. But still, a revolutionary crisis must ever be unpropitious to trade. In the violent transfer of authority from hand to hand, and the double jurisdiction which is then established, how many opportunities are offered for successful fraud! The villain then plies his calling with impunity, when, by merely passing from one province to another, he can elude the pursuit of justice. Even when the ordinary securities of person and property are but slightly weakened, apprehensions founded upon a knowledge of human nature, are sufficient to alarm the timorous sensibilities of commerce. Accordingly, our trade with China has experienced considerable stagnation; tea has not been brought down in sufficient quantities to meet the demand; and native merchants have hesitated, in the present unsettled state of the country, to take large quantities of British goods in exchange. Six months ago, a large stock of calicoes remained unsold, and this has been increased by later arrivals. While the war continues, those of our manufacturers who supply the Chinese market, may expect a slack trade; but, from the vigour with which the operations of the patriot army have been carried on, we may, perhaps, predict a speedy close, and in that case China may soon become, under a more liberal *régime*, a consumer of British goods to an extent much greater than a mere survey of our past intercourse would lead us to expect.

While civil war among the inhabitants of a distant empire has deranged one portion of our trade, more serious obstacles of the same nature have occurred nearer home. In the events which have chequered

the history of Europe during the past year, and which
are now assuming a still more threatening form, we
read a sad and humbling lesson on the uncertainty
of human happiness. The year began in the midst
of the brightest promise ; the fortunate past and the
still more fortunate future were a cheering theme,
and the coldest philosophy might pardon the jubilant
expectations with which the nation, glowing with
conscious triumph over difficulties that had long
retarded its prosperity, pressed on to realize the
greater good which seemed waiting to reward its
toil. Trade was busy, food cheap, the spirits of the
people buoyant beyond measure, we were at peace
with the whole of Europe ; well might the press pour
forth its chorus of gratulation and utter its prophetic
hopes, for it only gave utterance to a universal sentiment. Scarcely, however, had we entered upon the
year when its early promise began to wane ; a cloud
was seen in the east which grew darker and broader,
till it threw over every European state the ominous
shadow of war. We need not recapitulate events
which are but too fresh in the reader's memory ; it
is sufficient that the crisis of actual hostilities to
which we are at length brought was foreseen throughout the year, and exerted, towards its close, a repressive influence both on our home and foreign trade.
It has been surmised that the anticipation of hostilities has been more injurious to commerce than their
actual effects may prove to be. The probability of
this opinion depends upon our being able to confine
the war within its present limits. But should we,
happily, succeed in doing this it is still likely that
its injurious influence will be more powerful during

the present year than it was during the past. Several of the unavoidable concomitants of war have only just begun to operate, and others cannot fail to be developed which we shall have to take into account in weighing the commercial statistics of 1854. Hence, without attempting to fix the precise amount of injury from this source which has already accrued to our trade, we will, in a few words, point out that which may be expected to spring from it, if it is not speedily terminated.

The first effect of war between two states is to limit the sphere of their commercial activity. The intercourse which was previously carried on between them must soon be entirely suspended, or carried on under a neutral flag. Hitherto the maritime rights of belligerents have been so interpreted, as to enable them to seize all goods belonging to the enemy, whether found in hostile or neutral vessels. The maxim on which this right has been justified is, that our interest binds us to do an enemy all the harm we can, and, consequently, that the more wealth we can take from him, and the more effectually we can prevent him from carrying on profitable traffic, the better. This is a dangerous maxim for a commercial state, whose resources are drawn from that very traffic which it prohibits. Hence, during the present war a more politic and humane course will be pursued, and free vessels be held to constitute free goods. But though, under a species of connivance, commercial intercourse will still be carried on with the enemy, it will be grievously shackled. Even if the same quantity of goods is exchanged, our own ships will be thrown out

of employ, and that, not by the law of superior cheapness, which would tend to the profit of the nation,
but by artificial compulsion. But the rights of neu-
trals do not extend to the breaking through of an
efficient blockade, and blockades have hitherto been
the most common operations in naval warfare. A
blockade of Russian ports which merely opposed the
exit of Russian vessels of war, would be a very in-
efficient mode of bringing the question to an issue.
Hence it is impossible to prosecute the war without
a serious diminution of traffic. This has already
been felt to some extent; all kinds of produce for
which we are indebted to Russia having risen considerably in price. But war inflicts still greater
damage upon commerce; its effect is to weaken commercial intercourse generally with every state. The
spirit of trade is very sensitive; its keen eye discerns
dangers that are yet remote, and a thought is often
enough to crush its buoyancy. Unlike the prosaic
thing for which it is sometimes ignorantly mistaken,
it stands close to the region of the emotions, deals
incessantly with hope and fear, and builds its golden
castles on materials not less fluctuating than desires
which a storm of passion may dissipate to-morrow, or
take away the power of gratifying. War is a serious
element in commercial calculations, and especially
war between three of the foremost nations of the
world. Its dangers may now be confined to one
portion of the globe, but who shall predict its movements? Who shall mark out the course along which
the infernal tide will sweep to-morrow? A purchase
may be made, but ere the merchandise can reach its
destination, what markets may not be closed, or what

other circumstances may not arise to effect a ruinous change in its value? With the vast dominions of Russia and Turkey in a state of siege, an insurrection in Greece, Hungary and Italy in a precarious condition, a camp forming at Coblentz, the Baltic states arming to maintain their existence between the crush of mighty powers, commerce is obliged to go softly. But, besides limiting the sphere of commerce, and weakening its operations, war strikes at its very existence. There is no reproductive power in shot and gunpowder; wealth may be scattered by this agency, but not increased. War is a fruitless expenditure of the vital energy of nations; unlike the peaceful pursuits of industry, the greater the exertions that are put forth, the more complete is the exhaustion that succeeds.

But though the prospect of war has exerted a repressive influence on our trade, and the hostilities to which we stand committed cannot but expose it to still greater calamities, we find even here a striking proof of the benefit which Free Trade has conferred upon the nation. If, as the majority of persons assert, the present crisis imperatively calls upon us to enter into the lists with one of the mightiest potentates in the world, what is the gratitude we owe to that policy which so well enables us to take the step? What a different position we were in twelve years ago! With declining trade and an empty exchequer, what minister would have dared to propose an additional expenditure of five or ten millions? The prosperity which Free Trade has produced has created our steam marine, infused a spirit of enterprise into the measures of government, provided the purse which is to pay fifty thousand militia men, and a large addition to the regular forces. The powerful armaments which have been sent to the Black and Baltic Seas, and the gigantic preparations which are still being made for the prosecution of the war, coupled with the fact that, to meet the vast pecuniary outlay, no artificial methods have yet been resorted to, constitute not the least significant proof of the beneficial effects of Free Trade, and the unbounded might of commerce.

We have said that the majority of the people seem to regard the present crisis as one which imperatively obliges us to go to war with Russia. We are not called upon to endorse that opinion ; we may even be permitted very seriously to doubt its accuracy. The necessity, such as it is, has been created by our past policy, and it is one which will continually recur so long as the same principles are pursued. The political history of Europe for the last four centuries is a series of conquests and reactions. Almost every leading state, by pretending to check the aggressions of another, has itself attained to a degree of power which enabled it, in turn, to become the aggressor. This has always, sooner or later, led to another combination, and another catastrophe, though, as in the visions of the prophet, another beast has never failed to emerge from the troubled sea, more powerful and more cruel than its predecessor. A Charles V. or a Philip II. may, at an infinite cost of blood and treasure, be put down, but to what purpose is this lavish expenditure, since ambition only changes thrones, and we have instead a Louis XIV., a Frederic the Great, a Napoleon, or a Nicholas ? At every epoch the war-cry is the same. Again does Freedom come from heaven and summon the nations to her banner; again is piety invoked; again does Justice plead her rights and assume her awful frown; again does the past give up its treasures of poetry and heroic sentiment to garnish the carnage of the battle-field; but all in vain, man's very nobleness deceives him. Exhausted and breathless he lies, when the fight is over, the helpless victim of a new master, and Europe, after glowing with impassioned frenzy over a thousand wrongs, sits down at the feet of the latest despot, enslaved, and what is worse, befooled. It is worth asking, how far we are to proceed in this insensate course? Whether we have not cowered with false terror before thrones because we have undervalued the moral life and power of nations? Whether faith in the people does not teach us that in their political growth, a growth which is sure to accompany the extension of commerce, we shall not find the only efficient check upon the faithless ambition of governments? In a more comprehensive sense than that in which the words were first uttered, we may exclaim with Louis Napoleon, "*L'empire, c'est la paix.*" Peace is not only one of the many blessings which will result from the dominion of justice, but it is to a great extent the only condition on which that dominion can be permanently established in the world. Some self-sacrifice, some apparent sufferance of wrong, may be required in commencing a new era, for we cannot atone by a word for the errors of centuries, but if humanity and justice, better informed, do indeed point us to such a task, it cannot be too speedily begun.

While our trade has recently been exposed to the influence of anticipated hostilities abroad, we have, unhappily, been experiencing actual hostilities of another kind at home. The battles which have been fought on the banks of the Danube, have had a scarcely less important counterpart in the mutual struggles between capital and labour, which have been carried on so fiercely in various parts of Lancashire. It is necessary to advert to this contest, since, both in its origin and its results, it is closely connected with the present state and prospects of trade. In looking at the origin of the recent " strikes,"* we must distinguish between the cause and the occasion. The cause is to be found in wrong conceptions of the laws which bind alike the capitalist and the labourer, disputed grievances, and the exacerbation which so easily springs up between parties who imagine that their interests are mutually inimical, and upon this alone the mischief of the " strikes " is fairly chargeable. The occasion is an altogether different matter; this, when it does not spring from despair, is invariably found in the enjoyment of unusual prosperity. When work is scarce, the workman will not strike; he knows that scores stand ready to take his place, and chooses to put up with hardship rather than risk the loss of employment by attempting to obtain redress. The high price of labour is the only weapon with which he can assail the employer. Hence, a strike for an advance of wages never takes place

---

* The distinction between " strikes " and " lock-outs " is of no practical importance here, since the original movement was wholly on the side of the workmen; the employers have simply acted on the defensive.

unless the workpeople are pretty well assured that the state of trade will dispose the employer to grant their demands, rather than let his machinery stand idle. It is quite possible that they may be mistaken in their calculations, and, still more, that events may soon transpire which will annihilate the conditions of success, and force them to give way, but this does not alter the fact that the actual enjoyment of prosperity, and a belief in its continuance, supplied the motive which first induced them to commence the contest.

This is precisely an outline of the history of the Preston strike. We have already spoken of the scarcity of labour at the beginning of 1853, the upward tendency of wages, the continued erection of new factories, and the certainty that, in the absence of deranging influences, a general rise of wages would take place. In such circumstances, about the middle of the year, the workpeople in Stockport and its neighbourhood demanded an advance of ten per cent. After a short delay their demand was granted, and they resumed work. This victory at once confirmed the impression that the employers were reaping immense profit, and that the moment had come when they might successfully insist upon higher prices. Nothing could have been more ill-advised, even if the existing prosperity had continued. The process they wished to hasten was already going on, with the gradual but irresistible force of nature. The fact is, employers were secretly bidding for hands without each other's knowledge. Ten, or even twenty per cent. was not allowed to stand in the way of acquiring a good workman. It had become a common occurrence for a workman to go to his employer and quietly inform him that he had a situation offered him at a certain advance ; adding, that he did not wish to go, but of course must consult his own interest. Thus, all that " strikes" profess to do was being done in the calmest, most friendly, and most effectual manner, by the law of supply and demand. But this would not do ; an impetuous rush, it was said, would forestall the prize, and secure an equal advance of wages to all alike. The resolve was made in an evil hour. Bread was becoming dearer, the prospect of war grew every week more threatening, many of the Preston operatives had been employed for the Chinese market, and tidings were received that, as the last freights were unsold, no more need be sent for the present. But for these circumstances, it would have been the interest of the employers to give way, and this, probably, to such an extent as to have conquered that natural reluctance to suffer dictation in the management of their business which has led them to unite in self-defence.

While the origin of the " ten per cent. movement" places the industrial effects of Free Trade in a striking light, the exertions which have been made, and are still making, in its support, prove the comparative abundance of the pecuniary means which the factory operative has at his disposal. It is sad to think that the gigantic efforts by which the Anti-Corn Law League was enabled to put down one monopoly, have been rivalled by the working classes of Lancashire in their attempts to establish another; but this is no small tribute to the social influence of Free Trade. It is now, in the middle of April, thirty-seven weeks since the Preston strike began. The number of persons thrown out of employ at its commencement was 25,000, but by emigration to neighbouring towns and other causes, it has been brought down to 15,000. And this immense body of individuals, sufficient, with those members of their families whose age prevents them from being included in the estimate, to people a large city, have been sustained in tolerable comfort for nearly three quarters of a year, and that chiefly by the operatives of Lancashire. Though we do not wish unnecessarily to trouble the readers with figures, yet the subject is so important, and the proof it contains of the substantial prosperity of the working classes so decisive, that we make no apology for inserting the following account of all the money contributed towards the support of the Preston strike, distinguishing the weekly amount of the contributions.

Total Expenditure of all the Operative Committees in Preston, during the Strike, 1853-1854.

Week.	Total amount. £.	s.	d.	Week.	Total amount. £.	s.	d.
1	80	1	3½	20	3,237	5	11¾
2	381	6	6	21	3,366	12	4¼
3	561	17	5½	22	3,250	15	0½
4	671	3	8½	23	3,426	19	6½
5	707	12	6½	24	3,281	9	9
6	1,153	15	6½	25	3,711	9	7
7	1,317	5	9	26	3,572	12	6
8	1,684	8	6	27	3,592	19	7
9	2,521	9	5½	28	3,634	0	2½
10	2,569	5	7½	29	3,610	11	8½
11	2,830	18	3	30	3,480	19	3
12	2,832	1	2½	31	3,619	14	0
13	2,939	2	7	32	3,604	0	5
14	3,094	12	6½	33	3,553	4	10
15	3,089	2	5	34	3,337	0	5
16	3,169	5	10½	35	2,808	3	11
17	3,213	11	1½	36	1,819	8	10
18	3,253	3	3	37	946	15	0
19	4,012	1	8½	38	995	15	5½

It will be acknowledged that these figures are among the most remarkable that we have had to adduce in the course of this essay. These sums were contributed, be it remembered, almost exclusively by operatives, and chiefly by those residing in a single county. Granting that some degree of coercion has been exercised in order to make up this large weekly rent, it is impossible to explain the general fact without supposing that the bulk of the factory operatives are in receipt of good wages, and enjoying a large share of physical comfort. The threats of a Trades' Union, when addressed, as they often are, to recusant operatives, owe all their terror to the continuance of good trade; they would soon be disregarded if the cries of famine were heard at home.

If the commercial statistics for 1853 had shown a diminution of the prosperity previously enjoyed, and rendered it necessary to apologise for the supposed failure of Free Trade, the circumstances to which we have adverted would have furnished us with ample materials for doing so. Indeed, it would be puerile not to admit that we may have occasion to recall those circumstances at the end of. the present year. Free Trade is far from being possessed of any such talismanic virtue as would enable it to triumph over the decrees of nature and the follies of mankind. Divine wisdom has not seen fit to endow any principle, however just, with an efficacy for good which would permit us to violate every other with impunity. For the present, however, we have no use to make of existing drawbacks, save that of illustrating our immense success. Instead of framing an apology, we have to proclaim a new triumph.. Notwithstanding the mar-vellous rapidity with which our trade advanced between 1842 and 1853, the longest stride was taken in 1853. As we have brought down the statistics in the body of the volume to the most recent date, it is unnecessary to enter here at any length into a proof of this fact; a cursory glance will suffice. If we look at our imports, we find an increase in almost every article, and in some to a very considerable extent. Thus, among articles of food, we find, in excess of 1852, more than five thousand tons of butter, five thousand tons of cheese, two million pounds of cocoa, five hundred thousand pounds of coffee, twenty-three thousand tons of sugar, four million pounds of tea, sixteen millions of eggs, twenty thousand tons of potatoes, twenty-five thousand tons of rice, upwards of four million gallons of wine, and two million quarters of wheat. Of raw material, we find, in excess of 1852, more than twenty thousand tons of flax, ten thousand tons of hemp, a million pounds of silk, six thousand tons of tallow, twelve thousand five hundred tons of hides, eight thousand tons of cocoa and palm oil, four hundred thousand loads of timber, and twenty-six million pounds of wool. Raw cotton is almost the only article in which there is even a slight decrease as compared with 1852, and a reference to the price of cotton would show that this was owing to a comparatively deficient, though still abundant, supply; for we imported one hundred million pounds more cotton in 1853 than we ever did before, with the single exception of 1852. Looking at our exports, we find an increase in point of value, which, considering the prosperity of the years immediately preceding, is far beyond all parallel. The difference between 1848 and 1849 was more than ten millions in favour of the latter, but 1848 was not a very prosperous year, the value of our exports having been six millions less than in 1847. The year 1852, on the contrary, was a year of great commercial activity; the value of our exports rose to three millions and a half more than they had ever been, yet in 1853 their value advanced by more than nine millions.* Turning to the revenue, we find, notwithstanding the taxes which have been repealed, an increase under almost every head, with a clear surplus over expenditure of more than three millions. The capital of the national debt has also been reduced by eight millions and a half; three millions and a half more money has been coined at the Royal Mint, and a million and a half additional has been deposited in the savings' banks. The tonnage which entered and cleared the ports of the United Kingdom with cargo, was a million and three quarters greater in 1853 than in 1852; the tonnage of sailing and steam vessels built and registered in the United Kingdom, was thirty-three thousand tons greater in 1853 than the previous year, while twelve thousand more men were employed in connexion with our mercantile shipping. These brief facts speak volumes. It is unnecessary, after mentioning them, to say that 1853 was a year of great prosperity; they are themselves the most complete and eloquent affirmation.

If we turn from parliamentary documents to the exclusive organs of commerce, we find the same tes-

---

* It appears from the completed accounts, that even this prodigious increase is below the reality.

timony regarding the trade of 1853. The price of freight is one of the most generic tests that can be applied, and on this account the following statement, extracted from the " Economist," giving the current prices of freights from different parts of the globe, in 1852 and 1853, will be perused with interest.

Homeward Freights to the United Kingdom, 1852 and 1853.			
PORTS.	ARTICLES.	PRICE.	
		October, 1852.	October, 1853.
		s. d.	s. d.
Akyab	Rice, per ton	70 0	85 0
Alexandria	Beans, „ quarter ..	6 6	10 0
Belize	Timber, „ load	55 0	80 0
Chinca Islands	Guano, „ ton	55 0	80 0
Cronstadt	Tallow, „ ton	18 0	50 0
Dantzic	Timber, „ load	17 0	30 0
Galatz	Wheat „ quarter ..	12 0	24 0
Havana	Sugar „ ton	63 0	95 0
Marseilles	Flour „ ton	20 0	35 0
Memel	Timber, „ load	17 0	33 0
Odessa	Tallow, „ ton	55 0	110 0
Oporto	Wine „ tun	22 0	45 0
Maulmain..........	Timber, „ load	80 0	100 0
Rio Grande	Hides, „ ton	47 6	55 0
Sierra Leone	Timber, „ load	70 0	100 0

Glancing at the trade circulars, we find Messrs. Trueman and Rouse making the following statement respecting the chief article of colonial produce,— sugar. "Notwithstanding an excess of import of 23,700 tons, as compared with 1852, so great has been the demand for home consumption, in 1853, the deli-veries for Great Britain being 331,000 tons against 311,000 in 1852, that with even a less export by 9,600 tons, the stock of all descriptions is reduced 26,000 tons, as compared with the end of the previous

year." The consumption of tea in the United Kingdom, during 1853, is estimated by Messrs. Layton
and Hulbert at 57,800,000 lbs., against 55,000,000
lbs. in 1852; while the Messrs. Moffat say its consumption is still on the increase. With regard to
the silk trade, Mr. H. W. Eaton says, " Gratifying as
it was to refer to the silk trade in 1852, as generally
the most favourable year on record, it is not the less
so, to be able to report a further improvement in
favour of the year just closed, showing an excess
in the total consumption of 896,247 lbs., or rather
more than 15 per cent. over 1852, and 29 per cent.
over 1851. It will, at the same time, be seen, that
although the imports show an increase of 708,530
lbs.,* the total stock remaining on hand is 21,517 lbs.
less than at the corresponding period last year." Mr.
Eaton adds, that fewer failures have taken place than
in former years, and that the workpeople have been
in receipt of good wages, by amicable arrangement
with their employers. Messrs. Du Fay and Co., of
Manchester, speak of the cotton trade during 1853
as follows:—"The steadiness of prices through 1853,
shows that business had been carried on cautiously,
and production, even when the mills were all at work,
was by no means excessive. Since the 'turn-outs' and
'lock-outs' have taken place, the supply has been
found, in some instances, unequal to the demand;
hence the possibility of maintaining firm and rather
high prices, notwithstanding the political difficulties
and dear provisions. Not only manufactures, but

---

* The actual increase of raw silk is somewhat less than this
amount, but the joint increase of raw and thrown silk is very considerably greater, having been, in 1853, 1,050,203 lbs.

raw materials, drugs, etc., kept up, showing a regular consumption, notwithstanding all difficulties, and beyond all expectation."—Middling New Orleans cotton, which, in January, 1853, fetched $5\frac{1}{2}$ per lb., in December was $6\frac{1}{4}$. To this we may add, a quotation from the Report of Leonard Horner, Esq., Inspector of Factories, for the half year ending April, 1853, just before the commencement of the strikes at Stockport and Preston. Mr. Horner says: "In my last Report, I gave an account of the vast increase of factories during the two preceding years, and there is no cessation, for new mills are going up everywhere. It is not to be wondered at, that I should hear of a great scarcity of hands, of much machinery standing idle, for want of people to work it, and of a rise of wages. This scarcity of hands has led to a considerable increase in the number of children employed in my district, which indeed has been going on happily for a long time. I believe the workpeople were never so well off as at present; constant employment, good wages, cheap food, cheap clothing, as well as many cheap, innocent, and elevating amusements, brought within their reach."

We will only add to these statements one or two others relating to the present condition and prospects of the agricultural interests of the United Kingdom. The "Norwich Mercury" informs us that, throughout the eastern districts, employment for labourers was good during the past year, wages advanced considerably during the last quarter, thirteen shillings being the common weekly payment for good and steady hands. The present high prices of all sorts of grain have given a stimulus to cultivation, and steadily enhanced the value of agricultural labour, while the tone pervading the principal journals in the interest of agriculture is more hopeful than it has been for years past. An immense improvement is perceptible in Ireland. The "Galway Vindicator" says, "the breadth of potatoes sown this year in the West is one-fourth greater than any plantation known for the last twenty years. The value of land in Connaught is higher than at any period since the last war. The landlords, with a sharp eye, are taking advantage of this state of things, and the rents demanded are quite equal to those paid during the Napoleonic era. In short, farmers and landlords are looking up." The "Carlow Sentinel" for the first week in April adds the following information respecting the more important article of wheat: "It has been stated, we believe truly, that a larger amount of grain has been sown this year than during twenty years previously. Within a circle of twenty miles which we have recently visited, it is impossible to describe the amount of labour bestowed on cultivation, even to the 'headlands.' No waste is tolerated, and even hedgerows disappear to make way for the plough. So great a breadth of land under crop has not been known for a quarter of a century." To this is added the not unimportant fact, that the marriages contracted this year in the neighbouring districts, as compared with the past eight years, are as seven to one.

Having, thus, briefly glanced at the progress of our Free Trade policy through another year, to the commencement of 1854, we now leave the subject in the hands of the reader, anticipating with confidence the conclusion at which he will arrive. Relying upon the facts which have been adduced, we venture to affirm, that, whatever misfortunes may chequer our future course, the expediency of Free Trade must henceforth be regarded as triumphantly settled. The nation has made up its mind to enter upon a doubtful and perilous path; we stand now in full front of the awful contingencies of war, and our hopes, whatever buoyancy they may have derived from the experience of the last ten years, cannot but hover with some misgiving over the abyss in which the well-being of Europe may so soon be engulfed. Our confidence reposes ultimately in Him who, though in the midst of mystery, and on principles which we cannot always comprehend, yet doubtless wisely and beneficently governs the world. May He turn the hearts of men to peace, and guide us to a time when the liberties of man will rest upon a firmer basis than can be found amid the uncertain shock of arms! But whatever may happen, the advocates of Free Trade may assure themselves that they have been in the right. They have raised the nation from a state of ruin to one of growing prosperity; they have inaugurated a just and civilised system of commerce in the room of one which was as illiberal and selfish to others as it was fatal to ourselves; they have done much towards placing before the world the peaceful development of the industrial resources of nations in the position which was once occupied by territorial ambition, and thus turning into a new channel the dominant passions of mankind. There is only one brighter laurel after which they can aspire, that of seeing Europe, through their labours, so knit

together by the influence of commerce, that war would
be impossible. We are not over sanguine; we remember that it is only after a long disciplinary career
of defeats that moral victories are to be won; but
still, when we reflect that Free Trade appeals to those
interests which are immediate and tangible, interests
of precisely the same kind as those which are affected
by war; that calculations of expediency furnish, in
the present state of the world, powerful incentives to
right doing, and that there is a degree of commercial
development between states which would render
mutual hostilities equivalent to mutual ruin, we do not
despair. There is, moreover, still stronger ground for
confidence. If justice is the immutable law of the
world's progress, its outward triumph is secure;
centuries may pass by, but it will come at last. Meanwhile, the advocates of a just cause can well afford
to wait for their full reward. The consciousness of
what they have achieved anticipates all that posterity
can say in its praise. The inward triumphs of rectitude have no to-morrow; they are ever complete;
they are in their own nature as perfect and undying
as the principle on whose behalf they were won.

THE END.

Printed for W. and F. G. Cash, Bishopsgate Street Without

Books lately Published

BY

WILLIAM & FREDERICK G. CASH,

5, BISHOPSGATE STREET WITHOUT,

AND MAY BE ORDERED OF ANY BOOKSELLER.

Demy 8vo., cloth, price 12s.

THE WEST INDIES, before and since Emancipation, comprising the Windward and Leeward Islands.—Military Command. By JOHN DAVY, M.D., F.R.S.

> " This is an excellent book, full of useful practical information, moderate and sensible in its views, and written in a spirit of impartial justice towards a great and suffering interest."—*Morning Post.*

Foolscap 8vo., price 3s. 6d.

THE SILENT REVOLUTION; or, the future effects of Steam and Electricity upon the Condition of Mankind. By M. A. GARVEY, LL.D., of the Middle Temple.

> " This is a plain, sensibly written, and eloquent book concerning our social progress, from a condition of half-brutified people, to our present advanced state."—*Weekly Dispatch.*

8vo., cloth, price 1s. 6d., in paper cover, 1s.

"1793 and 1853,"

By RICHARD COBDEN, Esq., M.P. *A handsome Library Edition with a Preface by the Author.*

Foolscap 8vo., cloth, price 3s. 6d.

ESSAYS ON POLITICAL ECONOMY. By the late M. FREDERIC BASTIAT. Capital and Interest.—That which is seen; and that which is not seen—Government.—What is Money?—The Law.

> " They are written with beautiful clearness, and from abundant knowledge. * * It is a small volume, but worth a large sum."—*The Leader.*

Lightning Source UK Ltd.
Milton Keynes UK
UKHW020641231118
332756UK00010B/975/P